For Art's Sake

The Biography & Filmography of Ben Turpin

For Art's Sake

The Biography & Filmography of Ben Turpin

Published in the USA by:
BearManor Media
PO Box 1129
Duncan, Oklahoma 73534-1129
www.bearmanormedia.com

ISBN 978-1-59393-263-3

Printed in the United States of America.
Cover Design by Steve Rydzewski.
Book design by Brian Pearce | Red Jacket Press.

Dedicated with love to the wonderful memories of my mother

Table of Contents

The face on page 222.

Introduction

In the summer of 1935, Ben Turpin was asked by a writer for The Schenectady Gazette:
"Are the slapstick days over?"
Ben replied, perhaps prophetically, "No, sir. The public will accept them with relish as there
are too many now living who like to recall those pictures made in the early days."

August 20

Ben Turpin has been acknowledged as the first American film comedian and was one of the first to take the legendary slapstick staple, a pie in the face. He was one of the best of the slapstick comedians and the world's greatest cross-eyed comedian. Although he made a fortune exploiting his optical disability, Turpin despised the fact that his success was a result of his eyes. One of the hardest-working comics in the early days of motion pictures, Ben was in fact, old enough to have been the father and even grandfather to many of his fellow actors, including Charlie Chaplin, Buster Keaton, Harry Langdon, Stan Laurel, Oliver Hardy, W. C. Fields, Wheeler and Woolsey, and The Three Stooges. And he did it all for art's sake.

My introduction to Ben Turpin came at the age of twelve, exactly one hundred years after Ben's birth. As a kid, I always loved cartoons and old movies. One morning, I tuned into reruns of the old early 60's TV show *Funny Manns.* The program was a half-hour of fast-moving silent comedy clips of mostly unknown comedians accompanied by jumpy good music and the silly narration of comic Cliff Norton, a show I loved. Over time, I learned the silent comics included Mickey Rooney as Mickey McGuire, Harry Langdon, Charley Chase, Billy Bevan, Snub Pollard, Bobby Dunn, *The Ton of Fun* aka *The Three Fatties* (Frank Alexander, Hilliard Karr, and Joe Ross), and my one favorite of them all, the little cross-eyed comedian I'd spent weeks trying to identify, Ben Turpin.

Searching through countless movie books and asking anyone older than myself who the "little cross-eyed guy" might be, no one knew or remembered. Then one day in my local library, I pulled Daniel Blum's *Pictorial History of the Silent Screen* from the shelf and leafed through thousands of fascinating images until I hit page 222. I immediately saw him: BEN TURPIN! What elation! At last I knew his name!

I soon began my lifelong quest to obtain anything and everything on Ben Turpin: his films, photos, stories, and artifacts. Turpin was forgotten to time and undeservedly so for a man who contributed so much to make millions laugh. Going back later to the people and family who couldn't place my earlier description of him, they instantly recognized his name.

Over the years, I've often toyed with the idea of telling Turpin's story; after all, it had never been done. Most of what had been written was little more than the same recycled old sentences. Several years ago, I broke the ice with a multiple series of chapters on Turpin in my self-produced magazine, *Slapstick!* The fanzine was the bi-annual collaboration of fans, writers, and researchers the world over dedicated to the preservation of silent movie comedy. A truly talented, dedicated, and generous bunch of people.

After researching and documenting Turpin's story for over forty years, I feel as though I knew Ben, the clown, the comedian, the man. Prior to the movies, Turpin, then a fairly popular tramp comedian of the stage, was rumored to have been the inspiration of artist Frederick Opper's popular cartoon character *Happy Hooligan*. Whether that's true or not, Ben decided he'd bring *Hooligan* to life and take to the road with his impersonation. After three years of mugging, clowning, and crossing the eyes, he awoke one morning, shocked that his right eye fell out of alignment. He tried, but realized he couldn't simply *push* it back. Due to financial reasons and a full schedule of bookings, Turpin chose to live with the handicap. Perhaps one day he'd have an operation. He never did.

Turpin's long-rumored early associations with vaudeville entrepreneurs Sam T. Jack and Gus Hill have been unsubstantiated in my research; perhaps it was just something Ben himself never discussed. Although entrepreneur Hill later claimed he actually discovered Turpin, Ben never mentioned Hill. Nor had Turpin ever brought up his reputed association with Sam T. Jack. Jack's seedy burlesque shows and his problems understandably got no mention from Turpin. But Jack is known to have hired many specialty acts and Turpin could well have worked for both him and Hill. However, Ben soon entered the new, at first despised novelty of moving pictures as part-time actor and handyman. He labored long and hard until Charlie Chaplin, a new comedic rage, crossed paths with Turpin in January 1915. Ben was hired as second banana in Charlie's troupe. Weeks later, after living in Chicago for much of the last twenty-five years, Turpin accepted Chaplin's invitation and relocated to California.

Mrs. Hazel Buddemeyer, actress at the Essanay in Chicago from 1913 to 1918 recalled, "Ben Turpin was the swellest man who ever lived — just as funny off the screen as he was on."

Chicago Daily Tribune, April 24, 1960, pg N5;
Pursued by Silent Screen Ghosts by Erwin Bach

After appearing in a couple of the popular Chaplin Essanay comedies, doors opened for Ben. In 1916, his salary doubled when he joined Vogue Comedies, Inc. In his forty-eighth year (1917), he found his way to King of Comedy Mack Sennett, where Turpin would soon become internationally rich and famous over the next ten years and beyond.

The always youthful, enduring actor Eddie Quillan, who made his motion picture debut with Sennett in 1926, once told me, "Ben must have been the highest paid actor on the Sennett payroll...he was getting three thousand dollars a week–in 1926!! BOY! That was a LOT of money in those days. It's still a lot of money but especially then.

"Ben never trusted Sennett. When payday came–which was on Saturday–we'd go to the pay window in front of the studio and the first one in line was always Ben. We'd see his limousine drive up and the chauffeur would get out, open the door for Ben who'd be the first there. As soon as he got his check he rushed into the back seat of his car and the limo would speed away. I asked someone after I had seen Ben do this a few times, why he did this, and was told that Ben didn't trust Sennett.

"One period while I was there, it seems the Pathe people in New York started to rate the comedies from our studio. A two reeler that Billy Bevan worked in received a rating of 100% and Billy was going around the studio telling all of us at every chance he had. And when Ben got his results in, he started telling everyone, especially Bevan, that he just heard that he too received a 100%. Then Ben would add, 'Yes, two films at 50%' and laugh like a kid."

Letter to the author, April 27, 1987

"Charlie Chaplin and Ben Turpin were my favorite comics." — Milton Berle
The Sentinel, April 8, 1937, *My Mother's Boy* by Milton Berle

In real life among the world of physical comedians, Turpin had few peers. He was an undisputed master in the field of falls and took special pride in his self-coined fall, the *108*. The *One 0' Eight* was a complete flip, usually from a standing position, then hitting the ground on his back with a smacking thud. It was the best fall of Ben's repertoire of eight different tumbles.

His biggest fans, of which he took the greatest pride, were the children. To his regret, Ben never had any children of his own despite having had three wives. But Ben did whatever it took to make the kids laugh on stage, on screen, and through much charity work. Ben always enjoyed working and it was not until the serious illness and tragic death of his wife Carrie (for years believed to be his first wife) that he retired from the screen in 1925. However, fate smiled down upon Ben, as he soon met and married his third wife and discovered a renewed and revived interest in film and life. The fans were so glad of his return.

With his savings, Ben ventured into the real estate game, buying, selling, and renting properties and as a result, always had a steady income, no longer needing the movies. But with acting in his blood, he always longed to entertain. He never sat idle.

Throughout Turpin's career, he often acknowledged his debt to Chaplin, who gave him his real break and was the man responsible for bringing him out to California. Ben also thanked Sennett for making him a star. And Turpin always had the largest thank you for the ever-loving public, who spent their hard-earned money to be amused by his silly antics.

During the 1930's with new and additional fans who first noticed Ben in the comedies of Laurel and Hardy, W. C. Fields, Wheeler and Woolsey, and others, a star was born once again. Ben had shifted gears and a whole new following, a new generation, was his. However, it was a sad shock on July 1st, 1940, when fans and friends learned of his passing.

Acknowledgments

This book began as a biography, but having collected so many Turpin quotations and a good number of articles over the years, I chose to make the book a compilation, a chronological documentary, and decided to let Mr. Turpin and his associates tell much of it themselves rather than paraphrase. Every attempt at giving credit where credit is due as well as noting reference sources are cited whenever possible. My sincere apologies to anyone I may have omitted or failed to credit, but thank you. Most illustrations in the book are from my own collection, but special thanks must go to the friends and organizations who supplemented this book with rare photos from their personal collections: Sam Gill, Robert Birchard, Brandt Rowles, The New Orleans Public Library, Museum of Modern Art/Film Stills Archive, and others as credited.

I must thank some of the many kind people for their support, encouragement, assistance, and friendship over the years: Bryan Tinlin, Sam Gill, Rob Farr, Joe Moore, Steve Massa, Joan Myers, Elif Rongen-Kaynakci (EYE Film Institute, Amsterdam), David Kiehn, Rick Scheckman, Brent Walker, Steven McLaughlin, George Livingston of the Willard Library, Battle Creek, Michigan, Dino Everett, Claudia Sassen, Lavinia DeCastro-Walsh, Eddie Quillan, Don Marion (John Henry, Jr.) Davis, Hal Haig-Prieste, Madeline Hurlock-Sherwood, Walter Lantz, Robert Cushman, Bruce Calvert, Richard Roberts, Ed Watz, Jim Kerkoff, Marilyn Slater, Nicole Arciola, Richard and Marjorie Knies, Barbara Knies, Hazel Dietz, Greta Dixon, Bill Cassara, Bruce Long, William Thomas Sherman, Chris Snowden, Bill Sprague, Phil Posner, Michael Hawks, Lyn Todd, Lisa Huber, Robert Arkus, Bo Berglund, Randy Skretvedt, Cole Johnson, Geraldine DuClo of the Free Library of Philadelphia Theater Collection, Mike Paradise, Paul and Christal Kassig, George Reed, Jim Tanner, Ralph Secinaro, Michael Campino, Wayne Powers, Larry Baumhor, Simon Myers, Matt Vogel, Kim Pitylak, Ben Ohmart and Sandy Grabman and their staff at BearManor Media, Brian Pearce, Sheila Davis, my family (Mom, Dad, Rodney, and Diane), and last but not least, the man who did it all for art's sake, *Ben Turpin!*

"The guy who was hitting himself over the head with a hammer and wouldn't stop was not nuts. Quite the contrary. He was a very sane man, probably a genius.

"For 40 years or thereabouts I hit myself over the head with hammers, bed slats, rolling pins, leaped out of windows onto pavements, was knocked down and dragged about.

"You'd think, off hand, that I was miserable. I was the happiest man in Hollywood.

"The reason I can't be put in any category with the geniuses of Hollywood — not because of the simple fact it's overcrowded–is because I stopped hitting myself over the head with a hammer. That very fact made me unhappy.

"When I was being tossed about, mauled, manhandling other people and in turn taking my share, it was the heyday of slapstick comedy. Millions rolled into the box office and theater aisles. Those were the plush Teens and Twenties. It's almost a forgotten art now."

"The World Needs Laughs" by Ben Turpin,
Screen and Radio Weekly, October 22, 1939

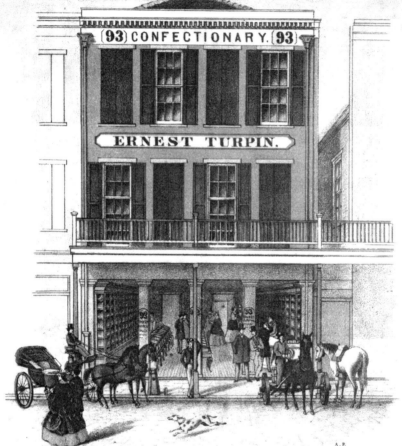

The Turpin confectionary empire, circa 1867, New Orleans.
COURTESY THE NEW ORLEANS PUBLIC LIBRARY

Ben Turpin
The Early Years

His antics, in the vernacular of the proscenium, are a wow. Comedy hokum of the broadest kind is his stock in trade. When the title of one of his pictures is first flashed on the silver screen, the kids in the gallery clap their hands with delight while the older ones downstairs settle themselves down in anticipation of twenty minutes of side aches. For Ben Turpin, the clown, is about to "do his stuff." [240]

Bernard *Ben* Turpin was born in New Orleans, Louisiana on September 19, 1869. His father, Ernest *Edward* Turpin, was the city's largest wholesale manufacturer of stick candy, rock candy, gum drops, chocolate, syrups, and more. One of the first to introduce taffy, Ernest was born in 1834 and, along with his younger brother Eugene, was born in Tampico, Mexico. Ernest opened his wholesale confection business in August 1854 at the age of twenty through the help of Ben's grandfather and namesake, Bernard Turpin (born c1811). Bernard was one of the best auctioneers in the entire state of Louisiana and exchange broker/president of his Importers Bonded Warehouse Co., auctioneer of everything from soaps to nuts, even slaves for a brief time. Most of the merchandise came from business liquidations, often including furniture, stagecoaches, food, clothing, and real estate, at his office at 55 Old Levee St. — later 93 Old Levee Street — or more often at the locations of his customers.

Bernard's building at 93 Old Levee would soon be the address of his son Ernest's candy establishment and one of New Orleans' most successful sellers of sweets. From its opening, Ernest was quick to advertise the availability of candies, jellies and jams, fruits in brandy, preserves, cordials, fancy toys, a variety of nuts, and lots more, much imported from Paris. *The New Orleans Courier* of July 11, 1860, advertised: "(Ernest Turpin's) establishment has been fitted up at great expense to enable him to manufacture, by the aid of steam, confectionary of the best quality, on the most extensive scale, and to compete in price with Northern manufactories. His candies, in particular, have given general satisfaction throughout the states of Louisiana, Alabama, Mississippi, Florida, Texas, and Arkansas." Business was good.

Ernest often advertised in the newspapers of the day, as in this example of July 1860, where he: *Begs the attention of the Public, particularly of Private Families, to his assortment of Superior Confections, manufactured by himself, and warranted Fresh. His Pineapple, Strawberry*

19

& Gooseberry Juices will be found a desirable article for the making of Syrups, of which article he has the greatest variety. His Cream Candy has acquired extensive celebrity. His Marshmallow Drops are manufactured in small quantities at a time, and can always be had from him quite fresh; whilst his stock of Sugar Plums and Assorted Candies are equal in quality to any imported, and furnished at the most moderate prices. Vanilla Beans, by wholesale and retail, constantly for sale.[30]

In 1861, Ernest enlisted with the Confederate Army at age twenty-six. On March 24, 1862, his father sold two-thirds of his interest in the candy business to Ernest and soon retired from the auction world in August 1867. That same year, Ernest moved into the store at 93 Old Levee (soon renamed Decatur Street in 1870), between Conti and St. Louis Streets, and expanded his inventory to also include fancy boxes, fancy papers, cornucopias, and much more. Interestingly, though the candy location was now stationary, the Turpin residence seemed to change often. According to New Orleans City directories, in 1867 the Turpins were living at 299 Dryades; in 1869, their home was at 332 Canal; and in 1870, it was 403 Canal. Ben later recalled being born on St. Charles Avenue and spending some of his earliest years on the 2000 block of Carondelet Street.

Young Ben's uncle was Dr. Charles Cyprien Turpin (born in New Orleans, 1816), who, at seventeen, was educated in Paris at St. Louis College, graduating with a Bachelor of Sciences degree in 1834 and Doctor of Medicine in 1843, then returning to New Orleans in 1842, where he made a specialty of the diseases of women and children. He was a member of *Athenie Louisianais* and had at various times contributed to different medical journals. He held the position of member of the Board of Health, of the medical board of the Eastern District of Louisiana, of visiting physician to the Charity Hospital, soon administrator of the Charity Hospital, and that of principal physician of St. Mary's Orphan Asylum and of the convent of St. Croix. He was a colleague of the eminent Dr. Joseph Jones of the New Orleans Board of Health and won distinction in the field of belles letters.[31]

Dr. Turpin died January 29, 1886, at age 70 after an illness of four days in his home at 240 Royal. A week or so earlier, he had read his paper on diphtheria, which was pronounced by his confreres of great interest and value. After news of his passing, the *New Orleans Medical and Surgical Journal* noted that Dr. Turpin had "no superior in this city" as a scholar and authority on French literature. The *New Orleans Times-Picayune* noted Dr. Turpin was most modest and retiring in disposition and never sought prominence, but his ability was so conspicuous that he was publicly recognized. "In the domestic circle he displayed that tenderness and warmth of sympathy which spring from a generous and loving heart, and by his departure his family and friends have experienced a loss which can be fully appreciated only by those who knew his admirable qualities." He left a wife and six children. Interment was at Metairie Cemetery.

Ben's great-grandfather Don Antonio Turpin came to America from Bordeaux, France and married about 1810 to Maria Henriette Tremoulet (born 1786; died January 8, 1867) in New Orleans.

On June 22, 1868, in New Orleans, Ernest married a twenty-eight-year-old Irish girl, Sarah L. Buckley. Back on October 28, 1867, their first child, daughter Ernestine E., was born and named after her father, who may well have anticipated a son. On September 19, 1869, Ben was born on St. Charles Avenue, soon followed by sister Octavia S. in February 1871. The children's earliest years were spent in the French Quarter.

Soon after the birth of Ben, Ernest put his candy empire up for sale. He advertised in *The New York Herald*: "UNUSUAL BARGAIN. An extensive Candy, Confectionary, Chocolate and Pastry Manufactory, in full operation, FOR SALE, on account of departure, after making a fortune." Mr. Turpin listed all the contents and equipment included within the store ending his ad with, "…A good opportunity to secure a fortune in a few years."[32]

Ernest sold the business in early 1871 to J. Villarrubia and J. A. D'Hemecourt and wished them success. On the heels of that, Ernest, always the businessman, bought the Pelican Job Printing Office at Poydras Street. It was one of the most complete and largest printers and binders of business cards, posters, invitations, pamphlets, catalogs, checkbooks, and more.

With Ben's grandfather Bernard's passing on August 19, 1873 (in Baden, Canton of Aargau, Switzerland at age 62), his heirs stood a large inheritance. Mr. Turpin owned a huge amount of real estate in the Parish of Iberville by the Mississippi River, including sugar plantations, uncultivated swamp lands, and more, which were all soon put up for auction. Ben would later inherit his grandfather's interest in real estate. Ben's grandmother, often in the background, died at age 96 in her home at Marais and Columbus, New Orleans, in October 1891.

Ben's mother Sarah allegedly "died" shortly after the birth of Ben's sister Octavia and the widower Ernest (now also known as *Edward*, presumably to avoid confusion with his similarly named daughter, Ernestine) moved his family to New York in 1876 when Ben was six or seven. Ironically enough, the 1876 *New Orleans City Directory* lists a Sarah Turpin as residing at 40 N. Rampart Street, with no further trace henceforth.

Ben later told writer Harry T. Brundidge, "My handle-moniker is Bernard, not Benjamin. When I was a very small lad, my old man took a look at some census figures and suddenly realized that he overlooked a bet. Why make candy in New Orleans, for a limited trade, when New York boasted some 2,000,000 prospective customers? *Bing! We went to New York!*

"I was brought up at 334 E. Fifth Street, down on the well-known East Side, but in those days the neighborhood was strictly Irish and German. No other nationality could light there."[1] The *New York City Directory* of 1876 lists the Turpin family's first residence at 162 E. Twenty-fifth Street. Later, the 1880 New York Census place the Turpins at 336 E. Sixth Street. The directory of 1884 and 1888 lists the 334 Fifth Street address that Ben recalled as Ernest Turpin's preserves business and documenting their home being at 315 Fifth Street.

Down on the Lower East Side, Ernest returned to the confection business by opening a small candy shop at 280 First Avenue. Soon working and clowning in the window of his father's store pulling taffy, Ben so amused customers that he often dreamed that maybe one day he'd be an actor. He later noted, "My father was a candy manufacturer and started a confectionary store near the Ables Theatre in New York. He put me to work early pulling big ropes of taffy looped over a huge hook on the wall, which went along fine until I started tossing ropes of taffy around incoming customers' necks. I had been doing comic leaps and jumps about the neighborhood for the kids, but this was my first attempt at being funny with adults. My attempt not only fell flat but I did too. Neither the customers nor my father appreciated my attempt at humor."[2]

"I attended grammar school No. 25 and was the life not only of the school, but of my whole neighborhood. I was in demand at every party, because I was supposed to be funny. I didn't have these goofy eyes then, but I'll tell you about them later.[1]

1879: *Stolen Sweets*

Ernest Stephenson, sixteen years old, of 404 East Eleventh Street, and John McGrath, a schoolboy, fourteen years old, of 217 East Fifth Street, smashed in the glass of a rear window in Ernest Turpin's jelly manufactory, 83 First Avenue, July 2nd, and stole a quantity of juices, syrup and candy. They then enjoyed a feast of "nectared sweets" and, becoming satiated, sold part of the remainder. As they were walking on Sixth Street they were detected with some of the stolen goods in their possession. Yesterday they were arraigned in Essex Market Court on the charge of burglary, and admitted their guilt. They said McGrath's brother induced them to commit the act. Justice Bixby held them for trial.

New York Herald, July 12, pg 9

"I got my education — such as it was — in New York.[3] When I was a boy I joined the Fourth Street German Turn Hall (East Fourth Street and Second Avenue) and became a very good acrobat.[2]

"When I was fourteen my father's failure in business necessitated my seeking employment. I went to work as a shipping clerk for Crouch and Fitzgerald, trunk manufacturers, a company that made jewelers sample trunks. I decided against the candy business, because I was fed up on it, and liked beer and cheese at the corner bar a lot better. I took to the place because it was a job, and I could make some money at it, and not because I had any desire to learn the trunk business.[1]

"I really don't know how many jobs I had, but my early ambition was to be a fireman. Every time I would see the Engine Company 25, I would go to the fire. I was thrilled. I would run to the engine house and be the first one to close the door of the fire department.

"I remember one job I had in New York City, during the big blizzard; I just can't remember the date (January 1886). I was getting three dollars a week at Ridley's, Grand Street, dry goods store (then one of the largest retail establishments in the world), as a cash boy. Then I worked at Hotel St. George on Broadway for ten dollars a month, room and board. In that hotel some well-known actors stopped there. I remember one, Jennie Yeamens, and I made some good tips there; but all the bellhops had to sleep in the cellar, next to the boiler room, and believe me there were some rats down there at night. I kept that job for three months.[2]

"Living on Fifth Street, the old gang I used to hang out with, every time there was a party, they wanted me to be with them. I was always very witty and funny; I could sing and dance.

"I kept on being the life of the neighborhood until I was seventeen, and then the old man called me in the parlor one night, looked me in the eye and said, 'Kid, you're gettin' pretty tough.[1] You ought to get away from here. Go out and see something of the world. Go West. There's a lot of chances there. Go to Chicago. Go anywhere!

"'I intend to sell my little business here,' he explained, 'and move back to New Orleans. I've laid aside a hundred dollars for you. Here it is; take it and get out!'

"'That sounds all right,' I told him; 'but what am I going to do when the hundred's gone?'

"'I'll tell you,' he answered. 'You get a job. Earn your own living, and don't come back expecting any more money from me, because there won't be anymore![3]

"'Now go out in the world and amount to something.' I took the hundred bucks and we shook hands. A hundred bucks was a lot of dough in those days — 1886.[1]

"Well, I threw up my job and struck out. I went as far as Jersey City or some other place — I can't remember just where it was, now — and got into a crap game with some fellows. In no time at all I'd lost the whole hundred dollars!

"Then I was in a fix! I was only a few miles from New York; but I didn't dare to go back home. I had never ridden a freight train up to that time — didn't know how, or anything about it. But I saw a train in the yards and climbed on, and the next thing I knew I landed in Chicago! I got off and brushed myself.[3]

"I arrived in the big city with no friends and no dear old gang to meet me. It was on a Sunday. Me and my grip started across the North Side.[2]

"My stomach was aching for food. I saw some fellows who looked friendly, so decided to get some advice from them.

"'How does a fellow get something to eat in this town?' I asked.

"'Hit the back doors!' one of the bunch replied (meaning a usually quick and easy handout from a generous homeowner).

"I did, and I got enough to eat pretty quick. It looked like an easy life. I didn't feel any wish to go and hunt a job and start to work as long as food came free."[3]

Still a young man, Ben decided he'd see the country before settling down. "I've been kicked off of more freight trains between the Atlantic and Pacific seaboards than any other five-year man in the business. What do I mean? Well, for five years I rode the rods, the tops of cars, the inside of empties, coal cars, lumber cars, empty cattle cars and got so used to saying 'Lady, would you give a poor young man a handout?' that I used to say it in restaurants after I went to work again.

"I could walk right up to a front gate and tell by the door of the house whether or not the lady had dogs. I'm telling you I had five years of that without doing a day's work.[1] *Five years!* Back doors were the best inventions I'd ever run across. They were automatic food producers for me. I didn't stay in Chicago all the time, but went all over the country, and I didn't ever pay any fare, either. I'd get tired of a place, or it would get tired of me, and then I'd take a notion to go somewhere else.

"'Well, I guess I'll go to New Orleans!' I'd say. And, by George, I went!

"Then perhaps I'd take a notion to go to Pittsburgh. There would always be a freight train handy, headed that way. All I had to do was climb on or under it. I bummed pretty near every place in the United States."[3]

Asked much later by interviewer Neil M. Clark in 1924 if he met any curious characters and other tramps along the way, Ben replied, "I certainly did! Tramps and thieves too! Mulligan stew was my daily bread. But it was a great experience. I wouldn't take a million dollars for it right today if it was offered me.

"Why not? Boy, it taught me human nature, that's why.

"I don't recommend tramping to anybody. You can't get away with it now. But in my younger days there were a lot of fellows who didn't know what a passenger train was for! Times have changed — they've improved.[3]

On July 10, 1890 at 10:30am an auction was held at Ernest Turpin's candy shop, 334 Fifth Street, near First Avenue by I. Horkhimer, Auctioneer. Mr. Turpin was retiring and wanted to clean house of stock and fixtures, manufacturing utensils, 5,000 bottles and jars of fruit syrups, juices, jellies, wines, extracts, honeys, and more in all varieties. Also ten barrels of sugar and molasses, 50 cases of condensed milk, 25 cases of jelly glasses, trays, ice cream freezers, eight large copper kettles, stoves, scales, a cider press, marble slabs, plated showcases, a new icebox, and more. After thirty-six years in the confection business he had enough.

About that same time, Ben was tiring of life on the road. "When I was twenty-two years old I decided that I had seen enough of the country. It was getting too tough to grab a ride or a meal.

"Well, I landed in Cincinnati after a three days' trip from St. Louis. I'll never forget those St. Louis saloons. Even a bum could eat in them.

"When I fell off that rattler I decided that now was the time to go to work, so I moseyed up town and looked around until I saw a sign in front of a restaurant that said, 'Dishwasher Wanted.' I went in and knocked that job off for myself, and what a dishwasher I was. I'm not boasting or anything, but I can still give the Mrs. of any kitchen a five-minute start and beat her doing up a mess of dishes. And my goblets will shine better than hers!

"I worked hard, and was promoted to a hash slinger. Then I began saving some money and bought a proper suit of clothes. At my work of slinging hash all I wore was pants, carpet slippers and a shirt. I was well liked around that place, and I made folks laugh.

"Well, I met some people that told me I was a pretty good comedian, and they asked me why I didn't go on the stage. The more I thought about being funny for money, the better I liked the idea and so I went on the road with a medicine show as the comedian at $7 a week and board. That was in 1891, I think, and I've been paid for being funny ever since.

"That was my first job."[1]

In 1921, Ben briefly recalled his Cincinnati days: "Twenty-five years ago I starved there. Today I star there on the screen. It's strange how time changes fortunes and circumstances.

"I always will remember a bandmaster named John Weber. He was a friend of the poor. He served free lunch with a glass of beer in those penniless days. About 4 o'clock in the afternoon I would line up with the rest of the purseless mob and have a hearty free meal.

"I soon played at People's Theater. John Heuck gave me the job. At Chester Park I later acted *Happy Hooligan* in a vaudeville stunt.

"I lived on Central Avenue, near a hospital.

"Cincinnati was the first place I ever bought and owned a regular suit of clothes. It cost me ten bucks and I bought it at a Fifth Street store. I walked up Fifth Street looking in every shop window at my reflection." Turpin could not recall the names of all the acquaintances he made in the five years of his sojourn here, a score of years ago.

"But they were all broke like I was then," he remarked.[17]

By 1892, Turpin settled in Chicago (or as early as 1889 if his 1892 Chicago Voter Registration file is to be believed), residing at 310 W. Jackson Street, and working as a clerk at 129 Market Street. Ben later claimed when he first landed in Chicago, "I looked around for a job, anything, so I went up Madison Street and took a job at the old Sherman House as a bell hop, at ten dollars a month. I worked about six months at the Sherman House, then I quit and got another job at (Albert C.) Swanson's Candy Store, 70 State Street, near Randolph. I worked there one year." Ben once recalled, "If you ever worked around a sweet shop you can appreciate how hard the work is after you have been there a while. At first it was great and I filled up on sweet goods.

"Later, however, I passed up anything that was sweet. Between working spells in the kitchen I used to juggle pans, brooms, and other objects. I got to be pretty good and stepped into an amateur contest. I won the money and from then on the theatrical bee put the stinger to me. That was the beginning."[33]

But with the urge to act, Turpin soon joined that traveling medicine show whose home base was in Olney, Illinois, about 250 miles south of Chicago:

"I think we were what you would call a versatile company. We sold patent medicine guaranteed to cure all human ailments. We sold a renowned soap; gave beauty contests to establish the high tide of pulchritude in the different sections through which we passed. But tooth pulling was the grandest thing we did.

"Usually we traveled from place to place in an old-fashioned covered wagon, with our advertising signs plastered all over the sides. On especially grand occasions we went on the train and slept in the day coaches. Whenever we would set up the platform and light the old kerosene torches, I always went on in blackface.

"After I had charmed the multitude with a song, the medicine man would come out on the platform to show the hicks the soap. This stunt was so easy it was foolish. He would first rub his hands over with soapbark which they couldn't see. Then he would pick up a bit of soap so tiny you could stick it in your eye.

"'Now ladies and gents,' he would say, 'I will show you what this wonderful soap will do.' He would soak his hands with the little speck of soap; then throw it away with a great gesture. When he put his hands in the water, the soapbark would make a lather that looked like an Alaskan snow bank. The hicks never failed to fall for that. He usually finished the demonstration by publicly washing the lamp black off my face, turning me to white as it were. It was guaranteed to cure man or beast with one bottle. That one bottle consisted of colored water and eight cents worth of salts; he sold it for a dollar a bottle.

"The beauty and popularity contest never failed to bring in the dough. We always bought a pair of lace curtains from a mail-order house for forty-nine cents. This magnificent article of art we agreed to give to the most popular maid or matron in Bingville. The votes cost ten cents each. The voting results, as the totals magnificently rose, were written by me on a blackboard that we carried. This was for dramatic suspense.

"The hicks from the farms and the sheiks from the village livery stable would contest furiously, buying votes for love and honor — for ten cents per vote. We never failed to clean up $20 to $30 on each forty-nine cent curtain.

"For obvious reasons we always saved the tooth pulling to the last. The medicine man, by use of a marvelous unction, invented by the famous Indian Chief Lo, guaranteed to yank the hugest and most vicious tooth absolutely without pain — payment strictly in advance.

"There wasn't any pain that anybody heard about. The people always yelled bloody murder; but I stood up on the front of the platform and drowned them out with my big bass drum. I need not say that we did not tarry for them to compare notes. After the last tooth was yanked, we stood not on the order of our going; we scooted.[4]

"I did all kinds of acts with that show, including going hungry."[1]

1892: Chicago Doctor Arrested — He Had No License to Practice in Wabash, Indiana

Wabash, Ind., Aug. 18 — Special Telegram — Dr. Turpin, of Chicago, was arrested here this afternoon for practicing medicine without a license from the county clerk. He is what is known as traveling doctor, going from town to town for a stop-off one day in each town, and had taken out but one license in Indiana, supposing that was enough. He was fined in the Mayor's court and immediately took an appeal, the purpose being to have the law which was passed by the last Legislature passed upon by the Supreme Court.[18]

Turpin told Neil M. Clark for *The American* magazine in 1924, "All the time I was knocking around, I didn't have any desire to work. Not a twitter! But, just the same, I was thinking down deep that maybe sometime I might be an actor. And here's what gave me the turn and started me off in the profession…

"One night in Chicago at a party, or some place where I was invited, I did some funny stunts and got them all to laughing.

"'Say, you ought to be an actor!' a fellow said to me.

"'Oh, I don't know!' I told him. But, just the same, that remark hit me where I was living and made me think some more.

"One day I was reading in a paper and noticed an ad of a fellow who wanted acts for his theater. I got hold of another chap and we turned busy; wrote a comedy dialogue and put in some dance and song stuff. What we doped out was a pip of an act. I'm telling you, we had hot stuff! We practiced it till we had it down fine, then we went around to see this fellow that had the ad.

"'You want acts?' I asked.

"'What do you think I advertised for if I didn't want them?' he came back.

"'How much do you pay?'

"'Twenty dollars a week for teams.'

"'All right, we'll be there. When do we start?'

"He told us, and we were right on deck!

"They gave us each a table in the dressing room, but I didn't know a thing about makeup. That's how ignorant I was! But out of the corner of my eye I watched the fellow at the next table. He was an old hand at it and I tried to do just what he did.

"No good! I got a great big gob of black paint under one eye. It was awful!

"That manager must have known we weren't actors, even before we went on; but he had to have the act, so he didn't open his mouth.

"It came our turn to go on the stage. The music played, and there were some people out in front. We walked on and started our line of conversation.

"Maybe we got halfway through, then I forgot every word I was going to say. I was silly with stage fright! The other fellow was, too. He quit right there, and walked off. I was all alone, with nobody to talk to, and I couldn't remember anything to say anyhow.[3]

"I just stood there tongue-tied. I was never so scared in my life. I didn't know there were so many people in the world as seemed to be looking at me from beyond the lights.

"'Go ahead!' somebody shouted from off-stage. But I just stood there. I started to shuffle about and turn a few flips and then I lost my footing and fell on my face.[5]

"I couldn't stand with my mouth open and nothing coming out, so I began to do any funny things I could think of — stunts with chairs and furniture, comic tumbles — what they call silence-and-fun.

"Pantomime, that's what it was!

"I got away with it, too! The house liked it, and gave me a big hand.[3] They roared with laughter. I was a success! Later I played that same house for $2,500 a week![5]

"The manager panned me, of course, for balling up the act, but I had taken so well that he let me go on with my pantomime stuff without any partner. He kept me at it for three weeks — at $3 a day — eleven shows a day. After two or three days I got over my stage fright, and then I was all right.

"That was my first job of acting. I was twenty-two years old when I tackled it, and that ended my days as a bum. I was an actor from then on. I improved my stuff, invented some stunts, and borrowed some from other actors. All the time I kept trying to do my stuff right, just the way that would take best with the public.

"I got bookings pretty regularly, and traveled everywhere — riding passenger trains now! As I got better, I made more money — twenty-five dollars a week, thirty, forty, fifty, sixty; but rarely any more than sixty. That was good wages in those days. It would've been better still if you always got it, but then some weeks you worked and got it; and some you didn't work and didn't get it. When you got it, you were rich. When you didn't get it, maybe you pretty near starved. Traveling and living expenses, and everything had to come out of it."[3]

In New York, 1892, Ben's sister Ernestine, then working as a clerk at 827/829 Broadway for Dr. Jaeger's Co., married a thirty-year-old bookkeeper, Julius J. Knies. A German immigrant who came to America just eight years earlier in 1884, Julius tragically died at the young age of 38 in 1900. Back on April 19, 1893, their only son, Julian Jerome Knies, was born in New York City. Years later Julian would take his best shot at Hollywood. Ernestine lived to 101, never remarrying and spending many of her years in New Jersey and her last years in Los Angeles. Shortly after the marriage of Ernestine and Julius in 1892, father Ernest Turpin retired back in New Orleans to a home at 258-1/2 St. Ann.

On February 22, 1893, the *Chicago Daily Tribune* reported a *Mr. Weiger Pfeifer was bound over to the Criminal Court in $500 bonds by Justice Woodman on the morning of February 21 on a charge of larceny. Bernard Turpin, who preferred the charge, said that he went to Pfeifer's residence at 997 Elston Avenue to collect $100 on a promissory note signed by Pfeifer. When Turpin presented the note, he says Pfeifer took it away from him and burned it up.* Mr. Pfeifer was a carpenter by trade and Ben may have worked for him.

1896: Train Wreckers' Work — Freight Derails Killing Three Men and Injuring Two Others
Milwaukee, Wisconsin, May 16 — Ties piled on the Chicago, Milwaukee and St. Paul railway, at Waldo, a few miles North of this city, derailed a Southbound freight train last night. Three men were killed and two injured. The dead are Engineer John O'Connor, Green Bay; Brakeman Emil Caspair, Milwaukee; John Miller, a tramp. The injured are Louis Tennis, fireman, hands and arms scalded and crushed; Ben Turpin, a tramp stealing a ride with John Miller, leg broken. The engine and seven cars were demolished when the train struck a pile of ties with which the train wreckers had obstructed the track. This is the result of several attempts to wreck the time freight, the passenger trains not having been molested, and seems to point to an organized gang of train wreckers who have a grudge against the St. Paul Road.[35]

On stage, Turpin was an impersonator, a juggler, dancer, acrobat, and equilibrist. One of Ben's equilibristic stunts was to sway on top of a dozen chairs and tables. He used to grimace while balancing. Mugging and crossing his eyes was one of his clowning stunts. He was constantly updating his stunts and material, learning and creating new dance steps and even dabbling in ventriloquism, making many friends along the way.

The Cincinnati City Directory of 1898 lists Benj. Turpin, *houseman*, living at 608 W. 4th.

On February 24, 1898, Ben married Miss Norma Koch (also known as Cook), a twenty-year-old German girl, in her hometown of Cincinnati, Ohio. For the next couple years, Cincinnati was their home. Turpin rarely spoke of Norma in his later interviews and articles, their apparently unhappy marriage having dissolved just after the turn of the century.
"About the time I was twenty-eight I got married and went into vaudeville.
"It didn't take — the marriage, I mean — and as for the other, that didn't put me on easy street by any means."[6]

The Cincinnati Directory of 1899 lists Bernard Turpin, *performer*, living at 412 Clinton.

June 6, 1898: That "King-Pin Dancer Ben Turpin" playing Fremont Park in Mayville, Kentucky for the week and held over for an additional two more weeks along with a variety of acts which included Monsieur Dubec and his Trained Animals; Master Albert Roslyn, boy tenor; The Famous Kline Children; George Edwards, comedian; Mlle. Maxine, great dancer; Grace Moselle; Bessie LaBelle; Prof. Raymond Mallison, great hypnotist and mystifier; Oma Vinelli, sweet singer from Maine; comedic songsters Nelson and Wilson in *The Barber Shop*; George Derious, funny old man; Grace Gilmore, the little magnet; Will Woodside, droll comic, and more.

On Tuesday, June 14, fire raged and gutted the rented home of entrepreneur Col. W. H. Fremont, where some of the actors had been boarding. Turpin, one of the boarders, and several others sustained losses, significant and minor, at the home on Second Street.
The *Mayville Evening Bulletin* wrote of Ben's Fremont Park appearance: "Turpin's repertoire seems never to exhaust" and "always funny. Turpin is undoubtedly one of the

finest dancers ever seen in Mayville. He is aptly termed 'the man with the locomotive feet.' The whole show is of the top-notch order."

1898 September: Ben playing The Casino (Cincinnati) with Bertha Burgess, Artie Fillmore, and Price Henderson.

Garage Haulers Fined (January 10, 1899)

Judge Gordon imposed a fine of $1 and costs on Ben Turpin and Beach Krum for hauling manure without a license. There's just one dumping ground inside the Omaha city limits and that is the set of cars provided by the garbage contractor, where a certain amount must be paid to him for hauling it outside the limits. If they do not unload on those cars the law provides that they must not deposit the contents of their wagons within three miles of the city limits. The minimum fine is $5, though fines of $1 have been assessed. These men failed to patronize the dump.[36]

On January 30, 1899, Ben's father, Ernest Turpin, died age 66 at his home, 1510 St. Ann, New Orleans, where he had returned to "retire" eight years earlier after leaving New York.[8] Ernest was last employed by his largest competitor in the confection business, Daniel Lopez and Sons of Canal Street. In 1912, after 62 years in business, the Lopez family closed the doors of their store for good because of bankruptcy. Ernest was buried in the historic St. Louis Cemetery. Years later, when fortune and fame were his in 1921, Ben returned to New Orleans to have his father's remains reinterred in a newer cemetery.

In 1900, Ben's sister Octavia, now age 29 and single, was residing in Erie County, New York. Census records list her as a patient at the Buffalo State Hospital, but give no clue as to when or why she was admitted. Octavia's whereabouts and her life beyond the institution, if any, is shrouded in mystery. Confidential hospital records were inaccessible to me.

Also unfortunately unknown are the whereabouts of Ernest Turpin's brother Eugene, Ben's uncle. It is known that he was working as a confectioner in New York City prior to Ernest's family's relocation there. On June 24, 1872, Eugene enlisted with the U.S. Army at age 34 in New York and was placed in the 7th Infantry. On May 11, 1875, he was discharged for a disability while stationed at Camp Baker near Helena, Montana. Statistics list him as being 5'-6", dark complexion, with black hair and black eyes. By 1879, he was working as cook at the New Orleans Insane Asylum. Census records the following year of June 4, 1880, list Eugene's occupation as a cook in the Parish of St. Bernard, Louisiana, his last known trace.

1899 September: "Ben Turpin has closed at the Auditorium, in Cincinnati, and opens with Harry Mills' Stock Company, Knoxville, Tennessee, September 11."[37]

It wasn't long before Ben had pieced himself together a vaudeville act, or variety, and hiked out to get himself a job. There were no vaudeville theaters at that time and variety was given in the dance halls connected with the big saloons.

Ben got a job working in a honkytonk in Houston, Texas. While the rest of the entertainers assisted in serving drinks to the thirsty cow-gentlemen on the floor, Ben put on a neat rough-and-tumble comedy tramp act. Sixteen to twenty shows a day were a mere nothing. He would follow the ballad singer, do his act, wait for the comedy soubrette to do her turn, preceding the ballad singer, and then go on again. He worked quite a few of these temples of alcohol and art.[7]

1900 June 25: Ben at the Palace Theatre, Houston, among other acts for the week.

The U.S. Census of 1900 documents Ben in Houston, Texas, possibly playing some honkytonk, and lists Norma Turpin, truly his wife, as his "sister." They soon separated, Ben going his way and Norma touring in the chorus of *Little Miss New York, Jr.* Norma's life soon came to a tragic end at the age of 25 on March 24, 1904, in the New York City Hospital of "acute endocarditis and nephritis" following nearly a month under the care of Dr. O. A. Province. Her body was returned to Cincinnati for a March 31 burial and whether Ben was still married to Norma at her death has been lost to time.

Ben Turpin is said to be the original Happy Hooligan from whom the famous cartoonist took his character. Mr. Turpin was in musical comedy for years and later went on the vaudeville stage.[38]

In 1900, illustrator Frederick Burr Opper introduced to the newspaper reading public his very popular comic character, *Happy Hooligan,* a long and lanky clown-like figure with a round, bald head topped with a tin can hat. He was often the butt of his own good intentions, which always happened, to the enjoyment of readers.

"My fortune was destined to change soon, for in 1900 *Happy Hooligan* was such a popular cartoon in the funny papers I decided to imitate the character."[2]

"One night I happened to see a fellow (possibly Ross Snow) doing *Happy Hooligan* on the stage. It was a new act.

"'I could do that,' I said to myself. 'I'm a long-necked guy and kind of funny looking.'

"So I got me a wig — bald you know — down to the fringe around the edges. I fixed up a tin can on my head and began to practice making *Happy Hooligan* faces, crossing my eyes and all the rest of the business. I was a knockout! I was *Happy Hooligan!*[3]

"I tolled back into Cincinnati and got a job doing my *Happy Hooligan* act in the Heck and Avery Museum there.[1]

"I put on a putty nose, stuck a card in the putty, and rushed out on stage. Everybody thought I certainly could balance things! The house laughed, but not at the card — my eyes had crossed in looking on the end of my nose.

"I did funny stuff for six or seven shows a day and got $3 a day which was a big increase over what I had been earning.[1]

"I started crossing my eyes for every show thereafter and my salary climbed steadily up to the fabulous sum of $45 a week. That was top money then. I was famous. My act got going better all the time and so I struck out for bigger fields by going to Chicago and working for Jones, Linick and Schaeffer in one of their theaters. I told them I was a comedian and talked big and they put me on.[2]

"That must have been about 1902. I (later) played theaters in Chicago for three years straight.[1]

"I went on with it, getting better and better, always practicing the fine points. That's the way I was, always trying to do it just right. I'd practice off the stage sometimes for hours at a stretch."[3]

1901 September: Turpin playing to "good business" at Robison's Olympia in Louisville, Kentucky with Harry & Bessie Allen; James McNamara; John Rooksby; May Brown; Alma Clifton; and Joe Livingston.

1901 September 22-28: Ben playing Heck's Wonder World Auditorium, Cincinnati, with Jennings, Renfrew & May Kennedy. Possibly Turpin's *Happy Hooligan* debut.

1901 October: Ben playing The Midway Theater, Cincinnati.

1901 November 19-24: Ben playing the Broadway Theatre, Houston, Texas along with Tillie Melbourne, Maud Grayson, Bella Hartland, Grace Hartland, Roy Duo, Billy Gibson, Ernest Bailey, Pauline Blossom, Charles Cross, F. McKenzie, and Charlie Flanders. Business was reported "excellent, owing to the high price of cotton and vast amount of work going on in the area."

1902 April 29: Ben back at the Broadway Theatre, Houston, to big business during this week of April 29. He returns for the week of May 6-11 to excellent business and returns once more for the week of June 11, again to excellent business.

In 1975, a Mr. Nick Riggs wrote his local tabloid, the *St. Mary's Oracle*:
"When Mother and Dad were living in Sistersville (West Virginia) during the oil field boom there in the 1890's, there was an oilfield worker, well known to Dad and Mother, who was a great comic and lots of good company; and he also entertained the customers of the Sistersville saloons, according to what Mother heard. He was in Sistersville for a long time, possibly years; then, when the oil boom busted, Mother and Dad moved down to the mouth of McKim Creek, and the comical oilfield worker left for other parts, and Dad and Mother lost track of him until Mack Sennett began his comedies in the early days of the silents. His name was Ben Turpin, and he became a world-famous screen star. Yes, Ben made the big time, and he could be said to have originated his comedy routines in Sistersville, and Dad & Mother were among the first to appreciate his talent. I doubt if the people of Sistersville are really aware of Ben Turpin being there in the 1890's, as this is the first time I have ever written anything about Ben and his early days."[40]

1902 June 14: Ben Turpin, in his acrobatic tramp act, has closed a six weeks engagement at the Columbia Theatre, Sistersville, West Virginia.[41]

1902 August 29: This night at 8PM the officers and crew of the U.S.S. Ranger, a steamer at Panama Bay, Columbia, hosted a dinner and entertainment for the men of the British ship, the H.M.S. Phaeton. Curiously, among the entertainers a fellow listed simply as "Turpin" appears in four acts including a "Buck and Wing Dance," which was a few minutes of mirth and fun with Turpin and Matthews, "Quartette, '*When a Boy I Used to Dwell*,' with Boden, Jones, Pinke and Turpin," and as *Happy Hooligan* in a sketch titled *The Katzenjammer's* along with enacters in character of *Alphonse and Gaston, Hans und Fritz, Uncle Heinie,* and *Officer McClutch*. It is pure speculation on your author's part that this Turpin may well have been Ben.[42]

"The Clever Character Comedian, BEN TURPIN, Comedian, Singer and Dancer" appearing for two shows daily during the week of January 26 (1903) at the Whitney Opera House in Fitchburg, Massachusetts. Turpin, the "Acrobatic Tramp Comedian," appeared along with several other acts, including The Can-Can Phrolikers — The Great 20th Century Novelty — and a Splendid Company of Artists including the Great Professor Nello, wonderful juggler and slack wire artist; Wood and Stone, comedy musicians; White and Sheldon, sketch artists; Cora Miskel and Her Pickaninnies; and 15 others. 2-1/2 hours of refined fun at every performance.

1903 week of February 23: Ben playing the Hub Theater, Milford, Massachusetts with Busch, Morrison, and Burwick and the Bell Sisters

1903 March 2: Ben playing Sheedy's Theatre (Fall River, Massachusetts) for the week along with Sully & Phillips; Payne & Edwards; Brothers Bolen; Laura Bradshaw; and Lorraine & Vinton. So popular was his act, Ben was brought back to Sheedy's two weeks later.

1903 May 25-30: Ben playing the Ninth and Arch Museum, Philadelphia. "Turpin, an acrobatic comedian, is another newcomer from whom much is expected." Others on the bill that week included Mr. & Mrs. S. Irving Boydell; Jacobs and Van Tyle; Marguerite Clemens; James H. Coyle; and the Franklin Sisters.

As for being stranded with shows in strange and awful towns, Ben asserted that he held the championship of the world. Once he was in some show and stranded out in Kansas. He had nothing but his trunk, a day's board paid in the hotel, and sixty cents in cash and was miles from anyplace where he could get a job or borrow money. It had rained for two days before and the town was ankle deep in mud, so Ben went up to the local hardware store, bought fifty cents worth of these iron mud scrapers at five cents each and also a screwdriver.

Going out into the residential area, he carefully screwed a scraper on a step at several of the most prosperous-looking houses. Then, firmly wedging a piece of mud between the heel and instep of his shoe, he would mount the porch and ring the doorbell. When the woman of the house appeared at the door, Ben would point out what he had done and ask her to buy it.

"But," the lady customer replied, "we have a doormat here, with 'Welcome' on it, and everything."

"Let me show you," would explain the versatile Turpin. He'd wipe his feet vigorously on the mat and then, going down to the steps to his five-cent scraper, would deftly remove the huge clot of mud caught under his instep.

"You see," he'd point out, "that mud would have been tracked all over your beautiful carpets and clean floors if it were not for my little scraper."

"How much?" would ask the woman.

"Twenty-five cents," would reply Ben.

"Sold!" If two bits were too much, he would sell them off as cheap as a dime.

With his fresh capital, he bought more scrapers, earning himself railroad fare back to civilization before the sun came out and dried up his principal asset.

1903 October 3, *New York Clipper*: Ben Turpin joined Adair, Gregg, and Adair Company in late September to do his *Happy Hooligan* act.

One day, during idle times and in search of steadier employment, Ben saw a want ad in a paper for a boy to handle props, act, and do a specialty act every night with the Mabel Paige Repertoire Company — "salary fifteen dollars a week, money for ticket wired." Ben wired for the job, the ticket was sent, and he joined in mid-October, 1903.

He reported to the manager, a pompous person, who promptly asked him if he could play a part. "What do you mean, 'play a part'?" Turpin asked.

"Why, speak lines! Carry a role!" explained the manager.

"I didn't get the idea," recalled Ben. "I can rustle props and do a specialty, and I guess I can speak a role, if you show me how. I'm a bright boy and trying to get along."

That Sunday night, Turpin played a part in *Tennessee's Partner*, rustled props for the rest of the actors, and went out between acts and did a specialty. He made a hit and kept the job. The Paige Company played each town every two weeks with a change of bill every night. Monday, *The Billionaires*; Tuesday, *Lend Me Five Shillings*; Wednesday, *The Road to Ruin;* Thursday, *Over the Hills to the Poorhouse*; Friday, *The Two Orphans*; and Saturday night, *East Lynne*.[7] One writer for the *Niagara Falls Gazette* at that time felt the company "One of the best."[43]

Kenneth McGaffey, in his article *Turpin Tribulations*, explained: All Ben had to do (for the Paige Company) was to go around town during the day and borrow whatever props and furniture was needed, haul it to the theater, put it on the stage, open the trunks and see that the actors received their proper costumes. Then rehearse his part, see that the scenery was all right, call the other actors when it was time for them to appear, play his part, and perhaps double in a couple of small roles, get out at the end of the first act and do his specialty, rush back and change his make-up and costume so as to be able to get ready for the second act. After the show, pack the costumes, move the scenery out of the way and get the furniture ready to be returned bright and early next morning.[7] Mabel Paige herself would soon enter the movies and spend much of her long acting career on the screen.

Tuesday, December 22, 1903, the new Mt. Olive Opera House opens in Mt. Olive, South Carolina. The attraction was Mabel Paige, supported by the Southern Stock Company under management of leading man Henry F. Willard. The house was crowded to overflowing and many turned away, their admittance denied. Immediately after the performance, Mr. R. J. Southerland, owner/proprietor, tendered the entire company a barbecue banquet. Guests included: Mabel Paige, Julia Phelps, Josephine Reimann, Marie DeTrace, H. F. Willard, Val Barras, Will Easton, T. Spencer Sprague, Robert Hyman, Ben Turpin, Frank Preston, Marvelous Hermion, and Mr. John Higgins, manager of the Goldsboro Opera House.[44]

1904 January 9, *New York Clipper*: Ben Turpin is with the Mabel Paige Southern Company, playing parts and doing his *Happy Hooligan* act. This is his tenth week with the Paige Co. and his act, he writes, has met with success.

1904 April 18-23: Ben playing in Brunswick, Georgia.

1904 May 6: *Hooligan's Troubles* playing Rohrraugh Theatre, Ottawa, Kansas

1904 May 2-21: Ben playing in Montgomery, Alabama.

The *NY Clipper* published a letter from Ben in an early June issue: "I am on my thirtieth week with the Mabel Paige Company, and have made good everywhere with my *Happy Hooligan* specialty. We close May 21st, at Montgomery, Alabama. I will play parks this summer, and am booked solid until the latter part of September."

Ben was with the Mabel Paige Southern Company for eight months as the company was soon advertising in a December 1904 issue of Billboard for his return! But he quit, went into Chicago, and for quite a while barnstormed around there, playing the variety theaters, occasionally breaking the monotony by taking a tour with some musical comedy, or 'turkey show,' as they were known. The actors would organize a company, play some town on Thanksgiving Day, when good business was always assured, and if they got enough money, they would continue on to some other town; if not, at least they had enough to buy turkey that night — hence the name.[7]

Shortly after the first motion pictures began to come out, enterprising showmen around Chicago rented vacant stores, filled the floor with seats, put up a screen and a small stage, and for a nickel or dime, would furnish those who sought motion pictures and vaudeville one reel of pictures, one song, and some other act. For this, Ben received $3.50 a day. Sundays he worked from eleven in the morning until eleven at night and once did twenty-five shows in that time. Incidentally, Jones, Linick, & Schaeffer, the Chicago firm for whom he worked at this trade, offered him, twenty years later, one thousand dollars for a one night personal appearance and Ben couldn't spare the time to do it. He was on vacation.[7]

"In my early days on the stage, I sure went through a hard mill. I remember one season I was the entire 'in person' act on the bill. They had a little one-reeler; then I'd give a comedy skit; that was the show. And we played it at least ten times a night, as the theater was small, filled up easy and emptied easier. I got $3 a night for my work and was glad to get it.

"Then I joined up with a showboat on the Ohio River. That was a lazy life. I guess I'd been there yet if I hadn't got filled up with malaria and had to get back to land."[9]

Ben came into the world with his eyes as straight as anyone's. He had the advantage of all the others in his *Happy Hooligan* portrayal and literally beat them by a neck, for Ben's neck was built on the lines laid down and denoted in that old-time song about *Annie Laurie*, whose neck was like a swan, and in addition to the length of expanse between collar and chin, Ben pretended to cross the eyes. He did this to add to the imbecile good humor with which Opper invested his cartoon.[10]

"Well, sir, once I started I kept playing that fool part for eleven years. Can you imagine it — *Happy Hooligan* for eleven years?"

After touring as *Happy Hooligan* for three years and having to look cross-eyed nightly for ten to twelve minutes (not to mention the daily matinees), one morning he awoke to the matutinal shave and discovered that jest had been turned to earnest.[5]

"My eyes were straight when I started, perfectly straight. I wasn't such a bad looking fellow. But all this practicing and acting *Happy Hooligan*, crossing my eyes to look the part, strained them pretty bad. One morning I woke up and looked in the glass. My right eye was crossed, and I hadn't crossed it!

"I rubbed it with my fingers — I thought I could push it back. But it wouldn't go.[3]

"*Happy Hooligan* made me cock-eyed. When I looked in the glass, there was that eye, cock-eyed. I didn't know what to do, so I just left it that way. You know, I played the part of *Hooligan* eleven years, and I had to roll my eyes around so much that I pulled a muscle loose sometime when I didn't realize it."[10]

"At first I cried. However, I got over that rather quickly and thought perhaps there might be something to that gag about 'everything is for the best.' I didn't worry much, even though I did give it several thoughts."[45]

"Aw, what's the difference, now I look more like *Happy Hooligan* than ever!"[3]

According to one interviewer, Turpin claimed he consulted surgeons and optical specialists, who told him that a minor operation would probably restore his eyes to normal condition, but the price of a permanent cure would be that he should abandon his impersonation of *Hooligan*. But by this time, Ben's imitation had become popular and besides, there were engagements to fill. He decided to postpone their straightening at least until the end of the season.[11]

"My eye muscles had been so trained I couldn't uncross the eyes without my having an operation performed, which I never did."[2]

Neil M. Clark wrote: "Incidentally, he does not see double. A lot of people seem to think he does. I asked Ben about it, and this is what he said: 'See double? No! That would be a fine fix, wouldn't it! Suppose I looked at a check and saw two checks?'"[3]

Over the years, various stories of the origin of Ben's cross-eyes were the subject of jokes, rumors, old wives' tales, and plain baloney. The man responsible for a lot of the eventual hype, Mack Sennett, eventually confessed to an inquisitive writer for the *Philadelphia Inquirer*, who wanted to know, "Was Ben Turpin made cross-eyed by a juggler's ball falling on his head?" Sennett replied, "He told me he woke up cock-eyed one morning and has been that way ever since."[39]

1905 September 11-16: Ben playing The Olympic Theater, Chicago, on a big bill with Felix, Barry & Barry; Carlin & Otto; Pauline Hall; The Four Musical Avalons; The Great Troba; Lindsay's Dogs and Monks; Ethel Robinson; Fox and Summers; Paulo & Marlow; LeMaire & LeMaire; Babcock Sisters; Paul LeCroix; Belleclair Bros.; and George K. Spoor's Kinodrome.

1905 September 18-23: Ben Turpin plays The Columbia, St. Louis, Missouri, with The Peking Zouaves; Felix & Barry; Mosher, Houghton & Mosher; and Pierce & Maizee.

1905 September 24-30: Ben playing The Haymarket, Chicago.

1905 October 9-15: Ben playing the Grand Family Theater, Hamilton, Ohio, with Don Carlos and His Trained Lion; The Freeze Brothers; Esher Sisters; Nellie Root; and movies.

1905 week of October 23: Ben Turpin, the comedy acrobat, playing the Bijou Theater, Oshkosh, Wisconsin, with Dadi, Illusionist; Jessika, the Country Girl; McSorley and Eleanor, Comedy Sketch Artists; and Broderick, the Tall Pine Tattler.

1905 November 18: Ben Turpin just finished with the Kohl & Castle Circuit, doing his *Happy Hooligan* specialty, and is booked solid until February 4, 1906.[46]

1905 week of December 4: Ben Turpin, Singer, Dancer and Acrobat doing his *Happy Hooligan* at the Bijou Family Theater, Bay City, Michigan, as well as starring as a member of the Bijou Players in a 3-act comedy, *The Troublesome Actors*, playing the *Squier*. Cast also included Mabelle Darr as the *Squier's daughter, Kitty*, Frank W. Shean as the *Troublesome Actor*, and Frank McSorley as the *Street Vender*. Alternating that same week, the Bijou Players also presented their play *Jesse James*. Although Turpin's participation in *Jesse James* is probable, it's unverified. So popular was Ben that he stayed the following week of December 11 with a new bill, which included The Three Mannings; Lindstrom and Anderson; and Miss Flo Morrison.

1906 week of January 1: Turpin again on the Bijou bill, this time with Dunbar's Caprine Paradox; Al Christal; Cook & Oats; Mrs. C.S. Humphrey; moving pictures. Business was good.

1906 January 15: Ben again at the Bijou to furnish laughs for the week in *Happy Hooligan and His Table*. Bill also included Nellie Revell, monologist; the Burke Bros., jugglers; Higgins and Phelps, comics; motion pictures and a sing-a-long. Miss Revell later went on to become vaudeville editor for the *New York Morning Telegraph* and soon general press representative of the Orpheum Circuit. Still later, in 1923, she wrote her autobiography, *Right From the Chest*.

1906 February 1: Miss Nellie Revell, Ben Turpin, and the dancers Jack Brown and Lillian Wright of the Bijou Circuit have been guests for the past week of Mrs. Belle Nunn, 817 Adams Street (Bay City, Michigan). *Bay City Times*

1906 February 12: Turpin in *Happy Hooligan's Troubles* at the Bijou Theater, Racine, Wisconsin played "fair" according to Wm. J. Mulrath's review in *Variety*.

Reviews of Ben Turpin's stage appearances have been scant and criticisms varied. Entertainment industry magazine *Variety* noted on March 10, 1906, at the Idea Theater, Fond du Lac, Wisconsin: "Ben Turpin in *Happy Hooligans Troubles*, big hit."

1906 March 26-April 1: Ben playing the Gaiety Theater, Springfield, Illinois, along with Anderson and Reynolds; Waverly and McRea; Trask and Cummings; and moving pictures.

1906 April 16-21: Ben playing the Olympic Theatre, Chicago.

1906 April 29-May 6: Ben playing the Main Street Theatre, Peoria, Illinois with Peter J. Smith, Carrie Belle Mille, Mexican Gonzales, McGee & Collins.

For a while, Turpin had been trying to get on the Western Vaudeville Association time without much luck. A couple of other people were doing a *Hooligan* act, but Ben could never attract the eyes of the heads of that organization long enough to see him work. One day, he happened to be in the office when the manager of a theater wired down for a comedy act to be sent for his opening show the following day. The manager had booked an act, but cancelled it at the last minute.

"I had about a dollar to my name. Not enough to pay my railroad fare to Marion, so there I was, with a job and no money to get to it. Finally, I took my suitcase and expressed it to Marion. Then, that night I sneaked down into the railroad yards and when the train slowed up, I jumped on and climbed up on the roof or deck, as it was commonly known. It was cold as the dickens, but I wrapped myself around a ventilator pipe and hung on. From up the pipe I could hear someone in a berth below snoring, and I wondered if I would ever be wealthy enough to be laying down there under nice warm blankets, taking life easy.

"When the train got into Marion, I slid down on the far side from the station and got uptown without being caught. I got my suitcase out of the express office, went up to a hotel that had a dining room in connection, cleaned up, ate a huge breakfast, for which I signed, and then took my stuff up to the theater. It being Monday morning, all the acts for the week were rehearsing, and the theater manager had on an awful grouch.

"'What's your act?' he asked me, as soon as I came on the stage.

"'*Knockabout Hooligan*,' I replied.

"'Oh, Lord!' he yelled. 'We had a *Hooligan* here last week, and he was so rotten I had to cancel him in the middle of the week. You'd better pack up and go right back to Chicago.'

"There I was, without a cent, in pawn to the hotel, and a long ways from home and money. You bet I put up an argument.

"'Maybe my act is different,' I said. 'It goes big everywhere I play it.'

"'Well, it better be good; if not, I'll close you after the first show,' he said.

"To make a long story short, I never worked so hard in my life. I pulled falls that I had never done before, and I made good. The manager had put me on to open the show — the worst place on the program — but before the middle of the week, I had the star-act position. He got over his grouch and wrote a nice letter about me to the Chicago office. When I got back there, with what was left of my thirty dollars for the week's work, I had a route booked and was kept pretty busy for some time."[7]

On May 26, 1906, The Police Gazette, NYC announced that Ben was booked by the Western Managers' Association until June 4. After that, he would join hands with Orra W. Nichols, accomplished bicycle rider, and the team would be known as Turpin and Nichols, their new act to be called *Hooligan's Mishaps On A Bicycle*.

1906 May 28-June 3: Ben playing the Savoy Theatre, Columbus, Indiana with Clayton and Hufford; The Clarence Sisters; and moving pictures.

1906 June 3: After a successful week at Oak Summit Park, Evansville, Indiana and having "took well" as per Robert L. Odell in *Variety*, Ben returns there June 18-21.

1906 June 30: Turpin and Nichols, comedy cyclists, are playing parks in the Midwest. They are scheduled to open on one of the Western Circuits shortly.[47]

1906 August 26: This week at the West End Park Theater, New Orleans, featured Fischer's Military Band; the Gonzales Brothers, Mexican Duettists; the Swor Bros; Charlotte Ravenscroft; and Ben Turpin in a "comedy acrobatic cycle act"[48] with no mention of the cyclist, Orra W. Nichols. "Ben Turpin, a new addition to the West End program, will set the sides to aching with laughter with his grotesque and comedy acrobatic stunts."[49] Orra soon teamed up with Russell Smith and they were a hit with a rube tri-unicycle act and the amazing powers of equilibrium.

1906 September: Ben Turpin, in a "new act," playing the West End Theater, New Orleans with Lavinia DeWitt, singer/cornetist; Fox and Foxie; comedians, Gonzales Brothers; Fischer's Band; and moving pictures. After a successful first week, Ben stayed an additional run. One writer noted, "Ben Turpin, the *Happy Hooligan* gymnast, is also one of the hold-overs, and continues to win applause with his make-up and his queer antics. In addition to this Ben does a couple of good stunts and fairly earns his pay as a laugh producer."[50]

The New Orleans Item, September 1, 1906, wrote of Turpin's West End performance: "When it comes down to getting applause, Ben Turpin, the comedy acrobat, also seems to be the real thing. In a *Happy Hooligan* make-up Ben capers around the stage in a way that keeps his audience in a roar of merriment all during his act."

1906 September: Ben appearing in Peoria, Illinois' Weaston Theater along with The Dalgren Sisters; The Rinaldos; McKinnon and Reed; Gene Rogers; and moving pictures.

The Deseret Evening News, Salt Lake City, Utah, October 20, 1906, made note of his Orpheum Theatre appearance: "Ben Turpin, acrobatic comedian, has a hilarious wrestle with a table in an act which deals with the troubles of *Happy Hooligan*." The October 23 *Salt Lake Herald* wrote: "Ben Turpin, the latest *Happy Hooligan* to arouse a smile, opens the bill with a knockabout song and dance turn with the assistance of a chair, table and a broom."

The Salt Lake City *Inter-Mountain Republican*, October 21, 1906, noted, "Ben Turpin in his appropriate makeup gives a very laughable version of the troubles of *Happy Hooligan*. With a table he manages to keep the house in a roar." Jay E. Johnson for *Variety* (Nov. 3, 1906) wrote of Ben's *Hooligan* as "well done." Ben was reengaged for a second week with one writer noting, "The Orpheum got off wrong on the first night on account of the non-appearance of two or three acts, which, however came up on Tuesday with a fairly, evenly balanced program, the exception being Ben Turpin, with some *Hooligan* stunts that were really slanderous on the happy one."[51]

An unidentified writer for the *Salt Lake Telegram* thought, "Ben Turpin in a *Happy Hooligan* make-up does nothing especially new in the way of knockabout comedy, but does it well."[52]

Early in 1907, Ben met Carrie LeMieux, a twenty-four-year-old stage actress and, according to Ben, within a week after just meeting, they were married on February 18,

1907, in Chicago. Another source suggests the couple were friends at least as early as 1905. On the marriage license, Ben claimed he was age 32, although really 37.

Catherina *Carrie* LeMieux was born on October 18, 1882, and immigrated with her family to Alpena, Michigan from Quebec in the late 1880's. Her father, August LeMieux (b1846, Cape St. Ignace, Canada; d1929 Alpena), was a mason by profession with six children. Their mother, Ellen, died in 1901. Writer Dorothy Wooldridge later noted: (Ben and Carrie) married in Chicago, two struggling actors uniting kindred sympathies. Before that, Ben had spent a lifetime as an ambitionless tramp, taking things as they came — joy and sorrow — all with the same shoulder shrug of abandon. He had cheered his comrades of the road with songs & dances, grimaces & humorous recitals. His minstrelry gained him mention, then a vaudeville contract.

Over the years of their marriage, in adversity and prosperity alike, Carrie would be Ben's valued companion and trusted counselor. He told how Carrie had stuck by him through all the lean years, cheered him, comforted him, cared for him, made him go to church and confession, ministered to his needs, helped him out with his *Happy Hooligan* act when he was playing cheap variety theaters. He told how she had said to him, "Never mind, Ben, better times are coming out there. We'll make it." Ben told Wooldridge, "I knew we'd make it, so long as she was with me. Why, I would have lived on soup bones to give her the necessities. She was the first woman to believe in me I had ever known."[12]

An anonymous writer for the *New Orleans Times-Picayune* later noted, "Ben and his wife were a quaint pair. Both old-fashioned, both devoutly religious, their wants and their lives were extremely simple in spite of Ben's enormous income."

August 15, 1926, pg 62

Soon moving into a home together at 361 N. Wells, Chicago, they were very poor in the first years of their marriage. Sometimes when there was no booking for them, Ben would leave her in Chicago and follow the county fairs as a taffy puller. He used to work the hot sweet over hooks on the outside of the candy booth and pull it until it became light-colored. Ben's duty was to attract a crowd by his antics and grand flourishes with the taffy. Sometimes he returned with a little carefully hoarded fund and sometimes he came back to Chicago via the brake-beams of a train. He and his wife were very poor, but they were content. Those who knew him say that Ben Turpin had always been humble of soul and it must have seemed a miracle to him that any woman could love him, the laughable, the unhandsome, the clown of life.[13]

1907 May 27-June: Ben in an acrobatic song and dance playing the North Avenue Theatre, Chicago along with The Tinkham Company Motor Cage; The Victors, boxing; The Roberts Four in *The Doll Making Dilemma*; Curran & Milton in a comedy sketch; plus illustrated songs and pictures.

Years ahead in the summer of 1921, just following a week's engagement at McVickers Theater, Chicago, Ben was interviewed by Carl Sandburg en route to visit a children's hospital. Sandburg noted, "Ben looked at a row of brick houses on Washington Blvd. with its long rows of stone steps and said, 'I used to scrub those steps for fifty cents a pair just fourteen years ago. Yep, I used to be a sort of handy man in this neighborhood. Cut the grass in the summer and shovel the snow in winter was my task — all for twenty-five cents. I remember how hard it was for me to save my first $100. In fact, I never did. Each time I found my bankbook registering about $30 along came a doctor bill and I had to start all over. No, I never did save that hundred.

"The first money I ever put away was when Mack Sennett handed me a thousand dollars upon my signing his contract. That went into the bank quickly. After that saving was not so hard. The little old bankbook whispered in my ear just before I left Los Angeles that my balance had just topped $50,000. Not so bad for a cock-eyed guy of 52 years who was scrubbing stone steps only a few years ago, who was a bellboy at the Sherman Hotel, who eked out a bare living in cheap vaudeville theaters for too many years to remember and who has stayed married to the same woman for almost sixteen years."[27]

Essanay
Slapstick of the Roughest Sort

"I'd married a girl who was making a man out of me, and it was a shame she had to live the way I did, with nothing that even looked like a home. So when I got this tip about the movies, I looked around and got a job with Mr. Spoor — the 'Ess' in Essanay, the big producers, you know."[3] Years later, Ben recalled, "I got into pictures back when the little nickel theatres were just beginning to spring up."[15]

"About that time things were getting pretty tough. I used to do eleven shows a day, sometimes more, and was paid $3. Shows were closing right and left during the panic and there I was without funds."[15] It is presumed that "the panic" began with Chicago's horrifically tragic Iroquois Theater fire of December 1903. Over 600 people died as a result of the catastrophe, mostly women and children, immediately forcing the total safety inspections of all buildings. Many theaters were closed temporarily for renovations while others were torn down forever.

"It was in the spring of 1907 while I was in Chicago that I secured my first job in motion pictures. I was walking along Clark Street one day when I met G. M. Anderson. We stopped to talk and he asked me how I would like to be a motion picture actor. I asked him what I would have to do and he told me 'falls.' I told him that *falls* was my middle name."

The Essanay Film Manufacturing Co. opened for business in a loft building above the Richardson Roller Skate Co. at 501 North Wells Street, Chicago, soon after their incorporation on February 5, 1907. The company name was devised from the surname initials of the two owners, George K. Spoor and Gilbert M. Anderson, *S an' A*. The two men soon adopted a similar Indian head from the then circulating American penny as their trademark. Spoor was an inventor and former proprietor of the National Film Rental Company, Chicago, when Anderson, an ambitious young actor with bigger dreams, approached Spoor with his ideas. Anderson arrived at an opportune moment. There was a scarcity of pictures for Spoor's vaudeville circuit and the growing exhibitors. By February 1908, there were 196 nickelodeons in Chicago alone. The two men decided to go into business together and Ben was one of their first employees.

"If I'd been handsome, I'd have been a dramatic actor right along, but with these eyes wished on me I had to find something to do that would keep me in a permanent job. I didn't know the ropes in the old days of pictures, so when Essanay offered me twenty dollars a week, I thought I was on the way to Paradise. You see I'd rarely earned much more than twenty-five on the vaudeville circuits. I used to do everything from mopping floors to camera-grinding for scene numbers. Anything to stay on that lot and earn a regular salary," Turpin remembered.

"'You'll get twenty dollars a week,' Anderson said, 'you carry your own props. But it's steady money every week.'

"That didn't look so bad to me. It would be better than fifty or sixty a week, some weeks, paying my own expenses, and making my wife go all over the country with me."[3]

"It was funny how I happened to start work in pictures," Ben recalled. "I had been on the stage since 1890 and for several years had been doing my *Happy Hooligan* act. I was a tumbler and as I had a long neck like the funny paper comic, I received many laughs along with my 'cocked-eyes.'

"(Anderson) engaged me for the first picture the Essanay put out, and believe me it was some tough work."[21]

"The first picture I ever worked in was titled *The Awful Skate* (or *The Hobo on Rollers,* released July 27, 1907). I don't recall the names of those in the cast, but I sure did a lot of falls." The film's inspiration was natural: a roller skating rink occupied the ground floor below Essanay and skating was a latest craze. Simply said, the comedy featured hobo Ben careening down streets on roller skates, bumping into moving men and outraged pedestrians, who were later paid two dollars each for their inconvenience. Cops and kids take chase and catch the hobo. Fortunately, this film still survives, though unfortunately, only about a third. That first film was a surprisingly overwhelming financial success, encouraging the new company to continue in their business venture, making moving pictures. They kept Turpin on as their company comedian and more.

"After *(The Awful Skate)* was finished, G. M. kept me on at a salary of twenty dollars a week. I soon found that I'd been engaged as a man of all work. We had to take some interiors so I built the stage. We had no stage braces so I had to nail it to the fence in the yard. I was also head property man, wardrobe man and had to carry the tripod at intervals."[17] This was just the beginning.

One early writer noted: *They were a strange-looking aggregation and the conductor on the Chicago street car didn't approve of the dozen passengers who just boarded his trolley, or the various articles they carried. Some carried washtubs, buckets, stepladders, pots, pans, flatirons, dishes, pieces of stoves, and various other articles of household equipment. All were loaded down like so many packhorses.*

It was the last one to board the car the conductor disliked the most — he was the smallest of the crowd and he carried the most. Under one arm he lugged a stepladder, rolls of wallpaper, a large brush, and in the hand of the same arm, he carried a big bucket of paste. Under the other arm, he had several small rolled rugs and a fifteen-foot roll of painted canvas. Around his neck were several coils of rope.

The time was 1907, the city Chicago, and the destination was "location" for a bunch of moving picture actors of the old Essanay studio.

The little man in the back was starting his first day's employment with the movie outfit. He had no particular title, but he was engaged to "act funny" in the pictures, escort the other players to "location," be sure that all the "props" were accounted for, act as timekeeper, sweep out the office, and in his spare time, assist in directing pictures. He was Ben Turpin.

For their first pictures, a platform was erected in an empty lot and the necessary furniture was rented or borrowed. Anderson, soon a major star in his own *Broncho Billy* westerns, recalled, "I take credit for Ben. When I met him he was playing little vaudeville dates, and he came out to the studio and was a janitor, he swept the floor. And he did that so nice and good, and he was so funny looking, that I thought he'd make a good comedian."[14]

After many bumps and bruises in the years ahead, in 1918, writer Harry Carr went *Looking Backwards With Ben* in *Photoplay* magazine: At (the) time, G. M. Anderson was just starting up in Chicago as a picture magnate and he gave Ben a job. At least Ben described it as a job. He doesn't know what it was.

"Them was the good old days," so Ben often sighs.

Every morning when Ben came to work, his first duty of the organization was to sweep out the boss' office. After that, he assembled the props to be used that day and they started out on location. In those days, the studio was in a back lot in Chicago. They didn't have any interiors. When they simply had to have some scenery that they couldn't find outdoors, they painted a piece of canvas and hung it on the back fence. Then the play acted in front of it. The trouble was the sun cast shadows on it unless the sun was just right. As they didn't like to have the shadow of an actor enveloping a whole mountainside, they had to wait for the sun to be right. Ben says that while they were waiting for the sun, he used to work in the shipping room with a hammer and nails, boxing up film for shipment. Oh, them was happy days![20]

Ben recalled, "I was doing carpenter work in the old days at the Essanay studio when we had to borrow properties and use barns for stages or any location we could get free. One day Manager Spoor saw me climbing over a fence with a bouquet of flowers. He followed me through a field to a little graveyard. I was kneeling over a grave placing the flowers on it and smoothing over the dirt when he came up. It was evident that his curiosity was aroused and he seemed deeply moved about something.

"'Ben,' he said, 'I'm frank to say I'm deeply touched. I didn't know it was in you to have such emotions. Let me buy some flowers for that mound. Whose grave is it? I'm sorry and would like to help you if I can.'

"For a moment I didn't know what to say, then I blurted out the blunt truth.

"'Gee, I don't know whose grave it is,' I replied. 'We needed the flowers for the stage and this is where I found them.'"

"Right then and there he engaged me for the next picture."[16]

Both Spoor and matinee idol Francis X. Bushman loved to repeat a redressed story.

"They didn't use automobiles to go to locations then," said Ben, recounting his early adventures to Harry Carr. "They sent us out in street cars. Every actor had to carry part of the scenery. Out of gallantry we let the ladies carry the tripods of the cameras while we carried chairs and screens and office furniture. Of course we had to go in all our make-up and we used to have some strange adventures. They didn't think much of picture folks in those days.

"I remember one time we had to make a comedy in which I had to fall in a fountain. Nobody would let us use a fountain so we went down to South Park Chicago and stole a location. I had just gone in with a grand flop when somebody yelled 'Cheese it!' Everybody else took to their heels and beat it with their cameras over their shoulders; but here I was, sopping wet, in the fountain. I came flopping out straight into the mitts of a policeman. Believe me, he was a big red-faced Irish cop and he didn't waste any words.

"I tried to tell him I was doing it for art's sake, but all he said was 'Come along.' They took me to jail and I was there four hours shivering in my wet clothes before I could get hold of anybody to bail me out. I didn't have a cent so when they let me out I had to walk home about a million miles in my wet rags."

Once, Ben was thrown out of a window onto a sawdust pile. At least that was the theory. The powerful and manly hero got too enthusiastic and tossed him clear over the sawdust pile. It was a regular home. Ben broke his hip. During the time of his convalescence, they let him work in the developing room turning one of the big drying drums, which then worked by hand power.

"One time they needed a cop's uniform and, being the regular goat, they sent me to go borrow one. You couldn't get police clothes at the costumers in those days.

"Well, I walk into a Chicago police station and gave them a happy smile. 'Good morning, gents, I want to know if one of you gents will be so kind as to lend me a police uniform.' That was as far as I got. One of the big police sergeants got up and grabbed me by the coat collar.

"'You can't ridicule a policeman in Chicago,' says he. And with that I was bounced on my bean out on the sidewalk."[20]

Writer Karen Kruse noted how Anderson was at least once even arrested for turning in a false fire alarm just so they could film Ben being chased by the horse-drawn fire wagons of Engine #78.[53]

Fellow co-worker and later gossip writer Louella Parsons recalled: At Essanay behind the scenes each day, Ben swept the dust upon where the great had trod. He was pleasant and he was reliable and he held the post for a long time. One day a comedian failed to appear for the filming of a script. The director was desperate. As he was pacing the floor in desperation, Ben popped into the room with his broom. The assembled actors burst into laughter. That was enough for the director and Turpin became a screen actor.[25]

In the early days, Anderson and Turpin, the Essanay's principal actors producing mostly slapstick comedies, would cruise around Chicago in the company car in search of inspiration. An epic known as *The Street Fakir* (re November 2, 1907), for example, resulted when Anderson spotted a piece of soap in a grocer bin:

Scene 1: Turpin steals soap by jabbing a nail attached to a string into soap and walks away with the other end of string in his pocket.

Scene 2: He cuts soap into little squares, wraps them, and sells them on the street corner, his gestures indicating that it's a new corn remedy.

Scene 3: Turpin moves to another corner, where limping customer catches up, angrily shaking the remedy at him. As Ben moves on, more and more customers join in pursuit and the close is a pell-mell chase with Turpin falling flat on his face.[16]

Most of the comedies were that simple and the crowds loved them.

While with Essanay during the day, Ben moonlighted most nights. He played the week of September 23, 1907, at the National Theater, Chicago, along with Charles & Minnie Gills, The Two Mannons, and The Popes.

A week later, September 30, Turpin was busy playing Howard's, Chicago, along with Roland Travers & Co.; Schepp's Dog & Pony Circus; Will & May Reno; Billy McRobey; Kohler & Victoria; Barlow & Nicholson; Genie Leslie; and moving pictures.

In October, Ben appears at the redecorated and repainted reopening of the Thirty-First Street Theatre (Chicago), along with Tetsuwari Japanese Troupe; Roland Travers and Company; Charles & Cantina Lawrence; and others.

Week of October 28: Ben playing Hyde Park Theater, Chicago with McBargh & Sharewood; Flossie Gibson; Dupree & Dupree; Knapp & Swanson; and movies.

Week of November 17, 1907: Ben as *Happy Hooligan* appearing at The Virginian, Chicago along with Grace Coyne, character change soubrette; Courtney & Jeanette, comedy jugglers; Daisy Lawrence's Dogs & Ponies; the Virginian Stock Company in *The Wild West*; and the VirginiaScope moving pictures.

At Essanay, Turpin continued to be featured in the comedies and was often involved in the films' construction and direction. He may well have also had a hand in, in some aspect or another, any and all of the small company's early productions.

Oh, What Lungs! (re July 1, 1908): A comic from the Essanay people which never fails to get a good laugh and in some theaters is applauded. A weak-lunged individual goes to a doctor, who announces himself as able to cure that ailment. The treatment is applied and the individual emerges from the office with a pair of lungs strong enough to move anything by the mere force of blowing. The situations are very amusing and the comedian of the Essanay studio, Ben Turpin, scores another success. *MPW*

Ben later recalled, "In late 1908, Francis Powers was directing the great actor Henry Dixey, in *A Christmas Carol*. Dixey was so important a personage that he rode back and forth from the Sherman House hotel in an automobile.

"One morning, Powers came over to me and said, 'Ben, go and make up for the King's jester.' I did as I was told and walked nonchalantly down to Mr. Powers, carrying the little jester bauble with the Punch & Judy head.

"'My God! Powers, what is that? I couldn't work near such a face!' was Dixey's wild comment. Powers had not warned him. So I was rushed back to the prop room without further ado."[24]

By November of '08, the Essanay comedies had become so popular, the company was soon dubbed *The House of Comedy Hits*. Each new comedy, western, and dramatic release seemed better than the last and their films so financially successful, the company soon moved into a new, much larger and well-equipped plant.

Ben recalled, "Late in November (1908) Anderson came to me and said that we would leave for Los Angeles, on December 3. We arrived soon after that date and were the first company to come to this city. I remember we had a hard time getting actors and Mr. Anderson was compelled to pay extras $10 to $15 a day. Our first picture was called *Tag Day* and crowds used to surround us and stare in wonder while we were at work.

"One day we were working in Eastlake Park when a woman approached Mr. Anderson and asked what was the matter with me.

"'Oh,' said Anderson, 'he's only crazy. Just watch and you'll see him jump in the lake. That is one of his usual stunts when a spell strikes him.'

"Just then I was given the go signal and jumped in. Then when I came out I had to do it over again; the cameraman had run out of film. And do you know I would not be surprised if that woman still thinks she saw a crazy man whose delusion was that he should jump in a lake every time he saw one."[22]

Tag Day and *Bring Me Some Ice* (re February 17, 1909): In these two films, the Essanay folks show great improvement. Although they stick to the comic, which in fact is the best work for them, they seem to abandon the long chases and the too-silly stunts. The details are carefully worked out; the actions are natural and well-timed. The photography is greatly improved and by taking these films in a warmer climate, the Essanay Company brings out some fine tropical scenery. The hearty welcome given these films proves that comic productions can please without being silly or a general destruction of property. *MPW*

Anderson recalled in 1964, "*Tag Day* was the first movie in Los Angeles history. We were using Westlake (now MacArthur) Park as a location, and Ben had to jump in the lake and grab a duck for one of the scenes. He'd scarcely hit the water and got hold of the duck when policemen surrounded us. They took us all to jail for creating a disturbance. When we got out we finished our picture in Boyle Heights, dodging the lawmen. But I never tried to make another movie in Los Angeles."

Westerner, July/August 1972, pg 62

In 1917 writer Beatriz Michelina noted those earlier films, "It must be remembered that, at this early date, motion pictures were still a novelty in themselves and the first crude Essanay comedies, showing the principals chasing each other around the block, squirting the hose on unsuspecting passersby, or hurling pies and other missiles, were hailed with delight by motion picture patrons. It was the weak beginning of a big enterprise.[23]

In these days when movies were still in their infancy, Ben wrote of his art in *Moving Picture World* magazine, April 3, 1909, a rare instance of a player writing about the industry:

"This is a great life. I have been in the moving picture biz working for the Essanay for two years, and I must say I had many a good fall, and many a good bump, and I think

I've broken about twenty barrels of dishes, upset stoves, and also broken up many sets of beautiful furniture, had my eyes blackened, both ankles sprained and many bruises, and I am still on the go. This is a great business.

"I shall never forget how about a year ago I engaged a fellow to play a part in one of our pictures; he was to be thrown into the water, and I asked him if he could swim, and he said yes, so he was engaged. I, being a comedian, was to throw him into the water, which I did. The moment he hit the water he went down, and as soon as he came up he began to holler, 'Get the boat! Get the boat!' He came very near drowning. The moving picture operator was still grinding when the director hollered him to stop. We finally got the boat and got him out. The moment he got on shore he started to run, and we haven't seen him since."

Turpin continues, "The hardest picture that I ever worked in, when I got mine, was called *Midnight Disturbance*, where a dog, and a bulldog at that, has to catch a pad which is attached to my waist, so he missed the pad, and he caught a piece of my flesh. I upset some of the scenery and we had to take it over again. On rehearsing the dog so as to catch the pad, I was bit several times, but the director only says to me — 'Well, Ben, does it hurt?'"[26]

A Midnight Disturbance (re March 24, 1909): A burglar (Turpin) has entered the top story of a flat by means of the fire escape and has the misfortune to arouse the occupants. They give chase, forcing the burglar to return to the fire escape for an exit. Being closely pursued, the thief is compelled to enter the next window below, arousing the tenant in his hasty endeavor to get away. The pursuers are joined by the person disturbed and the culprit is again forced to make the fire escape. In and out of the windows, on and off the fire escape, the unfortunate burglar is pursued by the ever-increasing mob through the hallways, knocking everyone down that comes between him and his freedom. At last his nemesis appears in the shape of a bulldog, who follows him with a persistency that brings about his capture. A policeman figures prominently in the picture as well as a gentleman about to take a bath. The following crowd is dressed in a variety of costumes that adds greatly to the comical events. All the action takes place either in the interiors or upon the fire escape in midair. Length, 525 feet. *MPW*

Moving Picture World noted, "A very laughable ten minutes. This is the film in the rehearsals of which their comedian, Mr. Turpin, lost some of his skin while the tenacious bulldog was being trained to hold on to the seat of his pants. The sketch is a good one and gets the laughter, but is rather drawn out, and some of the scenes could have been cut down without injury to the whole."

On the other half of that release was another split-reel comedy with Turpin, *The Energetic Street Cleaner*: "A bit of comedy from the Essanay studio which affords an opportunity for their popular comedian to show his quality. A man is given employment in the department of street cleaning and goes about his work so vigorously that everything that comes in his path is swept away, including people. Few films are greeted with more laughter than this. It is lively and the sport is clean." *MPW*

Ben continues his tale, *Life of a Motion Picture Comedian*: "Once I was working in a comedy in Chicago. It was midwinter and the wind blew icy cold. They had a scene in which a tramp was flung into a fountain. I was the tramp. There were so many formalities to be gone through before permission could be got to use the fountain in the public park that the director decided to chance it before the park police came along. We got busy, and two husky men flung me in, and — it was cold. I came up spluttering, then — 'Look out — the cops!' somebody yelled. And the outfit bolted, leaving me in the basin of the fountain. The cop grabbed me, and sent me on a long, freezing ride in the police wagon. For four hours I sat in the police station waiting to be bailed, but no one came, and at last they kicked me out. I hadn't a penny, so I had to walk five miles through the streets of Chicago, dripping icicles, at the head of a procession of small boys. At last I got back with wet tramp clothes and a red nose. And the company actually said it was the funniest thing that ever happened to me."[26]

Anderson told *The Denver Post* in 1909, "Our studio in Chicago occupies a whole floor, and there we make all interior scenes, and maintain a picked permanent company of players. During the summer we make outdoor pictures in and around Chicago, but when fall comes, I take a photographer, property man and several principals, and follow the warm weather."

Unfortunately, many of these earliest Essanay films are probably gone forever. Anderson tells why: "Our films will be sent to the head office in Chicago, and from there they are leased to 'renters,' as the jobbers of the moving picture industry are called. This lease calls for the return of the films after six months, for then they are worn out, and the company takes the means of protecting the people against spoiled pictures. The 'renters' then lease them out to the picture shows at so much a day.

"The first run of the films, of course, are seen in the cities at the best shows, and on down the line until the expiration of six months finds them delighting the Podunk populace. Then they are sent back to Chicago, and 'melted up,' for there is a lot of silver in them. The Essanay Company, for instance, nets about $2,000 a year from this melting process alone."

Those few films having escaped the fiery inferno have surely since decomposed unless saved by a fortunate fate or the caring film preservationists. To the best of this authors present knowledge of the earliest Turpin comedies (1907-1909), *The Awful Skate, A Disastrous Flirtation, A Case of Seltzer, The Neighbor's Kids, The Haunted Lounge,* and *Mr. Flip,* are the only few that survive, complete and/or incomplete. Here's hoping additional titles will surface.

The earliest of all Turpin films, those produced during his first two years with Essanay, are those hardest to document. Most actors and their studios didn't announce their players' identities, often acting in full or near anonymity. Players in those days were ashamed to tell of their association with movies, as the public didn't care for actors much at first. The early periodicals almost never mention Turpin nor any actor or actress among the cast of particular film titles. That soon changed with the eventual public acceptance of moving pictures, their sudden favor and the curiosity of the picture going public.

However, it is known that Ben was Essanay's chief comic and can be presumed the star of a great number — if not all — of the company's comedies in the first two years. Such films as *Hired, Tired and Fired,* an Essanay release of September 23, 1908, may well have been a Turpin comedy: "This picture portrays the various manners in which a young fellow (who evidently was born with a decidedly lazy streak in his make-up) secures work, gets tired and is fired without unnecessary delay. He is employed to help move some furniture, and the listless manner in which he handles it soon secures his discharge. Then in rapid succession we find him a waiter, a bartender, etc., from all of which positions his lack of energy soon leads to his dismissal. Finally he becomes a policeman, which job he holds without making any particular effort — in fact, this seems to be the only position he is able to hold."

Another Ben Turpin possibility was the film *Never Again* (re Sept. 23, 1908): "A comedy of excellent merit has been made out of this very popular and well-fitting expression. How often have you allowed yourself to do something and then vowed never again to repeat the experience? Such is the case in this subject with our principal character, who, after tolerating the excessive heat all day, thinks he sees an avenue of escape when he reads a circular announcing that you should 'Keep Cool by Going to Coney Isle.' He makes up his mind to go, little imagining he would have been much better off had he stayed at home. He hires an auto to take him to the boat landing, but it breaks down and he has to help in an endeavor to pull it out of a hole. He does not succeed in doing this, and in order to catch the boat he has to run, managing to get the boat as it leaves the pier. The boat crowded, he is squeezed to a pulp by two very fat women. Finally he arrives at the island, after that he has all kinds of trouble, which continues until he decides he has had quite enough of 'Cool Coney Isle.' He starts for home, and then finds all the boats and cars have gone and he has to hoof it. When he arrives in the city he spies a sandwich man advertising the cool breezes of Coney Isle, and what he does to the sign is a caution." *Billboard*

Yet another Turpin probability was the July 14, 1909 split-reel comedy *The New Cop*: "An undersized man, gifted with much ignorance, but who has a pull with a local politician, secures a position as a policeman. He is given a book of rules and told to enforce the law on his beat, and his efforts in trying to arrest innocent people are extremely ludicrous. A man is trying to get into his own home and *The New Cop*, thinking he is a burglar, pounces on him. A man carrying a bundle of laundry is intercepted. A painter going up a ladder is pulled down. The new cop goes on doing these ridiculous things until he meets a bulldog on the sidewalk. This proves his Waterloo. The policeman tells the lady her dog must be muzzled. She becomes very indignant at his intrusion and lets the dog loose. The cop immediately beats it and the dog gives chase. The cop runs into the police station with dog hanging on to him, begging aid from the sergeant. The sergeant takes the star from the cop's uniform and forcibly ejects him and the dog from the place."

The Rube and the Bunco Men (re April 14, 1909) is another lost film, although, in a rare instance, we do know it starred Turpin. *Moving Picture World* wrote: "There are numerous funny situations developed as the picture unfolds which cannot be described. It is a good bit of comedy and gives the Essanay funny man, Turpin, an opportunity to display his powers, which he does to good advantage."

The Sleeping Tonic (re June 2, 1909) is "an Essanay film which allows their comedian, Turpin, to do some more of his funny stunts. He can act the sleeping part quite as well as he does the livelier parts which have so often fallen to his lot, and the places he selects in which to fall asleep bring him several different kinds of trouble. In a few places the photography is weak." *MPW*

Of the very few surviving Turpin films…

The Haunted Lounge (re January 6, 1909), *Moving Picture World* noted:

"This is a story briefly told, but brimful of clean laughable comedy. We consider this one of Essanay's best efforts." In his haste to escape from the clutches of the law, a tramp

(Turpin) rushes into a secondhand store and hides in a folding lounge. An old maid later purchases the lounge and, after having it delivered to her house, discovers the lounge moving. Frightened, she sells it to a neighbor. The neighbor, after a similar experience, sells it to someone else. The lounge changes hands continually until it is sold back to the secondhand dealer where it is bought by the same policeman. Getting it home, then trying to sleep upon it, the lounge moves with the policeman clinging to it. After riding it around the room, the lounge heads out the door, down the hall and stairs and into the backyard. Here the policeman decides to burn the lounge and after it is burned to ashes, beholds the tramp standing in the center of the ash heap unharmed. The police arrest him for disturbing the peace.

Mr. Flip (re May 12, 1909): A young man (Ben), after dressing himself in extraordinarily bad taste, sallies forth to conquer the fair sex. He first enters a dry goods store, endeavors to start a flirtation with a saleswoman, receives a slap to the face and gets ejected. He next enters a manicuring parlor, telephone office, a lady barbershop, a bar room then lunchroom, and in each instance his fate is the same as experienced in the dry goods store. Unfortunately that's where the extant print ends. The missing footage contained: We next find him occupying a box seat at a vaudeville show. A soubrette is doing a song and dance, and, after starting a flirtation with her, he sends her a bouquet with his card, requesting that she meet him after the show. The actress has her colored maid keep the appointment, and places her coat and hat upon the maid, covering her face with a heavy veil. The young man, waiting at the stage door, meets the wench, and together they enter a cafe. After ordering a sumptuous repast, *Mr. Flip* endeavors to embrace his companion, and, in doing so, her veil is disarranged, revealing the fact that she is a Negress. He is roughly ejected by the waiters in attendance. He meets his Waterloo at the hands of a bevy of laundry girls. The surviving print of *Mr. Flip* is unfortunately missing its second half.

A Case of Seltzer (re July 28, 1909): In one of Ben's last comedies made in his first two years at Essanay, *Moving Picture World* wrote: "A lively comedy in which a masher (Turpin) is soundly thrashed and his dandified appearance seriously damaged by a vigorous application of the contents of a number of seltzer bottles. One might wish that other cases of this kind might be as summarily dealt with. Such a film affords little chance for dramatic action. The interest is centered in the roughhouse which constitutes the bulk of the action."

After two years with Essanay, Ben and Carrie found their perfect apartment at 1401 Wells Street in the heart of Chicago and close and convenient to the studio.

"My wife and I wanted to set up in housekeeping, so we found a little flat that we could get for nine dollars a month. Then we selected some furniture — maybe two hundred and fifty dollars' worth — but I lacked fifty dollars for the first installment. That shows how hard up we were. I went to Mr. Spoor and told him I wanted to borrow fifty dollars.

"'I'll give you the money,' Spoor said, 'and take it out of your pay, five dollars every week.'

"'All right,' I said, 'just so you're a good fellow and don't take out ten dollars a week. We couldn't eat if you did!'

"So, at the end of two years I wanted a raise and I asked for more money.

"I went to Mr. Spoor and told him I thought I was worth twice as much as I was getting.

"Spoor said he believed the public was getting tired of seeing me in pictures.

"'No,' he said. 'The truth is, Ben,' he added, 'I think you're getting stale in the pictures. Now suppose I just pension you off — give you twenty-five dollars a week, and you stay out of pictures.'

"I looked him straight in the eye, and I knew then if I did what he said, Ben Turpin was a goner. He was through. 'I won't do it!' I said.

"He was obstinate and wouldn't give me twenty-five dollars a week and a chance to stay in pictures. So I went back on the road again."[3]

"I quit, tried vaudeville for a while, worked extra in pictures and (eventually) returned to Essanay. Spoor let me cool my heels plenty."[15]

Years later, Ben told *The Oregonian*, "I was the best actor and handiest man the Essanay had."[9]

1909 May 29: Ben Turpin, who posed for many motion pictures for Essanay for the past two years, has decided to reenter vaudeville the coming season.[54]

Ben later remembered, "I went the round of variety houses for three more years. It was the same old grind I had gone into movies to get away from, and I soon got sick of it."[3]

When there were no bookings, Ben would travel with the county fairs, pulling taffy or clowning in circuses when necessary to make a few bucks.

See Comedian in Pictures and In Real Life (October 30, 1909)

An audience in the Star Theatre in Aurora, Illinois recently enjoyed the novelty of seeing a moving picture comedian in real life and pictures on the screen. Ben Turpin, formerly employed by the Essanay company, showed at the Star Theatre in a *Happy Hooligan* act. The picture following his act was the Essanay's *Breaking Into Society* in which Turpin played the leading part. In his comedy, the funny little man appears at his best and his antics caused much applause.

Though Ben's double act was not announced, many in the audience had recognized him in the picture and applauded as loudly as they had when he amused them as *Happy Hooligan*. The novelty of the double performance attracted large crowds and packed the little theater during every performance.[11]

Breaking Into Society is one of the funniest farce comedies the Essanay Co. have released. It is a full reel comedy and is a big laugh from start to finish.
The Woodland Daily Democrat, December 29, 1908

The comedy picture, *Breaking Into Society*, showing where an Irishman inherits millions and goes in for society to find later that he was the wrong man, is very funny.
Mansfield News, February 16, 1909

1909 August 28: Ben & May Wallace form a team opening at Palais Royal, Chicago.
Variety

1909 November 10, *The Piqua Daily Call* (Ohio): at The Bijou Theater, last half of the week: Blue Feather Orchestra; Al Hessie, Comedy Juggler; Motion Pictures; Ben Turpin,

Tramp Comedian; Eddie Adair & Co.; Yankee Octette, assisted by Edith Henne, (11 people) the only act in vaudeville carrying its own Musical Director, Special Scenery, and Electrical Effects; and more motion pictures.

1909 November 16, *The Xenia Daily Gazette* (Ohio): Ben Turpin, who presents the star act at the Orpheum Theatre the first three nights this week (November 15-17), is one of the best vaudeville comedians in the business. He often is employed by the big motion picture companies to act in comedy sketches for pictures. Several pictures in which he appeared have been shown here. He appears in a *Happy Hooligan* act.

1909 December 10-12: Orpheum Theatre, Mansfield, Ohio, The Son and Murray Amusement Co. present a Great Array of Comedy Features…Ben Turpin Company presents *Hooligan and Susanne* in *Furnished Rooms*. "Ben Turpin and Company put on a *Happy Hooligan* sketch which reminds one of the syndicate stuff in the colored supplements of the papers. *Happy* has an ideal makeup for his work and with a little trimming the act would be much better for all concerned." Others acts on the bill included: Joe Ellis, the Happy German Comedian; The Norwoods in their new Black Face sketch *The New Cure for Rheumatism*; Ross & Shaw in *In Jungle Town*; and the moving picture, *The Gold Seekers Daughter*.

1910 January 6-8: Ben Turpin in *Happy Hooligan and Susanne* at the Grand Theater, Massillon, Ohio, 3 shows daily (2:30, 7:30 and 9:00) along with Oehlman Musical Trio; Royer & French; May Evans; & motion pictures. "Ben Turpin in *Happy Hooligan and Susanne* are very funny and are bringing forth rounds of laughter. There is nothing educational about this act. It is just one of those kinds that make a person forget his troubles."[55]

1910 February: Ben, now working for the William Morris Agency, playing one week at the President Theater, Chicago with Lavigne & Jaffee; Owen & Hoffman; and The Prentice Troupe. The following week, Turpin playing the Comedy Theater, Chicago with Anders & Randall; Loretta Tivans; Grace Robin; Clayton & Drew Players; and The Four Mognanis.

1910 April 16: "Ben Turpin, who has been a 'film' comedian for Essanay, has been booked for a tour of the Moss and Stall time, starting August 8th."

Variety, pg 27

1910 April 20: Census records list Ben Turpin, an "actor in theatrical show" and his wife Catherina, "no profession," as living at 1401 Wells Street, Chicago.

1910 May 30-June 4: Turpin playing the New Murray Theater, Richmond, Indiana, along with the Busch Dever Four; The Booth Trio, comedy cyclists; and Gus Williams, German character comic.

Week of June 6, 1910: Turpin playing the Star Theater, Muncie, Indiana.

Week of June 13, 1910: Grand Theater (Hamilton, Ohio): *The Sexton's Dream*, a magnificent, spectacular singing & pantomime production; Don & Mae Gordon Trio, sensational cyclists; Ben Turpin, original tramp comedian; and two high grade and excellent films. "Turpin, the original tramp comedian, with a new line of jokes, songs, etcetera — whatever that is — will no doubt be a big scream."

The Independent Moving Picture Company, or simply the IMP, of New York City was founded by Carl Laemmle in the spring of 1909. Florence Lawrence, Gladys Hulette, King Baggot, Mary Pickford, Owen Moore, Thomas H. Ince, and George Loane Tucker were but a few in this pioneering company over the next few years before IMP evolved into the long-enduring Universal Pictures.

For a brief time away from theater and taffy, Turpin also spent time with the IMP at least as early as October 1910. Ben did not get his start with the company, as Laemmle liked to boast in later years.

The Hobble Skirt (re October 27, 1910), an extremely rare IMP short, was discovered in 2008 by UCLA. Escaping the ravages of time and despite incidents like the large Universal vault fire of October 1924 at Fort Lee, New Jersey (destroying many of the company's earliest film prints and negatives), this survivor features an unmistakable Ben Turpin in comic lead. *The New York Dramatic Mirror* thought: "This is pretty near the limit for foolish farce. The story has not the first indication of plausibility, and the different situations therefore fall flat. The incidents that follow fail to raise a laugh in any instance. Seriously, this sort of stuff is damaging to IMP's reputation."

With a review like that, one wonders if Ben made additional comedies for the IMP. However, in January 1911, Turpin was still associated with the company, as when Richard V. Spencer's *Moving Picture World* column, Notes of the Los Angeles Studios, asked:

Imp Coming? — Mr. Ben Turpin, representative of the Independent Moving Picture Company, was in this city (Los Angeles) recently on business. While here he talked with local directors. Local studio gossip is to the effect that Mr. Turpin is looking over the ground and sizing up the climate, preparatory to establishing a Los Angeles studio for the IMP Company.[56]

A short time later, Spencer wrote, "Turpin, who had spent several weeks in the city looking for a studio site, has gone back East. While here Mr. Turpin began the erection of a studio at the corner of Lake Shore Drive and Temple Street, about a mile from the Edendale studios. Shortly afterward, for some unknown reason, work was called off, and Mr. Turpin went back East."

Moving Picture World, Feb 4, 1911, page 253

Trailblazing director Thomas Ince, then also employed by IMP, later elaborated on Ben's trip to California: "Turpin reported that the General Film Company was endeavoring to prevent all independent organizations from using the motion picture and was seriously hampering their operations, so the plan was abandoned. Cuba was decided upon as a fruitful location."

One by one, members of the prestigious film companies, such as some of D. W. Griffith's Biograph players, made the move to IMP for more money. Some of the biggest stars of their day, Florence Lawrence and Mary Pickford were a few of many who would sign with Laemmle. Pickford, joining IMP by January 1911, made two pictures for the company before setting sail for their new Cuba location. Before setting sail, Mary married her leading man, Owen Moore, another former Biograph player, on January 17, 1911, in Jersey City. The couple worked for three months in Cuba before returning to America.

Interestingly, Ben and wife Carrie are listed among the Manifest of Alien Passengers sailing March 4, 1911, from Havana on the *S.S. Saratoga*. They arrived in New York three days later. Among their fellow passengers were several IMP personnel, including King Baggot, George Loane Tucker, William Daly, Isabelle Rae, David and Anita Miles, and others.

Ben later wrote, "I recall once, Mary Pickford was filming a scene laid in Havana. As she poised on the edge of a boat ready to leap into the sea, the grind of the camera was halted and I was substituted in her place, attired in long curls and feminine dress. I made the leap."[15] The film was possibly Mary's lost one-reeler, *The Fisher Maid* (re March 16, 1911).

1911 Chicago Directory: Turpin, Bernard, *actor*, home: 1401 Wells

1911 February 13-15: Ben scheduled to appear at President Theater with Levigne & Jaffe; The Prentice Four; and the Owen Hoffman Company.

1911 mid- or late August: Ben as *Happy Hooligan* playing Chester Park (Cincinnati) with Spellman's Royal Troupe of Performing Bears; John Fay Palmer & Ray Lewis, travesty stars and dancers; the Prentice Trio in *The Rube and His Two Girls*; Henry Swan, singing comedian.

The Theater by Len G. Shaw (*The Detroit Free Press*, August 26, 1921):

George Sidney, then the star and owner of the *Busy Izzy* musical comedy company and recently the star of *Welcome Stranger*, had sent his manager on a hunt through the small theaters of Chicago in search of talent. In the Virginian theater, Madison and Halsted streets, the scout came across Ben Turpin. The latter was doing a bicycle and table tumble act and in all of the 10 shows a day was risking the breaking of his neck. Sidney saw the turn, and between star and manager, they engaged Turpin for the splendid salary of $65 a week to do his specialty, his wife to act as maid to Carrie Webber, in private life, Mrs. Sidney. Sidney and his show started out from Chicago and their route took them north into the country of the woodsmen and the copper miners. Business was bad. Winter came on early and the troupe had tough sledding to carry on from day to day. As the receipts dwindled, Sidney's conviction that the cross-eyed comedian was a jinx mounted.

The climax was reached in Stevens Point. The box office had yielded $12.35, not enough to get the troupe out of town. It was then that Sidney said to his manager: "For the love of Pete, give that cross-eyed guy two weeks' salary and his railroad fare back to Chicago. He'll have us all stranded in some poorhouse if you don't. I tell you, he's a jinx, a lemon, the champ of hard luck. Get rid of him or I'll get rid of you."

And Ben was fired. Fired for having the cross-eyes that had made millions laugh. But Ben made good his prophecy of that winter morning in Stevens Point as the blizzard whirled about him and pierced the little tan overcoat: "I'll be somebody someday — you see if I don't.

"Goodbye, boss, I know it ain't your fault that I'm getting canned. Sidney thinks I'm hard luck; that I'm a jinx because I'm cross-eyed. But I'll be somebody someday — you see if I don't. It ain't because I'm cross-eyed; it's because I'm funny; yes, sir, funny, that's what I am. That's why he's firing me — and I know it. But you'll hear of Ben Turpin someday."

Then the 6:10 am train pulled into the little railroad station at Stevens Point, Wisconsin, and Ben Turpin, dressed in a funny little tan overcoat and brown derby and with Mrs. Turpin clinging to his arm, climbed aboard the day coach that was to carry him back to Chicago and the ten-shows-a-day vaudeville circuits.

That was in 1911. There was a reunion backstage at the Adams Theatre Wednesday night (ten years later in Detroit, September 1921), where Turpin is appearing in person this week. The other party to it was Frank Whitbeck, who, ten years ago, dug Ben out of the little Chicago variety house and who is now manager of the Miles Theater in Detroit. It was their first meeting since that memorable winter morning in Wisconsin when Whitbeck regretfully helped Turpin and his wife on the southbound train and the comedian assured him with all the picturesque eloquence he could summon that he did not blame him for the discharge.

"Ain't I made good, Frank?" queried Turpin as they parted.

Whitbeck cheerfully agreed that from being fired out of a starving road company to drawing a weekly stipend of four figures was making good with a vengeance.

Ben's earliest known *Busy Izzy* participation was at their Grand Theater (Rockford, Illinois) show on October 10. Ben and Carrie traveled with the show daily through Illinois, Wisconsin, and Minnesota before leaving the company on November 13, 1911.

Meanwhile, Ben's old employer, Essanay, opened a Western Branch in April 1912 at Niles, California after Anderson's exploring San Rafael, San Diego, Denver, and other natural backdrops. Anderson continued in his successful *Broncho Billy* westerns as well as producing the comedies of *Hank and Lank* (Augustus Carney & Victor Potel), which soon evolved into the *Snakeville Comedies*. This popular series of rural one-reelers featured Carney as *Alkali Ike*, Potel as *Slippery Slim*, Harry Todd as *Mustang Pete*, and his real-life wife Margaret Joslin-Todd as *Sophie Clutts* and many were directed by Roy Clements. Carney, similar in appearance to Turpin and with the company since 1910, left in January 1914 when his success went to his head. Essanay replaced Carney with Eddie Redway.

Late August 1912: Chester Park (Ohio) Opera House features Ben Turpin; The Prentice Trio; Henry Swan; and John Fay Palmer and Ray Lewis.

Just as this biography was going to press, filmmaking Professor Dana Driskel of the University of California, Santa Barbara discovered most of a rare and long-forgotten Turpin comedy, *The Hidden Treasure*. This little split-reeler, also known as *The Philanderings of Puddinfoot Pete*, was produced by the American Flying A Film Company at their new studios in Chicago and released November 30, 1912:

Bill Binks sold his ranch and came home in high glee, carrying the currency, for Bill didn't believe in banks. Bill tried to think of an unusual place to hide that currency and finally hit upon an old pair of boots; then Bill betook himself off without saying a word to his faithful helpmate. *Puddinfoot Pete* (Ben), awakening from a delightful slumber beneath the sheltering side of a barrel, stretched himself and made his way to the "eats." Repeated knocks at Bill's door so incensed Bill's wife that, in desperation, she hurled half the articles from the kitchen at poor Pete and he wound up with the boots.

Getting into the boots, Pete found a giant stack of bills. Recovering from his faint, he set out upon the task of making the world happier and incidentally spreading Bill's bills wherever there seemed no joy. He hired an automobile and set out for a restaurant. What Pete did to the chicken and the sugar is a scream. With a full stomach, he hailed forth once more and, seeing a woman grinding an organ, fell to dancing, much to the happiness of all concerned. He left a small package of bills behind him and sailed forth in quest of all sorts of funny adventures.

Passing a grocery store, Pete stopped dead. Perspiration broke out in great beads on his forehead, for there staring at him in the face were forty boxes of soap, neatly arranged on the storefront. Pete didn't hesitate. Calling an express wagon, he paid for the soap and personally saw it taken to the wharf. Then he carefully piled it up and made one grand plunge into the middle of it, and thus did Pete get back at an old enemy. He wound up the day in a remarkable manner. Out of a new building, friends carried an injured workman. Pete followed them sadly home. To the wife he gave what remained of the money and after a brief interval of desperate misery, struck up a tune and went back to sleep on his lumber pile.

Moving Picture World, November 23, 1912

Why Turpin made his way to American may have just been a matter of needing work. Surely he had friends in Gilbert P. Hamilton and A. M. Kennedy, both former Essanay associates, who may have helped Ben find employment. However, Turpin's association as actor or otherwise with American is unknown this early in my research, although it is known Ben also starred in *Mrs. Brown's Baby* (re December 21, 1912). Two years later, another American split-reeler with Turpin (undetermined whether a re-release or a "new" comedy) was released.

1913 March 24: Turpin appearing at the Hippodrome, St. Louis, Missouri for the week along with Mme. Bedini; the Hamada Family; Little Nemo; Dixon, Bowers, and Dixon; Anna Burt; Will Hart; Fiechtl's Tyrolean Singers; McCrea; Davenport and Company; and the Brammons, all to booming business.

1913 May 24: Ben and Carrie place an "At Liberty" ad in the *Billboard:*
Comedy Team — Man and wife Knockabout act; play parts; experienced in Burlesque or Musical; bass drum. Contact: Ben Turpin, c/o Empire Theatre, Indianapolis.

1913 September 20: The Bell Opera House in Benton Harbor, Michigan The Treat of the Season with the Reilly and Woods Big Burlesque Co. with Dave Meyers, Ben Turpin, Anna Golden, & Ida Stanley.

That winter, late 1913 or early 1914, Turpin returned to Essanay.
— "At last I went back to Mr. Spoor and asked him to give me my old job again. I was ready then to take almost anything. You see, I was nearly fifty, and you couldn't call me a great big howling success, even if I had been making good money on the boards right along.

"'All right, Ben,' Spoor said. 'You stick around. I'll see what I can do for you.'

"I went down to the reception room and waited. I came back every day for two weeks — and waited. Nothing turned up. Finally I went to see Mr. Spoor again.

"'Look here,' I said, 'you promised you'd see what you could do for me. I can't wait any longer. I've got to eat!' Well, he said then he'd give me a chance, and he took me on at my old salary of twenty a week. And I was glad to get it!

"They had another comedian who was getting seventy-five dollars a week, and that was tall money. It was the middle of winter, and you know how those breezes blow off Lake Michigan! There was some ice floating around in the lake, and the first job they handed out to me was a corker.

"'Ben,' they said, 'you run down to the lake, and this fellow' — the comedian getting seventy-five per — 'he'll be chasing you. You jump in. He goes in after you.'

"'That's an order! I thought. But I didn't say a word. I was glad to do it, for it was a chance to make good.

"When we got down to where they were going to make the picture, the man who was to chase me into the lake began to protest.

"'See here! I'm not going into that lake in this kind of weather,' he said. 'You wouldn't go in yourself and you know it!'

"'Wouldn't, eh?' Phooey! This director runs and jumps in, overcoat and all!

"The director crawled out of the lake and they wrapped blankets around him. Then they went ahead and got all set to make the picture. I ran, like I was supposed to, with the comedian after me, then into the lake I went. But all my work was wasted. The comedian wouldn't jump in, after all. He isn't a comedian anymore!"[3] Rumor has it that the comedian was the recently hired Eddie Redway.

"Shortly after, director Francis Powers told me to make up for a cabby. He was directing Francis X. Bushman (soon one of Essanay's biggest stars) at this time. Powers had a hansom cab in a particular scene and wanted a driver. I put on the high hat and long coat and took my seat on the box. They shot that scene nineteen times. Every time the cameraman began to grind, Powers became so overcome with mirth he couldn't proceed. I didn't know what he was laughing at then, but later concluded, when I learned that he was laughing at me, that if I could make him laugh so heartily, I could make others do so. I made a serious decision then and there to plunge into comedy, and here I am folks — not so good looking, but very cute."[57]

Wallace Beery joined Essanay in August of 1913, first appearing in some of the *Smiling Billy* Mason comedies and George Ade Fables before developing his own character series as *Sweedie*, the big Swedish housemaid, with big Beery in full drag. Ben stayed busy in a number of these shorts, many of which were actually directed by the young and versatile Beery himself. Ben later told W. Ward Marsh of the *Cleveland Plain Dealer*, "He used to get me in little creeks and hold my head under water until I nearly drowned." Ben moaned, "Oh, he was mean to me!" Marsh went on to say, "Ben had shed tears. Honestly cried. I saw the tears. It seems that years before Ben had achieved his present day success, Wallace Beery, noted screen villian, treated him meanly, always carrying the scene of disaster for Ben just a little further than the script, the director, or Ben called for. And, he suffered. And, the tears came.

There were times when Ben was kicked too hard, other times when he was soundly beaten and still others when the playful Beery held him under water just a moment too long."[58]

Beery got his share as well. Not long after joining Essanay, he was to run out on a pier at Lake Michigan and then supposedly dive into the lake. A dummy was all ready for the immersion, but the director didn't get a chance to use it, as Beery was unable to stop, slipped, tripped, and went headfirst into the lake. The pier was all ice and, fortunately, the cameraman got it all on film.[59]

One day in March 1914, Beery was injured in a spectacular leap into a fire at the Essanay Argyle Street plant. He was taken to a hospital, though not too badly hurt. Apparently, he jumped from the rooftop of a shed at a second story level, missing the safety net and hitting one of the men holding it.[60]

1914 June 17: Essanay releases the first of a string of popular George Ade Fables, *The Brash Drummer and the Nectarine*, starring Wallace Beery, Turpin, Leo White, and others.

1914 August 6: Wallace Beery, Essanay's remarkable comedian, will be seen in a new series of pictures to be released under the head of *Sweedie*. These comedies will concern the adventures, humiliations, and embarrassments of a Swedish servant girl. The role just fits Beery, as he is capable of portraying the part of a domineering servant girl who thinks she is abused. The first of this series, *Sweedie the Swatter*, is typical of the others to follow.[61]

1914 August 21: Ben Turpin, one of the leading Essanay slapstick artists, calls himself the Francis X. Bushman of the comedy department. The only way which they are alike is that they are so different in looks. Bushman is very handsome, and Ben, well, he is awfully funny, anyhow. *Essanay publicity*

Hollywood columnist Louella Parsons was writing stories for the Essanay productions in those days and later recalled, "Essanay boasted the luxury of one office boy who was continually on the brink of being fired — only no one ever quite got around to it. For months I knew him only as 'Ben.' He was cross-eyed, homely, and the superstition of theatrical folk (they think crossed eyes an unlucky omen) did far more to keep Ben's job than his eager, running legs.

"One day Ben confided in me his ambition to become an actor. He seemed rather pitiful, the little cross-eyed man of forty-odd talking about his dreams. 'I know I could never play heroes,' he said, 'but I do think I could do comedy pretty well.'

"I was busy and only half-listening. 'Oh, forget it, Ben,' I advised.

He said, 'Yes'm,' and started to back out the door.

"'By the way,' I asked, 'what's your last name, Ben?'

"'Turpin, Ben Turpin.'"

The Gay Illiterate by Louella Parsons, 1944

Recounting her days with Essanay in an earlier article, *Movies Demand*, Parsons wrote "When E. Mason Hopper was the director of comedies at the Essanay, one of his favorite performances was to have a pie-throwing match. Can you imagine anything more unpleasant than to have a juicy strawberry pie flung right into your face, so that your eyes, your hair and your nose were red with the filling of the once-upon-a-time pie?

"I watched Ben Turpin get deluged first with water from an overflowing bathroom one day and then covered with a chocolate pie. There wasn't enough left of his face to recognize him after the scene was 'cut.' It took him exactly two hours to rid himself of the debris, and the cleaner took a week to get his suit in wearable shape. Yet Ben was called upon to do just such stunts every time he was cast in a comedy. Being hit squarely in the stomach or having 200 pounds walk over one is just too trivial to be mentioned."[62]

1914 September: Ben Turpin, the comical captain of the Essanay comedy police force, lost four perfectly respectable teeth in the new film, *Sweedie's Clean-Up*. *Essanay News*

1914 November: Ben Turpin, Essanay comedian, is congratulating himself over having a piece of his ear blown off and his face filled with powder. Ben, as the police captain, pursues Wallace Beery, who is fleeing in an auto in the comedy *Sweedie at the Fair*. Unable to catch Sweedie, Ben sets off a can of gunpowder under the auto and blows Sweedie up. Sweedie was thrown out of the machine unhurt, but Ben got the majority of the charge unintentionally with resulting facial alterations. *Essanay News*

1914 December 5: *Press Agent Says* — That Ben Turpin, the Essanay comedian, courts all the bumps and knocks he can get. "It means money to me," says Turpin. "Everytime I get smashed out of shape, I am just so much more valuable for my oddity. I was born peculiar looking, and after I had my teeth knocked out and my head pushed out of shape, I began to look like a caricature. I can't walk along the street without someone laughing at me. I should worry. That's what brings me my 'ham and.'" *Motography*, page 797

1914 December 26: *Press Agent Says* — That Ben Turpin, Essanay comedian, is mourning the loss of his pet mule, which has taken part in so many Essanay comedies. The animal finally became too old to take his parts well so had to be put in the "has-been" class. Retired to a farm on a pension, Turpin visits the animal every Sunday.[64]

Ben later recalled, "Just about then Charles Chaplin joined up with the Essanay.[3]
"Chaplin came to the screen in a film called *His New Job* and he gave me my first job. I really owe all my success to Charlie Chaplin and Mack Sennett.[65]
"*Broncho Billy* Anderson hired the little mustached man away from Mack Sennett at Edendale in California. Sennett wouldn't pay Chaplin more than $125 a week.
"I had to be an extra until one day Charlie asked me if I wouldn't like to work in some pictures with him."[5]
According to the research of film historian Bo Berglund, Chaplin's last day at Keystone was December 26, 1914. On Monday the 28th, Charlie, accompanied by Anderson, left San Francisco, where the two transacted some business, then headed for Chicago. Within the next week, Chaplin began work under his new employer, Essanay.
Chaplin later recalled in his *My Autobiography*, "The next morning I went to the casting office. 'I would like a cast of some sort,' I said dryly, 'so will you kindly send me members of your company who are unoccupied?'

"They presented people who they thought might be suitable. There was a chap with cross-eyes named Ben Turpin, who seemed to know the ropes and was not doing much with Essanay at the time. Immediately I took a liking to him, so he was chosen."

Turpin also remembered his first meeting with Chaplin. "After I got my chance and worked in some other pictures, pretty soon I thought I was the comedian. But one day a new fellow turned up at the studio.

"'Ben,' somebody said to me, 'meet Charlie Chaplin!'

"I didn't know who Charlie Chaplin was, but they put me on to work with him. He and I worked together.

"'Ben,' he said — he had a broad English accent — 'put on your — aw — make-up and let a fellow see — aw — how you look.'

"So I went in and got the piece of an old wig that was the only mustache I had. I stuck it on and changed my clothes and came out. Charlie took a look and began to laugh.

"'Haw! What sort of a funny-looking egg is this I've got to play against?'

"Charlie laughed some more and kept laughing. Every time he looked at me he started again.[3]

"The English comedian hired me to play in his first picture. He told Anderson, 'I'll take this cock-eyed kid to fill in a role.'

"He did. It was for a picture called *His New Job* (re February 1, 1915). Chaplin was a master, and still is, of pantomime and the art of hitting and falling. The film was made in Chicago. We were putting up a building in the picture, and I was his helper.

"Charlie knocked me down with boards, stepped on my face, dropped bricks on my head and pushed me out of windows.[5]

"You heard that gossip about Charlie having killed a man in a picture, didn't you? Huh? Well, that was me. I was the guy he killed. Some bump, believe me.[20]

"I not only got the chance to polish up my falls, but to learn how to keep from getting hurt. I've never been hurt (Ben's idea of *hurt* must have meant terrible pain or injury). You seldom are if you figure out your fall, time it right and use any sort of judgment.

"Delayed action is one of the funniest bits of comic business an actor can learn. If a phone rings, it can be very comical. Most players on the screen today answer an insistent telephone forthwith. But not in the school I studied in: You ignore the ring at first, then show curiosity, leisurely walk toward the phone and after studying it in some puzzlement, you pick up the receiver. I knew some of these things and Chaplin taught me others.

"A man with crossed eyes, has a decided edge over many others in any delayed and unexpected action (unexpected from the audience standpoint only — it takes sometimes days to work out an 'unexpected' bit of business). Charlie Chaplin taught me that all falls, running into doors and such, depend for their comic effect almost entirely on slow register of reaction on the face. The situation must invariably be given away on the face after it happens."[5]

The Clubman's Wager (re January 15, 1915)

An odd little rarity pops up during Turpin's Essanay days, a split-reel comedy for American-Mutual. The origin of this lost film, Ben's third known short for American Flying A, is unfortunately unknown as to whether a "new" film or rerelease of an earlier short: Four clubmen importune a tramp (Ben) to change a $1,000 bill to settle a wager. The experiences of the tramp in his efforts to get change make a series of highly comic situations.

1915 January 21: Ben Turpin, Ruth Stonehouse, Wallace Beery, Lester Cuneo, Royal Douglass, and other Essanay players took part in a charity act at Green Mill Garden, Chicago. *Essanay News*

Comedy Film Main Feature

His New Job, featuring Charles Chaplin in two acts, is the first of the series to be made by the Essanay Film Company, of which Mr Chaplin is now a member working at the Los Angeles studio. After signing the Essanay contract, Chaplin's first play was to be something new, so he chose the above title and started to work on the picture.

The comedy is declared by critics to be the funniest of all ever filmed. "This is the best comedy I have ever produced" is what Chaplin says about the picture. Mr. Chaplin is assisted by an excellent cast, including Ben Turpin, who with his ludicrously absurd physique, adds greatly to the fun. "The new surroundings and the clever actors whom I had to work with enabled me to make the greatest comedy of my life. I couldn't help laughing at it myself when I saw it on the screen."

This two-reel comedy is just what its title indicates. Mr. Chaplin built it up on the fact of his coming to the Essanay company, though he has instilled incidents into it that would make a Methodist deacon shriek with laughter. Mr. Chaplin produced the play without any scenario whatsoever, although he had carefully thought out the outlines of his plot beforehand. Most of the incidents and practically all of the little mirth-provoking tricks were extemporaneous, however, Mr. Chaplin originating them as the camera was clicking out the film. The result is that the comedy is the most original and the fun the most spontaneous and unstilted of any ever produced. Mr. Chaplin was ably assisted in his work by Ben Turpin, one of the oldest comedians in time of service in the motion picture business. The two men are nearly of a size and make a team that cannot be beaten. Turpin's absurd physique, together with Chaplin's peculiar capers and wonderful facial expressions, make them a pair unique to the motion picture comedy stage. This is a real comedy all the way through with 100 percent laughs.[66]

Chaplin recalled, "During my short stay in Chicago, Spoor did everything to placate me, but I could never really warm up to him. I told him I was unhappy working in Chicago and that if he wanted results he should arrange for me to work in California.

'We'll do everything we can to make you happy,' he said. 'How would you like to go to Niles?'

"I was not too pleased at the prospect, but I liked Anderson better than Spoor; so after completing *His New Job* I went to Niles."[67]

Ben continues, "Well, (Chaplin and I) played together for a while, but one day Charlie suggested that we go somewhere else. 'Come on, let's go to California,' he said. 'This bally climate is too cold, don't you know.'

"I went with Chaplin to Niles, California, where we made *A Night Out* (re February 15, 1915). Crowds followed Chaplin whenever we went to Oakland and San Francisco. He was a great idol of the public and still is, but not in the same measure as in those days.[5]

"He was making up a company, and put in a word for me. I went to see the manager.[3]

"Anderson offered me a contract for two years at twenty-five per week. Nothing to worry about, he couldn't discharge me — I couldn't quit — and always a steady living for twenty-four months, hot or cold, stormy or sunshine! And besides, I wanted to go to California.[25]

"I reached for a pen with my fingers shaking. 'Where?' I asked. Anderson pointed to a line near the bottom of the page, and it was all I could do to see it with my right eye. The left was off the job looking far into the future. Just for a bluff, I swirled the penholder around like a man getting ready to write fancy cards. Then I wrote — just as firm — *Bernard Turpin!* That settled me for two years.

"When I came out, there stood Charlie. I stretched out my hand. 'Shake!' I said.

"I was feeling pretty good. It looked like a great chance, and I owed it to him.

"'I want to thank you, Charlie,' I said.

"'How much did you sign up for, Ben?' he asked.

"'Twenty-five a week!' I told him. It was five more than I was getting, and I appreciated it, but Charlie nearly fell over backward. I found out later he was signed up for $1250 a week!

"I signed up for two years at twenty-five a week, without anything said about a raise. Then at last it dawned on me that I had sold myself for a mess of pottage. I began to hear of salaries. I discovered that I had made more than three million for the Essanay — actually cleared that much on my pictures…and I was living on a clerk's salary. We had hard work in those days — slapstick of the roughest sort.[5]

"A few months later I was featured in my own pictures at $30 a week."[24]

Chaplin's longtime cameraman Rollie Totheroh, who began their association at Essanay's Niles studio, later told Sam Gill, "Ben wanted "equal time' with Charlie and salary to match. When Charlie saw Ben getting as much of the show and publicity as himself, he let Ben go after having him brought him out to Niles from Chicago."

Clown Princes and Court Jesters, Kalton C. Lahue and Sam Gill, 1970

Ben recalled, "I got to thinking that as I was a chief comedian and the shipping clerk and property boy, scenery shifter and janitor, not to mention being telephone girl and scenario writer, I ought to have more money. I braced up my nerve and asked them for forty dollars a week. By gosh, I thought they were going to faint. They took it so hard that I was laid off for a couple of weeks. I couldn't bear to witness such grief. When I came back they said very sadly that they had decided to sign me up for a couple years at thirty dollars per week. But after a while they raised me to fifty a week. I thought I had put a pretty slick one over."[3]

Writer Harry C. Carr, soon a publicist for Mack Sennett, was sharp to notice Ben in the Chaplin's: "There is Ben Turpin whom Chaplin selected for important parts in his reels. Turpin is almost as funny as Chaplin himself and divided honors with him in some film comedies. Here was another instance of Chaplin's astuteness."[68]

Turpin played his third and last role in Chaplin's comedy *The Champion* (re March 11, 1915), Charlie's last film in Niles. Hardly noticeable, Ben trudges through a rowdy crowd in the bleachers, walking over everyone while peddling his peanuts, including G.

M. Anderson. Leo White, often Charlie's foil and another reliable and dedicated Essanay player, later remembered, "If I wasn't an acrobat, my neck would have been broken a dozen times." About the making of *The Champion*, Leo recalled how he was pounded on the head with a heavy weight, ducked under a shower bath, and shot through a door twenty feet into a yard, tumbling heels over head.[72] A few months later, during the production of Chaplin's *A Night at the Show*, a heavy woman who plays the part of a fat princess, at 350 pounds, fell on Leo and all but crushed his breath out. *Essanay News*

Everyone had their troubles in the making of moving picture art.

Elaborate Program is Planned at Niles

Niles, March 13 — Preparations are now well under way for the entertainment and dance to be given on the night of St. Patrick's Day at Connor's Hall here. The affair is given under the joint auspices of the Catholic churches of Niles and Decoto, of which Rev. John A. Leal is pastor. The two churches have combined in an effort to raise funds with which to build parsonage for the pastor. This event is expected to assist in the building fund. Perhaps the evening's greatest attraction will be Ben Turpin.

1915: Ben Turpin is something of an acrobat as well as a comedian. In the comedy *Curiosity* (re March 29, 1915), Ben plays the part of a madman. He sets up a table and juggles brooms, chairs, and other pieces of furniture in a way that would make a professional juggler envious.

A Coat Tale synopsis (re April 1, 1915):

Ben Turpin is hurled into a lake in the Essanay comedy, *A Coat Tale*. He is hunting for a bargain coat he gave his wife, in which he pinned a hundred-dollar bill and which his wife hurled out the window. *Essanay News*

On April 8, 1915, Chaplin moved to Los Angeles, where he continued his contract with Essanay, taking Edna Purviance, Bud Jamison, Paddy McQuire, and others as well as adding new players, such as Snub Pollard, and leaving Niles and Turpin behind.

1915 May 19: Ben Turpin says that after having been killed off in *The Undertaker's Uncle* (re April 29, 1915), he was resurrected and leaped out of his coffin quicker than he ever expects to again. Victor Potel crawled under the coffin and bored a hole through with an auger, which struck Turpin in the back.[69]

The Undertaker's Uncle (re April 29, 1915) review:

At last the efforts of Victor Potel and Harry Todd have been rewarded with a third partner equally successful in making the orchestra ring. No less than Ben Turpin is the undoubtedly ludicrous gentleman who adds new life to Snakeville doings. All this is no disrespect to the powers of Margaret Joslin, bless us. The Snakeville characters are in continuation, for the girl is again the object of both men. A note early in the reel informs the girl that the uncle of the undertaker has left much money to the other. The "other" is naturally delighted, but the undertaker seizes the opportunity of a chance tramp and dresses him up as his uncle. This is the character Turpin takes and it keeps the remainder of the reel in a turmoil of laughter. *MPW*

1915 July 5: Ben Turpin, the comedian of the Essanay at Niles, is considered by devotees of the motion pictures to be unsurpassed for his ability to put over a laugh. Turpin has appeared in Livermore and in Niles to two occasions for the benefit of churches and lodges and those who saw him then want to see him in the Parade of the Horribles, July 5.[70]

The Bell Hop (re August 12, 1915) review:

Ben Turpin has never been any funnier than as a bellhop in this offering. It may also be said that seldom have audiences enjoyed a picture more than this when, to quote a house manager, "they laughed as they might at a Chaplin picture." The reason for this is psychological in part. The entire production was gone at in a fresh and enthusiastic spirit, which reflected from the screen. The main reason, though, was the clever work of Mr. Turpin, who possesses both funny gestures and the unexpected in exhibiting them. Except in appearance, though they are both short, he is much like Chaplin. The groundwork of their success is alike. Also, it is one of the funniest single presentations seen since Chaplin has become famous. The plot dresses the lead in a bellboy's uniform, where, in a hotel whose rules are not too strict to allow sufficient latitude to the versatile guide, he extracts an unusual measure of mirth. Moreover, it is new blood in the lead, an encouraging event at all times.

Here's Looking at You, Ben (1915 August 13)

Straight from Niles, California comes a slapstick refutation of mortality that ought to relieve anxious hearts. Ben Turpin postcards *The Chicago Tribune* with emphasis: "It has been reported around Chicago by moving picture fans that I was killed by a blow on the head with a mallet by Charles Chaplin in a picture called *A Night Out*. No, sir, I am still alive and doing fine at the Niles Essanay studio. I am not in the Chaplin comedies, but I am playing in the new western comedies. I wish you would report the above sometime in your paper, as I have many friends in dear old Chicago, my home town." That clears away another rumor.[71]

1915 August 15: Ben Turpin got his head stuck in a fence during the making of the Essanay photoplay *Broncho Billy Steps In* (re August 13, 1915) and had a difficult time extracting it, to the joy of the other players. *Essanay News*

1915 August 21: In baseball, the Niles Essanay Indians will play the Fruitvale Kriegs. "There will also be a crowd of rooters, mostly actors, with the club. Gilbert M. Anderson will be in charge of the club and there will also be Harry Todd, Victor Potel, Ben Turpin, plus a number of others to root for the Niles boys."

A Married Man's Troubles (1915 September 14)

Ben Turpin declares that married life in the photocomedy is anything but one glad, sweet song. In the Essanay comedy, *Others Started, But Sophie Finished*, his mother-in-law literally mops up the floor with him, while in *Snakeville's Twins*, he is a poor downtrodden man who is forced by his wife to care for the twins while she washes for a living. Ben never gets a chance to rest.[73]

1915 September 24, unidentified film review in part: Mr. Ben Turpin, in another picture on the program, showed himself to be a comedian of very promising ability. He's been working with Mr. Chaplin recently and has acquired some of his methods, but he also shows an originality that promises well for his future.[74]

If He'd Slipped (1915 December 11)

Ben Turpin took a desperate chance recently while working in a comedy called *The Merry Models*. He went thru all kinds of acrobatic stunts while standing on the sill of a window 14 stories high. The scene was taken in one of the tallest buildings in San Francisco. *Essanay publicity*

Chaplin completed his last short for Essanay before the end of the year, *A Burlesque on Carmen*. Missing were the familiar tramp clothes, shoes, cane, and derby in favor of a military uniform. The studio upheld its December 1915 release and, over the next few months, added and padded an extra two reels to Chaplin's film, trimmed from 16,000 feet of new footage featuring Turpin and others directed by Leo White.

According to most research, Ben did not appear in Chaplin's original two-reel *Burlesque on Carmen*. Turpin, however, is in the released four-reel version, but never in any of the same scenes with Chaplin in this film's extant footage. Ben remembered it differently: "Sometime later the company decided to pad out an old two-reeler of Charlie's and make a four-reeler of it. I had worked in it, and they needed me. But I had learned some things about taking care of myself, so when the manager came around to me, I was ready for him.

"'All right,' I said, 'I'll work. But I want two hundred and fifty bucks a week!'

"'Two hundred and fifty! Ben, you're crazy! What's the idea?'

"'I mean I want two hundred and fifty a week, or I don't act!'

"Well, they gave it to me, and tore up my old contract. I worked with them three weeks more and finished the four-reeler."[3]

Snakeville's Champion (re December 16, 1915) review *(in part):*

This comedy, based on a burlesque wrestling match, does not differ in any material from the numerous similar pictures already on the market. Ben Turpin, Lloyd Bacon, and Margaret Joslin maintain their good comedy character work. Bacon, the world's greatest wrestler, arrives in Snakeville and offers to meet anybody in a match. Ben starts training and challenges the champ. He wins the first fall, but Bacon scores the second. Ben wins the third and deciding fall by tickling the sole of his opponent's foot.[75]

In April 1916, Chaplin brought suit against Essanay and VLSE for a permanent injunction against the distribution of the film, *A Burlesque on Carmen*, charging that the four-reeler would ruin his reputation. Also, the release of *Carmen* in four reels (instead of two) was a violation of Chaplin's contract with Essanay and that Turpin was employed in some scenes for the purpose of completing the four reels. One source claimed that Chaplin was averse to having Turpin in his cast, as proven by Charlie's last six films, which did not feature Ben. Theater owners were even siding with Chaplin and offered to delete the new footage and project Chaplin's film as originally intended. However, Charlie didn't let

Essanay interfere with his new contract with the Mutual Film organization and plunged into a series of shorts that are regarded as his best. Under Mutual, Chaplin jumped to an amazing $10,000 weekly.

With the $750 for his work on Essanay's *Carmen*, Ben said to himself, "'Here's where I get me a business manager!'

"I got one, a dandy, too. I certainly owe him a lot. Among other things he taught me how to save. I had never saved a penny before. He got me a contract for a year (with the Vogue Film Company) at one hundred dollars a week.

"'Now, Ben,' he said, 'I'm not going to charge you any fee for this contract — not if you do what I say. You've got to save sixty dollars a week out of this hundred — sixty every week.'

"That was a starter. Everything I've got today I owe to his teaching me to save, when I was nearly fifty years old."[3]

Author Donald Parkhurst, in his fine appreciation of the Essanay Studio at Niles, noted Ben's popularity in the small town: Ben Turpin, the jovial, cross-eyed comic, was another favorite. Ben was pulled in once, along with Anderson himself, by constable Frank Rose as they were splashing around in a Niles Canyon pool, chasing wild ducks in violation of game laws. But these were harmless antics. Ben is still remembered for his hilarity in jumping off buildings, being submerged in horse troughs, or posturing as September Morn in the local parade. He was tossed into every water trough in town. Much later, in 1934, when an ex-policeman had opened a service station on the old studio site, the good-natured Turpin made the trip from Hollywood to pump gas and attract business. There are people around here who will never get over having their windshields wiped by that crazy guy with the crossed eyes.

The differences between the experiences of Turpin and Chaplin are remarkable — two men, both comedians, working for the same studio and in the same town, one who loved the place and the other who couldn't stand it. If anything, it was Turpin who had the right to complain, for he was paid only $25 a week and watching Chaplin receive $1,250.[76]

Louella Parsons later noted in 1924, "Ben Turpin was an errand boy and extra man and when he was in a picture with Chaplin, Charlie, after seeing the picture, said he would never again make a picture with Ben in it. And he never did."[77]

Ben Turpin Takes Tumble Down Stairs *(1916 February 8)*

Ben Turpin, who plays the part of *Bloggie* in Essanay's western comedy, *It Happened in Snakeville*, accidentally fell down a flight of stairs while working in that picture. Several people rushed to his assistance, expecting to find him badly injured, but the wiry little comedian jumped to his feet and dashed back up the stairs, ready to proceed with the scene. Turpin says he has fallen so many times in photoplays that he's as tough as a rubber ball. *Essanay News*

February 16, 1916, dawned bright and clear and a good day for filming. The Essanay crews worked through the morning, took their usual lunch break, and decided to shoot a few more scenes while the afternoon sun was still bright. The name of the picture is not known, for it never got to the theaters. While the crews were at it in mid-picture, a telegram arrived from Chicago and the show was over. No one today knows exactly what the telegram said. But immediately the actors and the cameramen trudged back to their lodgings and began to leave. The next morning, Niles found itself utterly bereft of its one claim to a major industry and was stunned by a stillness which it hadn't known for years. Some must have been deeply affected by this strange turn, their minds full of questions which, to this day, have not been fully answered. Some sort of inquest is in order, for the breakup of the Niles Essanay studio was a major happening, not just for the town and its aspirations, but for the whole of Northern California and for the motion picture industry. In 1933, the studio buildings were leveled and the grounds cleared. By that time, it was torn down for scrap and most of the nitrate-base films in its vault had been stolen.

Turpin, years later, joked, "I want everybody to know that I was not a poor, bare-foot newsboy, as so many of my other millionaire friends of today were. I never sold papers. The only reason I ever had for the possession of a newspaper was to use it to wrap something in.

"I entered the picture business because I had to either work or go hungry, and when I was broke it happened that the old Essanay Film Company, was the only place I could find that was in need of unskilled help. What I did is nobody's business, but I made up my mind that I would be before the camera someday, and waited my chance.

"From a menial position around the studio, I was advanced to the prop room one day after I had showed some initiative."[78]

Years later, in August 1921, Ben told Carl Sandburg, "I was hurt 19 times in two years while working for Essanay."[27]

But things were looking better for Ben…

Ben Turpin, The Essanay Player (1916 February 12)

A fortnight ago, I published the incomplete portrait of *Bloggie*, the new name for an Essanay comedian, and offered a prize to the first sender of the real name of the artiste. Imagine my astonishment when Monday morning, after the Saturday of publication, nearly two hundred postcards were piled up on my desk, and, wonder of wonders, only thirty-six of them were wrong! No finer tribute to the keenness of *Pictures* readers could possibly be given.

The name of *Bloggie* is Ben Turpin, and I award the prize to H. Broughton, Coliseum Picture House, Leeds, whose correct card was the first one I looked at. His reply was, "There is only one such neck on the screen, and that belongs to Ben Turpin."

During the following days, shoals of late cards came to hand and quite a funny article could be written around some of the guesses. They included Dick Turpin, Mr. Turpin, Benjamin Turpin, Old Turpin, and Von Turpin (This last evidently thought of Tirpitz); Hughie Mack, John Bunny, Henry Ainley (poor Henry!), and Ford Sterling, whilst many readers seemed determined to drag in Billy at all costs. Thus they gave Broncho Billy, Billy Reeves, Billy Ritchie, and Billy Armstrong.[79]

Vogue

Hard Knocks in Vogue Comedies

Ben later told, *"The name of my next company was the Vogue Film Company, and they gave me $100 a week. You see, they just asked me what I wanted and I named that figure (never dreaming I'd get it) but they took me on and very soon I got myself a business manager and all the trappings that now befitted my position. Let me tell you, it paid to have all that extra front."*[28]

The Vogue Comedy Company was organized in October 1915 by Samuel S. Hutchinson and Charles LaFrance to fill the Mutual Film Corporation's comedy void left by Mack Sennett's Keystones when Sennett signed with Triangle in the summer of that year. LaFrance had assembled Pricilla Dean, Russell Powell, Milburn Morante, Lillian Leighton, and William Scott for the initial Vogue comedies. Joining the following month, Paddy McQuire (b1889), former musical and burlesque comedian, who most recently completed nine months in Essanay's Chaplin company. The five-foot-nine-inch, brown haired, blue-eyed comic spent five years with the Kolb and Dill Company before joining Bob Hughes American Burlesque Company, where he toured the world over for two years before joining Essanay in February 1915. Like Ben Turpin, McQuire (often erroneously spelled McGuire) was also born in New Orleans according to the 1917 *Motion Picture Studio Directory*.

Hutchinson soon had a disagreement with partner LaFrance and ended their association. Hutchinson continued and next acquired the services of Henry "Rube" Miller, a thirty-year-old from Trottswood, Ohio, brown haired, blue-eyed, a long and lanky (5'-9", 147 lb.) ex-clown with Forepaugh & Sells Circus. Rube entered the movies in 1912 with Keystone, where he, like many others, soon learned to direct. Gaining much additional experience, he soon found his way to Vogue in January 1916. According to Rube, his on-screen costume was derived from the shoes of Billy Emerson, his hat once worn by Tony Pastor, his vest Dan Daly's, and his coat once belonging to Ezra Kendall. After a year of starring, writing, and directing for Vogue, Rube went to Lehrman Knock-Out (L-KO comedies) and soon joined Fatty Arbuckle's Paramount comedies before fading into obscurity around 1920.

1916 January 8: The Vogue Comedy Co. moved last week from the quarters they shared with the Signal Company to the old OZ Studios, which have been refurbished and painted. Here Jack Dillon and Rube Miller will make slapstick of the most approved order. Dillon is scoring quite heavily with his one-reelers and is quite a find.

1916 March 4, *Reel Life*, page 2: Mutual President John R. Freuler, well pleased with his acquisition of Essanay's comedian Charlie Chaplin, told the press:

"I consider this (*the signing of Chaplin*) the most important transaction in the recent history of the motion picture industry. It carries a wide significance in relation to the policy of the Mutual Film Corporation. It is a step — a very long one — but there will be more. Negotiations for other great stars have been in progress for weeks and months. When certain present contracts expire you will see these famous stars appearing in Mutual Pictures. There is a great deal more to come."

1916 April 22, *Reel Life*, page 12: Ben Turpin, late of Essanay and one of the best-known comics in picture work, will appear shortly in his first Vogue-Mutual release.

In 1935, Turpin elaborated, "On a train southward I met S. S. Hutchinson, Santa Barbara millionaire who had become interested in pictures. He had Mary Miles Minter under contract along with several others who were to become stars.

"'How much do you want?' Hutchinson said.

"'I'll take a hundred,' I replied, meaning $100 a month.

"'All right, here's your first week's salary,' and he handed me a hundred.

"That's the way things happened in those days. Although the salaries were increasing, improvements in the art of taking pictures were slow. There was absolutely no system yet in making the pictures. It was several years after I entered pictures before I ever heard of a script, or scenario. When some official of the company decided to make a picture, he would call all the players, cameraman, office boy, and what-not, together, tell them what he had in mind and in about an hour, between ourselves, a picture was ready to be 'shot.' Everyone made up his or her lines and 'business.'"[15]

Sifted from the Studios: Vogue Films, Inc. *(1916 April 29)*

In the new comedian, Ben Turpin, Vogue Films Incorporated has secured the only actor in whom Charlie Chaplin is said to have expressed interest from a competitive standpoint. Vogue prints are big money-makers and the company will, if present earnings are continued, show one of the most satisfactory earning sheets of all the manufacturing companies for 1916. *Motography*

Vogue Adds Big Guns *(1916 May 6)*

Ben Turpin, formerly with the Essanay and who has appeared in a few Chaplin pictures, has been signed by Vogue Films, to add his comic ability to the already formidable forces of this organization. Ben will appear in forthcoming Vogue comedies under the direction of Jack Dillon along with Paddy McQuire, Rena Rogers, Arthur Moon, and Louise Owen.

Motography, page 1024

Rena Rogers, Ben's leading lady and the "Little Blonde Lady of the Screen" at Vogue, soon became the wife of director Frank Borzage about this time.

Vogue's Battery Of Comics — Ben Turpin Will Add His Antics To Those of the Other Comedians In This Active Company (1916 May 27)

Ben Turpin, the well-known comedian, has been added to the force of funny men who appear on the screen under the Vogue brand and future releases will show Mr. Turpin in new laugh-provoking comedies. The first picture in which Turpin will appear will be *National Nuts*, to be released May 28 and is under the direction of Jack Dillon.

The comedy was filmed during the opening season of the Coast League and the game was between Los Angeles and Salt Lake. Turpin will be seen as Peerless Frank Chance's greatest twirler. When he appeared on the field, 18,000 fans wondered, but the next moment it dawned on them that a picture company was at work and all eyes were focused on Turpin, who, dressed in a suit large enough for a player three times his size, "wound up" and delivered his own unique expression of baseball comedy.

In addition to Turpin's comic ability, the Vogue forces already include Mr. Paddy McQuire, who has familiarized the American world with the antics of the characterization of Bungling Bill. Paddy has a most careless disregard of safety first and will take a fall out of a third or fourth story window with the same nonchalance that he will submit to being run over by an automobile. Rena Rogers also contributes her share to these comedy scenes and is an able assistant in all fun making. Arthur Moon assumes all the heavy roles of the plays and can alike enact the heavy lover and heavy villain parts.

Motography, page 1200

Some Late News Concerning Comedy

Ben Turpin is to be featured in a series of comedies, now in the making. These should be good. Turpin was shown in the earlier Chaplin comedies, but couldn't be continued in them because his methods were too much like those of Chaplin. Instead of feeding the star, as they say in vaudeville, his work was in conflict with Chaplin's. Very few movie comedies are making good enough to be featured longer than two or three weeks at any first class movie theater. One of the few exceptions to this is the comedies starring Mr. and Mrs. Sidney Drew. These hold up because they are bright little plays, aside from the real comedy which raises the audience to the laughing point once or twice in each story. There is no rival to Chaplin and the only comedies which get an equal number of laughs are some of those featuring Roscoe Arbuckle.[80]

Delinquent Bridegrooms (re June 18, 1916) synopsis:

Bloggie and Bill, tramps, steal two dress suits that belong to Thompson and Brown, who are to marry the Widows Moon and Dolan that afternoon. Thompson and Brown see the theft and pursue them, but they make their getaway in a stolen auto. They are arrested for speeding and brought to the station house and jailed. Thompson and Brown, garbed in the discarded rags of the tramps, are mistaken for them and are also jailed. From here on, things happen with the rapidity of a Gatling gun, during which time the son of Widow Moon kidnaps the minister and makes him marry Rena Thompson and himself. *Motography*

Sifted from the Studios: Vogue Films, Inc. (1916 June 24)

Good news comes from the Coast to the effect that the original plan, including the purchase of studio grounds in California and possibly a factory site in Chicago, will be carried through. The demand for the Vogue product is increasing each week, due largely to Ben Turpin, who is now conceded in the trade to be one of the best slapstick comedians in the U.S. Two-reel comedies are now being tried out and the demand has been instantaneous. *Motography*

Sifted from the Studios: Vogue Films, Inc. (1916 July 1)

There is no question in the minds of the management of the company but that Vogue comedies will show net earnings in excess of 50 percent for the year. While they have taken on the more expensive program and highest paid stars, such as Ben Turpin, the popularity of the Vogue releases has been exceptional all over the country. It is pretty generally understood that this company, with its very small capitalization of $100,000, will eventually be increased to yet a much larger figure. With Thanhouser out of the Mutual production program, Vogue now partially fills that vacancy and has an opportunity to greatly increase its earnings. Purchases at anywhere near the present market we feel will very decidedly repay the investor. *Motography*

1916 July: "The popularity of the Vogue releases has been exceptional all over the country."

Motography, July 4, 1916, page 47

Chaplin Case "Off Again — On Again" (1916 July 8)

Some time ago, considerable litigation was started by Charlie Chaplin when he sought to restrain V.L.S.E. from releasing in four reels the *Burlesque on Carmen* in which he was starred. When the injunction was denied, the great little comedian appealed the suit for damages. This suit was also decided in favor of the defendants, according to advices received from the V.L.S.E. offices in New York. Chaplin is now being sued by the Essanay for violation of his contract made at the time he worked in Carmen.[81]

1916 July 8: The Vogue-Mutual studio will shortly begin work on the first of a series of two-reel comedies, one of which will hereafter be released each week. These will not interfere, however, with the one-reel comedies now being produced at the Los Angeles studios.

Motography, page 82 (in part)

1916 July 22: Mutual has divided the Vogue comedy players into two companies. Rube Miller will direct one company with Roy McRay as assistant and with Ben Turpin and himself as chief funmakers. Lillian Hamilton, a new acquisition, Harry Huckins, and Owen Evans make up the cast. Henry Kernan and Jack Gaines will direct the other corps. Paddy McQuire, Arthur Moon, Ed Laurie, and Gypsy Abbott have the leads.

Reel Life, page 14

Vogue, Inc. Makes Special Feature Comedies
All-Star Cast to Produce Exceptional Two-Reelers (1916 August 5)

We have no less an authority than Charles Chaplin for the assertion that Ben Turpin is one of the few real funny men on the screen. And it is a part of the previously unwritten history of the film business that a producer who was using Chaplin and Turpin in the same cast had to take Turpin out because he proved too much of a lead himself to play with Chaplin. It was a case of just too much comedy in one subject.

Some Liars (first of the new two-reelers, re August 13, 1916) synopsis:

Rube is the boss of his house. Ben's wife, played by old friend Eva Thatcher, is the boss of his house. They meet in a nearby saloon. A general fight follows. Later, their coats, one with Ben's address in it, are found on the pier. Their wives mourn them, not knowing that they were rescued by the motorboat police and given thirty days in jail. They return to find their wives in mourning, but, fearful of entering, pass themselves off as a couple of nuts. One cop, noticing their strange actions, starts to arrest them when their wives appear on the scene and fall all over them in their joy at seeing them again. Then to put themselves in right again, both explain their long absence by the weirdest of stories ever concocted. The yarns were good, but Ben's wife suspects him. At this moment, notice comes from the police captain stating that if they pull any more similar stunts, they will go back to the coop for thirty days. Their wives, wised up to the situation, roundly thrash them and lead them home.

Who is one of the greatest, best, and most popular of screen comedians?

"In my opinion," said Charles Chaplin, "Ben Turpin is one of the few really great comedians in motion picture work." Way back in the spring of 1892, Ben began with an old medicine show. He followed in this business until the early 1900s, when he joined a repertoire company. In the character role of *Happy Hooligan*, in the play of that name, Ben invaded the larger cities and overnight became a national character. Later, Turpin played opposite Charlie Chaplin, in which comedies he was a riot himself. Ben is now seen in his own company for Mutual, *Doctoring a Leak. Mutual publicity*

The Vogue studios are situated in the center of beautiful grounds that formerly surrounded the mansion of ex-Senator Cole of California. J. R. Crone is the general manager of the company.

1916 August 20: Latest News from Movie Land by Mae Tinee: Ben Turpin, whom press agents quote as being a "bundle of nerves," fell fifty feet the other day when the flagpole on which he was balanced broke in half. Outside of being thrown through a glass door against a marble statue, the fall was rather "commonplace." Poor Ben Turpin.

Chicago Daily Tribune, pg D3

1916 August: Ben Turpin, Vogue comedian, did a fall down three flights of stairs in the Hotel Stowell in Los Angeles one day last week. For a picture, of course. Soon after, Ben became entangled in the rear end of a Hollywood street car one recent day and suffered more from humiliation and lack of clothes than from injuries sustained, so he afterward confessed. *Mutual publicity*

The Stolen Booking (re 1916 August 29)

Ben and Rube Miller steal the suitcases of Kelsey and Ryan, two prominent legitimate actors, and find a contract and a wallet containing two dollars. They leave the place to join the troupe, which left some time before. They arrive in a small town and pose as Kelsey and Ryan and are informed that the troupe had been driven from town, but they suggest that Rube and Ben produce a benefit performance and, gathering a few of the townsfolk, they start rehearsals, taking the leading parts themselves. A series of amusing incidents follow and finally, Ben and Rube are forced to leave town; thus ends their career as famous actors. *Motography*

Doctoring A Leak (re 1916 September 17)

Dr. Kripple phones for a plumber to repair a broken pipe in the bathroom. The maid also phones for a plumber and when Ben arrives with his kit of tools, he wastes his time flirting with her. He goes downstairs and turns off the water and when Rube, the second plumber, arrives, he turns it on, thinking he is turning it off. A patient comes to the house and, thinking Rube is the doctor, seeks his aid. Rube poses as the doctor, but is discovered by Ben, who also poses as the doctor. With water rising, Rube and Ben get into various difficulties and finally, when the real plumber arrives, he opens a sewer outlet in the cellar, which lets out all the water, taking Rube and Ben in the rush. *Motography*

Vogue-Mutual Notes *(1916 September 2)*

Ben Turpin, Rube Miller, Paddy McQuire, and Arthur Moon, comedy leads of the Vogue-Mutual releases, are to appear at a big charity entertainment arranged by a prominent Los Angeles woman, the proceeds of which will go to the city's poor. Each will appear in the make-up he wears in the roles assumed in Vogue-Mutual comedies.

Motography, page 544

Ben Turpin Takes A Tumble *(1916 September 23)*

Life to Ben Turpin, the nervy little Vogue comedian, is just one chance-taking episode after another. Ben has probably been thrown from trolley cars, run over by autos, bitten by dogs, fallen down more stairs, and been kicked by more horses than any comedian in the business, yet he always comes up smiling and ready for something new. Last week, he was called upon to crawl into an ash pit under a red hot fire and went through with it as though the incident was an everyday occurrence. Early this week, the little fellow was called upon to stage a fight on the edge of a smokestack 194 feet from the ground. As no other actor would take the chance with Ben, he was compelled to use a dummy. In throwing the latter over the edge of the stack, Ben missed his foothold and fell. He would have landed on the ground if his rare presence of mind had not come to the rescue. Ben grasped the small ladder that had been strung from the top of the stack and although badly bruised, managed to keep from falling the entire distance; however, he insisted on finishing the scene. The man has no nerves. He is all nerve.

Moving Picture World, pgs 1982-3

Just a week later: Ben Turpin just doesn't care what he does or what is done to him. The latest stunt was to allow himself to be saturated with gasoline and set on fire.[82]

1916 October 28: Albert Ray, former actor, director, magazine writer, and brother of actor Charles Ray, was added to Vogue as a scenario editor to assist Hugh Saxon under Frederick Palmer, managing editor of the scenario department. Also added, Robin E. Williamson, former director of Florida's VIM Co. joins to direct. During the last two weeks, there have been some changes in casting at the Vogue. Ben Turpin, who has been playing for the past few months with Rube Miller, will appear with Paddy McQuire in a series of world-beaters. Robin Williamson will direct this company (first release, *The Wicked City*). Rube Miller will head his company alone. He'll direct as formerly with the assistance of Henry Kernan. In the studio's supporting cast, members of which are chosen to play with either Paddy McQuire and Ben Turpin or with Rube Miller as occasion demands, are Gypsy Abbott, Lillian Hamilton, Arthur Moon, Margaret Templeton, Owen Evans, the company's dare-devil, and two fat men whom everyone loves, Larry Bowes and Edward J. Laurie.

Motography, page 983

Ben's leading lady, Gypsy Abbott, the 5'3", black haired, brown-eyed girl, was born in England in 1894 and spent eight years on stage, including three years in Chicago stock and ingénue roles with Nat Goodwin. She also spent two seasons singing and dancing with the Pantages & Orpheum circuits and entered the movies with Balboa and starred with Carlyle Blackwell, Henry B. Walthall, and others before joining Vogue. She soon married director Henry King in 1916, eventually retiring from the screen.

Young Lillian Hamilton also worked as leading lady in the Vogue comedies. She began her acting career on the legitimate stage playing child parts. Entering the movies, she first appeared in Universal productions, then ten months with Selig, and next spent over a year with the independent Premier Company playing various parts in Western dramas. When Premier folded, she returned to Universal for four months before joining Vogue in July 1916 with three years of screen experience behind her. She stood 5'4" with brown hair and blue eyes.

Arthur Moon, often the rival or villain in the Vogues, was born in Garden City, Kansas, March 23, 1889. Educated in Salt Lake City, Chicago, and Columbia University, he had much stage experience. In 1915, he entered the movies with Universal, where he remained for eight months. On January 1, 1916, he joined Vogue. Moon stood 5'11" with black hair and brown eyes. He and his wife died in October 1918, a result of the infamous influenza epidemic, while on a vaudeville tour in Helena, Montana.

Wanted — A Doll With Taking Ways (1916 November 23)

Ben Turpin, Mutual comedian, is looking for a blue-eyed woman with light hair and a baby smile. She walked off with his brand new $50 cigarette case the other day. He promises faithfully to close his eyes, hold out his right hand, and ask no questions.

Chicago Daily Tribune, page 12

Reel Stars In 'Peril' at Film Exchange (1916 November 25)

Nell Craig, popular movie actress, narrowly escaped asphyxiation in a fire that damaged the building of the General Film Co., Opera Place and Elm St., early Saturday.

Ben Turpin and Rosemary Theby, who happened to be in the building with Miss Craig, experienced similarly narrow escapes.

Miss Craig owes her life to the fact that she was concealed on a shelf some distance from the flames in the basement. Turpin was saved by the prompt work of the firemen, while Miss Craig, who was scattered thru five reels, escaped by lying quietly in the fireproof vault.

Celluloid's So Tender

Being on the film, the movie stars were much more liable to death by overheating than in the flesh, as celluloid is much quicker to melt than cuticle.

The fire, police and firemen say, was caused by a defective gas furnace. A leak is supposed to have caused the first explosion, wrecking the furnace and allowing gas to escape into the basement.

In the basement were movie films that had been discarded, Harry L. O'Rear, manager, said. Robert Eggleston, 20, of 661 Elm St., Covington, night shipping clerk, discovered the fire. He was on the third floor with John Ross and William Redmond, film inspectors.

Eggleston, to save films stored in the upper floors, ran to the basement as flames were shooting into the stairway and closed a fireproof door.

The broken gas pipes on the furnace caused a blaze which firemen could not reach because of the fumes.

Frank Kroll, equipment superintendent, and Capt. Leonard Westcott, Co. 45, donned smoke helmets and shut off the gas supply.

The loss amounted to several hundred dollars.

Cincinnati Post, page 8

Jealous Jolts (re December 31, 1916) synopsis:

The village queen loves Ben, a hay baler. Paddy, a cowboy, loves the girl and he is the one favored by her parents. Ben hides in the doghouse one night and it is lassoed by Paddy and Ben is given a thrilling ride, nearly ending in disaster. He escapes, however, and is knocked out and pressed into a bale of hay by the cowboy. Gypsy's father steals the hay and she is starting to feed the horse when she sticks the pitchfork into Ben. The next day, Ben is buried alive by Paddy. The girl is tied to the chair by her father, but escapes and, in doing so, sets the house on fire. She is pursued by her father and Paddy. Ben, who escaped and donned a diver's suit, which he filled with free air, causing him to ascend to the clouds, is shot at and falls at the girl's feet. The constable comes upon them and later they are married while Ben is chased by his former wife, a washwoman.

Another mishap has befallen Ben Turpin, comedian with the elongated neck. His latest misfortune occurred at the Vogue studio, where he attempted to make an aerial flight as a human balloon. At a height of about thirty feet, something went wrong with the apparatus and Mr. Turpin alighted hard upon his feet, thus wrenching the ligaments of both legs. The comedian now is propped up in bed. It will probably be two weeks before this human bundle of comedy will be seen in a picture, but it is safe to say that his thousands of admirers will be waiting eagerly to see the great favorite once more frolic upon the screen.

Ben Turpin Hurt in Human Balloon Act
Noted Film Comedian Drops Farther Than He Expects To (1916 December 10)

Keeping up with the public demand for realism, the Vogue Comedy Company has built a cobblestone house, equipped with excellent lighting facilities and constructed with artistic finish for use in the Mutual comedies featuring Paddy McQuire, Ben Turpin, and Rube Miller. It has been set in the very middle of the company's attractive grounds at Los Angeles. The rooms have been finished in different styles of architecture so that if the director wants variety, he can move his setting to another room. The attic is to be equipped with one of the most complete storerooms ever gracing a studio and a wardrobe room will be installed on the same floor.

Everything is progressing merrily at the Vogue-Mutual Laugh Factory. The work of Paddy McQuire and Ben Turpin, now playing together, however, has been temporarily interrupted by an injury that overtook Ben the other day when he was trying to play the role of a human balloon. In a drop of thirty feet which he was supposed to make, the apparatus went back on him and he landed feet foremost, giving him a thorough jouncing, which has laid him up in bed for a couple of weeks.[83]

American Film Company Looking for Scripts (1916 November 22)

The American Film Company is in the market for scenarios. "We want great big compelling stories written especially for our stars," said R. R. Nehls, manager of the American and the other producing companies, Vogue and Signal, with which S. S. Hutchinson, president of the American, is associated, at the Chicago plant of the American the other day.

"Our demand for comedies is small, since we have a large scenario staff to prepare material for Rube Miller, Paddy McQuire, and Ben Turpin at the Vogue Studios. But that should not discourage authors with good scripts. Everyone is always ready to snatch up anything that is really good."[84]

Ben Turpin Wishes Movie Censors Were In — "Change Them Rules!" Can't Kiss, Can't Kill,
Can't Beat, or Tap A Till, Can't Hug Very Long, Censors Say, "Oh, So Wrong" by M.R.A.R.

Some of the saddest things ever seen on the screen are many of those so-called comedies. A genuine comedy is a different proposition and this style of picture is arriving nearer to perfection every day. One of the best film comedians we have is Ben Turpin and he recalls the time, and that only a few years ago, when no one realized that a comedian was worth anything. All that was needed to make people laugh was to have a chase in which the participants constantly fell over each other. It was then very hard to get anyone to play in comedies. The regular actors then felt it beneath their dignity and only the down-and-out would consider it. His first associates in comedy were a motley crew, consisting mostly of the stage carpenters, piano movers, plumbers, and their families.

"It is queer," said Mr. Turpin, "what a few years will do. Now comedians are pulling down a king's ransom in the way of salary and are some of the most successful actors on the screen."

As sometimes happens when people risk their lives to give realism to funny situations, Ben now and then takes a tumble. He was trying to impersonate a human balloon when the apparatus went back on him. In the 30-foot drop, he landed on his feet, but received such a jolting that he was laid up for a couple of weeks.

The spectacle of a coward braggart being exposed in one of the time-honored but legitimate tricks for creating comedy and a very fine example of this was given by Turpin in one of his plays, *His Bogus Boast*. In this funny film, the admiration of the ladies went to Ben's head and, not content to let well enough alone, he boasted of his prowess as a hunter, although he had never been further West than the Hudson.

His popularity with the ladies inspired the men with jealousy, just as his overdone yarns aroused their suspicions. One of them bribed the butler to furnish the motive power for a large bearskin rug that started towards Ben. As the animated rug approached him, all thought of damage to his rented suit, the hero-worshipping women, and his own reputation for bravery were forgotten in his intense desire to escape and that quickly. His efforts were side-splitters. In common with producers, manufacturers, and fellow actors, Mr. Turpin has a few things to say regarding the censor.

He last expressed himself on this subject in verse:

Can't kiss, can't kill, Can't beat, or tap a till.
Can't hug very long, Censors say: "Oh, so wrong!"
Can't laugh in a church,
Or whip a child with a birch
Nor tie a can to doggie's tail,
For if I do, I go to jail
Oh, Censor Board, I love you well,
But still I wish you would, Change them rules!

Who says a comedian does not have deep and noble thoughts lurking behind his frivolous exterior?

Ben Turpin, the Vogue comedian, has returned to work. His injured leg doesn't bother him anymore. Everyone is glad, for little Benny is a good-hearted, cheery chap.

Motion Picture Classic, February, 1917

1917 Los Angeles Directory: Ben Turpin, *photoplayer,* home: 5742 Camerford Ave.

1917 March 4: Gypsy Abbott, Vogue player, has been across the Mexican border with her company. On the return trip, there was a mix-up of suitcases of which Miss Abbott good-naturedly took as a joke. The joke ended, however, when she reached the office of the federal authorities and found that the suitcase she was carrying contained several thousand dollars' worth of smuggled opium.[85] Gypsy soon left the Vogue, maybe due to this prank.

Falling — On and Off the Screen by Robert Francis Moore *(1917 March, in part)*
"Can you do a fall?" That's the first question asked of an aspirant to screen comedy. Now, that doesn't just mean can the candidate just fall down when told, but can he do it without hurting himself in such a way as to get a big laugh? Now that is where the art lies.

Being an ardent comedy fan, I often wondered just how some of these remarkable tumbles were accomplished without serious injury to those participants, but I determined to talk to some of the brightest luminaries in that branch of the profession and get some firsthand information. One of the newer tumbling comedians, whose rise to fame has been rapid, is Ben Turpin, of the Vogue Comedies.

"Are you one of those to whom the body-smashing art comes natural?" I asked.

"Yes and no," Ben replied. "I always had a fondness for that kind of work, but several years ago I joined a circus troupe as a producing clown, and, naturally, that job gave me a chance to practice a fine line of neck-breakers. That's really where I got my experience. I don't rely much on science in taking falls, for really the most scientific tumbler in the world may easily hurt himself. My motto is: Throw yourself into the game and trust in Providence."

Moore continues: Some of the greatest exponents of slapstick tumbling are those whose names never appear on the screen programs. These are the famous Keystone Cops. I was talking the other day to one of the directors of that studio and he made the statement that this brand of grief-killers had done as much and more than any star to win popularity for Keystone comedies.

"Why," he said, "in the old days, when there wasn't enough body to the scenario, when the 'gags' were falling flat and everything was going wrong, the never-failing remedy was to call in the 'cops' to pull the picture thru." These are picked men, daredevils ready for anything, from driving an automobile through the side of a house to shooting the same machine off a fifty-foot pier. And there isn't any fake to what you see, either. Keystone maintains its own hospital and it is surprising how few cases are treated there. And of course, there is the usual quota of bruises to be dressed and an occasional sprained ankle, but nine times out of ten, the performers get away clear. I asked the director how he accounted for this. "It's because we tell them where to fall," he said.

"Sometimes they miss their mark, and then someone gets hurt; but they get hardened to it, and we have some on our payroll whom you couldn't kill with a steam roller."

Motion Picture

Ben, too, would soon find his way to Keystone.

In his interview with producer Henry *Pathé* Lehrman, Barnet Braverman noted, "Mack Sennett wanted Ben Turpin and offered him $200 a week. Turpin didn't believe anybody had that much money to pay, or would pay it. Hutchinson said, 'I won't let anyone dictate to me. I won't pay it.' So Turpin went over to Sennett and exhibitors gave Hutchinson to understand they would not take his other pictures if no Turpin, so the Vogue studio closed."

1917 April 15: Ben Turpin, Mutual-Vogue comedian, was asked what he thought about the war the other day. Here are his views: "All these foreigners who are living in this country and are not satisfied with the methods of our President should return to their countries and fight. They will be made perfectly at home by wearing American uniforms, eating canned beef and hardtack, becoming entangled in American-made barbed wire, and finally being punctured by American-made bullets."[86]

1917 April 29: Ed Laurie, the fat boy of the Vogue-Mutual studio, fell on Ben Turpin during a scene the other day and put the comic out of business for several seconds.[87]

With his later success in the Sennett comedies, the Ben Turpin Essanay and Vogue comedies were bought up by enterprising young companies, who retitled and rereleased films such as: *Forced to Work* (originally *For Ten Thousand Bucks*), *The Porter* (*The Wicked City*), *High Art* (*Picture Pirates*), *The Country Lover* (*Jealous Jolts*), *The Skyrocket* (*Masked Mirth*), *The Janitor* (*Shot in the Fracas*), *Barnstorming* (*The Stolen Booking*), *Why Men Leave Home* (*Some Liars*), *The Animal Tamer*, *His Wedding Day*, *The Close Shave* (actually one of Turpin's last Essanay shorts, initially known as *The Barber*, shelved and never released until 1921), *The Nut Crackers*, and others, often confusing their initial origin.

1917 April 14: Ben Turpin leaves Vogue for Keystone after his present picture, *Caught in the End*. Ben will be missed, for he is a big favorite with his fellow artists.[88]

After completing over thirty comedies in one year for Vogue, Ben recalled, "At the end of the year I said to my business manager: 'We're going around to see Mack Sennett, you and I. I think maybe he's anxious to have a little talk with us.' Mack did want to talk to us and I've been with him ever since."

Mack Sennett
For Art's Sake

Ben told writer Inez Wallace in 1934, *"Mack Sennett phoned me and asked if I'd come to work for him. I knew I could get even more money. My manager and I talked it over and decided to ask for $200 a week. We did — and again we got it without any argument. It was unbelievable. There seemed to be no end to what these movie men would pay."* [65]

A farewell party was given Ben Turpin, former Vogue comedian, by his fellow players at the Vogue. Ben is leaving to join the Keystone forces and will be sadly missed. The party was given at Lillian Hamilton's house and proved a gala affair, breaking up in the wee hours of the morning. Among those present were Mr. Ben and Mrs. Carrie Turpin, Lillian Hamilton, her mother Mrs. Hamilton, Al Ray, Paddy McQuire, Hugh Allen Saxon, George Crone, John Oaker, Mr. and Mrs. Robin Williamson, Mr. and Mrs. Lawrence Bowes, Owen Evans, Walter Newman, Linney Templeton, and many other Vogue favorites. The evening and the morning, too, were voted a huge success. In response to loud applause, Ben made a speech and for an encore did a hula-hula dance.

Motion Picture Classic, June 1917, pg 75

In March 1917, Ben entered the gates at 1712 Allesandro Street in Edendale, California, Mack Sennett's Keystone, the most successful producer of comedies at the time. Charlie Chaplin, Harold Lloyd, Roscoe "Fatty" Arbuckle, Mabel Normand, and Gloria Swanson were but a few of many personalities who'd been associated with Keystone by this time. Many others came and went over the years, including Harry Langdon, Carole Lombard, Mal St. Clair, Sally Eilers, Del Lord, Frank Capra, Larry Semon, Erle Kenton, Andy Clyde, Eddie Quillan, and more.

Gene Fowler, in his Sennett biography *Father Goose*, wrote: "One day a scrawny, cross-eyed fellow named Ben Turpin applied for a job. Sennett was very superstitious and kept his fingers crossed all the time Turpin talked. Mack wanted to hire Ben, but feared that ill luck might follow. Finally he put him to work as a janitor. Later he allowed the angle-orbed aspirant to take a trial ride on the back step of the patrol wagon.

"'None of our cops are game enough to jump from that step and land on their backsides,' said Sennett. 'If you do a good, high fall from that step and don't break your tail, I'll give you a job in pictures.'

"Turpin got on the patrol, leaped until the horizon could be seen below his flying rump, then landed hard. He got up, caught the patrol and took another sensational pratfall. Again he jumped and landed. And again, and again. In fact, Sennett and (Fred) Mace had to restrain him from more leaps. 'It was pretty good,' said Sennett, with characteristic understatement, 'The job is yours.'" Though the story's a good one, scholars over the years have noted, however, Fowler's Sennett-collaborated biography is peppered with much more fiction than fact.

Turpin himself recalled his first day at Keystone to writer Gordon Gassaway for *Picture Play* in 1920: "I sat and sat in Mr. Sennett's office until I noticed he began to wiggle and twitch in his chair. Then he turned to me and exploded:

"'Well, what do you want?'

"'I want a contract,' I said.

"'All right,' Sennett said, 'But take those eyes out of here and stick 'em in a bucket of water or something until we're ready for you.'"

According to author Kalton C. Lahue in his *Mack Sennett's Keystone, The Man, The Myth and The Comedies* and his interviews with Sennett's business manager, George W. Stout, when Mack became interested in Turpin after seeing some of the Vogue comedies, he had Stout locate and hire Ben. Lahue states, "Stout made numerous attempts to contact Ben over the next few months, but the Vogue studio rebuffed each by refusing calls for Turpin, censoring his mail deliveries and otherwise attempting to keep Ben unaware that Mack Sennett wanted to talk with him. Vogue suffered a fear prevalent (and justifiable) among producers — whenever a screen personality found someone as important as Keystone initiating a feeler, he either broke his contract or demanded more money, and Vogue executives were determined that if they could help it, neither would happen to their relationship with Turpin. But something as important as this can't be kept a secret forever, and Ben finally learned through the grapevine what was going on.

"Turpin suddenly appeared in George Stout's office one day minus his identifying brush mustache. As Ben had not given his name, Stout failed to recognize the little comic and so treated him as just another applicant looking for work around the studio. When he reached the inevitable question, 'What can you do?' Turpin offered himself as combination carpenter and janitor. Turning away from Stout and bending over, Ben reached into a pocket, pulled out his moustache and fastened it in place. Straightening up, he whirled around to face Stout with his eyes crossed magnificently and announced, 'I'm Ben Turpin!' Elated that they had finally made contact, Stout reached into a desk drawer, pulled out a contract and shoved it in front of Ben. Turpin signed on the dotted line without even questioning the salary offer and Stout excused himself, rushing off to tell Sennett the good news." Ben once told it that Sennett called him to his lot and initially offered him $125 a week.

Turpin grabbed the chance, but when Sennett wanted to put him under a five-year contract, Ben decided to take the papers for the deal to a lawyer friend to see if they were all right.

"I didn't know much about such matters and my friends said not to sign. I went back to Sennett, who raised the ante $25. I was still advised not to accept. Then Sennett added $50 more. I was ready to go through with the deal, but my attorney refused to allow it.

"Well, the dickering went on for several weeks and the outcome of it was I signed up for $200 a week for two years, with an option of a $50 a week increase every six months.

"That was the most money I ever dreamed of making."[15]

Whatever the truth, Turpin's original six-page Keystone contract survives, signed and dated March 16, 1917. According to the terms, Ben was to start work at Keystone exactly one month later on April 16 at one hundred and ninety-five dollars weekly for the first six months. It was agreed that Keystone "hereby engages and employs Ben Turpin for a continuous period of six months beginning on the 16th day of April, 1917, as a motion picture actor to act, play, pose, perform and take part in motion picture rehearsals, acts, parts, scenes, settings, roles and plays as ordered by the employer at the studio or studios of the employer in California or on designated location or at any other place required by Sennett for the agreed weekly salary of One Hundred and Ninety-Five ($195) dollars to be paid weekly by Sennett to Turpin." Ben later recalled, "Every six months the pay envelope got heavier until it was a burden to haul it to the bank and I asked for checks. I stayed with Mack Sennett until 1927, proving that it pays to stay with one concern."

On March 31, 1917, a charity baseball game benefiting the American Red Cross was played at Washington Park, Los Angeles, featuring Hollywood's Tragics vs. Comics. Umpires were Barney Oldfield and James J. Jeffries. The Tragics included Wallace Reid, William Desmond, Franklyn Farnum, George Walsh, Eugene Pallette, Antonio Moreno, Crane Wilbur, Jack Holt, Jack Pickford, Hobart Bosworth, Wheeler Oakman, Lew Cody, Wm. S. Hart, Herbert Rawlinson, and George Beban. The Comics: Charlie Chaplin, pitcher; Eric Campbell, catcher; Charlie Murray, 1st base; Slim Summerville, 2nd base; Bobby Dunn, short stop; Hank Mann, 3rd base; Harold Lloyd, left field; Chester Conklin, center field; also Max Asher, Edgar Kennedy, Billie Ritchie, and Rube Miller. Ben Turpin, Sennett's newest comedian coming in from right field, lost his pants during the heated game. Ten thousand spectators were there. One spectator wrote, "Ben Turpin and Hank Mann put on a wrestling bout in the middle of the diamond. Mann finally ends with a toehold, the toe between his teeth. They got up and Mann cracks Turpin on the jaw. He is out cold, necessitating the presence of the cops to carry him off."[89]

Ben remembered, "You oughta seen them give me the ha-ha and the bass razoo on this very lot when I first came to work for Mr. Sennett. I felt like a turtle in a goldfish bowl, as the fellow said, and got about as much privacy. They followed me around just to laugh at me." Lahue resumes, "Ben's expectations of great things to come went unfulfilled as he reported for work day after day, drawing his paycheck weekly for sitting around. Finally, he was assigned to the group of second-string comics who were making the so-called 'bogus' Keystones." ("Bogus" meaning those one-reel Triangle-Keystone shorts where Mack Sennett supposedly supplied the talent and technicians for those actually Triangle-produced shorts as opposed to the Sennett-produced two-reel Keystone comedies).

1917 June 13: In a forthcoming Triangle comedy (*Sole Mates*), Ben Turpin and Florence Clarke stage a soul kiss that should be perfect. At least, there were sixteen retakes before the director (Herman Raymaker) pronounced it just right. *Sennett Weekly*

Turpin's earliest known films at Keystone included the lead in a one-reel Triangle-Komedy, *Sole Mates* (re July 29, 1917), and a small bit in the Mack Swain and Ethel Teare two-reeler, *Lost — A Cook* (re August 12, 1917), where Ben shows up as a wedding guest who can't stay away from the punch bowl. Prior to these he worked in a one-reeler *The Automaton Figure*. Lahue notes Sennett saw the latter film, "liked it and ordered that the one-reeler be expanded to two. Thus *The Automaton Figure* became a Sennett Keystone release subject, *A Clever Dummy*." He adds, "Viewing a good print of this film today, the difference in cast members found in each reel is apparent and the inconsistencies in its plot development can be attributed to this padding.

"Nonetheless, Ben was now a starring member of the first team and his screen personality began a gradual transformation that would accelerate into full stardom in the early twenties, when he became the highest paid comic on the lot until the arrival of Harry Langdon."

The July 9, 1917 issue of the *Mack Sennett Weekly*, the company trade journal of news, new releases, publicity, bathing beauties, and everything Sennett for the exhibitors, was quick to announce "Ben Turpin New Style Comedian" and is said to be "the only cross-eyed actor in the movies. Whether this is true or not, he is doubtless the funniest, and in this new Keystone *(A Clever Dummy)*, appears in a role which tests his genius as a laugh maker to the limit." Sennett's publicists were quick to sell their new comedian to the market with a barrage of hype, penning such things as: "They say that when Ben cries, the tears roll down his back. Which may or may not be true. One thing is certain, however, and that is, that when you see Ben, you'll laugh till you cry." The publicists grabbed us with headlines such as "Cross-Eyed Comic is Great Pitcher," stating: "The Mack Sennett-Keystone Company has a baseball team which boasts the most extraordinary pitcher on record. He is Ben Turpin. Ben is one of the few human beings who can see in front and behind at the same moment. This is invaluable in baseball as many a venturesome soul discovered who tried to steal from second to third while Ben was winding up."

A Clever Dummy (re June 15, 1917) synopsis:

Many a man and many a woman have done strange things for love, but it is believed that Ben took the cake when he decided that he would impersonate the dummy in order to be near the object of his affection, Claire Anderson. It made no difference to him that the lovely blonde sported an engagement ring that had put a dent in her fiancée's (James Delano) bankroll. To be near her was Ben's desire. But instead of achieving his goal, he landed in a nailed-up box that landed on the railroad tracks in front of an express train. To be sure, Claire rescues him, but she doesn't throw her arms around his neck and cry "my hero!" Not in this story. A lot of funny things happen to Ben and to the dummy. They are so much alike that one can't tell them apart and each makes a tremendous hit. Some of the funniest scenes in the picture occur when the show is put on. Eventually, the dummy and Ben come face to face, a fact which starts a new series of cyclonic emotions, which wind up with a bang and a real Keystone finish. *The Los Angeles Times* wrote: "Ben Turpin has already a big name as a comedian, and *A Clever Dummy* is said to be one of the most hilariously funny Keystones which that company has ever turned out. The subtitles are especially clever, is a promise."

July 22, 1917, page III 1

Almost immediately after the release of *A Clever Dummy*, Ben's old employer, Essanay/ General Film, were out to make a further profit from their earlier productions by reissuing and retitling some of their earlier shorts, *Two Laughs* and *Pete's Pants*. The company wrote, "An innovation in the Black Cat series of 25-minute features released through General Film is the appearance of Ben Turpin, comedian, in an out-and-out comedy, titled *Two Laughs*. All of the Black Cat pictures have been comedy-dramas, but Essanay made room for the Turpin comedy in this series because of its splendid fun. Turpin has never appeared to better advantage, is the verdict of General Film, than in this release. It is called *Two Laughs* which is completely a misnomer by reason of the laughs numbering many, many times that." Mr. J. L. Goral of the Variety Theater, Buffalo, New York commented that *Two Laughs* was "A very good comedy. Turpin is a fair drawing card. Scenery and direction, OK."[90]

More comedies were to come and other enterprising showmen would also join the bandwagon of buying up the rights to these older Turpin films and rereleasing them over the next several years, both legally and illegally. The Sennett company thought well enough of Ben to say, "Turpin is as funny off the screen as he is on it. He keeps the whole company in a state of giggles all the time the camera is working. Ben is as slow and sad as a fox terrier. He has the effect of a restless young cyclone."

Mack Sennett Weekly, July 30, 1917

The Pawnbroker's Heart (re August 19, 1917):

Ben next reprised his role as a janitor in the Chester Conklin film, *The Pawnbroker's Heart*. In a pawnshop, Chester and Ben did their best to get their salaries with as little effort as possible. Peggy Pearce comes in and secrets herself with her boss, Glen Cavender, in an effort to get her job as his maid back. It starts something, for Mrs. Cavender (long and lean Caroline Rankin) and Peggy's husband, Chester, don't get the angle. A band of crooks plan to rob the pawnshop. Clothing store dummies play an important part and two bags, one with and one without cash, figure in the plot.

Ben later recalled a typical Keystone situation during the filming of *The Pawnbroker's Heart*: "They were slamming dummies against a wall, but the heads broke off all of them. They were short of time on the scene and didn't have any more dummies, so I told the directors to use me; they did, and my head wasn't broke — but it made an awful dent in the wall!"

Keystone News Notes (1917 August 26)

Ben Turpin of the Keystone company tried to enlist. "Can't use you," declared the recruiting officer. "You're cross-eyed." "Sure," retorted Turpin. "I'd make a great scout, for I can see before and behind at the same time."

Shortly after Ben's arrival on the Keystone lot, Sennett ended his bittersweet two-year association with Triangle, next signing in July 1917 to have his productions distributed by Paramount. As a result of a strenuous court battle, gone was Sennett's further right to the name Keystone, but he retained the studio in Edendale. When Sennett left the Triangle-Keystone concern, it was not certain whether or not his entire company of funmakers would go with him. Most of them decided in favor of their old boss, including Polly Moran, Charlie Murray, Mack Swain, Chester Conklin, Bobby Dunn, Louise Fazenda, Glen Cavender, Slim Summerville, and Ben Turpin, to name a few in the new Paramount-Mack Sennett Comedies. Triangle continued to produce its own new Keystone Comedies, which now had nothing to do with Sennett. After several comedies, the new Keystone gave in to its competition and closed its laugh factory. Sennett's comedies, according to his own testimony, would be produced independently of every other organization, being released through Paramount. One two-reel comedy would be released every two weeks. Production beginning at once.[91]

Ben's first work in the Paramount-Sennett Comedies was in support of Mack's bigger stars at that time, Chester Conklin, Polly Moran, Charlie Murray, and Louise Fazenda. In the first released Paramount-Sennett short, *A Bedroom Blunder*, Ben turns up in the second reel as the front desk clerk at a seaside hotel who mixes up the rooms of Charlie Murray and Mary Thurman, resulting in some sticky situations for the stars and their movie spouses. Even director Eddie Cline gets in on the on-screen fun.

The *Mack Sennett Weekly* (July 30, 1917) next gave mention to another favorite director: "The actors all like to work in Vic Heerman's pictures. Victor is fastidious and immaculate in his clothes and fastidious and immaculate in his work. He is quick and clever and sympathetic with a rare instinct for dramatic effects. He has a peculiar facility for getting the best work out of people." Heerman was soon at work on Louise Fazenda's first Paramount release, *Are Waitresses Safe?*

Are Waitresses Safe? (re November 18, 1917) synopsis:

It all starts in a bakery and restaurant, where one finds Louise Fazenda juggling china and Ben Turpin doing his best to hold down his waiter job, but with disastrous results. Partly, his downfall is due to Slim Summerville, who is as tough as he is stringy, the bitter and unscrupulous rival for the hand of Louise. Ben has the inside track. Comes then a drunk (Al McKinnon), who tries to do everything he's asked, but can't control his feeling nor his feet with the result that he materially assists in landing Ben and Louise among the homeless thousands. But it's not for long, for we find Louise installed as the prize roustabout in the mayor's home. It was a nice job and the mayor (Gene Rogers) had a lot of confidence in Louise. So much, in fact, that he and the mayoress went away on a trip and left the house and the family jewels in her care. It was too good a chance to give a party.

Many a woman have succumbed to less temptation. So Louise fell and it was some tumble. The old mansion never before staged a party like that which Louise and Ben gave. The family jewels glittered as gloriously on her neck and bosom as they ever did on the proud lady who owned them. Slim and his gang hadn't been invited, but they went just the same, which led to the merriest little free-for-all that ever happened. Even then, it wouldn't have been so bad had not the mayor and his party returned at the inopportune moment and landed in the middle of the melee. There is an exceptionally large and clever cast in addition to the stars and between the drunks, the iceman, and the gangsters, to say nothing of a refractory soda fountain, the fun is fast and furious. Teddy, the famous Great Dane, is in the picture, too, and Pep, a Maltese cat who is a new Mack Sennett find, while new and novel gags of the sort that only Mack Sennett Studio knows how to make are almost countless. Louise Fazenda has long since been conceded the funniest woman on the screen. *Are Waitresses Safe?* will be her first Mack Sennett Comedy and virtually a pace setter for those which are to follow. *Sennett Weekly*

Newsy Notes from Movieland by Daisy Dean *(1917 December 18):*
Ben Turpin bases his claim to immortality on these interesting facts:
He can't make his eyes behave. He is one of the foremost funmakers of the day.
He has halted more loose custards with his facade than any other comedian in the pictures.
He can write a film story as competently as he can enact one.
Turpin is slightly past forty, is thoroughly domesticated and is a rabid football and baseball enthusiast.[92]

In a simple review, theater owner Charles H. Ryan of the Garfield Theater, Chicago noted of the next Sennett release, "*Roping Their Lover* is a western burlesque comedy that went over OK. Not quite as many laughs as the usual Sennett but there are a few thrills. Ben Turpin is rising fast as a comedian. His work is natural." *Motography*

Of his next comedy, *Sheriff Nell's Tussle* (re Feb. 24, 1918), Ben recalled, "One day I was doing a scene where Billy Armstrong was to hit me with a prop statue. It was supposed to be one of those breakaway things made out of plaster; you can break them with a flip of your finger. Well, some bonehead prop boy got mixed in his dope and handed Billy a statuette made out of solid marble. In his hurry he didn't take notice of the weight, and when the director gives him the signal he gives me a thump with all his might on my bean. The next I knew I gave a yell and grabbed him by the throat. At least I thought I was grabbing him by the throat. I heard my wife give an awful yell and I realized it was her and not Billy Armstrong I was choking. I had been cuckoo at home in bed with a doctor and a trained nurse for two days."

Anaconda Standard, July 28, 1918

1918 March 16: Ben Turpin of the Paramount-Mack Sennett comedies knows what it means to sacrifice himself to art. In a new comedy, he is required to make a fall on a hard board floor. In making the picture, he took the tumble with such fidelity to his art that he broke the floor. The crash so startled the cameraman that he forgot to grind. Then he told Ben it would have to be done over again. "Can't do it," said the comedian, laconically. "Why not?" he was asked. "I'm all full of splinters," replied Ben and he made for his dressing room. *Motography*

About this time, Ben's wife was seriously injured in an auto accident while driving from church. Ben, ultimately believing the accident the cause of her eventual illness and tragic death, is discussed later in this book.
In the Sennett comedies, it wasn't unusual for Ben to pop up in the films of Mack's other comics; after all, they were all under the one and same roof. Ben is known to have made surprise appearances in the Chester Conklin film *His Smothered Love* (re May 5, 1918), Charlie Murray's *Love Loops the Loop* (re June 2, 1918), and others. In turn, these same stars also popped up in Ben's films.

Saucy Madeline (re April 22, 1918) synopsis:
All the trouble arises through the unconquerable jealousy of Charlie Lynn, who is the keeper of a bowling alley. Ben Turpin, a small town roustabout, comes there to work and

just because he can't make his eyes behave when Polly Moran is around, her jealous husband is on the verge of apoplexy several times. The climax comes when Polly, in her charitable zeal, volunteers to take part in a benefit for the Old Bowlers' Home and selects a costume more pleasing to the eyes of the audience than to her jealous husband. The spectacle of Turpin, who is an entire orchestra, a call boy, and bowler, is highly diverting. *Motography*

Too Realistic for Ben Turpin (1918 April 22)

Ben Turpin wears a large goose egg bump on the top of his head as a souvenir of *The Battle Royal*. In one scene, Charles Lynn is supposed to whack him over the head with a boxing glove fastened onto the end of a long pole. In some way, the glove slipped off the pole as Charlie raised it over his head. The result was that Ben got the full force of the bare club on his head. He went down like a log. The camera, as a result, got one realistic thrill that wasn't in the script. *Sennett Weekly*

1918 Los Angeles Directory: Ben Turpin, *photoplayer*, home: 5560 Santa Monica Blvd.

1918 May 5: When Ben Turpin, the cross-eyed comedian, was knocked out in a fight a short while ago, the first thing he said when he came to was, "Where's a mirror? I want to see if my eyes are still crooked." Ben explained that they got that way through his being hit on the head while in vaudeville and a doctor told him that if he ever got another crack like that it might jar them back into shape.

Oakland Tribune, pg 18

The Battle Royal (released May 20, 1918) review:

Ben Turpin is introduced as a victim of financial depression. His inability to pay his landlady results in his being forcibly cast out in the street, wrapped up in his steamer trunk. That's when Charlie Lynn and Polly Moran take pity on him. The picture was directed by Richard Jones, who staged the action in a fast and furious manner. *MPW*

Two Tough Tenderfeet (released June 16, 1918) review:

A feature of the current program is the Mack Sennett comedy, *Two Tough Tenderfeet*, featuring that cock-eyed walloper Ben Turpin, one of the most laughable fellows on the screen. Like all Sennett pictures, this one is fast and furious and provides a most enjoyable half hour. Too much cannot be said in favor of the Sennett comedies, which are the rage of the country. As a producer of mirth-provoking films, Sennett is the ace of aces. He has a large following of picture fans here who seem to take as much interest in his comedies as they do in the big feature pictures.[94]

Ben Turpin and Charlie Lynn are two exceedingly tough individuals. Their adventures land them in a desert, where they successfully escape lions, wild men, jackrabbits, and other fierce creatures and reach a frontier settlement, which was so tough that the two tough tenderfeet are made to feel themselves mere amateurs in the line of toughness. Ben falls in love with Polly Moran, the female sheriff. *MPW*

The trio of Polly Moran, Turpin, and Charlie Lynn were soon gaining in popularity in the Sennett comedies. Ben went from Moran's co-star to equal billing and eventually star status with each successive short. Sennett publicist Harry Carr noted the three "would bring laughs to a German drill sergeant. Their fun is unctuous and uproarious. Not the least of their strong points as comedians lies in the facts that they are good friends off the screen, and generous collaborators on the screen. They all work for the good of the picture and the result brings down the house."

Much later, in 1929, Carr also recalled, "Sennett put Ben in a series of comedies with Polly Moran and a man whose front name was Heinie. His teammates were jealous of Ben. One of the daily entertainments of the studio was to stand around the front gate when they came together for the day and hear the names they called each other — the result of a long night's patient thought and research. Ben lived under one never-ending dread. His eyes had been crossed as a result of a blow to the head. Every time anything cracked against his distinguished skull — which was pretty often — he flew to a mirror in the fear that his eyes might have been straightened again. They were his meal ticket. During the course of the long array of battles in this unit the management got a terrible 'mad' at Miss Moran. In fact it was decided to dispense with her services. A shriek protest came from the 'trade.' The exhibitors who were our cash customers protested that all their patrons demanded the girl who rode bucking broncos in the Sheriff Nell comedies. 'The girl who rides' was one of the big sellers of pictures. So Miss Moran came back with an advanced salary and a grim smile. Grim because she never had ridden. All the broncos were busted for her by doubles."[95]

1918 June 5: Charlie Lynn and Ben Turpin, the "Heavenly Twins" of the Mack Sennett Comedies, have a mutual admiration society. Ben thinks that Charlie is the world's greatest comedian and Charlie is prepared to prove Ben is the man who invented laughter.

Albany Evening Journal

She Loved Him Plenty (re August 11, 1918) review:

Just a rollicking farce, so exaggerated in characters and incidents as to be almost form-less, yet filled with ingenious devices from that unfailing Sennett font of invention. Sennett seems to be afraid he will not provide enough material and runs over the edge with a rapidity of action that makes it almost impossible to keep the sequence of events. One has barely time to grasp a situation and laugh before it is rushed off to make room for another and these follow one another is such quick succession that much of the purely humorous, the amusing side of human nature, is entirely lost.

What is needed in these tremendously active Sennett productions is a diminution of speed so that the audience mind can have brief periods of relaxation. High tension is all right by itself, but combined with the speed of movement beyond that of average comprehension, it may prove a strain on attention and hinder its own purpose. Some of the Sennett farces have enough sensational material to supply twice as much film as is used, but they usually get plenty of laughs and, in that respect, *She Loved Him Plenty* is no exception. Charles Lynn and Ben Turpin make a great team for acrobatic farce and Polly Moran can easily travel where either of them dares to go. The farce will win, but what this character of release can stand, what most of the five-reelers cannot, is a little letting up of speed. They travel too fast. *MPW*

With the completion of *She Loved Him Plenty*, Polly Moran ended a three-and-a-half year association with Sennett. According to the news reports, she was to entertain troops overseas. But with the end of the war, she soon set sail for Australia, where she was to begin a long vaudeville tour. Sennett writer John Gray also left at this time. Both would eventually return, Gray within the year and Moran not for eight years.

1918 August 17: Ben Turpin was one of many celebrities who attended this night's entertainment and masquerade ball at the Shrine Auditorium, Los Angeles. The event was given under the auspices of the Motion Picture War Service Association. Attendees also included Theda Bara, Thomas Ince, D.W. Griffith, Cecil B. DeMille, William DeMille, Wallace Reid, Bryant Washburn, Lila Lee, Fred Stone, Jeanie MacPherson, Charlie Murray, Jack Mulhall, George Beban, and many others. Helping America's fallen heroes proved a financial success that night.

Sleuths! (re September 22, 1918) review:

A gentleman crook who walks into a private detective office and gets away with all of the money belonging to the proprietors, and also with their pretty stenographer, is one of the characters in *Sleuths!*, a two-part Sennett-Paramount featuring Ben Turpin and Charles Lynn as the two gumshoe men. Tom Kennedy plays the part of the crook and Marie Prevost is the good-looking typewritist. The ability of Messrs. Turpin and Lynn to do funny falls, pull comic faces, and keep the nonsense moving and the spectator on the broad grin is given continuous proof during the action of this comedy. F. Richard Jones, the director, has been apt at inventing new bits of business and the production is worthy of its well-known trademark. *MPW*

Ben's Bean and Tree Collide

Ben Turpin claims to be the hard luck comedian of the world. Every picture decorates him, so he claims, with a new scar or a fresh bump. *Hide and Seek, Detectives* is no exception to the rule. Ben was sliding across a park lawn in one of the scenes when a palm tree got in the way. It was the kind of palm that had knobs and stickles, as Ben discovered.

Mack Sennett Weekly, November 25, 1918

Rubbernecking in Filmland by Giebler: *Murray Shoots Turpin Abaft the Turret*
Atop the tank Victory in Central Park, Los Angeles to sell Liberty Bonds, October 1918

Charlie Murray was the announcer and he started off by introducing Ben Turpin as the greatest cock-eyed comedian in the world and then, to show what a soldier does with guns bought by bonds, he shot Ben just abaft of the turret — on the tank — and Ben did one of his best comedy falls. Louise Fazenda made a few well-chosen remarks that were received with great delight by the crowd. Myrtle Lind, Phyllis Haver, Ford Sterling, and Chester Conklin, without his walrus mustache, also spoke and Mack Sennett made quite a lengthy and telling speech and everybody, including Sennett's dog Teddy, hustled for bond sales and put them over in great shape.[96]

Rubbernecking in Filmland by Giebler:

Filmland is full of gloom and germs. Everyone you meet has a different cure for the Flu or a sure-for-certain, double-back action, ball-bearing preventative for the Flu, but in spite of this, everyone you meet has either just got over an attack of the Flu or is just getting down with it. It certainly didn't look like the Flu was making any difference at Sennett's. They were going right ahead with their laugh-makers the same as if things were normal and every theatre in the country running full blast. Eddie Cline was busy with *Hide and Seek, Detectives*, a rib-tickler, with Ben Turpin, Charles Lynn, Tom Kennedy, and Marie Prevost as support.[97]

Turpin's first big article/magazine spread appeared in December 1918's *Photoplay*, an interview conducted by Sennett's publicist, Harry Carr. Ben told Carr, "I worked around a few joke factories and then I came to Mack Sennett's.

"It's a great life," said Ben meditatively about his movie career. "I've been in the hospital twenty-five times. I've had my teeth knocked out four times. One time they got me up on a rope over a canyon and somebody let go of the rope, dropping me about the distance you fall out of a balloon. I've been hit by a peevish lion and chased by temperamental dog actors.

"In one of the Mack Sennett comedies the villain was to hit me with a trick statuette. He grabbed up one made out of solid marble by mistake. I just remember everything turning black then I got mad and socked the guy. He let out a yell and I found it was my wife. I had been in bed a week.

"Another time, I was acting in Sennett's comedy, *The Battle Royal*. There was a scene where a fellow was to swat me with a club padded on the end with a boxing glove. The glove slipped off and hit me on the top of the head so hard that I went down through the floor." Despite his mishaps, Ben is still in the ring. To see Ben at his best, you should see him in the intervals between making the pictures. He never turns off the jazz. When not imitating D.W. Griffith or Cecil B. DeMille, he is pretending to be a little innocent heroine lost in a shivering snowstorm on the sidewalks of New York. One of Ben's favorite diversions is to get down on his hands and knees and imitate Teddy, the Sennett dog. The only one who never laughs is Teddy, who gives him a look of terrible disdain and walks solemnly away.

Between pictures, Ben is found at Katy's. Katy runs a little cafe on the corner near the studio. Ben takes a seat at one of Katy's best tables and spends the day there. He quarrels with Katy over the best way to mix batter. He plays horse with Mrs. Terrence O'Grady's children while the mother is in passing the time of day with Katy and maybe borrowing the shade of a slice of butter. When the iceman comes around, Ben gives his imitation of a pig stuck under a fence and the iceman goes out cackling. Ben has a little joke with the postman when he comes around and a merry quip for the edification of the egg man. Somewhere around eleven o'clock, the barber from up the street drops in and he and Ben talk war. Ben has a hoarse croaking voice and his terrible sarcasms about the Kaiser would carry to Berlin on a clear day.[13]

Hide and Seek, Detectives (re December 15, 1918) synopsis:

Ben and Charlie Lynn are detectives who pay more attention to their enjoyment than to their business. When they both fall in love with the same girl, Marie Prevost, and find they have a rival in big, burly Tom Kennedy, who resents their interference, events happen every minute. They lasso Kennedy, but he makes his escape in a novel fashion and he proceeds to massacre his rivals in Wild West style. The boys can't keep running around after him forever with a pair of lassos, so they invent a plan to have him hanged for killing a poor old bum they find in a park. Tom's trial certainly makes a new world's record for speed and it lands in a way that will be one of the big laughs in this comedy.

Cupid's Day Off (re January 12, 1919) review:

It may be *Cupid's Day Off* as far as this Sennett-Paramount comedy is concerned, but it is also Ben Turpin and Charles Lynn's day on. Also, Alice Lake, in a neat but not elaborate suit of fleshings, gets in on the excitement. Heretofore, running a shoe store has been considered a quiet, respectable business, but Ben and his partner make the interior of their emporium of fashionable footwear look like the finish to a feature number at a smart cabaret.

They also put new life and the joy of winning into a gambling joint until they are discovered cheating. This so shocks the proprietor and his regular customers that they lose their faith in human nature and send for the police. And so the merry game is kept up! There have been funnier comedies bearing the Sennett trademark, but this is a good average buy and exhibitors know what that means. *MPW*

East Lynne With Variations (re February 23, 1919) synopsis:

The story of *East Lynne With Variations* is a delicious satire on the good old standby of our front-seat-in-the-gallery days. It's all there — the deserted mother with her child in her arms followed all around by a fiendish wicked snowstorm, the heroine lashed to the rails by the scoundrelly villain, the young woman fastened to the buzz saw of a lumber mill and about to be reduced to mincemeat. And hist! The wicked villain with a mustache and cigarette — the noble hero and the persecuted heroine. There are two drunks sitting in one of the boxes of the theater who get so excited that they insist upon helping out the action of the melodrammer. In the middle of the play, the head sceneshifter gets jealous of his wife, who is the leading woman of the show, and drags her from the stage. Nothing if not resourceful, Ben rushes down into the audience and kidnaps a beautiful young woman to play the leading woman's role.

Then comes a startling climax when the snowstorm is shut down by a queer accident. An equally tragic catastrophe jazzes up the ocean when a storm and a submarine play at cross purposes. This is an entirely new angle on an old-fashioned melodrammer company rather than a satire on the melodrama itself. *Sennett Weekly*

The Hard-Luck Twins by Harry C. Carr *(1919 April)*

How a well-known team of screen comedians turned their troubles to good account, Charlie Lynn and Ben Turpin had just posed for a close-up back of a picket fence in the Sennett Studio. You know Charlie and Ben, of course. Charlie is the one with the drooping mustache and Ben is the one with the funny eyes.

"You may not know it," said Charlie, "but you have to be a natural-born, dyed-in-the-wool, name-blown-in-the-glass, hard-luck genius to do this sort of thing. You — "

"That's right," interrupted Ben. "Take me, for instance, "I – – "

"Shut up!" said Charlie, reaching for a sledgehammer. Ben subsided. "The test is whether you're the sort of person that always has a jinx following you," Charlie went on. "If you're always getting busted up and hit over the bean and stepped on, the best thing to do is to capitalize on your misfortunes and become a comedian. Some men go through hard luck for years, working at the wrong trade. But I discovered early where my talents lay.

"I was a scene-shifter in a theater, and my first job was to drop a bag of gold onto the stage. I got the signals wrong, let go too soon, and as a result the leading lady was laid out cold. What happened to me was still worse. But it showed me what I ought to do."

"I had a worse one than that," said Ben. "I was a taffy puller at the country fairs, and one of my stunts was to pretend to hit someone in the crowd with the long hank of the stuff, which I'd jerk back and swing over the hook with an artistic swipe just in time to miss him. Well, one day I made a swipe at a fat man. But I wasn't looking where I was throwing, and wrapped the hot taffy around his neck. He turned out to be the chief of police of the town, and I left the village that night. I turned up in Chicago and made a beeline for the movies. And I've been in 'em ever since."

But capitalizing one's calamities doesn't chase away the jinx. For though Charlie and Ben have learned a lot about how to fall down or how to take a wallop with the least amount of injury, they still seem to keep running into hard luck every now and then. In fact, Charlie got bumped so many times and so badly that there was a time when he lost his nerve and he had to take himself in hand very seriously in order to get his confidence back again. And Ben seems always to be pursued by some sort of trouble as bad as having a chief of police, wearing a muffler of hot taffy, chase him off from a fairground. If there's any chance for things to go wrong in a piece of slapstick work, Ben usually manages to get the worst of it. He's like the "innocent bystander" who's always getting hit.

"We're the two most prominent graduates ever turned out from the University of Hard Knocks," Charlie said to me as he started off to answer a summons from Mack Sennett.

"We certainly are," added Ben as he turned to follow. "And if anyone wants to know what we think of our jobs," he concluded, "you can tell 'em that it's great to live for one's art, but it's hard on the teeth." *Picture Play*

Author Emma Lindsay Squire visited Sennett's studio for the April 1919 *Motion Picture* magazine…

At lunchtime I joined Chester Conklin and Ben Turpin, who were making their way to the little upstairs restaurant at the studio. Chester was feeling his head sympathetically and Ben was examining the bump, though his eyes were directed, as nearly as I could judge, towards the farther end of the studio.

"Don't worry," Ben said consolingly, "the worst is yet to come — Mack says there'll be a 'retake' of that scene after lunch." Some comforter is Ben.

"Tell me something about the funny side of making comedies," I suggested when we were seated at a table in the restaurant.

"There ain't no such animal," said Ben, eyeing me sorrowfully — at least he may have been looking at me — it's hard to tell — "it's all hard work — nothing funny about it except the laughs you get out of the screen!" Chester was still coddling his bump.

"That schoolhouse scene looked sort of roughhouse," he said, "but that was mild in comparison with what I generally go through. This afternoon I am wiped all over the place by the mother of this pupil — and believe me, it's not going to be a pink tea affair either.

"But that's nothing — yesterday I was thrown in a tank of water exactly fifteen times before the director was suited; after that I was dipped in a flour barrel, then soot was blown over me. The whole thing took from eight in the morning until three in the afternoon without a stop of any kind, and as I was coming across the street to the studio, feeling like a German worm, a dame comes up to me and says: 'Oh, Mr. Conklin, I'd know you any place — you have such a funny expression.'"

Ben looked at Chester — or at me — or at both of us — and shook his head.

"That ain't the worst," he told us gloomily. "Tank stuff is easy money; gee, I wish they'd pick out a nice soft tub to chuck me into — I'd think I wasn't drawing me pay. Look at me now; I'm forty-nine years old, and been in the hospital twenty-five times.

"I've been hit on the head with an iron horseshoe, knocked silly with a barber pole, stepped on by horses, and run over by machines. Once they were to hit me with a five-foot 'breakaway' statue of light material, and the prop man got a real one by mistake — and say, when I come to, I didn't know whether my name was Ben Turpin or Mary Pickford!"

"Oh, well, as to that," Chester chipped in, not to be left out of the recital of sorrows, "I get my share of rough stuff too. I've been knocked cold by a real prizefighter in a picture, and I've been run off a high dock into the water by an automobile; besides that, I've jumped from one high building to another without a net underneath, and once when I was chasing around a ten-story building I fell off and was caught on the awning two stories below. Once I had to wear false whiskers dipped in a smudge pot to make them look as if they were on fire. They really caught on fire, and I had to go thru the scene with those things burning my face raw — then it had to be done over again. The fans laughed their heads off at that stunt, but maybe you think it was funny to make? — Nix!"

"Sure, it all looks funny," interpolated Ben, "but how many fans know what we go through to get the right effect? It gets my goat to sit behind a Percy-boy who tells Mabel — 'Oh, no, they don't really hit him — they just pretend to; oh no, that isn't a real fall — it just looks like it.'

"Say!" he broke off suddenly, "if you wants to know whether the falls are real or not, look at this!" He rose from the table and moved over to a cleared space in the room. Without the slightest preparation, he leaped into the air, turned a backward somersault, and came down flat on his back with an awful smacking thud. I gasped for breath, but he was on his feet before I could utter a word. The other actors went on eating, merely glancing up as he brushed himself off; it was evidently Ben's little way of keeping himself in trim for his work.

"That's an easy one," he said as he rejoined us. "I can do eight different kinds of falls, and they're all real, believe me!"

I believed him.[98]

Regarding falls, Ben knew few, if any, peers. Sennett wrote in his *King of Comedy*, "A 108 is an acrobat's term for a comic fall which only the most skillful athletes can perform without lethal results. One foot goes forward, the other foot goes backward, the comedian does a counter somersault and lands flat on his back.

"I've seen Turpin perform the 108 not only on streetcars but on concrete sidewalks — if there was an audience handy to whom he could announce himself as $3,000-a-week Ben Turpin."

Years earlier, Sennett told Gene Fowler in *Father Goose*, "The Leaping Lena feats of Turpin aroused the envy of the other cops, all of whom were great and furious tumblers. This led to impromptu contests to determine who could endure the most fantastic falls. Sometimes the comedians would vie with one another on the sidewalks of Edendale, much to the amazement of the civilians.

"Turpin did not confine his leaping practices to the lot or sidewalks. He used to simulate a high-diving epilepsy and fall from the platforms of streetcars. The trolley crews would be terrified. Once he staggered to the tracks and sun-fished directly into the path of an approaching car. The motorman ground the brakes and Ben rolled from the right-of-way just in time to escape injury. He quickly wriggled beneath the trucks of the now-stalled car and pretended he had been run over. Someone called an ambulance, and when the doctor leaned over Turpin to examine him, Ben opened his very cross-eyes and almost scared the surgeon to death. Tramway officials requested Sennett to keep Turpin off their tracks.

"'He's a menace,' said the Inspector. 'He breaks our motormen's morale.'"

In an article discussing falls, director Eddie Cline, who worked with Ben and went on to direct Buster Keaton, W. C. Fields, and many others, told the media, "The best of 'em all was Ben Turpin, or the craziest, which amounted to the same thing. I'll bet if Ben walked in this office right now and I said 'Do a 108, Ben,' he'd try it if it killed him. And Turpin's 69 years old.

"A 108? — well, that's a little number that Turpin invented and named. He used to claim that there were eight kinds of falls, and this was the one topper of all of them. To go into a 108, Ben usually got hit or kicked — and hard — from behind. Then he'd go into a three-quarter front somersault in the air and land flat on his back.

"Sure it hurt him, sometimes. We all got to be expert in snapping each other's vertebrae back into place, because in the early days $3 was a day's pay and it was even more painful to squander it on a doctor bill. Most people don't know that Turpin's eyes were crossed from an injury in a fall. He used to do a vaudeville act — and, incidentally, he worked with a tomato can for a hat, and that suggested the comic strip character *Happy Hooligan*. Anyway, he was doing this vaudeville act, and it ended with a headspin off a ladder. One night he lit too hard on his head, and when he woke up he was cock-eyed. He thought he'd never act again. But he found it was a lucky accident, after all, and before he retired Ben was making $3,500 a week. He has a house in Beverly Hills and a $100,000 trust fund and he is sitting pretty."[99]

The Saddest Spot in Los Angeles — Where The Comedies Are Made by Karl K. Kitchen
The morning I arrived at (the Sennett) studio, the cross-eyed Ben Turpin and his side partner, Charles Lynn aka Charles Conklin, were engaged in hitting each other over the head with rubber mallets. They were at work on one of their typical scenes in which the comedy husband returns to his comedy home to find his comedy wife in the arms of his comedy false friend — with the inevitable exchange of comedy blows. I have witnessed many sad sights, but this spectacle of Turpin and Lynn rapping each other's heads with rubber mallets was the saddest proceeding that was ever my misfortune to gaze upon.

"Making these two-reelers is one-tenth inspiration and nine-tenths perspiration," said Mr. Sennett after watching the edifying slugging match between Ben Turpin and Charles Lynn for several minutes. "It's very different from making film dramas, where you have a scenario and know what you are going to do. Here we have to think up new stunts, try them out and find out if they are funny on the screen. Of course I plan out the stories in a general way; but their effectiveness is largely dependent upon their treatment. It is up to the various directors, with the assistance of the principal comedians, to evolve new stunts and work them out. And I want to tell you that it is the hardest kind of work."

"But have you ever stopped to analyze them?" I asked.

"Of course nothing is simpler. Nearly all the comedy films we make are based on the triangle of the old-fashioned French farce — the wife, the husband and the husband's false friend. In fact, if we attempt anything else, it doesn't work out. Toward the end of each picture we have what is called a rally or a speeding up of the action, usually a chase of some kind, in order to bolster up the interest of the spectators. Most of our pictures are made on this basis. Occasionally we try out other plots, but, as I say, they don't come out satisfactorily. Just at present, for instance, we are making an experiment with a comedy with a beautiful woman for the central figure, with two rival suitors furnishing the laughs, but we won't know how funny it'll be until we get it finished. I'm very much afraid we'll have to go back to the husband and wife and the false friend," he sighed. "Pretty hard lines, isn't it?"

"It's pretty hard lines for the people who have to see them," I admitted, recalling some wasted evenings in so-called temples devoted to film art. For the first time since I arrived at the studio, a smile appeared on Mack Sennett's face.

"It's a wonder that I am not in the psychopathic ward of some hospital!" he confided. "You can't imagine the strain I'm under turning out one of these comedies every two weeks. Some of them are pretty bad, but on the whole they are a lot better than they used to be."

At the conclusion of our repose, we went to the projection room to see the previous day's run. As six or seven takes of each scene were run off without subtitles or anything to give me an idea of their connection, it was about as jolly as seeing the same movie six times in succession. One scene revealed a comedian braiding an older gentleman's long white beard with the tail of an old skate and then hitching the nag to the rear of a fast moving flivver — with the obvious results. Another scene showed what happened in a blacksmith shop when the smithy dropped a red hot horseshoe into the hip pocket of the comedian. The smoke which arose from the operation, coupled with the efforts of the comedian to dive into a water trough, made us smile the first time it was flashed on the screen, but after it has been run off five or six times, it could not have tickled the risibilities of the most loyal Sennett fan. Repetition is deadly, especially of stunts of this kind.

"I'd like to do better things than this," said Sennett seriously. "I'd like to make smart, dress suit comedies — stories with some subtleties, but I can't if I want to stay in business. Movie audiences want this kind of stuff, slapstick comedies with pies, seltzer bottles and all that sort of thing. When we try anything else people walk out on them. Besides, it is much easier to make the high-class comedies. I have spent more time and money in trying to get a mouse to run up a girl's skirt — just one stunt in a two-reel comedy picture — than some producers spend on an entire picture. Cultured people naturally despise these custard pie effects, but you must remember that cultured people don't buy many tickets to the movies. It's the great masses of the public that support the movies. The men and women who make up these masses want to see things on the screen that happened or might happen to their neighbors. For instance, Mr. Bill Smith happens to know that his neighbor, Mrs. Brown, is having a little flirtation with Jones. So when he sees a comedy picture in which the husband returns, it recalls to his mind what is going on in his neighbor's home and how funny it would be if Brown returned and actually found Jones there. It is necessary to give the public situations that they understand and that they can adapt to their friends and neighbors. And as you know, the many well-directed and well-placed kicks are funny simply because they illustrate the downfall of dignity."[100]

The Foolish Age (re April 13, 1919) cameo

Ben and Heinie were surprise members of Chester Conklin's choir in addition to Louise Fazenda, Paddy McQuire, Garry Odell, and Phyllis Haver on piano. In the middle of their rendition of *Sextette from Lucia*, Ben on trombone and Heinie on sax make the most of a sour solo.

Trying to Get Along (re July 6, 1919) cameo

Ben and Heinie appear in the opening reel of this Charlie Murray comedy as a couple of freeloading diners at Charlie's cafe. Heinie makes a slick and sneaky exit, stiffing the unknowing Ben with the check. Unable to pay, manager Murray bats Ben over the head, who flips a 108 and, now unconscious, is dumped into a city trash truck.

Turpin in a Burlesque (1919 July)

Mr. Sennett is personally directing Ben Turpin and Charlie Conklin in another of their uproarious burlesques of life in a one-night stand theatrical company. This one presents Ben as the youthful romantic lover, the villain, and most of the other parts of a great war play that was the theatrical sensation of twenty-five years ago. Ben as the dashing conqueror of youthful feminine hearts, as the fastidious romantic matinee hero, is a figure truly amazing. It promises to be one of his funniest efforts. *Sennett Weekly*

Treating 'em Rough (re August 3, 1919) cameo

Ben pulls a surprise appearance in this Louise Fazenda short. He plays one of several peculiar strangers who pop up from a trap door to Louise's country store cellar. With a leaking liquor bottle under his arm, he states, "I'm glad it's gone dry," and walks an inebriated zigzag out of the store, dripping a trail of booze behind. This film marked the Sennett debut of Billy Bevan, the durable and soon popular comedian and later character actor who had a long career in motion pictures.

1919 September: Ben Turpin, Charlie Lynn, Charles Murray, and others make a personal appearance at Sid Grauman's Theater in Los Angeles in conjunction with the showing of their latest Sennett comedy, *Salome Vs. Shenandoah*. Contemporary reports state that each and every show for a week was sold out to capacity.

Maxims of Ben Turpin

It doesn't matter where (they think) you're going, so long as you're on your way.

Never let your right eye know what your left is doing.

In the slapstick, a tooth in the head is worth four on the set.

It isn't half as funny to be sad as it is sad to be in the comedies.

Laugh and they hand you the ha-ha; weep and they greet you with the he-he.

The early bird was never meant to be a chicken.

Eyes may be the windows of the soul…but you'll need a periscope to get next to mine.

1919 October 19: Ben Turpin has signed a contract for another two years with Mack Sennett and will continue in the Paramount-Sennett Comedies. Turpin's experience has been unique. After a career of many years in comparative obscurity on the screen, he has suddenly become famous in a year. He got a job in Chicago with one of the early day film companies. Ben said he helped with janitor work, heaved scenery, was chief comedian, and helped carry the props when the company went on location. Once he broke his leg doing a comedy stunt, they let him wind film in the laboratory as vacation. He got $20 a week. Once, when he asked them to raise him to $40, the studio almost expired. He put in several years of screen work, but it was not until he joined the Sennett company that his real possibilities were seen. All the Turpin comedies are carefully built up to his personality. *Sennett publicity*

Ben Turpin's Careless Optics *(1919 November 4)*

The optics of Ben Turpin, Mack Sennett comedy star, have not always been of the careless, cross-purpose variety. Ben says so himself. Here's his explanation: "I played *Happy Hooligan* on the road and I used the trick of crossing my eyes to help along the comedy. One morning, after a show, I got up and looked at myself in the glass — and fell back with a start, because I could not believe it was me. Goodnight! Somebody had put a crimp in my act last night. Wonder how could I get that way! And I looked at myself again. My eyes were certainly crossed. Then I realized that I had done my little stunt once too often. Now, however, I have insured those eyes for $10,000 to cover the loss to me if they should ever straighten out again."[101]

A Costly Cry

"The best laid schemes of mice and men gang aft agley." No one, perhaps, at the present moment is more convinced of the truth of this saying than Ben Turpin. It seems that Ben recently arranged a charming surprise as a birthday present for his wife. Mrs. Turpin's mother, you must know, lives in New York and she and her daughter have not seen each other for some years. On the birthday morning, Ben arranged with the telephone company to connect the telephone at his wife's bedside with the flat of his wife's mother in New York. Neither knew of the plan. Ting-a-ling went the telephone. Mrs. Turpin took down the receiver and there was her mother, 3,000 miles away, talking to her. "And," says Ben ruefully, "my wife was so surprised and moved that she began to cry. Then her mother began to cry at the other end. Neither one of them said a word, but they sat there and sobbed at each other across the continent for about a quarter of an hour at twenty dollars a minute!"

1919

"Close-Ups" of Movie Stars (1920 January 4)

Ben Turpin, comedian with the quizzical eyes, has written a sketch production to be presented at a benefit in Los Angeles called *Drink To Me Only With Thine Eyes.*

Mansfield, Ohio

The Star Boarder (re January 4, 1920, cameo) review:

Mack Sennett's latest concoction in slapstick is when the laughs are all counted about on average with the product from this studio. It starts off with promise of being a real hit, but later degenerates into the usual stuff from the same old bag of tricks, both as to the plot and business. In giving the comedy a good sendoff, Ben Turpin, Baby John Henry, and the Mack Sennett dog, Teddy, are mainly responsible. Turpin plays a cigar salesman.

J.S. Dickerson, January 31, 1920

***Six Ben Turpin Comedies Now Being State-Righted** (1920 March 6, in part):*

Cameo Film Company, 64 W. Randolph Street, Chicago, takes advantage of Turpin's popularity and offers several of Ben's Vogue comedies, reissued and retitled as *The Harem* (adapted from *Poultry a la Mode), A Cheerful Liar (His Bogus Boast), He Looked Crooked (Why Ben Bolted), The Leading Man (Hired and Fired), The Landlubber (A Deep Sea Liar),* and *The Plumber (His Blowout).* The comedies are of the knock-about, slapstick type and are typical of the work which has earned for this eccentric comedian such popularity among his fans and the exhibitors throughout America.[102]

***Ben Turpin On Way Here** (New Orleans, 1920 March 7)*

Ben Turpin, one of the most noted comedians of the screen, is on his way to this city for the dedication and opening of the new Liberty Theater. He is a native of New Orleans, according to word sent out from the Sennett studios, and begged a chance to see Royal and Canal Street for a little while. Before coming here, however, Ben stopped in Arkansas to visit some friends and may not get here until the middle of the week.[103]

***Ben Turpin On Vacation** (1920 March 7)*

Ben Turpin is enjoying a vacation. When last heard from, the whimsical comedy star of the Sennett Studios, and the handsomest male in captivity, was floundering about in the wilds of Arkansas, trying to find a way out. He was in transit to New Orleans, his natal city, whither he said he was bound in order to bask upon the street corners and give the girls a treat. *Sennett publicity*

Ben Turpin, who has been spending a three-week, well-earned vacation in the east, is on his way back to his comedy duties at the Sennett studios in Los Angeles.[104]

Secrets of the Movies (unid. syndicated question & answer column, 1920 March 31)

Q: How did Ben Turpin become cross-eyed?

A: He wasn't born that way, he acquired it. To most anyone else, it would have been a tragedy, to Ben it finally meant fame and riches. In his youthful days, Ben was a juggler of heavy weights. One day doing his act, he tossed up an extremely heavy weight and forgot to catch it. It hit him on the forehead. When Ben came to, he was cross-eyed and his success as a juggler spoiled. Then he became a taffy puller in Cincinnati until Mack Sennett finally saw him. Ben's chief fear these days is that something will fall on him and knock his eyes straight and then he will have to start another career all over again.

The Billings Gazette (Montana)

1920 cApril: Ben appears in the short subject *Movie Stars at Home* along with footage of Charles Ray, William S. Hart, and other favorites.

1920 May 3: Ben Turpin has returned to the studio after a three week vacation spent in the east. He says he would have stayed away a month if he hadn't met a doctor who claimed he could straighten his eyes. Ben fled the town for fear the optical expert might accomplish this dread purpose while he slept. *Mack Sennett Weekly*

1920 May 8: Mack Sennett will continue all production in his Hollywood studios, although officials of his organization announce alterations and additions that will materially increase facilities and equipment for filming of super-comedies.

Motion Picture World, pg 1067

1920 May 19: Turpin signs a 54-week contract with Sennett for $231.50 per week, commencing May 22, 1920 and ending May 28, 1921.

Married Life (re June 15, 1920), five reels for First National, synopsis:

The plot opens at a football game in which all the principals make their appearance either in the college throng of spectators or as heroes on the gridiron. Phyllis Haver sits with Heinie Conklin, known in the story as Joe, brother of the no more infamous Jack Dalton. Ben is disclosed doing mighty deeds of valor against the opposing team. Jimmy Finlayson is seen on the sidelines waiting for some unfortunate player to get hurt and allow him a place in the game. Phyllis and Heinie are engaged and appear as fond lovers, but he soon reveals his true character a la the melodramatic tribe of Dalton and bets against his own team. Then, to ensure winning, he steals the signals from his team and gives them to the opposition. Kalla Pasha sits on Ben and Eddie Gribbon leaps upon him. Thereafter, Ben is carried hors de combat from the field and Finlayson's time has come.

The game is going against them and Heinie rejoices in true villain style, but his iniquity avails nothing against the puissance of Jimmy and his fellows, who wrest a tenth-hour victory and return champions. Heinie's villainy is exposed by Bert Roach, captain of the rivals, who claims the signals didn't work. Phyllis departs on the arm of the champion, Jimmy, and soon wedding bells resound and the pair is married while the title reads: "Their Day of Days, but to others it was just a wedding."

Matrimonial life for Phyllis and Jimmy would have been no different than ordinary had it not been for two factors in troublemaking, Ben Turpin and amateur theatricals. Ben, who is introduced as Rodney St. Clair, is enrolled as the hero in the melodrama that Phyllis has written for a society benefit. She calls her play *The Last Installment*, probably the worst play that was ever written. Jimmy is violently opposed to its presentation, saying it will damage his reputation. Phyllis, in tears, asserts it has proceeded to the point where she cannot back out and that "the show must go on!"

Jimmy threatens her with divorce and finds sufficient grounds in the rehearsals of the amateur show, for Ben appears as Chesterfield, the hero, and rescues Phyllis from the clutches of the villain. So many kisses are exchanged that Jimmy becomes righteously suspicious that it isn't all for art's sake. However, *The Last Installment* comes to performance before a thronged theatre with Ford Sterling, Charlie Murray, Louise Fazenda, and others of the Sennett principals watching the show and applauding or commenting as their fancy moves them. Rodney St. Clair is omnipresent. He saves the heroine on an average of three times an act and there are 4 acts. Finlayson, the husband, arriving late at the theatre, leaves in disgust at the 953rd kiss and after untold mishaps to scenery, props, players, and performance, Turpin is hurt by a fall and is removed to a hospital, where the real trouble begins.

The villain, who, though she is married, has never given up on Phyllis, gets on the job, and arranges that the attending surgeon shall be the jealous James Finlayson. Jimmy's intentions are clear enough. He will dispose of the hated Rodney St. Clair while the latter is under chloroform and live unmolested thereafter with his now distracted Phyllis. But Heinie has other plans. He proposes not only to get rid of Rodney, but of Jimmy as well, and so he notifies the police of what is about to happen at the hospital and substitutes illuminating gas for the chloroform. The sleeping form of Ben rises like a balloon and floats aloft and when the cops arrive, the operating table is empty and nobody knows what the answer is, not even Jimmy, whom the police and his wife accuse of murder. The villain gloats evilly over the mix-up and leads in the police chase for Jimmy, who falls out of a tenth story window, ultimately taking refuge in an aeroplane into which, just as it is starting, the villain leaps.

Phyllis and Ben are ultimately landed in the flying machine and the fight becomes general until thrilling episodes nearly overwhelm the beholder. The flight and fight are transferred to terra firma and little John Henry, Jr., becomes involved logically in the trouble and supplies what is probably the most fearful thrill in pictures. Ultimately, the doctor's innocence of murder, Phyllis' innocence with Ben, the latter's innocence of evil intent, and Conklin's villainy are all established to the happiness of everybody concerned and, with a maxim of good advice, Ben takes his leave of the reconciled Phyllis and Jimmy.

Which Are The Funniest? (*Married Life* publicity, 1920)

Which are the funniest parts of the human body to picture fans — the eyes or feet? A comparison of Charlie Chaplin's pedal extremities and Ben Turpin's twisted orbs would be worthwhile. If we are to judge from the number of laughs that Ben gets in the newest Mack Sennett five reel comedy, *Married Life*, funny eyes have the day.

1920 July 17: Ben Turpin taking another vacation.

Motion Picture World, pg 331

Neilan and Stars Arrive In Oakland (*July 20, 1920 in part*)

Special preparations are being made to handle a capacity crowd, which is expected to turn out to see the baseball team of stars led by Ben Turpin and Charlie Murray in their meeting with the Oaks. The park will be policed by soldiers and no seats will be reserved. The entire day's program, with the exception of the banquet, it is announced, will be free.[105]

Turpin As Orator (1920 August 7)

Ben Turpin will make his debut as a public orator, it is announced, this evening at the Kinema Theater. The "cockettish" comedian is expected to give his views on the subject of matrimony if properly persuaded. This will mark the final day of the showing of Mack Sennett's *Married Life* at the house.[106]

1920 October 3: Mack Sennett and Ben Turpin were back east not long ago, "somewhere in the hills of Kentucky." As they left the hotel one day, the landlord told them they had better leave town. Sennett wanted to know why. The landlord said the natives knew he and Ben were revenue agents for the United States. Sennett had a good laugh, but Ben was worried. Sennett asked the landlord why the folks around those parts took him and Ben for revenue agents. He got the sharp answer. "Didn't you tell this here feller this morning that you was goin' out and take some stills?" Mack and Ben haven't recovered yet.[107]

Married Life Scores Success at the Star

Owing to the wonderful success of Mack Sennett's five-reel super comedy, which opened yesterday at the Star Theater, the management announced this afternoon that this production would be shown an additional two days. *Married Life* is a super comedy in every sense of the word. Ben Turpin, whose previous efforts have won him an enviable place in the hall of comedy fame, introduces a new brand of comedy and, with the excellent support of practically all of the Sennett comedians, presents five reels of fun. Hardly had the film started at yesterday's performances that the audiences started laughing and it was just one continuous laugh after another. So many requests were received for a continuance of the picture that arrangements were made to show it for four days.[108]

Married Life reviews:

There is no reason that I can see why Mack Sennett should not do well with five-reelers — better, in fact, than he has been doing with short comedies. His *Married Life*, with just a bit of a story, is a good start. And if his next one has a little more story and a little less repetition, he will be realizing the promise he has always given of being the greatest director of screen farce the pictures have produced. It keeps Ben Turpin pretty busy looking both ways for Sunday and also a new place to fall for five reels, but fortunately for him and for us, neither Ben nor his pathetically comic eyes are overworked in this particular opus. The incident of the operation in which Turpin inhales illuminating in place of laughing gas and proceeds to float all around the hospital is sure to threaten any audience with convulsions.

Married Life is a five-reel Mack Sennett farce done in the broadest slapstick fashion. We admit our liking for two-reel Sennetts, but, in truth, this five-reeler bored us, although there are many ingeniously devised laughs. *Married Life* is described as a domestic satire, but in reality, it merely relates the episodic adventures of "a man's man," played by the slant-eyed Ben Turpin. The thing is ridiculously amusing — at times. But two reels are enough for this sort of thing. *Motion Picture Classic*

May Get Chance To Rest Eyes (1921 February 10)

Ben Turpin, he of the funny criss-crossed eyes, is about the happiest man in filmdom at the present time. Mack Sennett has given him his opportunity to prove that he is a real comedian and could even be a laugh provoker if he did not cross his eyes. Ben's "big chance" came in *Married Life*, the latest Sennett five-reel comedy. In this tremendously funny picture, Ben is the big feature and his work is of the legitimate type that marks him as a comedian of the first water.

Nothing rouses the wrath of Ben so quickly as the implication that his comedy status is based on the fact that he can throw his eyes out of plumb and that if he refused to perform this feat, he would lose his job as comedian with the Sennett company. That Turpin's gifts of comedy are authentic and unrelated to the manner in which he crosses his eyes is known to all who take the pains to consider the art of this inimitable comedian.

Ben Turpin was a successful funmaker even before he attempted to cross his eyes. It started eighteen or twenty years ago when Ross Snow was playing *Happy Hooligan*, F. B. Opper's good-natured hero. Ben, then in vaudeville, saw a performance and almost at once realized that through the peculiar formation of his neck, the long slender one thrust upward from the sloping shoulders to join the homely but pleasant face surmounted by an old tin can, that he possessed one of the very necessary physical qualifications for the role of *Hooligan*. He lacked the sloping shoulders, but this was an obstacle that he could easily overcome. He determined to play this role and he noted the crossed-eyes of the happy-go-lucky tramp. Nothing daunted, Ben crossed his eyes and his make-up was perfect. He was a howling triumph with his audience from the very start and from that time on, they would not accept him in anything but a cross-eyed role.

As the public expected it of him and his good sense prompted it, Ben became a martyr to art and portrayed only the parts of gentlemen with twisted orbs. He continued playing the roles of kindly spirited, misguided persons of the *Happy Hooligan* type until you might as well have asked David Warfield to give up *The Music Master* as to try to get Turpin to desert him. At least that is what his friends and the public at large thought, but they did not know Ben's real feelings. Deep down in his heart, he resented the fact that everybody thought that he could not play anything but a cross-eyed man's role. He yearned for an opportunity to prove that he could be funny without twisting his eyes out of shape.

Then came his golden opportunity; *Married Life* offered it. Mack Sennett, in looking over his company for a suitable member to handle the leading male role of Rodney St. Clair, the sturdy lover, selected Ben, and although the latter played it with eyes crossed, the success of his work in this part proved that he could have made just as big a comedy hit in it without resorting to this old practice. And now Ben is vindicated — he can make them laugh with eyes normal — so who knows — perhaps he will do this very same thing and give his poor tortured optics a needed rest from their comedy contortions.[109]

Film Specials Announces Release on December 1 of "Jolly Comedies"

Film Specials announces that "their series of comedies will be ready for release December 1, 1920." The new comedies will be titled "Jolly Comedies." The first release will be *The Nut Crackers*, in two reels, produced by G. M. Anderson, featuring Ben Turpin and directed by Jess Robbins. The second release will be called *Neptune's Step Daughter*, in two reels, produced by the Macdon Pictures Corp., featuring Gertrude Selby and directed by Frank P. Donovan. These will be sold on the states' rights market, according to the Film Specials report. The films were another attempt at reissuing earlier Essanay releases.

Warner Brothers Will Re-Issue Ten Essanay-Charlie Chaplin Comedies

Warner Brothers, of 220 West Forty-Second Street, New York, announce they have purchased from the Essanay Film Manufacturing Company negatives for the following Charlie Chaplin comedies: *A Night Out, His New Job, A Night in the Show, The Tramp, A Woman, The Bank, Shanghaied, Police, Triple Trouble*, all two-reelers, and *In the Park*, a one-reeler, making ten in all. A high price was paid for these subjects, and they will be reissued on states' rights basis, one each month, beginning January 1, 1921.

Entirely new prints will be made; they will be re-subtitled and an entirely new and up-to-date line of paper and accessories prepared. In addition, Warner Brothers have also purchased from the Essanay Company twenty Ben Turpin subjects, which will also be states' righted with new prints and paper, probably on the basis of one every two weeks. The subjects include: *A Quiet Little Game, Some Bravery, A Waiting Game, Taking the Count, A Safe Proposition, The Undertaker's Uncle, Versus Sledge Hammers, The Merry Models, Bloggie's Vacation, Special Delivery, The Bell Hop, Countess Bloggie, Pete's Pants, Two Laughs*; also *Snakeville's Debutantes, Snakeville's Champion, Snakeville's Hen Medic, Sophie and the Fakir, Others Started, But Sophie Finished*, and *Snakeville's Twins*. These are one-reelers.[110]

1920 December 17: Ben Turpin and Phyllis Haver, stars of Mack Sennett's First National comedy, *Married Life*, acted as best man and bridesmaid at a genuine wedding performed on the stage of the Victory Theater in Los Angeles the other day. The wedding ceremony took the place of the usual prologue at the cinema. Justice Summerfield tied the knot. All were pleased, according to reports.[111]

Stars Laugh at Scheme to Lower Salaries — by Ben Turpin (1920 December 19)

"For some reason or other I cannot agitate myself over the imminent peril of seeing some obscure shop girl usurp my place on the screen. Where in the world is there a woman so lost to the charming vanities of her sex as to aspire to a Ben Turpin role? I have no fears in that direction.

"As far as the economies of the question are concerned it seems to me they will continue in the future, as in the past, to adjust themselves. Take my own case, for instance. My salary appears to be an accurate reflex manifestation of my value when regarded as a marketable commodity in an industry where the law of supply and demand operates as freely as it does in the motion picture business."[112]

A Small Town Idol Goes Over Big by Esther Wagner (1921 February 21)

When I walked into the Sigma Sunday afternoon to Sennett's *A Small Town Idol*, loud cheering and clapping of hands greeted my ears. To hear the audience, you'd think it was some melodramatic masterpiece and the hero was on his way to rescue the girl from the bloodthirsty villain. And here they were cheering Ben Turpin because he was on his way to save Phyllis Haver from none other than Jim Finlayson. Can you imagine an audience getting excited about a comedy? It wasn't an ignorant-looking audience, either, and everyone from the kiddies on up enjoyed it. Giving away the plot of a comedy is not only worse than useless, it is foolish. Real comedies have no plot; that is, they don't as a rule, but this *Small Town Idol* has more or less plot, concerning Ben Turpin, who loves the village belle. He is wrongly accused, leaves town to forget, comes back a famous movie star, then is wrongly accused again and almost lynched.

In the nick of time, however, the paper is found and Ben is saved. There are some beautiful Babylon scenes in which over five hundred Sennett beauties appear; there are several weird and snaky dances; good photography and sets to recommend it. Phyllis Haver is pretty as ever. Ben Turpin is more cross-eyed, if anything, and in this picture has a cross-eyed mother. So if you want to laugh and don't need the deeper wells of humor from which to draw, see *A Small Town Idol* and have a good time. It's Sennett's best work so far.[113]

A Small Town Idol review *(1921 February 23)*:

Mack Sennett has again demonstrated to the world that he is the King of Comedy. There is a harmonious blending of story interest and humor which stamps this production as the comedy king's greatest creation. *A Small Town Idol* has attracted the attention of some of the greatest critics in the country. They have praised the production as the greatest of its kind. Despite the fact that former Mack Sennett feature pictures have had plots which were not quite as strong as the average picture, *A Small Town Idol* proves an exception to it. Sennett has made the picture with the intention of making the story end of it the strongest and intermix the comedy. The cast includes all the Sennett favorites. Ben Turpin, the celebrated comedian, is seen in the title role as the small town idol, Phyllis Haver and Marie Prevost have the stellar feminine roles, Jimmie Finlayson plays the part of the villain, Bert Roach, Charlie Murray, Billy Bevan, Al Cooke, and many other favorites have important parts. In the early scenes, Ben Turpin is the hero of the track and as the jockey rides his mount to victory.

From there begins the story of the small town idol who, confronted with a mass of circumstantial evidence of his general evil tendencies, deems it necessary to leave his country home. Ben not only leaves behind his home, but a brokenhearted mother and fiancée. He aspires to more noble deeds and the restoration of his friends' opinions through a new start in the city. The metropolis is also unkind to him. He has some amazing adventures among crooks and then becomes a "double" in a motion picture organization. In this capacity, he alternately provides riotous humor and realistic thrills. Plunged into the very depths of gloom, Ben attempts suicide, but even in this, he is foiled. He is finally made a star and becomes the hero of *Two Gun Sam*, a picture within a picture. He returns in triumph to his hometown to make a personal appearance.

Overcoming plots formatted by his enemies against his life and character, he reaches the goal for which he originally sets forth — to win back the affections of the village belle and justify his mother's faith. Ben is superb in mock and real heroics, he has many humorous antics, and he deftly glides from comedy to dramatics with admirable sympathy.[114]

Twelve years later into the unforeseen sound era, the film was rereleased as a two-reeler to a new generation. As early as 1933, *The Hollywood Reporter* wrote, *Small Town Idol Just An Antique*: "Dusted off from the studio files, *A Small Town Idol* is still a relic, despite the monkey-gland treatment attempted through sound effects. It carries a number of laughs and interests one in the manner of an old daguerreotype. The laughs are all *at it*, rather than *with it*. It is unfair to use the names of Marie Prevost, Ramon Novarro and Andy Clyde in billing this featurette. They are stuck in and have no place in it. The others play legitimate parts, but it is nothing to be proud of, and since this picture was made, all, excepting Ben Turpin, have changed radically.

"The exhibitor who plays the short must know his audience. To play this type of picture once or twice is a novelty. If your audience hasn't had them before, it may be worth a try."

May 24, 1933

Screen Knight, Ben Turpin, Is Home for Visit *(1921 March 16)*

In part, Turpin told an unidentified reporter for *The New Orleans Item*, "I've had all the ups and downs a man who follows the game must expect. It's been a grand experience, full of thrills, pleasant and otherwise and all the other things that go to make up an exciting life. If I had my choice, I'd go through it all again.

"About six years ago I was in two pictures with Charlie Chaplin. My association with him put me right in the front rank. I'm signed up now with Mack Sennett for a couple of years and after that I may retire."

Asked by his interviewer if he'd noticed much change in New Orleans, Ben replied, "Oh, these big buildings make it look like an up-to-date city. But you can't change the people. They are and always will be the same kind-hearted Orleanians that I knew and liked.

"I take a couple of months' vacation every year, and have just come from Hot Springs. In ten days more I'll be back at Los Angeles tumbling before the camera. Before I go I will visit the graves of my parents, who are buried in the old St. Louis Cemetery."

While in New Orleans, Ben also took part in the *Elks' Tag Day*, a fundraiser to help the families of four firemen who lost their lives in a recent tragedy. A fifth fireman was recuperating in Charity Hospital. Climbing a tall ladder with a comedic shimmy, Turpin appealed for donations and the money poured in.

On March 18, Ben and Carrie, still in New Orleans for Ben's personal appearances, told the newspaper, *The New Orleans States:* "I enjoy being a comedian and have no desire to be a tragedian or a leading man. Next to working in pictures I'd rather be a farmer. At my home in Los Angeles I have a good size garden. I also have an automobile with a cross-eyed steering gear. And when I get through my day's work at the movie studio I get into my car and hustle home to don my overalls and get to work in my garden where I raise cross-eyed peas and other things and chase cut-worms from my orange trees with a hoe.

"I am also quite fond of playing golf and believe I can claim the championship of the cross-eyed golf players of America." Mr. and Mrs. Turpin expect to remain in New Orleans for several days, devoting themselves to recreation and visiting friends and relatives, including two cousins of Mr. Turpin, Misses Felice and Mamie Rodrigue, who reside on Dumaine Street.

Newsy Notes From Movieland by Daisy Dean *(1921 March 22)*

One question persists above all others in the fan mail addressed personally to Ben Turpin or to the publicity department of the Mack Sennett comedies and that question is whether Ben is actually cross-eyed or whether he distorts his gaze only during the period of picture making. The photograph of Ben Turpin as a baby and his mother (in *A Small Town Idol*) would seem to prove that Ben's eyes are a hereditary adornment and that nature crossed them from the beginning of things. That, however, is a fictional assumption not borne out by the facts.

Ben's eyes are crossed, but not hopelessly. They became so after he had forced them into their angular direction through much vaudeville work. As impersonator of *Happy Hooligan* many years ago, Ben deliberately crossed his eyes many times a day for the benefit of his lifelike personification of Opper's fantastic hero. His eyes became fixed and it is not likely he will untangle them, although he is assured he can do this with the aid of a surgeon when he wants to. He is identified on the stage and screen as a cross-eyed hero and were he to submit himself to an operation and straighten his eyes, he would only force them back artificially and perhaps render it impossible for a second operation to straighten them out again. At present Ben and Mrs. Turpin are vacationing in the south and east.[115]

Ben Turpin Buys Tomb (1921 April 1)

Ben Turpin, recently here on his first time in years, was delighted with the reception New Orleans gave him. Turpin made one investment while here and it was the tribute of a son whom fortune has favored to a father who did the best he could with the means he earned. The father was employed by A. Lopez, who conducted a famous confectionery on Canal Street. Upon his death, he was buried in one of the old St. Louis Cemeteries. During his visit, the film comedian purchased a tomb in the new St. Louis Cemetery to which the remains of his father were moved.[116]

New Orleans by O. M. Samuel *(1921 April 1)*

Ben Turpin is appearing at the Strand (New Orleans) this week, following the Sennett super comedy, *A Small Town Idol*, in which he is featured. Turpin employs the jockey costume worn in the film and indulges in anecdotes of the screen and stage. His stories are well-told and his stage personality appealing even if a trifle bizarre. Ben indulges in his famous fall for the delectation of the auditors.[117]

What Is Ben Turpin's Hobby? from *Secrets of the Movies (1921 April 30):*

Driving his flivver limousine, Ben may be cross-eyed, but he is an expert driver and, according to Mrs. Turpin, he takes more pride in his ability to run, repair, coax, cajole, and persuade his flivver than he does in his movie acting. Then, too, Ben gets a lot of fun out of the fact that only he himself knows where he is driving and his fellow drivers on the road are always completely at his mercy. Ben does not always go in the direction in which he is looking.

1921 May 8: Ben Turpin, who has been one of the real luminaries of the Mack Sennett comedies for some time, is now to be a star in name as well as fact. This means that when *Love's Outcast* is put out by Associated Producers, Inc., Turpin's name will be printed above the title of the comedy instead of under it.

1921 May 22: Ben Turpin is back on the set again and will work in a five reel production with Mabel Normand under Sennett's direction. *Sennett publicity*

Orphans In Joy Riot As Guests of the Los Angeles Times — Thousand Kids Pay Long, Loud Tribute to Screen Stars at Never-to-be-Forgotten Cinema Treat by Grace Kingsley
(1921 May 22 in part)

The *Los Angeles Times* entertained some one thousand kids from various orphanages at a special performance of Mary Pickford in *Through the Back Door* and the Sennett players in *Home Talent* and everybody was inside watching the show. Ben Turpin and Phyllis Haver, in the flesh and blood, performed a dance in which Turpin cut up his very best capers for his youthful audience, ripping off the comedy for a yell while Charlie Murray stood by and made a good number of wisecracks as announcer.

Ben fell hard for the kids — in both senses. He did his funniest falls and he also stuck around and handed them out their presents of toys and candy during intermission. And maybe those players have listened to more noise from audiences, but I doubt it, for the youngsters fairly tore the rafters off. Maybe other manual manifestations of joy have made the players happier, but I don't believe that, either. And maybe other applause has been more sincere — but I know that isn't so.

"I think Ben Turpin's just as good an actress as Mary," said a little girl in a stage whisper.[118]

Perfectly Ridiculous! by Ben Turpin

Hereafter, should anyone tell you it's unlucky to have crossed eyes, just refer him to me! I'll show him a bank account and a contract that prove conclusively there's not a shadow of truth in it. It's perfectly ridiculous!

For the benefit of the unduly superstitious, let me elucidate:

I have a wonderful appetite. I get plenty of salary to gratify it.

I am embraced by all the prettiest — and least dressed — girls in California.

My clothing bill is small, for I buy clothes to fit my face.

It's easy for me to do my work, because I look so funny I don't have to act it.

And my wife isn't jealous — how could she be?

There are many other lucky things in my bag of tricks, but I won't enumerate them; these are the principal ones. Show me, if you can, any man, I don't care how straight his eyes may be, who has any more living luck than I have! True, I have an ingrowing chin and a more-than-comfortable mouth, and my hair can't be marcelled, and tailors don't rave over my form. But that's more of my luck. All these things fit in with my eyes. Did I not have these characteristics, my crossed eyes would make me conspicuous and I am really quite sensitive and self-conscious.

Speaking of my sensitiveness, I have, with much difficulty, trained myself to control my temper when I meet people who take a look at me and hasten to cross (that's not as long ago as you might think) their fingers and spit. In my youth, I received several valuable aids to the control of temper. I remember one lesson in particular. My instructor, though superstitious, was healthy. And he was big. That's one of the times that my eyes brought me bad luck. I had to pay my own doctor bill. There's no sense in reviewing my past life — I am too fond of liberty. What I did before I wandered into Sennett's studio a few years ago is nobody's business but my own and a few persons whom I won't name. I came to the studio as a carpenter.

One day the assistant to the assistant to the property man wasn't on the job. The property man needed some flowers. He saw me watching a bunch of bathing beauties and thought my eyes were directed at him, so he sent me after the flowers. I was broke and couldn't buy them at the florists, so I wandered into a cemetery. As luck would have it (those crossed eyes led me), I found a grave with a fresh floral piece on it. I borrowed it, the blushing movie bride used it, and then I returned it. As I was trying to straighten the piece over the grave, the director, having followed me into the cemetery, yelled at me.

"What you doing? How come?"

"Oh," I replied, looking at him with my eyes directed toward a church half a mile away, "I borrowed these for that wedding scene you just directed, and I'm returning 'em to the owner. I don't suppose he'd mind, though, if I didn't put 'em back," this was an afterthought.

"I'm damned," he said. "I never knew before a human being could look so inhuman. Hold that until I get a camera!" And that's how I went into the movies.

Do you think now that crossed eyes mean bad luck? Tell me, why should I be put into a class with black cats, hearses, walking under ladders, stumbling over a threshold, and all the other black arts of superstition? *Perfectly ridiculous!*

Pantomime, 1921

Mr. Turpin Enchants His Many Fans by Mae Tinee

Ben Turpin, the cross-eyed lamb, does certainly have his followers! The minute a new comedy featuring him is announced, his admirers invest in 2 cent stamps and write me to know:

"Didya see Ben Turpin's latest?" "Say, ain't he a bird?" "Didya like Ben Turpin in his latest?" Now me — I — perhaps I haven't seen the bird. But I read my mail and say — "Well, it looks like it's up to me to cast an eye." So I goes and I — well…

She Sighed by the Seaside gives our lop-eyed darling the opportunities of his life. It casts him as a lifeguard and provides gentlemen for him to upset and a beauteous lady to save. This last act he accomplishes with great aplomb and flair, as it were. He dives into the dusky deep, lighted cigar smoking intrepidly. He emerges from said dusky deep, same cigar (possibly same cigar) still smoking merrily, and the damp but undamaged damsel on one arm. Both Miss Prevost, who wears a decidedly décolleté white satin bathing suit, and Mr. Turpin "pull," as the police reporters say, considerable original stuff. Miss Prevost knows when to smile and she can take punishment with the same sang-froid as does Dempsey. Mr. Turpin is airy and lithe and homely and has a good comedy sense.

They are supported by well-known Sennett favorites, including the bibulous appearing gentleman, who is a photographer (Al Cooke), and the suave villains (Heinie Conklin and James Finlayson). If you want to laugh, *She Sighed by the Seaside* will see that you do it.[119]

Alas, Girls! Handsome Ben Is As Married As He Looks by Ben Turpin

"Let the galled jade wince," I don't care who it hurts — the fact is, I'm married. And have been married for so many years that my wife doesn't mind it anymore. She's the only person in the world — beside myself — that can tell which way I'm going and why. I wouldn't break the news of my matrimonial estate so abruptly if I had the art of a writer to hint and suggest and qualify and finally come out with it in nobby literary style. I know that a million girls will lament the fact. But if they feel too bad about it, they may write to Mrs. Turpin, 1055 North St. Andrews, Los Angeles, California, and perhaps she will comfort them and reconcile them to a life without me.

As I was saying, I'm married, and the Turpin household consists of the boss (that's my wife), two dogs, and a parrot that has the damnable habit of shrieking at 4 a.m., "It's eight-thirty, everybody on the set!" That's the real lowdown on my secret hobby. I am a born agriculturist or else that parrot has made me one. For, I ask you, what conscientious pictureplay actor could possibly get a wink of sleep with a near-human voice like that of a director through a megaphone bawling, "Eight thirty — everybody on the set!"

I got into the habit of getting up about 5 a.m. to please that parrot. Mrs. Turpin, who has all the thrift of my ancestral folk in France, suggested a way to kill time till breakfast. I could work in the garden. "All great actors," she told me, "all great men, in fact, have hobbies, and the most popular kind is gardening. It gives them a chance to get their pictures in the *Ladies' Home Journal* and other papers; it improves their dispositions by contact with nature in her blossoming moods; it is a good appetizer now that there isn't any other kind and it helps around the house a great deal," (meaning, of course, that if you are out in the garden you are not around the kitchen hollering for food). So I put in my time from 5 until breakfast and thereafter until it's time to leave for the studio, working in my garden, of which, all joking aside, I am genuinely fond and considerably proud. For pets and as consolation for the presence of the parrot, which I haven't found heart nor opportunity to murder yet, the two dogs of the Turpin ménage serve me faithfully. They are not high-grade dogs with long pedigree and short tails. They are just dogs, 100 percent mongrel, mixed, content with their lot and my never complaining pals. [120]

1921 May 13: Ben Turpin can't look his wife straight in the face when he tries to tell her why he comes home late. When he takes friends for a spin in his car, only Ben knows where they're going because Ben looks two ways at once. His eyes became permanently crossed when he forced them into that condition 10 times a day while he was acting the part of *Happy Hooligan* on the stage. Ben isn't sensitive about his eyes. He made such a hit in Sennett comedies that he has been made a star. He was featured in *A Small Town Idol*. His first starring vehicle will be *Love's Outcast*. As long as Ben can star and collect a star's salary on his affliction, he intends to steer clear of surgeons and their knives. "Some day when I am ready to retire and live like other people do, I'll have my eyes made like other people's," says Ben, "then I'll look the world square in the face and go straight."

The Lowell Sun (Mass.), by James W. Dean

Home Talent review:

Mack Sennett has spared neither time nor money in making *Home Talent*, his latest five-reel comedy. He has been most generous with his comedians, giving each and every one plenty of footage. If you don't feel inclined to laugh at Ben Turpin, why, there's Charlie Murray, or perhaps you'll take Phyllis Haver or Dot Farley. They're all there, every one of them pleasing and you will have to be in an awful humor if their antics do not amuse you highly. *Home Talent* has a plot that concerns a hotel proprietor (Murray) who has heaps of trouble with some of his boarders, who, it happens, are stranded vaudeville performers. Their board bill grows lengthy and Murray demands action. So they plan a wonderful theatrical venture in which they star the proprietor's daughter, little Phyllis. The show is a huge success — almost. There are beautiful Roman scenes where girls are sold in the slave marts and it is in the filming of these scenes that the Sennett bathing beauties come in for their share of glory. Glorious, symmetrical girls, every one of them.

The Sennett players are all in good form, but Ben Turpin is the star, without a doubt. His work is just as sincere and at the same time comical, as always. I think *Home Talent* is better than *A Small Town Idol*, which you surely remember, although the former is shorter by two reels. And the audience, of which I was one, gave much evidence of having a mighty pleasant time.

Lima News & Times-Democrat (Ohio), May 31, 1920

To Sell Signatures Of Harding Cabinet — Auction Will Be Feature of Affair Given By Disabled Men (in part)

An elaborate musicale and dramatic program has been arranged under the direction of Miss Esther Marr Bushan. Charlie Murray will be master of ceremonies. Among those taking part in the program are: Harry A. James, monologist; Antoine Dahl, pianist; Orlkioff, Russian concert violinist; Alma Stetzler, dramatic soprano; girl whistling chorus from the Southern California School of Artistic Whistling; University of California Glee Club; Mme. Robert Fenton Fowler & Miss Rose Mulholland, duet; Mlle. Helen Louise, French ballet dancing; Carmel Myers, Bebe Daniels, Ben Turpin, Mabel Normand, and other motion picture artists, all helping to raise funds for the Disabled Veterans.[121]

Ben Turpin Series Planned for Associated Producers (1921 May 28)

Included in the activities mapped out by Mack Sennett for the ensuing year are plans for a Ben Turpin series to be released by Associated Producers, Inc. The hero of *A Small Town Idol* will be disclosed in perhaps twelve two-reel fantastic comedies in which his genius will be revealed from as many angles as he has direction of vision.

Already Started. The first of the series is well under way and will be ready for release by Associated Producers in the near future. Mal St. Clair is directing it under the supervision of Sennett. Included in Turpin's support are Phyllis Haver, Harriet Hammond, Billy Bevan, and George O'Hara. *MPW*

Turpin a Hit in Love's Outcast

That Mack Sennett, the "King of Comedy," has shown foresight and knowledge of public taste in starring Ben Turpin is reflected in the reception accorded the "strabismic" (CROSS-EYED) comedian in the vehicle *Love's Outcast*. This two-reel comedy, which is scheduled for release by Associated Producers (July 3, 1921), played a prerelease engagement of one week at the California Theatre, Los Angeles, recently, co-headlining the bill with the feature and walking off with the comedy honors. The picture was a big hit.

"Ben Turpin is the bright, particular star of this two-reel Sennett comedy, which is genuinely amusing without the aid of any slapstick byplay. Most of the action takes place in a courtroom, where Ben's supposed wife is suing him for divorce. The defendant is charged with being a gay deceiver, who proves irresistible to women. The trial is made very funny by the clever acting of the handsome Mr. Turpin and the picture ends in a roar of merriment when the defendant proves his innocence by showing that he had risked his life saving the correspondent from a vicious bull which found in her company. The scene of that encounter with the bull is immense. Ben rides him and then throws him and Paul Revere has nothing on him — Turpin, not the bull. The subtitles are humorous. At the finish, the happy wife says invitingly to Ben, 'Come home and throw a few bulls for the children.'"

Moving Picture World, August 13, 1921, pg 729

Turpin told an interviewer regarding the new Associated Producers comedies in 1921: "What I would like to do in pictures is to burlesque the present big features. Or the old familiar plays. *Uncle Tom Without the Cabin* was a big success, and so was *Home Talent*. I think *Love's Outcast* will be good, and we are sure putting in a lot of work on these specials of mine, because, after such a long time of hard knocks, I want to put my best work in them. Roy Del Ruth is my director, and he is a good one. Mr. Sennett and all of us lay out the story, and then Roy and I work out the gags. It takes about a month of hard work to make one of these two-reelers, just as long as it takes to make a big feature, and if a thing isn't right, we do it over and over again."

Turpin Travels *(1921 July 21)*

Ben Turpin is headin' east! His first stop will be Chicago!

He's going out with his first of a series of Ben Turpin specials that have been made for distribution by Associated Producers that includes *Love's Outcast, Love and Doughnuts,* and *She Sighed By the Seaside.*

A former Sennett comedian told me some time ago that Ben is shy; that he always looks out the window before he answers the doorbell. Perhaps his timidity is forcing him to bring Mrs. Turpin along with him on the trip. Perhaps it isn't shyness at all; maybe he doesn't dare venture far away from home without taking someone along who looks in the direction they're going! He's scheduled to visit the larger cities; therefore, one may conclude that Cleveland is included. We're big — and we're getting along in years — 125 tomorrow. Ben is due back on the coast later next month. He appears in Chicago tomorrow.[129]

Sycophants Bow Before Riches of "Cross-Eyed Ben" *(1921 July 24)*

Chicago, July 23 — Fancy-vested, diamond stick-pinned agents who used to kick Ben Turpin downstairs if he held out for more than $15 a week for his "turn" in vaudeville were lined up in platoons, fawning and servile and clutching at his sleeve yesterday when he alighted from a train. "Cross-Eyed Ben" Turpin, the butt of village jokesmiths, the kerosene circuit ham, was back with fame and riches to lift the mortgage, humble the haughty select men, and shake hands with lowly friends. The famous Turpin, the Joe Jefferson of the cock-eye, was gracious with them all, even the haughty booking agents now grown to movie magnates. When he had escaped from their clutches, he was greeted by thousands of movie fans. He will remain in Chicago for a week or so.[123]

His Eyes Insured for $100,000 *(1921 August 6, in part)*

While starring with Mack Sennett, Ben had his eyes insured for $100,000, the money to be returned to him if they ever become straight.

Movie Weekly magazine, page 14

Turpin Visits Chicago (1921 August 6)

Ben Turpin visited Chicago for the first time in over six years, Friday, July 22, where he was met by Ben Beadell, representative for the star, who is planning a tour of personal appearances — the first he has ever made. The famous comedian, whose career is of special interest to Chicagoans because of the fact that it started here at the Essanay studio, was hailed with enthusiasm at the station and was given generous recognition by the dailies. Mr. Beadell announces July 24 as the first booking date of Turpin's tour, when he will appear at the Strand Theatre, Milwaukee, for one week. Following that, he will appear at McVicker's for one week and, beginning August 8, at the Rialto.[124]

Ben's personal appearances in or around Chicago included The Strand (Milwaukee), July 24-July 31; McVickers, August 1-August 7; and The Rialto, August 8-August 14, 1921.

August 3, McVickers Theater (Chicago) *review:*

Ben Turpin in reality drew them in, held them out by the hundreds, and then wrung every drop of applause conceivable upon his entrance after a two-reeler in which he is featured had been run off on the screen. But Ben seemed to disappoint the folks a bit, for at the conclusion of his seven minutes, his reception was very mild. The folks had seen Turpin — saw him do a few back flops — listened to an antiquated monologue of the Atlantic Gardens vintage — watched him clown as leader of the orchestra and conclude his turn with a portrayal of "meller drama" characters. The house had had enough and as a matter of fact, a bit too much, which was readily evinced at the conclusion of his act. Turpin is a movie actor and probably was a capital acrobat and tumbler — but as a monologist, never did shine. It would really be more advisable for him to do a few of his "grotesque" falls — toss his brown derby around a bit and then tell the audience something about his studio experience. It seems as though Turpin garnered all the applause of the bill as his reception on his entrance was bigger than the applause accorded all the other eight acts collectively.[125]

He Makes Eyes 'Cause He Can't Make 'em Behave by Mae Tinee

It sure seemed like the old days — following a manager behind the scenes, object being to interview an actor in his dressing room. Even the smell was natural and I tripped over a property stool and was crazy about it. The actor? Ben Turpin. They'd told him a lady was coming and he had his neck craned through a crack in the door, looking for her. He didn't need to turn his head because he is so constituted that he can see in all directions not immediately behind him. We greeted each other cordially and came right to the point:

"Permanent!" he said, looking at me and vice versa.

"Wave?" I said, looking at his hair, pretending not to understand.

"Nope. Eyes," he told me. "Always just as you see them now." He handed me gallantly to one of the two chairs in the room, took the other, which was in front of his dressing table, and started to make up.

"Born that way?" I asked sympathetically. He smeared a hectic flush over his cheekbones and shook his head.

"Nope. Used to be a juggler. You know — juggled three balls. One of them rubber — you know. The rubber one hits you on the head and you click the other two together, so the audience thinks you got a real rap. One of them hit me, and it wasn't the rubber one.

When I came out of the hospital I could see the boats in the Chicago River and the trains pulling out of Illinois Station. Been like that ever since."

"Oh, well," I said cheerily. "Oh, well —"

"Lucky day for me," he said. "Say" — he whirled about — "do you know what I was making when I was out at Essanay?"

"No," I said. (I didn't.)

"Twenty dollars a week," said Mr. Turpin, impressively. "And Mr. Spoor lent me $50 to pay down to an installment house. That's the way I got my flat furnished. We didn't feel able — my wife and me — to get a regular kitchen stove, so we just got one of those little laundry stoves — you know — and fried eggs and things on that.)

"I'm a wonderful man, Miss Tinee, been married to the same woman fifteen years!"

"I'll say you are!" I said. "I bet you like her."

"I bet I do, too," said Mr. Turpin, with great finality. He added, "I wish she was here. But I'll bring her over to *The Tribune* to see you."

"How'd you find out how funny you were?" I wanted to know.

"Well," he said, plastering on his famous mustache, which isn't permanent. (He's clean-shaven and has gold in his teeth.) "Charlie Chaplin told me to go and make up, and when he saw me he laughed till he almost bust, and he said he wouldn't work with me, because I was the funniest man he ever seen and he'd be damned — pardon, lady — if he'd work with me.

"But I did a couple of pictures with him. Mack Sennett saw them.

"It started him thinking. Then people began asking where the long-necked, cross-eyed guy was, and Sennett told me to come on over. I did, and when they asked again he said I was with him.

"He gave me 200 bucks to start. Want to know how much I'm getting now?"

"Too polite to ask," said the lady reporter.

"Tell her," said the press agent, who was also there.

"No, don't," said the lady reporter. "For I probably wouldn't believe you or die of envy if I did. I suppose you have houses and lands?"

"House and yard," said Mr. Turpin. "Livestock — one parrot and a dog. The dog is cock-eyed, too."

"He never IS!" I exclaimed.

"Well, I bet he is," Ben laughed. "Only he never juggled. He was born that way."

We chatted a while longer and then it was time for the funny fellow to go on and do his act, which consists of a lot falls and some jokes that are funny and some that sound funny because he cracks them. My advice to you is to go right on pulling for Mr. Turpin. He's homely and rejoices in the fact; he's cross-eyed and thinks he's lucky; he has no education and will tell the world he hasn't; he and what is known as "the big head" are stranger and I bet he'd give friend or foe his last dime if he thought they needed it. That's Ben Turpin — old funny face![126]

Fire Fighter Ball Players Bar Ben Turpin As Umpire; Against Cock-Eyed Arbiters

Chicago, Aug. 10 — Baseball players from the New York fire department, who arrived yesterday to engage the Chicago firemen in a series of games, put up a tremendous kick when they learned Ben Turpin, the celebrated movie actor, had been tentatively chosen as umpire.

"Not a chance," said Chief Kenton of the Gotham squad. "Turpin is too efficient. With his cross-eyes he can watch the batter and the base runners without twisting his neck. My Babe Ruths are not accustomed to cock-eyed umpires."

After a heated argument, the Chicago men agreed to withdraw Turpin as umpire and relegate him to the subsidiary job of batboy. Turpin has been aiding the Chicago firemen in raising the $100,000 for the Firemen's Mutual Aid and Benefit Association. Ninety thousand dollars of this amount already is in. The games today and Friday will be played at the White Sox Park and, Thursday, the teams will appear at the Cub Park. The Gotham players were accompanied by numerous politicians and a street parade was staged to acquaint the public with what is being done.[127]

1921 August 18: Charlie Chaplin plans to rest six weeks. He finished his latest comedy, *The Idle Class*. Once before, he rested too long and ALMOST lived to see Ben Turpin and Harold Lloyd run off with the affection of the fickle movie fan.[128]

Ben Turpin On Stage (1921 August 20)

"Meeting the public need hold no terrors for the screen comedian," is the verdict of Ben Turpin, who has just embarked on a tour of personal appearances in the Middle West and whose reception at McVicker's, on the Jones, Linick, & Schaeffer chain, proved that his Chicago friends are legion. "It may not be so advisable for the star whose reputation depends upon personal beauty," he suggested, "but I don't have any of his worries. On the contrary, it is my ambition to get just what he would do anything to avoid getting — a laugh out of the public."

And Ben Turpin got what he went after. A few famous flops, a few famous gags, a few famous glances, and the public was his. His stage appearance was preceded by one of his latest pictures, *She Sighed by the Seaside*.

Funny Ben Turpin Coming to Adams In Person (1921 August 21, in part)

Ben Turpin, whose crossed eyes have won him a fortune and who within the past two or more years has risen to an envied position among screen comedians, is paying Detroit a visit this week and is appearing in person three times daily at the Adams Theater. Brought here at a large price, Turpin will prove to Detroit audiences that he is just as funny-looking in real life as the camera makes him appear.[130]

Signs of the Times (1921 August 28)

Ben Turpin is having unusual experiences on this, his first tour of the country in a series of personal appearances. The Mack Sennett "comique" was not always thus — not always did Ben travel in Pullmans with compartments at his service and the best and most obsequious attention showered upon him, nor was it always his expectation to be met at depots with welcoming throngs through which he was to make his way, past batteries of cameras, to a waiting limousine and then whisked off to the best hotel in the city.

Take, for instance, Chicago. Recently, the Sennett hero of the crossed vision was visiting there and making personal appearances. At the depot, he was met by a multitude of film enthusiasts, personal admirers of his quaint, original humor, and newspaper representatives eager to photograph him and interview him.

As he sped along State Street in the limousine of a great theatrical magnate, Ben, seated beside his devoted wife of many years, pointed out an old "movie house." Fifteen years ago, Turpin was doing an "acrobatic single" in that place, juggling cannonballs, safes, and paper napkins ten times a day.

"I was certainly a 'ham actor' in those days," commented Ben. "But," protested Mrs. Turpin, who hasn't become entirely reconciled to the bright lights that break about the throne of a comedy prince, "we weren't unhappy in our little North Clark Street lodging house."

"I've been happier since," said Ben, laconically surveying the mate to his own limousine, "and don't forget that I was the guy that had to do the worrying about the price of the next meal."

Then he wandered out to the Essanay studio on Argyle Street and when he wasn't working as janitor, he filled in as "double."[131]

Ben Turpin to Give Show for Newsies (1921 September 2)

A theater party for (Toledo) News-Bee carriers will be given in the Rivioli Theater on Saturday (Sept. 3) at 10 a.m. Ben Turpin will entertain the newsies with a sketch called *Nonsense in Silence*, which was used by him in a picture but never presented from the stage.[132]

Bees Like Ben Turpin (1921 September 8)

Ben Turpin, movie star, got "stung" yesterday at the Indiana State Fair when he permitted Frank N. Wallace, state entomologist, and C. O. Yost, state apiary inspector, to decorate him with a swarm of bees. The little insects picked out one of Ben's handsome eyes for the point of attack. The demonstration was staged at the exhibit of the division of entomology of the state conservation department. Mr. Turpin is appearing at the Circle Theater this week.[133]

1921 September 9, *The Indianapolis Star (Indiana):* Through the courtesy of the Circle Theatre, Ben Turpin, America's Handsomest Man, will appear tonight informally at the Casino Gardens on West Bank of White River, North of Emrichsville Bridge. Open Air Dancing on Pavilion overlooking White River. Café Service. 1-12 p.m. No cover charge for dinner guests. Chicken dinners and a la carte service. Phone reservations if possible. Featuring the celebrated Miami Six Orchestra.

Movie Secrets Are Revealed (1921 September 11)

Q: What screen actor earns $2,500 a week almost solely because of his eyes?

A: Optical strabismus, or cross-eyes, earns for Ben Turpin the princely salary of $2,500 iron men per week. Without discrediting Ben's dramatic ability, there is little doubt that he is paid this salary because of the fact that he is the proud possessor of the only pair of cock-eyes in the movies. Eight years ago, Ben was doing small parts in vaudeville and burlesque shows for twenty-five dollars a week.[134]

In an interview with Gladys Hall titled *Eye-Eye!* for *Motion Picture Classic* magazine, Ben told her, "I'm a good Christian and so is my wife. This is my business and I do it. I make people laugh, and to laugh makes them happy, and I'm proud to do it. I never meant to be a movie star. It happened to me, but since it has, I'll do the job right, cost what it may." And speaking of costs, he snapped, "I paid nine thousand dollars last year for sending out my pictures."

Hall ended with her impression of Ben: "He has value. He is undoubtedly and quite terribly sincere. He is honest and in earnest and he walks in the fear of the Lord which, in these days, is something. He is good and he loves his wife. Bathing girls haven't turned his head — only his eyes. He has balance, appearances notwithstanding."[135]

Ben Turpin's Mission In Life Is To Create Laughter

Ben Turpin has probably added almost as many good hearty laughs to the lives of motion picture audiences as his old friend and former playmate, Charlie Chaplin.

"When I was a kiddie," says Turpin, "it was my greatest ambition to make people laugh, and like many another fond parent my folks used to encourage me in my mimicry. When the neighbors would visit our old home in New Orleans I was invariably trotted out to do my childish bit.

"Later on this propensity developed, until it reached the stage where I was hurtled right across the footlights on the burlesque stage. Of course, the branch of the gentle art Thespis I selected was that of comedian. But I tried to instill variety into my work, and it was not long before, no matter how serious I would try to be, audiences gave me the laugh the minute I appeared before them.

"For a long time I did not know whether they were laughing with me or against me. It was in this frame of mind that I joined the old Essanay Film Company, along with friend Chaplin.

"I had long before given up the old dream of every comedian — the desire to play romantic leading roles — and had settled down with a vengeance to be funny. From then on my resolution was to furnish the grim old world with as many laughs as possible.

"No, my unruly eyes had nothing to do with this change of heart and desires. Mack Sennett was extremely good to me in providing me with vehicles that gave me ample opportunities to develop this desire to the utmost, and I shall continue to work upon the risibility's of the film fans as long as I can deliver the goods.

"My one pet theory is that laughs are better than medicine. There are already too many people in this world who are ever ready to eat up the scenery with dramatic wailing on gravities of our daily existence; there are too many pessimists. They would not matter so much if they did not insist on croaking their gloom preachments to the unwilling listener.

"And it is to offset these sad-eyed calamity howlers' deadly work that I am exercising my turbulent eyes in my comedy films." Turpin will be seen in person during the week of September 26 at Gordon's Scollay Square Theatre, Boston.[136]

Ben Turpin at the Globe (1921 September 13)

Followers of the screen who have laughed heartily at the antics of Ben Turpin, the eccentric comedian, were at the Globe (Philadelphia) yesterday to see him in person and accentuate their favoritism. Ben appeared in a comedy act surrounded by several other players who simply aided him in provoking laughter, for the act was one of those hilarious affairs that, devoid of artistry, was nevertheless amazingly humorous and gave the rubber-necked, cross-eyed comedian plenty of chances to display his abilities. Others on the bill included the Dancers Supreme, the Texas Comedy Four, Faber and Bernet, Miner and Evans, Ubert Carlton, Leon Stanton and Company, Seymour and Jeanette, and Frances and Frank.[137]

Ben Turpin Deplores Gay Life of Movies
Film Actor Knows Arbuckle and Says Miss Rappé Was Beauty (1921 September 14)

Ben Turpin, he of the roving eye, whose Adam's apple is as active in private life as on screen, deplores the gay life of the movie studio.

"I don't hand the gay life a thing," said this film actor, who is now in Philadelphia and who knows "Fatty" Arbuckle well. "I don't know much about it because we don't mingle. No gay life for me."

Then he discussed "Fatty" Arbuckle, whom he knows fairly well, and Miss Rappé, whom he knew slightly.

"I always put Arbuckle down as a good fellow," he said. "It was a thump to me to hear he had gotten in such a scrape.

"As for Miss Rappé, I often heard people speaking of her when I was out on the Coast. She was a beautiful girl."

Turpin is a little fellow with a slight frame, which was enhanced today by a suit of checks, the black and white variety. A hat of British origin and of racy lines sat on his head at a jaunty angle and a blue and white tie of impressionistic design cried aloud over a waistcoat of light tan.

There followed in Ben's wake a whimsical odor of — sweet lilac.

Phila. Public Ledger, pg 3

Ben Turpin at Cross Keys (1921 September 20)

There were innumerable admirers of Ben Turpin at the Cross Keys Theater (Philadelphia) yesterday to see the famous cross-eyed screen comedian in person. He had an act that showed him to be a real comedian and scoring a big hit. He remains today and tomorrow. Other acts comprised Everette's Monkey Circus, Schwartz and Clifford, Faber and Bernet, Phillips and Travers, the Hennings, and the Eastlakes.

Philadelphia Inquirer

Actress Theda Bara was also in town at the time, making a couple personal appearances. On Saturday, September 17, she had an accident at Philadelphia's Allegheny Theater resulting in the cancellation of her tour for the next week. Ben covered for her as well as fulfilled his own bookings at the Broadway and Cross Keys theatres.

Ben Turpin Claims He's Permanently Beautiful —
Gloriously Cock-Eyed Comedian Runs from Doctors and Specs Vendors —
Don't Want to Be Cured (1921 September 25)

Ben Turpin, the Mack Sennett Adonis, is the only known person that sells his affliction with honor. Ben is hopelessly, permanently and gloriously cock-eyed. While others similarly afflicted spend their money and their energies in efforts to unscramble their vision, Ben flees surgeons and doctors for fear they might cure him in his sleep. For the astute Mr. Turpin has turned his misfortune into profit. If cross-eyes are an affliction, Ben isn't aware of it. One doesn't pity John D. Rockefeller his oil stock. But because you do pity Ben his affliction, you render them, to him, like so much stock in Standard Oil. Ben "cashed in" on your sympathies. America's "handsomest" man wasn't always cross-eyed. There was a time when it was possible for him to follow the line of his vision. Once he could look his mother straight in the face and lie like any good little boy. Now he can't look his wife in the face even when he's telling her why he came home late. Ben Turpin's "beauty" is known everywhere that movies are shown, but few ever get the chance to look him in the eye. He's supposed to have come from aristocratic French lineage (though it is surprising how said aristocratic lineage and movie fortunes go together). He is a native of New Orleans, born to that city about fifty-two years ago. I suppose you know the story of how Ben used to juggle. Only once, he missed and when he came to, his eyes were crossed. And thus he has ever since remained. Millions of movie fans have argued pro and con on the question, is he really cross-eyed? He is.

The New Sentinel (Fort Wayne, Indiana)

Ben Turpin of the Funny Eyes Here Next Week (1921 September 25)

Ben Turpin, beloved by thousands, will be a visitor in Boston a week from today. The famous cross-eyed comedian is coming here primarily to consult a specialist regarding eye trouble. Anticipating the possibility of an eye operation, Turpin will make personal appearances before Boston theatregoers at Gordon's Scollay Square Olympia Theatre. Ben fears that it may be necessary for him to remain in a dark room for a long period while his eyes are under treatment and he wants to appear before the Boston public before his career as entertainer is temporarily halted by the physicians. The famous screen comedian had planned to visit the Hub today, but illness caused a postponement of his departure from California and caused a delay in his traveling plans. In order that Boston theatregoers may see him as he actually appears in comedy scenes before the camera, Ben Turpin will bring with him the costumes he has worn in many of his screen successes. And, in order that his stage appearances may seem perfectly natural to his audiences, the comedian will display on Gordon's Scollay Square Olympia stage all the grotesque facial and eye contortions and all of the funny falls and stumbles that he has exhibited on the film.[140]

⇒ His next stop Cleveland, Ben met writer W. Ward Marsh of the *Cleveland Plain Dealer*, who noted: Ben Turpin is one of the few screen stars who is merely accenting naturalness when performing before the camera — and I make that statement without apology to our guest of honor this week. Nature may not have made him a beautiful creation, but she certainly has done wonders for him. Ben is funny, as those of you who have seen him in Lowe's Park or State or the group who watched him luncheon in the Carlton Terrace Monday will testify. Ben walks with the same melodramatic swagger — with the exaggeration. His eyes are somewhat tamer than in pictures; nevertheless, his screen appearances are emphatic pictures of his everyday life if first impressions may be advanced. Monday noon, I stood in front of the State. Walter Lusk of Assoc. First National, for whom Ben is starring, had planned a luncheon and Ben had been detained at his hotel. Shortly, Ben came up the Avenue in company with Lusk and Fred Desberg of the Loew theaters. Long before I could note Ben's eyes were different from others or before that neck was in clear outline, I had spotted Turpin. His walk, had it been describing his conversation, was telling of a burlesqued melodramatic dissertation of foolishness.

Attired in something nattier than a brown sport suit, soft hat, and highly polished oxfords, Ben nervously (all his movements are of sudden nervous reaction) came into the zone of introduction. The first move Ben made at the luncheon was to pick up the individual salt and peppershakers, form binoculars, and look over the admiring eaters in the Terrace. Shortly, the orchestra struck up *Bright Eyes* and Ben, sparkling, demanded that it follow the selection with "Cock Eyes."

Then a waiter inquired "whether there was anything Mr. Turpin would like?"

"Oh, whattye got?" asked Ben in comic tones (that is, as comic as a severe cold would permit). "No, never mind those — bring me some nails!" Then, turning to the headwaiter,

"Don't they dance here? Get me a girl; I want to dance before I eat."

Introductions were forthcoming and Ben and an unidentified girl did a duet, after which he returned to his table fit for his luncheon, but his cold prevented him from eating much.

Ben's sentences are short, pointed, and are usually snapped out.

"Are you traveling alone?" I meekly inquired.

"No, not me!" came the burlesqued mellow answer. "Got my father-in-law, my sister, and my wife along. Never travel alone. Always take my wife with me" — and then as a sudden afterthought — "have to do that!"

Ben was told about the State's orchestra and the stage settings were described to him. "Better be getting down," he said. "I'm never late. I want to look things over. Say, I'm all bandaged up," pointing to his back. "Had been doing handsprings, doin' 'em right along. Doing 'em in Boston. Flipped over the lights into the orchestra pit. Busted up a bass viola and hurt my back. Not turning flips now, but I can do 'em…*easy!*"[29]

Two years later, Marsh elaborated on that earlier interview: "Tears were pretty freely and generally distributed that afternoon. Another moist strabismic attack overtook the bashful orbs when their owner recounted an affair, his husky voice growing huskier with every word and sob, which he saw up in New England. The greatest fit of sobbing came when Ben related, brokenly, what happened when he slipped at a handspring on a stage a few days before he arrived here. It seems Ben was up to his tricks when not only his eyes played him false, but his feet. He went over the footlights, head first, into a bass drum or something and almost broke his back.

"He spoke in a hoarse voice and when he mixed tears with his rasping voice he was not easily understood.

"That story, if I remember correctly, was interrupted several times by sobs and tears. He was fairly grief stricken because he was afraid his audience would think he had been drinking something worse than coffee. And the tears, which came often during an hour's talk, were not prompted by alcohol or its various compounds and mixtures."[141]

Ben Turpin Is Greeted at the Capitol Theatre (New York, 1921 September)

Ben Turpin stepped off the Twentieth Century Limited yesterday and went directly to the Capital Theatre, where he appeared in connection with the presentation of a film made behind the scenes at the Mack Sennett studios, showing informal glimpses of the various popular studio characters. He is scheduled to appear throughout this entire week at 3:45, 8:15, and 10:15.

Ben Turpin is the owner of the oddest pair of eyes on the screen. He can look in two directions at once and he is obliged to do so in order to see the big crowds who flock to see him at the Capitol. A novel type of film is called *Behind the Scenes at the Mack Sennett Studios* and shows interesting and informal glimpses of the famous Sennett Comedy Company, introducing such well-known studio characters as the celebrated Bathing Girls, the dog Teddy, the cat Pep, sundry tame animals and "wildflowers," and the comedian, Ben Turpin, himself. In connection with the presentation of this film, the comedian will make his personal appearance at the Capitol next week.

This is his first visit to New York, which he is making expressly for this engagement, and his appearances at the Capitol will be his only public ones during his visit. Ben has won popularity with movie fans with the most individual pair of eyes on the screen and this will be the first opportunity offered the public to get a close view of them off the silver sheet.

Turpin At Capitol; New for Times Square — Big Picture House Trying "Personal Appearance" — Comic Does Little (1921 September 30)

Ben Turpin's Capitol appearance is prefaced by a single reel entitled *Behind the Scenes at the Mack Sennett Studios* in which Teddy the dog, Pep the cat, the goat and the bear and the more noted of the Sennett beauties, including Marie Prevost (now with Universal), Phyllis Haver, Mildred June, and about a score of others, are shown fooling around with a couple of A.K. photographers in the still department. Someone suggested that the two A.K. guys might have been H.O. Davis and Mack Sennett themselves with the aid of make-up. Turpin is in the picture and the orchestra plays *Bright Eyes* for his appearance. The film is quite unfunny and only serves to introduce the comic.

For Turpin's appearance, the orchestra again plays a couple bars of *Bright Eyes* and Turpin slides to the center of the stage, takes the baton from the leader, and offers a burlesque imitation of Sousa leading the men in *Stars and Stripes Forever*. That lets him out. Some of those present expected to hear him quote from the one volume he confesses he ever read, *The Life of Tracy the Outlaw*, but he did not. In vaudeville, Turpin says he's been receiving $1,500 a week. For the week at the Capitol, Ben's "managers" say he is getting $1,000. At any rate, it is pretty soft for Turpin to take down a grand a week during the time that there is nothing stirring on the Sennett lot and the other "comics" are with the lay-offs.[142]

Louella Parsons (1921 October 2, New York Telegraph)

New York to Ben Turpin is bounded on the north, south, east, and west by the Capitol Theatre. Ever since he arrived last Sunday, his route has been a straight line from the Astor Hotel to the Capitol and back again. They even took his morning last Monday and made him pose for a picture on the Capitol Roof. When I saw him, he was gently reminding the photographers, press agents, and admiring ensemble he was but a human being and when the noon gong sounded its merry chime, he wants his chow. He might have had it, too, but when I came upon him at this inopportune time, he had to stop long enough to talk Essanay. He was one of the old crowd and considered himself in affluent circumstances when the cashier handed him $20 every Monday evening. He returned to Chicago a hero, wined and dined and feted. And he says exaggerating the cast in his eye and making himself more cross-eyed than nature intended brought this change in his fortune. They didn't realize in the old days Ben's brand of humor was funny enough to be starred. Everyone liked him at Essanay and laughed at his jokes, but he was never in the Francis Bushman-Bryant Washburn class.

It took Mack Sennett to capitalize Mr. Turpin and the little comedian says he will never cease being grateful.

"I owe everything to Mr. Sennett. What chance did I have until he featured me?"

"How did you happen to go to the Coast?" I asked Mr. Turpin after we had discussed all of the old crowd and laughed at some of the old-time jokes.

"Mr. Chaplin added me to his company. He wanted me for *A Night Out*, so I thought it would be time to broach the delicate subject of a raise. G. M. offered me $30 per; I jumped at it.

"'Say, Charlie,' I said to Chaplin, 'thanks to you I have a two years' contract with Essanay.'

"'Great,' said Charlie.

"'Yep,' I said, pleased with myself. 'I am to have $30 a week.'

"'What!' cried Chaplin. 'You fool! Do you mean you signed for $30 a week?'

"'Sure, don't you think I am lucky?'

"'Lucky? I think you need a nurse! I thought you were getting at least $300. Why didn't you come to me before you signed that foolish paper?'" That, Mr. Turpin says, was the beginning of his dissatisfaction. Then he played in *Carmen* and was so funny Mr. Chaplin is said to have told him:

"See here Turpin, you are funny enough to be starred yourself." Mack Sennett thought so, too. He sent for the comedian and offered to pay him six or seven times $30 just as a starter.

"Oh gee," moaned Turpin, "I got myself all tied up on that contract with Essanay."

And because he had come to the Essanay with Gilbert Anderson when the company was first organized, he felt he couldn't be disloyal. Chaplin, who liked the unaffected little comedian who wanted to be loyal even when it meant his future success, said to him: "Don't mind about that contract. There isn't anything for you here anyway. I will fix it for you." And he did.

Turpin, who never had any illusions of his importance with Essanay, had a terrible feeling his former employers didn't mind losing him and so he moved to the Vogue lot with a very clear conscience. Mack Sennett was clever enough to see the funny side of Turpin. Ben exaggerated the crossed eyes and let him do all the clownish tricks that always brought a laugh to both the members of the staff and the lounge lizards at the Essanay plant.

The result was sure and certain. For three years, Ben Turpin has been gaining in favor until he is now considered the favorite of some of our most discerning film fans, among them Agnes Smith, who considers no boudoir is complete without a picture of Mr. Turpin. The ladies who admire Bernard may consider it a crushing blow to hear he never travels without his wife. He feels it isn't safe in these days when the movie scandals are so numerous. Mrs. Turpin was in an automobile accident some years ago and was injured in such a way she has not been able to hear a sound since that tragic day. No one could see the little comedian with her without being touched by his solicitation for her welfare. He consults her on his photographs, his engagements, and, one suspects, even on the matter of his clothes.

"Got the same wife," he told me. "Been married fifteen years and I'm satisfied and so is she." Although she could not hear, we did not doubt Mr. Turpin's boast that he had made her happy. She has diamonds, good clothes, and is looked after in her affliction in a tender manner that should put a long credit mark after his name. Duty, you say. Probably, but there is something more than duty that makes a man as thoughtful as the funny little cross-eyed man in the loud, checkered suit.

In all his life, Ben Turpin never had anything please him as much as his return to Chicago. He played next door to the theatre where Francis X. Bushman and Beverly Bayne were playing. In the old days, Mr. Bushman was the star and Mr. Turpin was just an extra man doing utility jobs for his benefactor, G.M. Anderson. The box office receipts prove the Turpin attraction brought in more money than any other similar entertainment in the history of the Windy City. It wasn't the idea that he was as good an attraction as Bushman and Bayne that pleased him. It was the reception given him by his old friends and neighbors that made the warm glow come to his cheeks and put a sunny, happy feeling in his cardiac region known outside of medical journals as his heart. To cap the climax and to add to the joy of the occasion, Aaron Jones presented him with an Elk's gold card.

"Say," said Mr. Turpin. "I just wanted to bawl. Mr. Jones has always been on a pedestal with me. I worked for him once and they don't make them any whiter than Aaron J. Think of his noticing me. It was the finest thing that ever happened to me. And, say, no one could get that away from me without dynamite."

"Over his dead body," suggested one of the numerous gathering, who were suggesting it was time to take another picture. But Ben was firm. He was going to eat no matter what and because I knew just how hungry he was, I left him in the hands of the crowd who are bent on working him to death.

"I want to see you again," he said, "if I can give them the slip," winking in such a manner that included the whole room and was really, I gathered, intended for me.

"The Mrs. and I will come over to your office. Gee, I want to see some shows, too. I am tired of work." When Mr. Turpin finishes his contract in twenty-one months with Sennett, he is going abroad for a long vacation and rest.

"Other plans with other producers?" someone hinted.

"Not me," answered Mr. Turpin. "I owe any success I have to Mack Sennett and you can bet your last dollar I am going to stick with him." His language may be more picturesque than elegant and he may wear loud, checkered clothes, but there is a heart of gold there and, thank Heaven, he hasn't acquired an English accent, nor does he talk of his valet and his great wealth. He saves his money and he says he isn't a star.

Yes, really — Ben Turpin is as real and natural as the old oak tree in the country school-yard. All the pretense and glitter that comes to most people making a good salary has passed right over his head. And because of this, I am for him and I hope he will continue to make people laugh as long as he lives and they live.[143]

Ben Turpin Plans to Leave Movies (1921 September 26)

New York — Ben Turpin, the filmdom "Roly-Poly"-eyed screen comedian, is going to quit the films — that is, in just 21 months from today. The boy who has made millions laugh with his funny antics in Mack Sennett comedies has a contract with the producer which runs for a year and nine months more. After it is ended, Ben and wife plan a world tour. He needs a rest. This flying trip here is his first real vacation in four years and it has been seven since he set foot in New York. With Mrs. Turpin, he returns to Los Angeles in the latter part of the week, where, after a short breathing spell, he will resume his picture making.[144]

Ben Turpin Greets Friends In Person — Comedian Back in Boston After Long Absence — Cross-Eyed Star Tells How He Makes Spectators Laugh

Hundreds of "fans" gathered in front of Boston's Hotel Touraine yesterday afternoon to welcome Ben Turpin, the Sennett comedian, who is visiting Boston for the first time since he entered pictures. Many years ago, Ben was in Boston as an acrobat at the old Austin and Stone Museum, but since he became one of the best known cinema comedy stars, he has seldom visited the East and had never returned to the Hub till yesterday. The crowd cheered both Mr. and Mrs. Turpin as they entered an automobile exactly at 2:30 to take a city tour. The party also visited Brookline and Cambridge, making stops at Franklin Park, where Turpin visited "my brothers, the monkeys," and at Harvard. Last night, Ben made his initial appearance at Gordon's Scollay Square Olympia Theatre, where he showed the capacity crowd how he does his funny falls and other stunts in the movies.

Mr. Turpin and his wife will spend a week in Boston. Ben will make daily appearances at the Olympia Theatre. He will next go to Chicago to meet his admirers. "I never realized how popular I was until I started making my personal appearances," said the actor. "I had a wonderful time in New York, but I expect an even more wonderful time in Boston. I'm on the lookout for all the pretty girls who have written letters to me and I hope I shall see them all. No, Mrs. Turpin isn't jealous. She's a very sensible woman."

Mr. Turpin refused to discuss his well-known cross-eyes. "I'm very sensitive about them," he said. "And let me tell you that it was not my eyes which won me my present success. If anyone thinks it was, let some other comedian with cross-eyes try to hold down my job. My eyes have nothing to do with my present standing."

Mr. Turpin then went on to explain what kind of spectators he liked the best. "You have seen cross, hard-boiled old crabs who look as if they'd commit murder rather than give away a nickel or say any a kind word," he said. "They are just the kind I like to have in my audiences. If I can make them laugh, I can make anyone laugh.

"I met a waitress recently who is just the type I mean. She glared at me and yelled, 'What will you have?' I gave her my order and then asked her, 'Don't you ever smile?'

"'Don't have to,' replied the waitress coldly. Then I asked her if she had a bad night or had a fight with her husband or wanted to get married. 'No,' she snapped. Finally I asked her if she would like a tip. 'If you want to give it to me,' she said nonchalantly. So I told her to get her tip off the gas jet. And finally I made her laugh.

"It's easy enough for these dramatic motion picture heroes to act. All they have to do is walk in and do what the scenario says. I have to make up most of the acting. For instance, my director would tell me to go into a hotel room like this and get a laugh. How would you do it?" The reporter admitted that he didn't know.

"I would walk in, look at myself in the mirror as if I were very handsome, and have the mirror crack because I was so homely," answered Ben.[145]

Ben Turpin on Job for Jobless — Will Serve Good Supper at Ledoux Hotel

Supper, consisting of vegetable soup, ham knuckles and cabbage, devilled corned beef, boiled and mashed potatoes, homemade pound cake, coffee ice cream, black coffee, and fruit, will be served at 6 o'clock tonight to the guests of the Hotel Jobless, Urban Ledoux Church of the Unemployed at 31 Howard Street, by Ben Turpin, the film funmaker, who is now appearing at a local theatre. Clad in one of his film costumes, over which he will wear a baker's white coat and hat, he will walk from the theatre to the hotel, arriving in time to personally serve the meal, which he made possible by a contribution of $200. Mrs. Helene Lehman has purchased the food and will prepare it for the guests. Secretary Roy I. MacGregor announced that he will invite 20 representative businessmen of the city to be present. When the meal is finished, the cross-eyed comedian will display his many laugh-provoking tricks. He will also furnish other entertainment. Turpin will distribute 50 tickets among unemployed guests for his theatrical performance.[146]

Next, in Cleveland, W. Ward Marsh wrote: Ben Turpin has no secret from his three loves — he is married to his wife, he loves his work, and he's true to the public. And so, after looking one way and talking another, he managed to get a telegram off from Chicago yesterday to the Loew officials here, telling them to tell the public just what it may expect of him when he arrives in Cleveland on Monday.

Ben is amusing Chicago this week and right after his final appearance there Sunday night — providing the girls don't jam the streets at train time — he is coming right on here for appearances on Monday in Lowe's State and Park. Afternoon and evening in the State and evening only in the Park. The feature of Ben's number will not be his comedy as first announced, but will be leading the orchestra in the theaters. Ben has written a selection himself and he has called it *The Squirrels Are Chasing Me Yet*.

"The musicians never saw any music like mine in their busy lives," he wired yesterday. "In fact some of them will never see anything like it again!"

Besides this stunt, Ben has a short reel of film, showing him in some of his new and funny sets. And he will offer a short monologue which he puts over the footlights. (Caution: Husbands must not be jealous of Ben; Ben may be flirting with another man's wife. Wives must not think Ben is flirting with them — she may be some other woman — on the other side of the house. Little things like that should always be borne in mind when Ben's around. He's playful — but he's married!)

Ben, of course, promises to appear in his makeup and further promises to roll his eyes often and in different ways. In a recent interview in the east, he is quoted as saying that his "goose neck" is growing longer and more elastic. All this proves he has no secrets from his three loves. He has told his program for entertaining us.[147]

Notes from the Palmolive (1921 October 16)

That Palmolive popularity has reached such a stage that even celebrities of movieland pay us visits when passing through the city surprises us not in the least. But when Ben Turpin, comedian, arrives and insists on a shampoo and a real shave, we think we may be excused for deviating from the usual conventional form of hospitality to a slight air wanting to show off our goods and demonstrating the real thing to him. Ben was real pleased with his shampoo and cream.

Should you have missed his visit, we'll say he was most entertaining to the employees and kept all in bursts of laughter.[148]

A Cross-Eyed View of New York — Ben Turpin Looks at the Great Metropolis from Several Angles by Beverly Crane

"Take your choice and concentrate," instructed a dynamic personage.

"Don't look both ways or you'll be floored," grinned an ex-pugilist.

"The crossing at the bridge — when 'they' be eyes — is most deceptive," prattled the ingenue. All were talking about Ben Turpin and, in their respective ways, endeavoring to give us a little advice about how to look at his puzzling orbs. They weren't especially instructive or even facetious. The first, however, we found to be the more useful of the verbal offerings, for Turpin is a rather dizzy person to hold speech with if you try your utmost to gaze into both eyes at the same time.

We saw Ben at the Astor Hotel, recognizing him with little difficulty. Without his makeup and minus the exaggerated twist he gives his eyes when working, he would pass in a crowd without ever being discovered. We found a forsaken nook on the balcony floor and there, save for a brief interruption by Mrs. Turpin, we remained until the clock chimed the half hour. Ben's voice was mighty husky — nope, not night air, just too much speaking and too many personal appearances. We had no trouble looking at the eccentric comedian at all; we just took our choice and concentrated!

"I'm supposed to have a thirteen-week vacation," he said, "but if Mr. Sennett asks me if I'm rested when I get back, I'll just pass away!"

"But you are certainly making a lot of new friends," we offered.

"Yes. I suppose so. But I'll be happy to get home. All this," he gestured broadly, "is not new to me. I lived here years ago. I don't enjoy going out every night. I've lived that kind of life. I'm a man of fifty-two years. When I'm home I get up at five o'clock in the morning, have a swim and a round or two of boxing with my Japanese chauffeur, breakfast, and by nine I'm at the studio and ready for work. At four-thirty I'm through; at eight I'm in bed."

This is a quiet life with a vengeance, but it explains why Ben, a man of fifty-two, looks like a man of forty; why he is capable of cavorting around as spry and sprightly-like as the young ones. Ben's present makeup is a relic of the old Essanay days, when he was a member of Charlie Chaplin's company. Ben was engaged at the studio to play character roles at the lowly stipend of $20 a week. He played them straight — no mustache. One day, Charlie was in a grand rush for a character man. He told Ben to put on a makeup in a hurry. Ben didn't have the kind of makeup that he knew Charlie wanted and he certainly didn't have time to go and get a mustache. He devised a scheme all his own and it worked famously. What he actually did was cut a mustache from a wig and paste it on. When Charlie caught one glimpse of him he sat down and roared.

When Chaplin decided to go west, he persuaded Turpin to go with him. Ben was reluctant to leave Chicago, it being, after all, home. He and his wife had just built a neat little bungalow and furnished it to meet with their simple tastes. But a livelihood was a livelihood, so Ben went west.

"I've had big offers to leave Mack Sennett. I had one offer recently that would have meant a quarter of a million salary for me. But why? Charlie Chaplin and 'Fatty'

Arbuckle — before the scandal — are the only two ex-Sennett comedians who have made a success away from Sennett. I get a good salary and I'm happy with Sennett. I consider him the greatest producer of comedy today. I just signed a new two-year contract with him. Because I did this before my old contract expired I got a nice little bonus. Yes, I enjoy my work in pictures, but it's mighty hard. To make a two-reel comedy takes on the average of six weeks. And do you know how long it took to make *A Small Town Idol*? Seven months! I never was so sick of anything in my life as I was of that picture. The same old thing, it began to seem like, every day.

"It's easy to play in dramatic pictures. It isn't so hard to make people cry. But try and make them laugh! Mr. Sennett sees every foot of film that is taken. If he laughs — fine! If he doesn't — it has to be re-taken."

"And you'll be glad to get home," we said as the clock chimed the half hour.

"Indeed I will," rising as we did. "God bless you and give you all success," Turpin said in parting and we took one long last look at the most famous pair of eyes in the world before leaving the little comedian.[149]

Ben Turpin is a Riot — Keeps Audiences at Loew's State and Park Theatres in an Uproar — Eyes Won't Behave and His Legs Just Won't Stay Where They Should Be *(1921 October 18)*

The loud chuckles and laughs that were heard coming from the lobbies of Loew's State and Park theatres yesterday were merely the results of the antics of funny Ben Turpin being performed inside. Ben, with his rolling eyes and funny legs and feet, kept the audiences in an uproar. He told funny stories, turned flipflops, led the orchestra in his inimitable way, and then for good measure danced Salome. It was just like going to the Mack Sennett studio in Los Angeles and seeing him perform in a picture.[150]

Turpin's Return Goes to State-Lake at $2,000 Per Week After Playing Other Chicago Houses *(1921 October 19)*

Ben Turpin played his third return engagement in Chicago last week at the State-Lake. On his original appearance at McVickers six weeks ago, he received $1,500 for the week, his second week at the Rialto brought him $1,200, it is said, and last week he returned to headline the State-Lake at $2,000 for the week. Turpin headlined the bills at both the Rialto and McVicker's and during the two weeks he was at these houses, business was very big. At the conclusion of the shows, he had no further bookings. A number of the small-time agents were delegated to offer him to the various picture houses here at a salary said to range from $1,200 to $1,500 a week. There were no bidders for his services and he was booked to play two picture houses by one of the independent agents. The houses located in Detroit and Cincinnati each paid $1,500 for one week.

Then Turpin was booked into the Capitol, New York, by S.L. Rothafel at a salary said to be about the Rialto figure when the bookers of the Orpheum, Jr., circuit thought he might be a good buy for them. Arrangements were made to have him make a reappearance in Chicago at their house, the State-Lake. After the opening performance Monday, the management was dissatisfied with his act and wanted to cancel his act at once and pay him for the week. On second thought, it was decided on account of the large and extensive advertising announcements and billing they had given Turpin, it might be better to retain him and revise his act. Turpin was then told to cut out all of his talk and simply lead the orchestra for his own offering with an added bit with DeHaven and Nice called The Flying Ginsburgs. This failed to register, but Turpin was allowed to finish the week.

Newsy Notes from Hollywood by Daisy Dean *(1921 November 8)*

Yes, Ben Turpin's eyes are really crossed. Now that the first and all-important question about Ben is answered, we can go on to the man himself. The next thing which was always asked as soon as it was discovered that we had seen the inimitable Ben was what does he look like. Turpin is a slight man and about five foot four. He looks very much as he does on the screen, only sans mustache and funny derby. His eyes are only slightly crossed, but he can roll them, and does, with startling effect. As he said with fitting gestures and striking a humorous pose, "I may not be good looking, but I'm awful cute."

Little Miss Fluffy Ruffles who looks with favor and fluttering heart upon the young and handsome heroes need not feel sorry for Ben Turpin and think him neglected and unloved, for he spends no less than several thousands of dollars a year to send photos to admiring fans. It keeps three girls busy taking care of his correspondence. Turpin is proud of his rise from a two-dollar-a-night acrobat and juggler to a high-salaried motion picture comedian. There is no veil drawn across his early career and there is no sham or pretense in his manner. Another thing Ben is proud of is his gold Elks life membership card. The life of a comedian is not all fun, according to Ben.

Some of the stunts result in accidents and during his five years at Sennett, he has been in the hospital so many times that he is "ashamed to look a nurse in the face." He has had more than one "new dining room set," his own way of telling about new teeth he has needed after some accident or other. Now, however, Mr. Sennett is rather careful of Turpin, for he is much too valuable to be allowed to run risks, and so doubles are sometimes employed for scenes which might mean a long delay in finishing a picture if Turpin were hurt. Turpin is really funny off the screen as well as on. He gave a short act on his recent "personal appearance" tour and the artist who made these impressions of him saw his act three times and laughed first, to say nothing of his uncontrolled mirth during the interview. Whatever we might have thought before, it has now been proved — Ben Turpin is funny.[151]

Love and Doughnuts by Peter Milne

"In a recent Ben Turpin picture the comedian appeared as a baker. He was shown 'holing' doughnuts with a mechanic's auger and going about his work in a perfectly serious fashion. A little later the subtitle 'Testing' was flashed on the screen, followed by a scene of Turpin testing his doughnuts by slipping them over a bar and chinning himself on them. The effect was utterly ridiculous, uproariously funny. And what was it? Really just an application of sound scientific methods, never funny when applied correctly, but as applied to a bakery more or less of a scream. Mr. Sennett and his staff will startle audiences into fits of laughter time and again by such methods.

"While on the subject of Ben Turpin it is only fair to record here that Mack Sennett has never received the credit due him for developing this cross-eyed Romeo. Turpin can be, and has been, quite a tiresome bore on the screen. He proved it a few years ago by trying to star himself without Mr. Sennett's guiding hand — and he failed. Certainly in his case direction enters into his success largely. Ford Sterling is another who once left Mr. Sennett's guidance to form his own company. But he also came back to the fold.

"The tricks of the slapstick producers are numerous. The familiar scene of the automobiles skidding all over a wet pavement is sometimes actually hazardous to those participating but more often it is filmed with a slow camera, the cars also skidding around rather slowly, with the result that the completed picture gives the impression of sheer and utter recklessness. In the Ben Turpin picture already mentioned, the comedian endeavored to eat asparagus and just as he would get a tip near his mouth it would curl away like a snake. Of course there are such things as wires and springs."[152] *Author Milne may have confused the popular Vogue reissues, which were circulating around this time, as "new" Turpin films. Ben worked for no one but Mack Sennett at this time.*

Ben Turpin — As He Is To Those Who Know Him (late 1921)

"It isn't every man fifty-two years of age who can go through what I have done in motion pictures and live to tell the tale as I am doing now. My dear fans, I want you to know that the short scene of forty or fifty feet of film which seems so easy to you requires me to work for many days — cruel, grinding labor while the cameraman may be taking thousands of feet of film to make that same forty as nearly perfect as possible.

"In the old days when I was a carpenter working about the Essanay studio, little did I think that I would become a victim of comedy, plying a hazardous way from one sensational role to another. Little did I think either that I would withstand the physical test of countless comedy fights, 'make-believe' street brawls which are more serious and disastrous than the real thing, nor did I ever dream that people would actually laugh at me. That you all laugh I know, because I have seen my own pictures at the movie houses, but that fact is still a mystery to me and I often wonder that anyone as serious minded as I really am could create mirth.

"Perhaps it is because I am so serious.

"I enjoy everything I do and I suppose I'm about the only living comedian who isn't anxious to be doing some other kind of work. Most of them want to be tragedians or anything they are least fitted to do.

"Next to working in pictures I'd rather work in my garden. You see I always drive the shortest way home so I will have more time for the garden. The folks kid me a great deal because I sit so straight at the wheel and lean forward when I am driving. They say I think the steering apparatus is a spade or hoe. Well, if more people used a hoe instead of a wheel, living in this world would be much easier."

Ben leaned out of the car and called to the traffic policeman as he made a wide turn. "Hello, Bill, which way am I going?"

"How d'you expect me to tell, you cross-eyed speedster," cheerily said the officer.

"That man oughtn't to be on the force," remarked Ben, "because he has a sense of humor. I always welcome a good joke on myself, I seem to have formed the habit in burlesque and vaudeville, where we had to keep adding to our fund of humor to enliven the script of the act we were doing." He is not slow to tell you that he is proud of his career and points to the significant fact that he has had to work earnestly for his laurels.

"In the hospital scene of *Married Life* you will remember, if you saw it, that I was dropped from a stretcher and from the ambulance onto the street several times. Those falls actually occurred and if I took one real fall I took a hundred in that picture and I must say that the street was not a bed of roses. It's very easy for a director to say to some big fellow, 'Jump on Ben, you can't hurt him — stand on him — make it real,' and other similar instructions but think of poor little me all that time. I have to take it all and never whimper."

Whereupon Ben looked off somewhere — no one could tell just where — and heaving a big sigh for so little a man, said, "Just the same there's a fascination about the work and the only time I rest is during the three or four weeks I spend each year at Hot Springs (Arkansas). If I didn't get that rest I'd doubtless be making comedies in another sphere."

Ben cares little or nothing for any kind of society except the friends that surround his home life. So little does he care for what people think that he will drive his limousine in his farmer's clothes or should a friend drop by unannounced when he is working, whisk him off to dinner and he considers the event quite natural and makes no apology for his appearance. Why should he, indeed? Is he not Ben Turpin and should anyone be surprised to see him in any sort of costume, even the most comical?

He is, in real fact, the personification of naturalness, is seldom bored and never embarrassed. How many men who have achieved success similar to that of Ben Turpin both in a creative way and in the art of making money would continue to live much the same as they did in the days before success when they were forced to save and live frugally? Doubtless very few. Yet Ben Turpin, well able to live on the finest in the land, buys his own groceries, plans every expenditure economically and is a master in the art of preventing waste. Far from being miserly, Ben is generous at every turn, but he insists upon getting value received for every dollar he spends and, be it said to his everlasting credit, is successful in the extreme.

"There is not a shopkeeper in Hollywood that I know of," asserts Ben, growing enthusiastic on his pet civic theme, "who doesn't consider the motion picture people his especially provided fortune sent by some kind of providence for him to thrive on. We are generally eaten whole although some are gently but thoroughly fleeced first. Hollywood would still be a scattered group of dusty roads were it not for the third largest industry in the world — motion pictures. The shops will do well to treat the people of that great industry fairly or the inevitable will happen — motion picture people will organize their own fair priced commissaries.

"I buy my own groceries and if I am overcharged I refuse to buy. I consider it the highest standard of good citizenship to resist the preying and knavery of shopkeepers who boost their prices without reason and solely because the people who buy from them will not resist.

"I consider that it is the duty of every American to equalize market values by careful buying and the prevention of waste at his own table. He should also produce something. It need not be much but he must contribute to the market to the limit of his ability to do so."

Ben says little at the studio about ideals of citizenship, but his neighbors take heed and one by one are following suit. Ben's example is bound to make itself felt. Ben eats a simple lunch at the studio cafeteria, generally in company with Walter Anthony or perchance with a group of the Sennett girls — Marie Prevost, Phyllis Haver, and the rest. He seldom fails to have an amusing bit of repartee with Charlie Murray and some of the funny Sennett titles actually come from the witticisms of this comic duet.

Unlike too many successful players, there is nothing "upstage" about Turpin. When not working in a scene, he sits by watching or talking in a low tone to some fellow player. He has no jealousies and few dislikes for anyone. He is simply a well-behaved cog in the smooth machinery of the Sennett productions. However popular the belief that comedies call for hilarity and good times behind the scenes, the fact remains that the Sennett studio is one of the best regulated in the business and Ben is an integral part of that good regulation — always thinking creatively, helping someone else, or advising where it is not interference to advise — teamwork. The Sennett players play as a team and Ben is one of the reliable "varsity" players, always on the job, never flinching, and determined to do his best comedy through to the last minute of play. He is fearless, eager to do, and indomitable and still greater things may be expected from Ben, favorite of countless fans as the years roll by.

Little Movie Mirror Books

Ben Turpin Fears The Worst —
Takes Out Insurance Against Chance of Eyes Becoming Straight (1921 November 17)

Los Angeles, Nov. 17 — Ben Turpin, none other than he of the interfering optics, must be afraid that some miracle is going to happen. He had taken out an insurance policy against the possibility of his eyes becoming straight.[153] *This was actually Turpin's third policy with the famous Lloyd's of London. The All Risk policy was in favor of the Mack Sennett Comedies Corp. in the amount of $25,000 during the period of November 19, 1921 and ending two days later on November 21. The provision:* To pay loss providing the eyes of Ben Turpin become straight from any cause whatsoever during the period of time. *It should be noted Ben was not the reputed first Hollywood celebrity to take out insurance. Years earlier Charlie Chaplin beat him with two feet.*

Man's Best Friend

Towser, Ben's little black dog of no particular breed and coincidentally also cross-eyed, was the gift of a lady in the east. The afflicted canine arrived with a note setting forth that she felt convinced that Ben was probably the only person in the United States qualified to understand the animal.

"There's Towser, a mutt that I wouldn't trade for any dog in the world. He's the only cross-eyed dog I've ever seen and his eyes are in exactly the same position that mine are." Sure enough, Towser's eyes had the true Turpinian cast and although no one could tell whether he was looking at his master or not, there was no mistaking the fact that his joy at greeting him knew no bounds.

"It's a wonder to me that he doesn't insure the dog's eyes, too," Mrs. Turpin said, explaining her husband's affection for the dog. Mrs. Turpin has a definite routine for her housework. While she prepares dinner, Ben feeds the chickens, dogs, and the parrot. Then he slips into overalls, boots, and a droll little hat, the real farmer kind, and plies the garden fork and the hose. When there is no work to do in the vegetable garden, he loosens the earth about the young fig trees and chases worms in the orange orchard.

"Mamma," he called to his wife, "come out here and see Billie." Billie is a big Plymouth Rock rooster that is very tame.

"Do you know he hasn't been here as long as Towser, but I do believe his eyes are beginning to turn in just like mine." This little joke provoked a real and prolonged laugh from Mrs. Turpin, who said that Ben would never cease inventing jokes about his eyes and that if he had his way, the whole world would be cross-eyed.

In the evening, the famous comedian plays his electric piano, the finest of its kind that money could buy. It is his capital joke to pretend to be playing the piano himself and he goes through the motions of playing so accurately and with such realism and temperament that he frequently deceives his guests, who are unaware that the instrument is mechanical. Not even Paderewski ever phrased more grandiloquently or shook his long locks with such artistic abandon. Ben sings, as he will tell you confidingly, "for my own amusement."

Ben Turpin is eternally the comedian. He simply can't help being funny and even when he attempts to become serious, his friends suspect a "new gag" and ask him if he is kidding them.[14]

Turpin Dons His Little Brown Derby (1921 November 19)

After 16 weeks of absence from the Sennett lot (due to his touring), Ben Turpin is back again and ready to begin work on his forthcoming comedy, which is scheduled to start soon.[154]

1921 November 19, *Billboard:* It is rumored that Ben Turpin intends paying a visit to this country (Australia) shortly. You can take this for what it is worth.

The Heartbreaking Game of Being Funny, When Laughing at Your Favorite Movie Comedian, Drop a Tear Of Sympathy for Him; He Needs It in His Business (1921 November 27)

Temperament doesn't enter into the making of comedy. Ben Turpin and Clyde Cook, not dissimilar in their working methods, offer little or no difficulty to their director in charge. Nor do they offer anything in the way of byplay to the hopeful newspaperman standing near. None of the comedy canneries are exactly cheerful places, but these respective haunts of Turpin and Cook are unquestionably the most dismal studios in Hollywood.

Turpin performs stolidly, in a matter-of-fact way, much as a bricklayer performs. There are no bursts of inspired comedy, no flashes of divine wit. The whole affair seems quite drab and colorless despite the fact that the finished product will probably make millions chortle in glee. He is making a living, he feels, honestly. That is all there is to comedy. He told me he doesn't read much, doesn't go to theaters often, and hardly attends picture shows.

"If I went to the movies when I got through here," he said, "it would be like a motorcycle cop going riding after hours of pleasure. There is no fun in seeing comedies after you've been making the things all day long — thinking up gags, breaking in new shoes, tripping over chairs, falling down broken ladders. Say, what makes you think comedy is funny?"

Turpin's elongated neck and popping, mis-mated orbs make him a comical figure, but there his humor ends. He is morbidly commonplace in his street clothes. In the studio quips, do not fly between comedian and soubrette; puns do not ricochet off the ivory shoulders of fair Phyllis Haver as the sawed-off Ben causes his eyes to perform for the relentless camera. There is nothing faintly suggestive of "carnival spirit," nothing even vaguely calling to mind the Joy of Endeavor. No one on the hilarious lot looks happy, as a matter of fact, unless the scenario specifically demands a smile.[155]

Insures Eyes For Huge Sum — Ben Turpin To Play Safety First
(1921 December 3)

Los Angeles, Dec 3 — Babe Ruth carries heavy insurance on his batting arm, Mischa Elman on his fingers, and Charlie Chaplin on his feet. Now comes Ben Turpin, funny cross-eyed man of the screen, to take out a policy for $25,000 on his crisscross orbs. This is the first time, so representatives of the Underwriters for Lloyd's, London, say that a person has taken a policy insuring cross-eyes against any accident or act of God which might straighten them, thereby blessing them with perfect orbs. Ben has been cross-eyed for many years. This visual condition, which in most people would be a misfortune, was accepted by the actor as the heavenly manna. While putting over a bit of slapstick comedy he was unlucky — or lucky — enough to bump his head with such a shock that his eyes were left as they appear today. He capitalized his affliction.

Now he's afraid his eyes will become straight again. The policy taken out by Turpin covers a period of one year. The premium, plus taxes and revenue stamps, totals $106.18.

1922: Secrets of the Movies (a syndicated Question and Answer column):

Q: Do you know who is believed to be the first slapstick comedian in pictures?

A: Ben Turpin was the first slapstick comedian in pictures. Turpin starred with the Essanay Company for two and a half years in slapstick. Then he joined Charlie Chaplin for a year after he became connected with Mack Sennett Comedies.

Ben Lands the Kale (1922 February 5)

Ben Turpin, who has the titular role in *Bright Eyes*, a new Sennett comedy for First National release, went to a New York bank to get a check cashed recently. The teller looked him over carefully and asked: "Have you any way to identify yourself?"

"Sure!" replied Ben. And he became cross-eyed and did his famous film fall.

"Now do you know me?" he asked.

"No," answered the teller. "But here's your money. You earned it."[156]

1922 February 11: Ben Turpin's comedy company laid off and will not start making pictures for another week. Billy Bevan's company is idle because of the illness of the director, Roy Del Ruth, with influenza.

1922 February 25: Ben busy on his next two-reeler, *The Robin's Nest* (work title of *Step Forward*), having recently finished *Bright Eyes*

Breakfast With Ben Turpin by Bob Dorman for *Pantomime*

"When can we have an interview?" we asked Ben over the phone.

"Come out to breakfast tomorrow morning and have some ham and eggs with me and the wife," said Ben. "Whenever you want me," added Ben, "you can find me on the front steps. I don't go out much except on Sundays. I'm strong for the front steps. It's a life-long habit of mine, sittin' out and watchin' the world go by. You see some funny things from a front door-step and I suppose people goin' by say the same thing when they look at me."

We arrived next morning just as Ben was going to the grocery store. His wife playfully pulled his ear as he marched down the steps of their bungalow.

"If you come back from that grocery store without the eggs, I'll pull your ear again," she said. Ben complains that he has a poor grocery store memory.

"It's a childhood growth," he says. "When I was a boy if they sent me to the store for a gallon of gasoline, I came back with a package of saleratus. Even now I still get all balled up when the grocer says: 'Anything else?' I just can't think on my feet in a grocery store when there's a lot of customers hanging around waiting for me to finish ordering."

Then, as an afterthought, Ben added: "I like a good breakfast. No grabbing off a cup of coffee and a bun for me. I get up good'n early, shave carefully and then sit down with the morning paper and eat leisurely. There were days when the wife and I couldn't afford a maid, but now we have one to serve breakfast. Give me a good grapefruit, ham and eggs and toast and a piping hot cup of coffee, and I start the day right." After breakfast, Ben turned on the phonograph.

"Dance? Sure the wife and I can dance," said Ben. "And don't think we can't do the new steps either. It broke us up pretty bad when the Toddle went out of fashion but we still have the waltz, and a variation of the fox trot to fall back upon. We turn on the phonograph when we want to dance at home. Some evenings I come home tired from the studio and find nothing more relaxing than a good book. But if the wife starts to play the piano when I'm reading I go off in a snore in about five minutes. A wife has to be an accomplished musician to be able to do that.

"I understand the Washington Johnnie has gone out," mused Ben. "Too bad, it was a good step. The wife and I are learning the Camel Walk now. We had just mastered the Tiajuana Jerk when that Frisco Johnnie step came in and we had to drop it. I like the shuffle too, even though it is jerky. But for a real natty step, give me the Palo Hop. With a fox-trot time it's a cuckoo."

Ben has two pets — "Cock-eyed Cecelia," his parrot, and "Cross-eyed Towser," an aged, gray-whiskered little dog given to him by an admirer some years ago. The dog has a slant in his left optical orb with a remarkable resemblance to Ben's moneymaking X-eye. Ben's parrot is never far off. You can believe it or not, but Ben wants the bird with him always. "I'm superstitious," says Ben. "That bird not only can talk, but it has human intelligence. It stays with me just like the warning-bird does on the back of a hippopotamus. The parrot warns me against strangers who may want to take my week's salary away from me — oil-stock sellers and the like. If one of those human birds of prey comes around, Cecelia will flutter her feathers and shriek: 'Get away from me with your stale crackers. Out, you soft-boiled egg. Vamoose, you son of a bum.'"

Clemenceau recently had the unusual privilege of unveiling his own statue — a function which usually takes place thirty to a hundred years after the distinguished one has been slid into a mausoleum niche — but Ben also has not been overlooked by his admirers. A company has recently been formed in Chicago which is putting on the market tens of thousands of Ben Turpin statuettes. They sent one to Ben.

"Best likeness I ever had moulded," says Ben. "Caricature? Ridiculous! It couldn't have been more faithfully cast if I had laid down and had plaster of Paris poured all over me and a death mask made of my face. My wife says it's even better than any photograph I ever had taken."

Ben's hobby is ventriloquism. He has a "stuffed lad," such as the professional ventriloquist uses, and can do some remarkable voice-throwing. If Ben ever left pictures, he could go into vaudeville with that ventriloquist act which he occasionally "pulls" for his friends.

"Yep, I get lots of fan mail," says Ben. "I once got a letter from a girl who said she admired me. I framed it. No others have come in since," he jokes. "However, the kids write me tons of letters. And that's the kind of praise I like. When my 'kid mail' slackens I begin to worry. Right now it's coming in fine. I don't ask theatre-owners, 'How did you like that last picture?' I sit tight and wait for the verdict of the kids."

Ben's best friend is Charlie Chaplin. They go duck hunting together on many weekends. (And here's a tip to those Eastern fan magazines: The favorite weekend sport of Chaplin, Thomas H. Ince, Mack Sennett, and Ben is potting the elusive mallard. No chance of a cameraman following them for a snap, however. The trips are incognito, sub rosa, entrenous. And always to a different rendezvous.)

"Usually on Sundays," says Ben, "the wife and I get into the car and go. I like an open car but the wife prefers a closed vehicle. As you see, we compromised by getting a closed car."

There's nothing "Ritzy" about Ben. When it came time to leave for the studio, he gave his wife a long and tender good-bye kiss despite the presence of the interviewer.

"No husband should leave his wife in the morning without a goodbye kiss," says Ben. "More divorces are caused by not kissing the wife good-bye than anything else. There's an art in it, too. First I kiss the wife. Then I turn my cheek and let the wife kiss me. We get double measure that way, and we both start the day feeling O.K."

They tell this story on Ben: Mack Sennett wanted him to sign a contract giving him more money. Ben said he didn't want a contract. "Don't need a contract," said Ben.

"Just tell the cashier to give me my money every week and that'll do. When people want to break up a partnership, contracts don't amount to much. You want to give me too much money, Mr. Sennett. I wouldn't know what to do with a salary like that. No man can honestly earn so much." That's not a press agent's yarn, either.[157]

Ben Turpin in Action *(1922 March 5)*

In the filming of *Step Forward,* Ben's cross-eyes got him in real trouble. He was rehearsing with a streetcar on a hill grade near Los Angeles. Ben was at the levers. A party of small boys watching the operation was lined up along the tracks. They began calling to Ben and he turned his head and commenced shouting back pleasantries at them. Then the wreck happened, a wreck which was not in the scenario. Ben's streetcar hit an auto, the impact throwing the comedy motorman from the platform to the street. Turpin was laid up for a week with a badly sprained shoulder as a result of the mishap.[158]

Ben Turpin Rides in Trolley to Keep Auto Dry by Constance Palmer *(1922 March 15)*

Ben Turpin was the cause of much excitement one rainy day last week as he entered the gate of the Mack Sennett lot. He was all dressed up in a brand new suit of golf clothes, the outfit including a loud, checkered cap. All he needed to complete the picture was a bag of golf sticks. He had come to the studio via the street car, which no doubt afforded the passengers their daily thrill. When asked why he used street cars on rainy days instead of coming in his big limousine and also why he wore golf clothes in the rain, he replied:

"I never drive my car in the rain. It might get wet. And by wearing knickerbockers today my other pants will be dry for tomorrow."

They tell another story about Ben in the old days at Essanay. He was a prop boy with ambitions to become a director. He told everyone about it so often that it became something of a nuisance. To quiet his importunities, one of the full-fledged directors loudly demanded a white elephant to be used in the picture he was making. The next day, his assistant came on the set without it, there being no such animal. But Ben said: "I'll get it. Just leave it to me." So the director gave him permission to absent himself from the studio all that afternoon. Not a word was heard of him until the morning after, when he proudly led a pure white elephant toward the scene of action. The animal was unnaturally white. Nothing living could have been so white. And it tottered. The company rushed up to examine Ben's find. "But — but — how did it happen?" stammered the director. "White enamel," replied Turpin proudly and leaned against the beast to hold it erect.

Listen to this, though: It's the true story of the way Ben broke into pictures. As I said, he was a prop boy. One day, they were taking a heavy emotional scene on one of the Essanay stages. Ben, ever busy, was fixing one of the props on the set. He didn't know the camera was grinding and no one noticed him. When the film was run off in the projection room, Ben's career as a comedian was started when the first titter ran like a wave over the spectators.

Philadelphia Evening Ledger

Ben Steps Lively (1922 March 26)

During the filming of *Step Forward*, Ben was badly bumped. During the rehearsals, William Beaudine, the director, tried to impress Turpin with the importance of stopping the car at a certain spot so as not to jolt too severely an automobile which, it was intended, should appear stalled on the tracks.

After trying it a few times, orders were given to "shoot" and the car with Turpin at the controls came tearing down the street with the comedian enjoying the thrill as much as the hundreds of onlookers who had gathered to see the movies being taken.

Well — after they had assembled the remains of the automobile and straightened the front platform of the car, Ben looked around, admitted he had had one of the fastest rides in his life, but didn't think the machine was within a block of him when he felt himself taking the air.[159]

Turpin Off (1922 April 16)

Still running true to form, Ben Turpin, cockeyed laugh producer in Mack Sennett Comedies, packed his odd-looking make-up into the crown of his brown derby, soaked it in camphor, said "good-bye, slaves," to his coworkers on the big lot, and with Mrs. Turpin, the other 90 percent of his family, boarded a train for Hot Springs, Arkansas. It has been the habit of Turpin for the past few years to take his vacation in the early months of the year. During his resting period at the Springs, Ben will boil out all the rust he has gathered in the last twelve months and come back full of "pep" and new ideas.[160]

Ben Turpin ss Pantages Headliner (1922 April 16)

Ben Turpin, the "tragic comedian," the guy who can't make his eyes behave, the fount of laughter and the spring of joy, will make his vaudeville debut Monday afternoon at

Pantages. What Ben will do to amuse the vaudeville crowds is a secret locked deep in his own bosom and not yet communicated even to Kathryn McGuire and Phyllis Haver, who will be his right and left bower in the act. It is possible that Ben's act has been discussed with Alexander Pantages, by whom the negotiations for the comedian's appearance were personally conducted, but "Pan," like Ben, knows the value of a secret well kept. So anyone who wants to know what Ben Turpin will do Monday afternoon will therefore be obliged to attend the Pantages matinee. The engagement is for one week only with the remainder of the Pantages circuit in prospect.[161]

Honor Ben Turpin (1922 April 23)

Hot Springs, Arkansas, is planning a "Ben Turpin Day" to celebrate the arrival of Mack Sennett's star comedian.[162]

Ben Turpin Umpires; Beauties Root (1922 May 17)

Irvington, May 16 — A baseball game between amateur teams was held Sunday afternoon in San Jose in which Ben Turpin was ump and the Mack Sennett bathing girls were rooters. The guests commanded more attention than the game when Ben Turpin, at his own solicitation, took up a collection among the fans for the fund to the restoration of the old Mission San Jose.[163]

Success On Stage (1922 June 6)

Surprising the most skeptical, Phyllis Haver, the beautiful and talented comedienne of the Mack Sennett forces, in her first real effort to entertain from the speaking stage, created a decided hit on a little playlet written by Willard Mack for Ben Turpin, Kathryn McGuire, and herself and put on at the Los Angeles theater. Alexander Pantages, head of the string of theaters bearing his name, has appealed to Mack Sennett for permission to book the act over his entire circuit.[164]

Summer Blizzards Created for Ben Turpin (1922 July 18)

Summer blizzards only happen in pictures, but at the same time, it will take an expert on photography to distinguish which of the snow shots were taken in the studio and which were actually taken in the snow country in the northern part of California. F. Richard Jones, directing *Home Made Movies*, the new Turpin picture, is injecting the same minute care and attention into this as he did with his latest feature production, *Suzanna*, starring Mabel Normand. The new picture promises to establish a level for comedy entertainment which will be difficult to surpass.

Turpin Soon to Be Seen in New Comedy Success (1922 July 23)

That theoretical law of average, which, it is claimed, governs the lives of humans and supervises their destinies, is ever attendant on studio folk. Nobody is more thoroughly convinced of this fact, probably, than is Mack Sennett's cross-eyed comedy star, Ben Turpin. Following the completion of *Step Forward*, Turpin took a six weeks' vacation at Hot Springs and, returning, had a further rest of two weeks before Dick Jones, Sennett's producing genius, began in earnest to put Turpin through his roles in *Home Made Movies*. This latest picture was finished on scheduled time and Ben was summoned to the studio to start immediately on another, also under the direction of Jones, who maintains the comedian will have to step lively owing to the fact that three more completed scripts are waiting for him. It will be many months before Ben Turpin will do much idle promenading.

Home Made Movies (re July 15, 1922) review:

A Ben Turpin classic with some good titles and some wonderful bits of slapstick. Turpin in a double part — as the young son and a grey-whiskered old father — will convulse any audience that takes its laughter straight. A cute bear cub, almost submerged in an aquarium and oblivious to everything but the fish, shares honors with the star. Neither of them ever looks at the camera, but for different reasons.

1922 August 20: Billy Bevan will appear without his makeup in future Sennett comedies. That means he's going to discard his soup-straining mustache. If anyone can show where such mustaches add comedy to a character, he or she is entitled to the bronze turkey feather. Snub Pollard and Chester Conklin would do well to emulate Bevan.[165]

1922 August: Ben Turpin and Phyllis Haver, after completing a vaudeville engagement with the Pantages Circuit, are back on the old Sennett lot with F. Richard Jones at the megaphone.[166]

Around the World On the Sennett Lot (1922 September 3)

Ben Turpin and Kathryn McGuire are cavorting amid the shadows of the Pyramids and the Sphinx in a travesty on *The Sheik* entitled *The Shriek*. Dick Jones directing.[167]

Ben Turpin In Person at Pantages Today (1922 September 20)

"The world today needs more laughter. Not only should there be a special Laugh Day once a year, but no day should pass without this greatest of health tonics playing some part in the life of every individual," said Ben Turpin, noted film comedian, who comes to the Pantages today in person with a novel sketch called *Look at Me*, assisted by Kathryn McGuire, beautiful film star.

"Although I don't care for the stage as much as the screen, yet each plays its part in helping make the world happy, and forget its cares. People don't realize what a great part comedy plays in helping keep them young and happy, and the motto 'keep smiling' should be made a part of everyone's life.

"Good comedy is hard to get. At the present time there are countless drama films, but very few comedy films. Sennett perhaps is the greatest exponent of comedy, and is also a hard man to make laugh. When one makes him laugh they know that laugh is a good laugh producer. At the present time the slapstick comedy with slinging of pies, and continual chasing is passing. In fact, Sennett has entirely done away with pie slinging. There is much talk at the present time of the Sennett girls coming back, and they will probably be featured again. 'Situation' comedies are now in demand, with real plot and background to hold interest.

"I congratulate Salt Lake on being one of the first to stage a laugh day. The next time I would suggest what is called a 'horrible parade.' In other words everyone dresses in costume and the day is made a street carnival event. Thousands of laughs can thus be created. I also want to say a good word for your city, for it is the most beautifully laid out city I have ever visited. Your wide streets are wonderful and your traffic well-handled."

Mr. Turpin visited Salt Lake fifteen years ago when on a vaudeville circuit in an acrobatic act. He was born in Louisiana and still speaks with a slightly Southern accent. Out of makeup and when not trying to twist his eyes, which simply won't behave, he looks a typical businessman. Unless one looks very closely, they do not notice that his brown eyes are slightly crossed. His eyes, like Anna Held's, have been his fortune and certainly have caused thousands of laughs. The noted comedian is married and laughingly said "has been true to the same woman for fifteen years." He likes his home in Hollywood and was loud in voicing disapproval of the terrible things said of the movie district. He declared many extras, or those representing themselves to be movie stars, who went to parties were greatly responsible for the terrible propaganda against California's moviedom. The Turpin act is only making a few of the many Pantages houses, going from here to Omaha, Kansas City, Minneapolis, and back to Chicago and the trip is only being made between pictures.[168]

Ben Turpin Will Entertain at State Penitentiary Today *(1922 September 24)*

As the inmates of the State State Penitentiary (Salt Lake City) cannot come to see Ben Turpin, that noted film star, who is playing at the Pantages, has graciously consented to go to see them. Today, Mr. Turpin will stage a special entertainment at noon, which will be given under the direction of Warden J.J. Devine. The talented comedian is a great favorite everywhere he goes and his screen plays have especially brought joy to those whom he will visit today. They were very anxious to see Mr. Turpin in person and through the courtesy of Manager Eddie Diamond of the local playhouse and Miss Kaye, this was made possible.

Ben Turpin On the Radio
Comedian to Speak to WDAF Audience Tomorrow Night *(1922 October 8)*

Ben Turpin, comical man of the movies, will speak over the radio to the audience of WDAF tomorrow night. Ben and his wife arrived yesterday for a week's engagement at Pantages Theater and he will make his radio debut from The Star's studio. Those who are familiar with the ingrown mustache, the terrified cross-eyed expressions, the nervous twitching of the lower jaw characteristic of Turpin, the comedian, might be disappointed in Ben. He really is not hard to survey. He is smooth shaven, has heavy gray hair, is tanned to an almost amber shade, dresses rather fastidiously, and if it wasn't for his eyes — you wouldn't know it was Turpin.

Ben will be one of the many features on a program crowded with variety. Leo's orchestra, an exceptional dance orchestra, will play popular selections. Several soloists will sing ballads and hit numbers; there will be a message from Roger Babson, statistical expert, and a talk on Fire Prevention.

Turpin Convalescing Following Operation *(1922 November 21)*

(Special to Exhibitors Herald) Los Angeles — Unbeknown to the motion picture colony, Ben Turpin, the famous cross-eyed comedian, underwent a serious operation at California Lutheran Hospital last week and is now slowly but surely recuperating at his home in Hollywood. Although in a serious condition for two days, according to report, he will

soon again resume the roles that have won him a prominent place in the motion picture firmament. The nature of the comedian's illness could not be ascertained at this time.[169]

Ben in Hospital (1922 December 3)

No, no, no. It isn't anything at all. Nothing to worry about. Just a minor, though necessary, operation. It won't even interfere with his work. Ben Turpin, taking advantage of the time afforded before starting on another Mack Sennett comedy, has conscripted a good-looking nurse and a private room in the California Hospital. Though he won't be doing his well-known "one hundred and eights" and other twists and flops, Ben will exercise his orbs by gazing at the floral offerings sent by sympathetic friends.[170]

The young, later movie director and Chaplin associate Robert Florey came from his native France in 1922 and Ben Turpin was one of his first interviews. Conducted during the filming of *Home Made Movies*, the interview was later abbreviated in Florey's book of stars, *Movieland*, in 1927. When Florey asked about Charles Chaplin, Turpin told his interviewer that he at first thought Chaplin was taking the work much too seriously and Ben didn't quite understand why, Turpin's experience being in those fast-paced slapstick and typically physical comedies at Essanay. By that time, in 1915 and having just finished a year with Mack Sennett's Keystone, Chaplin had something different in mind. Charlie was now producer, director, writer, with his name and reputation on the line and a lot more on his shoulders at $1,250 a week. Charlie surely didn't want to spoil any success he'd worked so hard for over the past twelve months with Sennett and here now was his opportunity to do even better at Essanay. Turpin learned a lot from Chaplin and always gave him credit over the years. Florey was an interviewer who, like many fans, overly enjoyed Chaplin and may have asked Ben too many questions about Charlie during that interview; hence, Ben's irritated responses. Florey even went as far as describing Turpin as a "foul-mouthed vulgarian."

Paraphrasing from Robert Florey's published French interview with Ben:

"Charlie was a likable fellow," Ben told Florey, "but, at first I didn't understand him too well. He didn't do things the way the others (at Essanay) did and was so demanding in his direction on the films we did together that it often drove me crazy.

"Charlie would say to me, 'Do this, don't do that, look here, walk like that, start again…'

"I didn't know then that we were creating art. I knew we weren't opera singers, but since Charlie appeared to know what he was doing, I stopped complaining and got to work.

"Until then, no one ever asked me to make faces and exploit my affliction so I contented myself in making the people laugh, and until then, I always made the crowds laugh without the eyes." In ending, Ben told Florey, "I have since proved that I could work without him and am now a star with Sennett and my films make lots of money.

"But I've often found Charlie to be a bit of a snob…"

Movieland by Robert Florey, 1927

Intermission

Young Ben Turpin soon after arriving in New York, c1877.

Ben posing for a Chicago photographer, c1887.

Prancing in Cincinnati, c1895.
COURTESY OF BRANDT ROWLES

Ben in make-up as Happy Hooligan.

Turpin as Happy Hooligan *with an unidentified player.*
COURTESY OF SAM GILL

Ben and fellow handymen at Essanay.
COURTESY OF SAM GILL

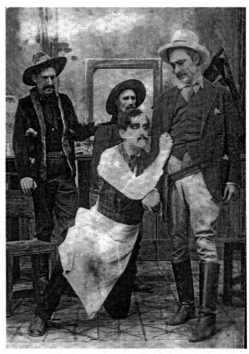

Ben and players in an early Essanay production, possibly The Younger Brothers, *1908.*

Turpin and Essanay associates reach California, December 1908, with unidentified female, Ben, Jess Robbins, and G. M. Anderson. COURTESY OF SAM GILL

Turpin in a rare starrer for American as a tramp who goes from rags to riches and back again in The Hidden Treasure, *1912.* COURTESY OF SAM GILL

Turpin in frequent tramp make-up. COURTESY OF SAM GILL

Essanay's and George Ade's Fable of the Brash Drummer and the Nectarine, *with Turpin, Wallace Beery, Leo White, and others, 1914.* COURTESY THE MUSEUM OF MODERN ART

Wallace Beery, 1914.

Wallace Beery in drag pushing her affection to Ben in one of the many Sweedie comedies for Essanay, 1914. COURTESY OF SAM GILL

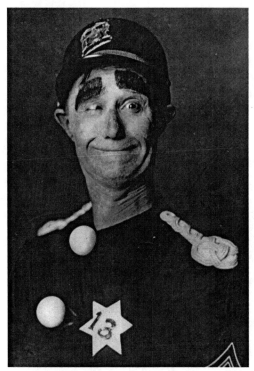

In uniform as Essanay's chief of police, 1914.

Ben and Carrie Turpin, Harry Todd, Victor Potel, Others Started But Sophie Finished, *1915.* COURTESY THE MUSEUM OF MODERN ART

Taking charge of his inept police patrol.

Patroling the waters of Lake Michigan. COURTESY OF SAM GILL

Ben Turpin, Essanay comedian, is mourning the loss of his pet mule, which has taken part in so many Essanay comedies. The animal finally became too old to take his parts well so had to be put in the "has-been" class. Retired to a farm on a pension, Turpin visits the animal every Sunday.[64] COURTESY OF SAM GILL

Ben meets Charlie Chaplin, His New Job, *1915.*

Ben and Charlie deserving A Night Out, *1915, much to Leo White's annoyance.*

Once owner of one of the largest autograph collections, Ben proudly shows his signed photo from friend Chaplin, in 1921.

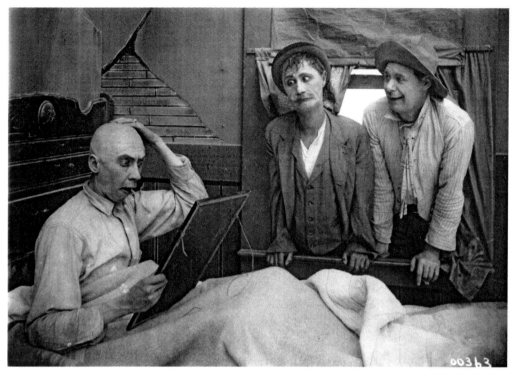

Victor Potel, Ben, and Harry Todd in Snakeville's Twins, *1915.*
COURTESY THE MUSEUM OF MODERN ART

Carrie Turpin, Ben, and Harry Todd in Snakeville's Hen Medic, *1915.*
COURTESY THE MUSEUM OF MODERN ART

G. M. Anderson, Victor Potel, Ben and others in The Convict's Threat, *1915.*

Turpin, Harry Todd and Victor Potel, The Wooing of Sophie, *1915.*

Unidentified Essanay comedy, Ben with Eva McKenzie and unknown player.

Snakeville's Champion, 1915, with Turpin, Lloyd Bacon, Harry Todd, Bob McKenzie, and others.

Final days at Essanay. Ben, Leo White and others break after a messy scene, early 1916.
COURTESY OF SAM GILL

A Waiting Game, *first released nearly a year after Ben left Essanay, December 6, 1916.*

Ben with co-star Rena Rogers on the cover of
Reel Life, *June 1916.*

Ben's first comedy for Vogue, National Nuts, *with Arthur Moon and Rena Rogers, 1916.*
COURTESY OF SAM GILL

Turpin cutting up with Paddy McQuire, 1916.

Ben and Paddy, Hired and Fired, *1916.*

Break between filming on one of the early Vogue's. Director Jack Dillon, Rena Rogers, Turpin, and Paddy McQuire on floor at center surrounded by cast and crew.
COURTESY OF BOB BIRCHARD

Carrying on out west in He Died and He Didn't, *1916.*

Rube Miller, writer, director, star and co-star.

Ben's 1916 fan photo later inscribed to friend, Clarence Hennecke.

Lillian Hamilton, Ben, and Rube Miller, Some Liars, *1916.*

The Musical Marvel, *with Arthur Moon, Gypsy Abbott, and Margaret Templeton 1917.*

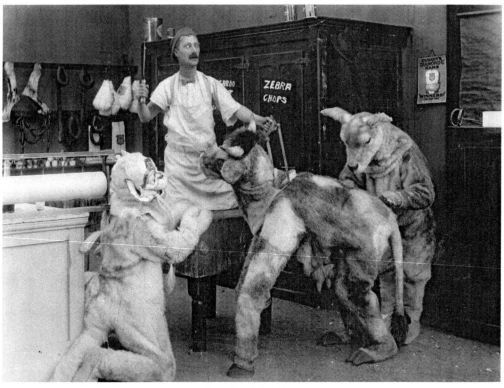

Haunted by the meat in his shop, The Butcher's Nightmare, *1917.*

Swarmed by lovelies and being attacked by a bearskin rug in His Bogus Boast, *1917.*

A Studio Stampede, *1917, re-released in 1921 as* Out of Control.

Leading his fellow Vogue players in song, Arthur Tavares, Harry Huckins, Owen Evans and Paddy McQuire. COURTESY OF SAM GILL

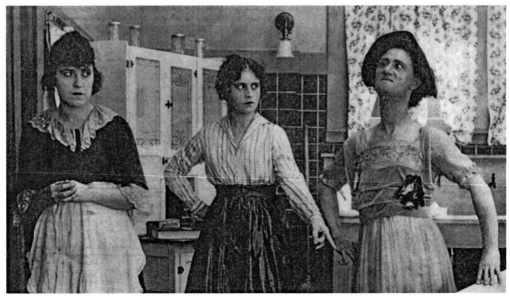

Why Ben Bolted, *1917, with Margaret Templeton, Gypsy Abbott, and Ben in drag.*

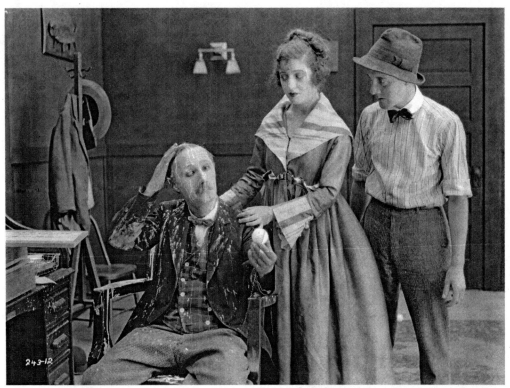

Ben's last for Vogue, Caught in the End, *1917, with Lillian Hamilton and unidentified actor.*

Vogue cast and crew pose for a last photo with Ben following scenes for Caught in the End.

Behind the scenes, Mack Sennett watches director Fred Fishback put Teddy through his paces. In the background, Phyllis Haver, Charlie Murray, and Turpin, 1917.

One of Turpin's first for Keystone, Sole Mates, *with Vivian Edwards and Alfred Gronnell.*

With pretty Mary Thurman in Sennett's first release for Paramount, 1917.

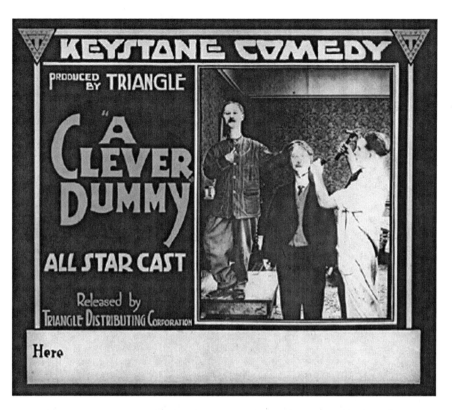

Polly Moran was just Roping Her Romeo; *either Ben or Slim Summerville will do.*

Slim Summerville trying to break up Ben and Louise Fazenda, Are Waitresses Safe?

Ben's newest fan photo, 1918.

Reunited with Polly Moran to capture Billy Armstrong, Sheriff Nell's Tussle, *1918.*

Cast and crew of Saucy Madeline, *seated left to right, Jack Cooper, Frank J. Coleman, Polly Moran, F. Richard Jones, Phyllis Haver, Charles Lynn, Gonda Durand, Turpin. Standing: Sloppy Gray, cameraman J. R. Lockwood, three unknown men, Gary Odell.*

Ben with a copy of the Sennett Weekly, circa January 1918. COURTESY OF SAM GILL

Polly Moran and Charles Lynn take pity on homeless Ben in The Battle Royal, *1918.*

Main cast and crew run thru scenes of Love Loops the Loop. *Left to right, Erle Kenton, Lloyd Campbell (director's assistant), Hampton Del Ruth, Walter Wright (standing), Judge Boyer (taking notes), John Grey (assistant editor), Wayland Trask, Mary Thurman, Ben, Charlie Murray, Laura LaVarnie, Harry Booker, and Teddy the dog, 1918.*

The Sennett comics doing their bit for the war effort in 1918, It's A Cinch. *Foreground, Tom Kennedy, Ford Sterling, Louise Fazenda, Chester Conklin; on stage, Mal St. Clair, Dave Anderson, Phyllis Haver. Ben and Charlie Lynn, far right.*

Charlie Lynn, Ben and Marie Prevost on the beach in She Loved Him Plenty, *1918.*

Ben and Carrie dressed to impress outside the Sennett Studio, c1918.
COURTESY BOB BIRCHARD

Ben and Charlie as Sleuths!, *nab Tom Kennedy with the help of Marie Prevost.*

Phil Whitman, Tom Kennedy, Ben, Charlie Lynn, director Eddie Cline and Marie Prevost enjoy a break between scenes of Hide and Seek, Detectives.

Hide and Seek, Detectives, *Ben, Marie Prevost, and Charlie Lynn.*

Ben and Charlie Lynn, soon back to his Charles Heine *Conklin moniker.*

Cupid's Day Off, *Charlie Lynn, Alice Lake, and Ben.*

Posing for a fan on a Los Angeles street, 1919.

Between filming, always time for a dance.

Ben and Charlie bring additional laughs to the Chester Conklin and Louise Fazenda short,
The Foolish Age, *along with Phyllis Haver, Kalla Pasha and James Finlayson.*

Turpin says his prayers in When Love is Blind, *with Marie Prevost and Charlie Lynn.*

In No Mother to Guide Him, *Fanny Kelly and Isabelle Keep watch Ben struggle with a block of ice, 1919.*

Menacing Kalla Pasha takes hold of Frank Hayes as Ben and Charlie Lynn prepare to take off in Yankee Doodle in Berlin.

Turpin pops up as an eccentric patient in the office of The Dentist. *Dr. Charlie Murray and Marie Prevost watch as two guards prepare to take Ben back to the nut house.*

Uncle Tom Without the Cabin, *1919, Ben, Marie Prevost, and Charlie Heine Conklin.*

Charlie Conklin, Charlie Murray and Ben during a personal appearance at Grauman's to promote Salome vs. Shenandoah, September 1919

Turpin on the cover of Film Fun *magazine, March 1920.*

The Star Boarder *with Bert Roach, Turpin, and Harriet Hammond, 1920.*

Between filming of Down on the Farm, *Ben, Kalla Pasha, Eddie Gribbon, Kathryn McGuire and the Sennett girls chase ducks, 1920.*

Jimmy Finlayson, Charlie Conklin, Phyllis Haver, and Ben in Married Life, *1920.*

Turpin portrait from his first starring feature, Married Life, *1920.*

Ben's success in Sennett comedies brought out many of his earlier films, the Vogue and Essanay shorts, including one never before released, The Close Shave.

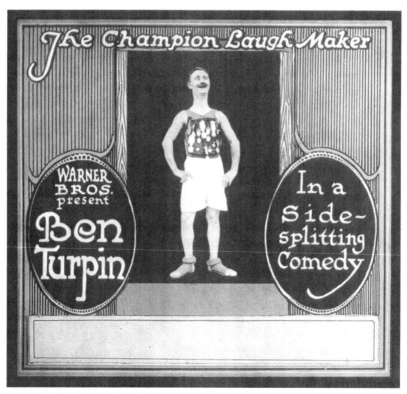

The Warner Brothers even invested in the Turpin re-releases.

Shelved for nearly a year before being released in May 1921, She Sighed by the Seaside *with Charlie Conklin, Jim Finlayson, Ben, and Marie Prevost.*

Ben and Marie Prevost in his next big feature, A Small Town Idol, *1921.*

Signs of fame with the sale of thousands of Ben Turpin statuettes.

Presenting his "stuffed lad" and sharing a favorite hobby, ventriloquism.

Ben and Carrie cooking up something for you.

The Turpins at home, dancing to the latest hits.

Cock-eyed Cecilia, Ben's pet parrot. COURTESY THE MUSEUM OF MODERN ART

Sitting on his front step watching the world pass by.

Turpin in the funnies, fame in the popular English comic book Film Fun.

Home Talent *with Jimmy Finlayson, Eddie Gribbon, Turpin, and Kalla Pasha.*

With old Essanay friend, Bryant Washburn.

In Chicago for the first time in six years.

Turpin on tour, Ben gets a smooch from wife Carrie in New York City.

Ben returns to Boston.

Loves Outcast, *Jimmy Finlayson, Kathryn McGuire, Jack Richardson, Ben, Bud Ross, and John Rand.*

Ben and Phyllis Haver in Love and Doughnuts, *1921.*

Ben and Towser, his cross-eyed dog and best friend.

Bright Eyes, *released December 21, 1921.*

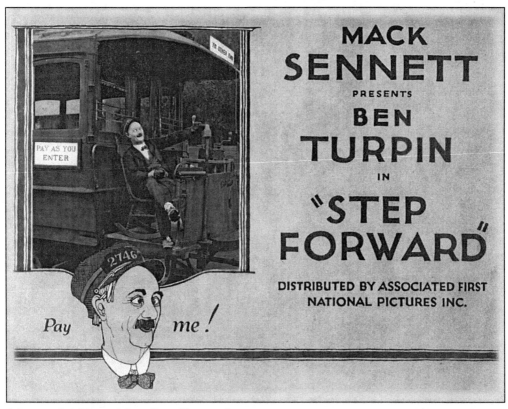

Movie title lobbycard from Step Forward, *1922.*

Keeping up with his fan mail in 1922.

Title lobbycard, Home Made Movies, *Turpin and Phyllis Haver, 1922.*

Ben welcomes Mabel Normand back home to Hollywood, September 1922.

Clowning in the Sennett cafeteria with F. Richard Jones.

Ben's Christmas greeting for 1922.

A Christmas Day appearance at Lincoln Park, Los Angeles, 1922.

Entertaining guests during production of The Shriek of Araby.

Kathryn McGuire finds it hard to resist Ben as The Shriek of Araby, *1923*.

How movies are made in Paramount's Hollywood, *with Kalla Pasha, James Finlayson, unknown, Hope Drown, Ford Sterling and Ben, 1923.*

Where's My Wandering Boy This Evening? *Looks like Jim Finlayson and Billy Armstrong found him in the company of that Pathe Vamp, Madeline Hurlock.*

Ben and his new leading lady, Madeline Hurlock, 1923.

Ben tries drinking himself to death during Pitfalls of a Big City, *1923.*

Ben and Cecile Evans in a game of checkers, Cameo, the Wonder Dog, *to play the winner. Kewpie Morgan, Billy Armstrong, Bud Ross and Madeline Hurlock in attendance before Ben falls* Asleep at the Switch, *1923.*

Ben as The Dare-Devil *with Kewpie Morgan, Harry Gribbon, Gordon Lewis, 1923.*

Pouring a cold one for Bud Ross in Ten Dollars or Ten Days, *1924.*

Ben on the street directing traffic for friend Officer Schultz during the Christmas holiday, 1923, at Western and Santa Monica.

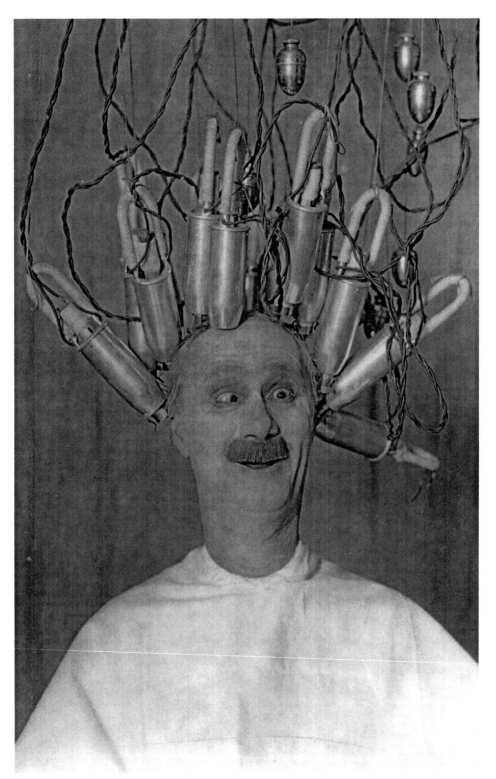

According to the caption on back, Turpin may have tried curling his hair but never thought of straightening his eyes.

Cast and crew in Lake Tahoe filming Yukon Jake, *1924. Kalla Pasha, Natalie Kingston, Turpin, Jack Richardson, director Del Lord and camera crew.*

Another love triangle, Ben, Alice Day and Vernon Dent, Romeo and Juliet, 1924.

Showing off his Mexican roots in this 1924 publicity pose.

Three Foolish Weeks, *1924.*

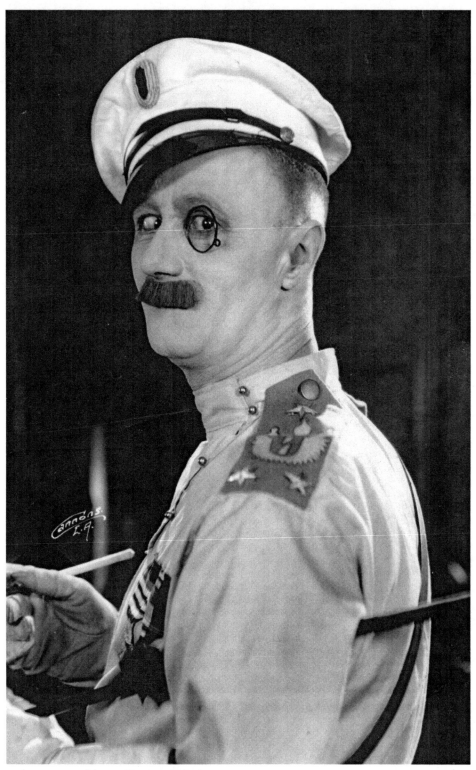

In full regalia, Three Foolish Weeks.

For publicity's sake, Ben with his cross-eyed 1925 Chandler.

The Reel Virginian, *1924, back with Alice Day.*

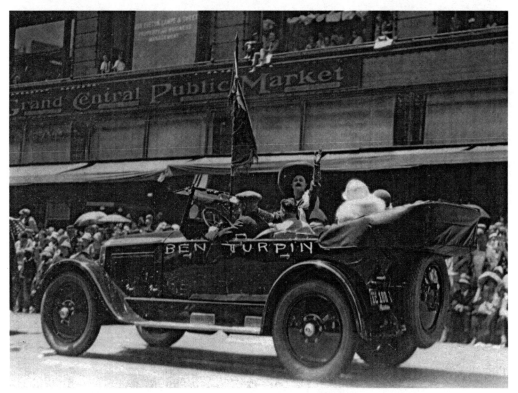

Ben in The Reel Virginian *garb for the fans during a Hollywood parade, 1924.*

Publicizing the next series of Turpin two-reel Pathecomedies, 1924.

Harry Langdon, Mack Sennett's new comedy ace.

The Turpins new home at 601 North Canon Drive, Beverly Hills, August 1924.

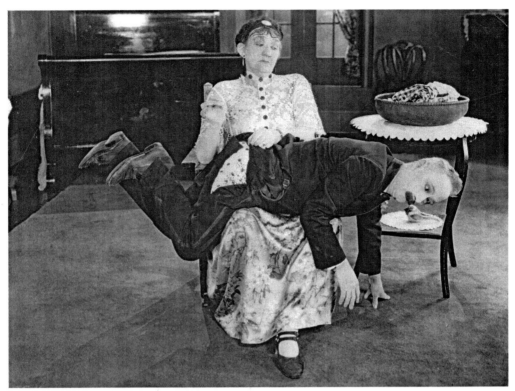

Begun in late 1924, Louise Carver helps sew up her boy's pants in The Marriage Circus, *released April 1925.*

A deleted scene with Blanche Payson from Ben's next production, A Raspberry Romance, *March 1925.*

Ben as The Wild Goose Chaser, *his last production before retiring.*

Carrie LeMieux Turpin in one of her last known photos.

Released as soon as it was completed, The Wild Goose Chaser, *January 1925.*

Lobbycard scene for one of Turpin's freelance appearances, Hogan's Alley, *1925.*

Babette Elizabeth Dietz, the third Mrs. Ben Turpin.

Ben and Babette, newlyweds, July 1926.

Closest family members surround the newlyweds, including sister Ernestine in striped dress.

Formal wedding portrait of Ben and Babette.

Ben Turpin, funny man of the films and his new bride, "a radiantly happy pair," as they arrived at San Francisco, July 9, 1926, where they would spend their honeymoon.

Mack Sennett

presents **Ben Turpin** *in*

"WHEN A MAN'S
A PRINCE"

Back again, cross eyes
and all, and funnier
than ever!

Pathécomedy
TRADE MARK

Announcement of Ben Turpin's return to Mack Sennett, 1926.

With George Gray and Bud Ross, When A Man's A Prince.

The Prodigal Bridegroom *better let go of Madeline Hurlock and start explaining to her folks,*
Vernon Dent and Patsy O'Byrne.

PG 265-6

MACK SENNETT
presents
BEN TURPIN
COMEDIES
Two Reels

Back to the screen after an absence due to illness!

Turpin has been missed. Movie-goers everywhere have been wondering "Where are those wandering eyes tonight?"

Folks used to think cross-eyes a misfortune. Turpin found them his fortune, for his erratic optics have trademarked him all over the world.

The youngsters in particular will hail these new Turpins with howls of joy.

Pathécomedy

Another ad trumpeting Ben's return to Sennett.

Not exactly the princess the Rajah was looking for in A Harem Knight. *With Louise Carver, Dave Morris, and Marvin Lobach.*

"Billy Gilbert", *Vernon Dent, Barbara Tennant and Ben in* A Blonde's Revenge, *1926.*

A Hollywood Hero unknowingly gets a little too friendly with Alma Bennett, wife of jealous Bud Jamison.

TRY OUR

ROMEO
NUT SUNDAE

A flashback to happier times before he was Broke in China, *with Ruth Taylor.*

Ben likes something about Thelma Hill that Andy Clyde doesn't appreciate in The Pride of Pikeville.

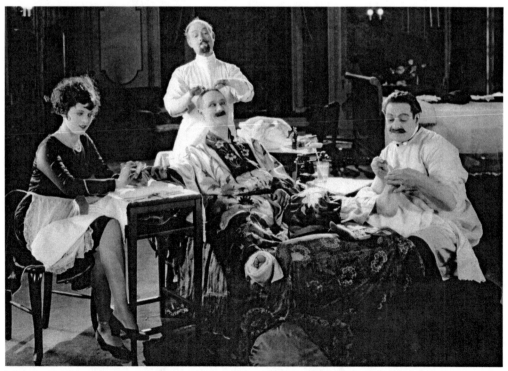

The Jolly Jilter *surrounded by his servants Lois Boyd, Bud Ross and Leo Sulky.*

MACK SENNETT

PRESENTS

Ben Turpin

The man with the in-growing eyes and hair-brush moustache in two laughter Specials.

As soon as his name appears in the headtitles on the screen people start to laugh, in anticipation. That means box office.

Sennett and Turpin, a great team for laughter and business getting.

Love Me and the World is Mine

Pathécomedy

DE MILLE PICTURES PATHÉ PICTURES PATHÉ NEWS PATHÉSERIALS

Sennett's ad for his last two Ben Turpin comedies, 1927.

Ben tells pretty Peggy Montgomery her face should be emblazoned on that can of peaches, from Love's Languid Lure.

Turpin's last two-reeler for Sennett, Daddyboy, *shown with Alma Bennett, 1927.*

Showing his support for 3-D photography.

Ben and unknown players in one of a few 3-D things he did for American Mutoscope.

A number of Hollywood stars gather for their trip to Atlantic City, summer of 1927.

Ben's nephew Julian Knies (aka Tommy Turpin), right, in a scene from an unknown comedy of the late 1920's. COURTESY OF RICHARD KNIES

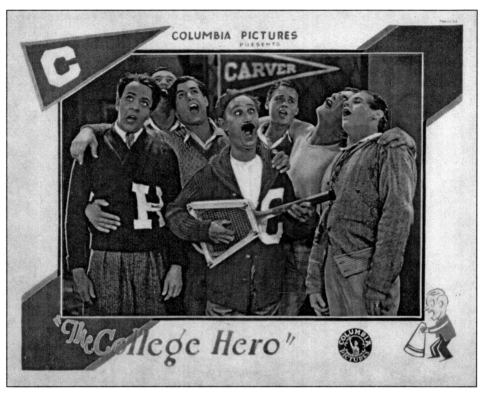

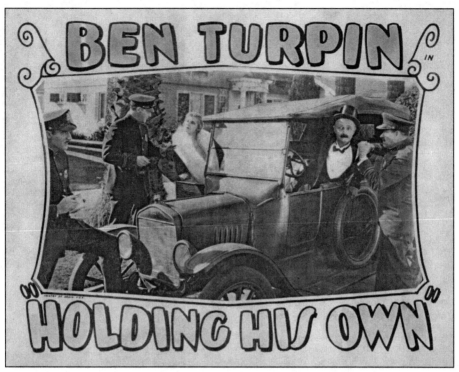

Lobbycard scene from one of Turpin's shorts for Weiss Brothers–Artclass.

Scene from Weiss Bros. A Cock-Eyed Hero *with Josephine Borio and some bad guys.*

Idle Eyes with Josephine Borio, Alice Belcher, Ben, Leo White and girls.

Clowning as a nurse for one of the Weiss Brothers shorts.

Enjoying a break during the filming of one of the last Weiss Brothers comedies.

Weiss Bros. Taking the Count *with Addie McPhail, soon Mrs. Roscoe Fatty Arbuckle.*

With popular comics of the silent era, Charles Conklin, Lupino Lane, Lee Moran, Bert Roach and Lloyd Hamilton in the Warner Brothers sound feature, Show of Shows, *1929.*

Major players in the Pathé feature Swing High, including Daphne Pollard, John Sheehan, Joe Lagnan, Little Billy, Bryant Washburn, Fred Scott, Harvey Leavit, Charles Richards, Chester Conklin, Stepin Fetchit, Ray McCarty, David Abel, Turpin, Nick Stuart, Sally Starr, Dorothy Burgess, Helen Twelvetrees, Joseph Santley, James Seymour, Eleanor Donahue.

Ben once again over the airwaves at Los Angeles station KHJ with Dorothy Burgess to promote Swing High, *1930.*

Bombardier Ben getting instructions from his commander Stanley Fields in Cracked Nuts, *1931.*

Working with two of his favorite film comedians, Stan Laurel and Oliver Hardy in Our Wife, *with Babe London and Blanche Payson, 1931.*

With Will Rogers in Ambassador Bill, *1931.*

Make Me A Star *with Ben, Joan Blondell, Stuart Erwin and Sam Hardy, 1932.*

W. C. Fields and Jack Oakie poke fun at Ben between scenes of Million Dollar Legs, *1932.*

Ben gets lost at Chicago's City Hall after calling on Mayor Murphy. He stops to ask James S. Stockwell for directions to Canada to get cock-eyed, November 1932.

Three Stars of Hundreds of Funny Films — Snub Pollard, Walter Hiers, and Ben Turpin, the three famous Hollywood Comedians, who appeared in person in Fanchon and Marco's comedy stage revue, 1932.

Ben's fan photo, distributed during the Fanchon and Marco tour.

Enjoying a break between shows.

Ben with Ruby Adams celebrate the opening of his San Francisco nightspot, May 1933.

Silent film veterans gather to help the premiere of J. Stuart Blackton's documentary, The Film Parade. *Lionel Belmore, Maurice Costello, Paul Panzer and wife, Bryant Washburn, Anita Stewart, J. Stuart Blackton, his wife and their daughter; seated Florence Turner, Kate Price, Bud Duncan, Mary Anderson, Flora Finch, and Ben, October 1933.*

With George Breakston and Vicki Joyce during a Christmas benefit, Shrine Auditorium, Los Angeles, December 18, 1933.

Some members of the Moulin Rouge Caravan, *Creighton Hale, Turpin, Nancy Welford, Jack Mulhall, Dorothy Dunbar, Tony Moreno, Anna Q. Nilsson, Roscoe Ates, and Mary Carlisle, 1934.*

From the Mascot serial, The Law of the Wild, *1934.*

A couple clowns pose with Ben when the circus came to Los Angeles, October 1934.

Ben takes aim at apple-headed Junior Coughan in The Little Big Top, *1935.*

Clowning with old friends Marie Prevost, Ford Sterling and Hank Mann between scenes of Keystone Hotel, *1935.*

Actor Warren William makes a surprise visit to the Keystone Hotel *set.*

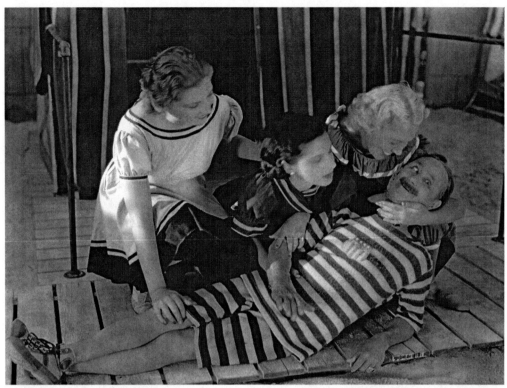

Lifeguards get all the girls, Ben got the Tic-Toc Girls, in Starlit Days at the Lido, *1935.*

Hollywood Stars On Parade, Leo White, Turpin, Mildred Harris Chaplin, Rex Lease, Clara Kimball Young and Franklin Farnum, October 1935.

Ben's giveaway photo during the Hollywood Stars On Parade tour.

Ben and Lee Tracy in Cinema Circus, *released January 1937.*

Actress Joan Woodbury and Ben at a Hollywood circus in September 1937.

Reunited once again with Chester Conklin for Hollywood Cavalcade, *1939.*

With Oliver Hardy in Ben's last film, Saps at Sea, *1940.*

Ben and Babette in one of their last photos together, 1940.

One of the last poses of Ben Turpin, 1940.

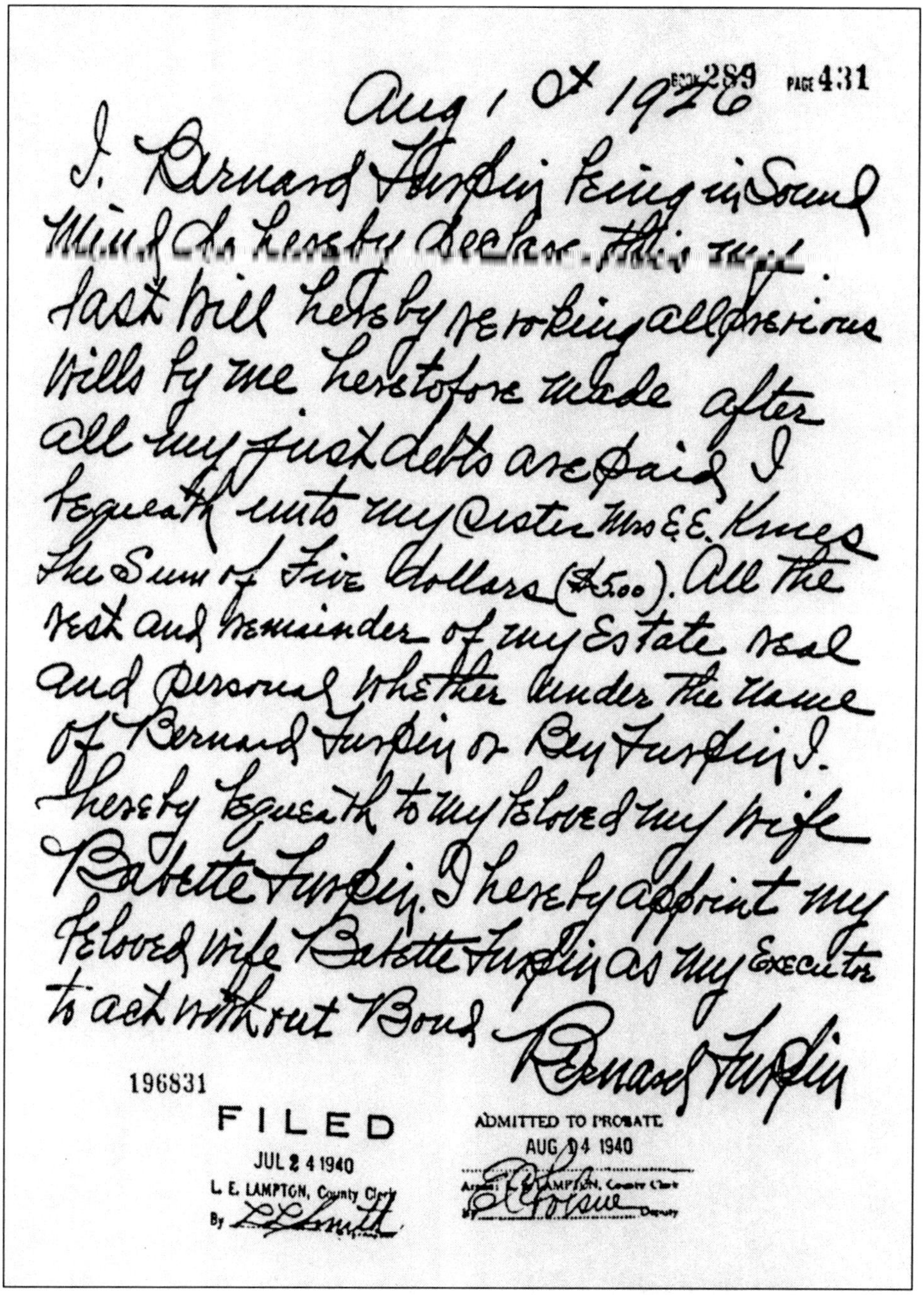

Aug 1 st 1926 BOOK 289 PAGE 431

I, Bernard Turpin being in Sound Mind do hereby declare this my last will hereby revoking all previous wills by me heretofore made. After all my just debts are paid I bequeath unto my Sister Mrs E.E. Kings the Sum of Five dollars ($5.00). All the rest and remainder of my Estate real and personal whether under the name of Bernard Turpin or Ray Turpin I hereby bequeath to my beloved my wife Babette Turpin. I hereby appoint my beloved wife Babette Turpin as my Executor to act without Bond.

Bernard Turpin

196831

FILED

JUL 2 4 1940

L. E. LAMPTON, County Clerk

By _____

ADMITTED TO PROBATE

AUG 04 1940

L. E. LAMPTON, County Clerk

By _____ Deputy

Turpin's disputed will of 1926.

Ben and Babette at home, circa 1926.

An almost unrecognizable pose of Ben's widow showing off her new nose and more in 1941.

Babette Turpin at age 90 in 1970.

A last hurrah, Ben makes the cover of Life *magazine September 5, 1949.*

57-89

Ben Turpin

The Shriek of Hollywood

"As for me on the screen, I'm just a goof. Everything I do is wrong, all wrong. That's why people laugh. I don't look right. I don't do right. I try to carve a roast and the dog gets most of it. I wear the wrong kind of tie, and it comes off in the peas. I try to propose to my best girl, and I say the wrong things. It isn't only comic looks that make a comedian. He's got to act comic too!"[3]

Ben Turpin, 1924

Following the completion of his last five-reel feature for Sennett, which began in May 1922, *The Shriek of Araby* — and met with mixed reviews (some suggesting the film would have been better as a two-reeler) — Turpin signs a new Sennett contract on February 19, 1923, for 42 weeks employment with the Pathé organization. The contract stipulated that Ben would not appear in more than nine photoplays during his employment with Turpin agreeing to $2,000 weekly for the first 26 weeks; $1250 the next five weeks; $750 the next two weeks; and $1500 the last nine weeks. Things were looking even brighter.

To Start Producing Campaign (1923 February 27, in part)
United Artists to Distribute Feature Productions from Sennett Studio

Following a short lull in production activities, during which time he reorganized the various departments in his comedy organization, adding several new writers to the scenario staff, engaged new directors, and re-signed some of the popular players who were identified with earlier pictures, Mack Sennett is again away to a flying start.

Through arrangements effected during a recent trip to New York, Sennett will release his feature productions through the medium of the United Artists' Corporation. Early announcement regarding the channel through which all two-reel comedies will be distributed hereafter is promised. The production campaign now underway will be a means of introducing many new personalities in Sennett pictures while at the same time not a few of the older favorites will be seen with a Sennett make-up on.

Ben Turpin, scrambled-visioned comedy star, will begin in a few days with the production of, what is claimed, one of the funniest stories ever written for him and surrounded by an all-star cast under the direction of Roy Del Ruth.[171]

Pathé Will Distribute Comic Film (1923 March 14)
Two-Year Contract Signed with Sennett, Producer of Screen Comedies

New York — E.M. Asher, personal representative in New York of Mack Sennett, producer of film comedies, tonight gave to the Los Angeles Times exclusive announcement of a two-year contract entered into today by the Sennett interests with Pathé for the distribution in the future of all Sennett and Ben Turpin comedies through the medium of Pathé.

The contract involves $2,500,000 and was closed here by Asher, representing Mack Sennett, and Elmer Pearson, on behalf of Pathé, after two months' negotiations. The Mack Sennett output represents twenty-one pictures a year — thirteen all-star Sennett comedies and eight Ben Turpin specials.

"The deal," Asher declared, "is the biggest of the kind on short subjects. It is a singular transaction, too, in that it is the first time distribution of Sennett comedies has been arranged for where they belong. Pathé is confining itself to short-subject distribution. Our experience has been that the big distributing concerns handling feature releases cannot at the same time satisfactorily distribute short-subject films.

"The contract Mr. Pearson and I just have signed for our respective concerns calls for the handling of all of Mr. Sennett's comedy pictures by Pathé for the next two years. The arrangement is, I am sure, a source of considerable gratification not only to our interests but also to Pathé." Formal announcement of the deal is to be made at Sennett offices, Los Angeles, tomorrow.[172]

Pathé Signs For Comedies — Exchange to Handle New Sennett Releases — Production Program Now in Full Swing (in part)

After weeks of conferences and negotiations, Mack Sennett has closed contracts with the Pathé Exchange, Inc., for the release of his two-reel All-Star and Ben Turpin comedies, placing at the disposal of the exhibitor a program of 13 two-reel comedies with specially selected casts and from six to eight Ben Turpin two-reel comedies.

With production of these comedies now in full swing at the Sennett studios and with several of them practically finished and waiting for the cutting room, the first Ben Turpin comedy to be released by Pathé will be *Where's My Wandering Boy This Evening?*, which is said to be yet another typically Sennettian burlesque.

Lavish Sets

The new contract with Pathé calls for the investment of greater production sums than Sennett has ever before had at his disposal. It is the intention of the comedy producer to invest the new pictures with more lavish settings and to concentrate on more distinctive production values and novelty innovations. Another departure in the program is the change from the old grotesque and over-exaggerated make-up to the true-to-life characteristics.

With this wide array of releases added to the Pathé exchanges, Elmer Pearson, general manager, following signing of contracts with Mack Sennett, stated that with the strength of the Sennett organization, these comedies are being produced with the object in mind that each and every one of them is to be an outstanding feature of each program on which they will appear.

Everyone Busy

Under the supervision of F. Richard Jones, who has recently assumed the duties of supervising director of all Mack Sennett productions, a corps of directors, technicians, cameramen, actors, and actresses have been working both night and day to turn out more releases. This means continued working on everyone's part. Reggie Morris, Chet Wallace, Roy Del Ruth, Mel Brown, William A. Seiter are on the directorial staffs, while a corps of technicians is building sets under Stanford D. Barnes. Herman Raymaker was contacted to direct Turpin's second comedy, but was too busy elsewhere. Director Erle Kenton, after a three-year absence, was brought back to direct Turpin in October.

The list of actors and actresses engaged for the various comedies included Ben Turpin, Billy Bevan, Harry Gribbon, Dot Farley, Kewpie Morgan, Eugenia Gilbert, Lila Leslie, Jimmy Finlayson, Billy Fay, Charlotte Mineau, Pricilla Bonner, Madeline Hurlock, Alberta Vaughn, and Billy Armstrong, while among the juveniles who figure prominently are Jack William Lucas, Josephine Adair, and Edwin Hubbell. John A. Waldron, general manager of the Sennett organization, stated yesterday that production will go on unceasingly and that new facilities are being built and added to the studio each day.[173]

Madeline Hurlock, making her Sennett debut in *Where's My Wandering Boy This Evening?*, was born to English-Italian parents on December 17, 1899, in Federalsburg, Maryland, a small town on the Eastern shore, and was the eldest of six children in a family to which she was strongly attached. She was educated in that state and later attended Neff College in Philadelphia. After college, Madeline joined a repertoire company with which she played in the Little Theatre in Philadelphia. Then followed a season's engagement at the Century Roof in New York and for a short time held a job as Miss Java. The young lady decided to try her hand, or rather her face and figure, in the movies. Mack Sennett, always on the lookout for beauties, saw Miss Hurlock on the screen and immediately signed her up to play vampire roles with Ben Turpin. Madeline had large, dark brown, expressive eyes and lustrous black hair and stood 5 foot, 3-1/2 inches tall.

Madeline told me, "Most of my films were made with Turpin. I didn't like him at first, thinking him what used to be called 'fresh.' As I got to know him, I found him friendly and amusing. He did not take himself seriously, nor did I take myself so."

Although believed to have made her motion picture debut with Sennett in 1923, Hurlock actually entered the movies at least as early as the summer of 1917 as an extra with Universal. In 1916, she met Sergeant Jack McGovern, a professional soldier of the Thirteenth U. S. Calvary, while he was in California. According to an article in *Moving Picture World*, August 25, 1917, "It was a great love match from the very beginning. So very recently valiant Sgt. McGovern got information that he is likely to be sent to France, so he wired for Miss Hurlock, and she arrived in Baltimore on Saturday night. She was met by Sgt. McGovern and some friends, and they immediately went to Ellicott City and were married." Divorcing in 1924, they "had nothing in common."

Madeline's whereabouts during the next several years are unknown and whether or not she remained active in films and/or confined to the life of a housewife may never be known; she wouldn't discuss it. Madeline is known to have appeared in an unidentified Lasky feature of early 1923 directed by George Fitzmaurice.

It is known, however, that early in 1923, Madeline Hurlock signed a contract for $150 weekly to appear in the Sennett Pathé comedies. Sennett himself spoke of Madeline to Theodore Dreiser in *The Best Motion Picture Interview Ever Written* for *Photoplay*, August 1928:

"I tried her out and most of us were puzzled at first because we put her in one thing and another and she didn't seem to do anything. Just stood around, as far as we could see. And we thought she was a total loss, or I did. But after a while we began to hear from exhibitors. They showed interest in her — liked her personality — asked who she was. Then I began to understand that there was something about the way she did stand around perhaps that was interesting to the public — her poise. So I began to surround her with the kind of material that would bring her out. And she herself, the more she becomes used to this work, is developing characteristics and stunts which are certain to make her into a sure-fire personality if she keeps on."

The small beauty was a busy actress at Sennett. She supported and made cameo appearances in many of the Sennett shorts with Turpin, Billy Bevan, Harry Langdon, Sid Smith, Jack Cooper, Billy Armstrong, Vernon Dent, Harry Gribbon, and others, all of whom, at one time or other, fell prey to her vamping ways. Another of her fellow actors, Eddie Quillan, once told me, "Madeline was a wonderful person to work with."

Madeline continues, "My directors were mostly Del Lord and Eddie Cline. I liked both of them. Harry Langdon was a worrier, Andy Clyde was a good actor, and a gentle, lovable man. By the way, Frank Capra was at the studio part of the time when I was there. He wasn't a director then, but what was known as a gagman."

Early in 1928, after five years with Sennett, Madeline left motion pictures for good. "I was fed-up with films and Hollywood, and could hardly wait to get back to New York. When I left (the studio, my weekly salary) was $750. Had I stayed on, it would have been $1000. In 1928, I went to London, Paris, Italy, and Switzerland — my first trip abroad."

Upon her return, Madeline met noted dramatist Marc Connelly, who was at the peak of his profession. They married October 4, 1930, but soon divorced after a few years when Madeline fell for their best friend, Robert Emmet Sherwood. They married in Budapest, Hungary on June 14, 1935.

"My husband was a well-known playwright. Among his plays are *The Petrified Forest*, *Idiot's Delight*, *Abe Lincoln in Illinois* and *There Shall Be No Night*. He won the Pulitzer Prize for the last three. He also won it for his book, *Roosevelt and Hopkins*. Oh yes, and an Oscar for his screenplay, *The Best Years of Our Lives*." She survived him upon his death in November 1955. In April 1989, Madeline died in her ninetieth year.

Mack Sennett has engaged the man who directed the first comedy in which Ben Turpin was featured to wield the megaphone over the crisscross comedian's second comedy released on the Pathé program. He is Herman Raymaker and it was almost eight years ago when this comedy director became acquainted with Ben's lureful orbs.

Rehearsals for the new production were conducted by Dick Jones, Supervising Director of Sennett productions. Filming began today. *But immediately halted when Raymaker was busy elsewhere.*

1923 September 17: Ben Turpin's *Pitfalls of a Big City* is a continuation of his *Where's My Wandering Boy This Evening?*, which was released recently. It looks to me as though Sennett had about 2,000 feet of celluloid left over from the "Boy" film and he has edited them into this comic. Whatever happened, *Pitfalls of a Big City* is funny. It has a burlesque sequence on *The Face on the Barroom Floor*, just as the first one did on *Where is My Wandering Boy Tonight?* and on *Foolish Wives*.[174]

1923 September 30: A big extra added feature, Ben Turpin in *Pitfalls of a Big City*, concludes a program of truly feature units. The Turpin picture being the very latest special comedy in which Ben is the featured player and is said to be the very funniest this unusual comedian has yet contributed to the screen. For those who enjoy Ben and his famous "eyes," there is surely some of the biggest laughs ever in this big comedy.

The Moberly Democrat (Missouri), pg 5

Pitfalls of a Big City (re September 2, 1923)
Ben Turpin as the honest "lad of the soil" who falls for a city-bred vampire extracts a few laughs from this well-known situation. Dot Farley appears as his cross-eyed mother, who eventually takes Ben over her knee and weans him away from the siren. Madeline Hurlock is the vamp who digs the pitfalls and Mack Swain is her big, burly husband. Jim Finlayson is Ben's father, who also becomes enmeshed in the city gal's toils. It was directed by J. A. Waldron and supervised by F. Richard Jones. The subtitles are well written and it's good, clean slapstick throughout with the usual chase at the finish.

The Expressions of Ben Turpin — Crossed His Eyes Once Too Often —
How Happy Hooligan Craze Made Turpin a Comedian (1923 August 4)
Almost every story written about Ben Turpin has given a different reason for the cause of his ability to look cross-eyed.
Here is the truth. While playing in *Happy Hooligan* for three years, he had to look cross-eyed from ten to twelve minutes each show (not to mention daily matinees) and one morning, he awoke to discover his jest had turned to earnest. Yet nothing arouses the ire of Bernard Turpin (Bernard is right) quicker than the intimation that he owes his comedy fame to the fact that his eyes are crossed. He resents the imputation that, if his eyes were straight, he would lose his job with Mack Sennett and be reduced to the necessity of retiring from the screen. This is very natural, for no man likes to believe that his success is the result of forces and qualities over which he has no control and goodness knows Ben, nowadays, has no control over his eyes.

Early Ambitions
Ben Turpin came into the world with his eyes as straight as any lad that ever came into the world and as a boy was noted for his wit and sense of humor. Like Charlie Chaplin, he was a born mimic and acrobat. His ambition was to turn these to account on the stage

and his first role was that of stage carpenter and property man, for he thought this was the first rung of the ladder and, at any rate, was within sight of the goal of his ambition.

The Happy Hooligan Craze

It was in Chicago that he gained his first chance to appear in a part. It was a very small part and his real chance came when a well-known cartoonist started the *Happy Hooligan* craze. Several artistes impersonated this character on the music hall stage, Ben Turpin among them.

The Price He Would Pay

Some days, Ben Turpin gave his impersonation ten times between the hours of noon and midnight. Soon, he couldn't straighten his eyes when the day was done. When he consulted surgeons and optical specialists, they told him that a minor operation would probably restore his eyes to normal condition, but the price of a permanent cure would be that he abandon his impersonation of *Happy Hooligan*.

But by this time, Ben Turpin's imitation had become famous and he decided to postpone straightening them out until the end of the season.

Later, Ben had received an offer to appear on the screen and as it was essential for his comedy parts that he should be the same laughable character he was on the stage, Ben Turpin has postponed the operation to the day he will retire.

With Charlie Chaplin

His earliest work on the screen was in Essanay comedies and later with Charlie Chaplin and he paid many tributes to that famous little comedian and Mack Sennett. He tells how the first time he met Charlie Chaplin, Charlie laughed for two hours and could not act at all. He was told to straighten up and get to business, but he said, "I can't. That chap's expression has me laughing, and I can't stop. If you want me to work, get him out of here."

Ben Turpin was born in New Orleans. Like most comedians, he is a better tragedian than many of our actors in heavy lines of straight drama. If you want to know just how sad he can look, you must see him in one of his comedies.

Real Hard Work

He is a hard worker and making comedies is hard work. He has been in the hospital thirty times for operations for breaks occasioned by rough comedy and not long ago, he lost four of his best front teeth because a man who was to kick him in the chest lost his bearings and aimed too high. Besides his cross-eye, Ben also owns a famous mustache. The first time he ever wore it, it was cut from the ends of a wig. He almost had the style patented, he avers, but finally decided that while other men might imitate his mustache, they could never hope to attain the eloquence of his eyes.[175]

More Punishment for Ben by W. Ward Marsh (1923 August 4, in part)

Ben Turpin probably has had more "screen trouble" than any other player. When a club has been yielded, Ben has been on the receiving end. When a blow has been aimed, Ben has furnished the jaw. When a pie has been hurled, Ben has let his curiosity get the better of his judgment, sticking his head around the doorway to greet the custards. When love has had to be made, Ben has made it — with the irate husband scowling in the offing, for an instant only. Alas, poor Ben!

Ben has always come to grief. He has been bruised, thumped, bullied, hanged, shot, and killed and all for the sake of making us laugh — which, because the troubles were his and not ours, we have done; haven't we? (Yes!)

Ben is now working on *Sidetracked*. It is to be hoped that Ben will be awake long enough to show his eyes. Advance material states:

In this new feature, Turpin steps out of his usual role of burlesque impersonator, playing a new and distinct character for a change. In *Sidetracked*, Ben is an all-round combination ticket agent, porter, soda water jerker, and announcer, but with it all, he finds time as usual to make use of his attractive orbs, flirting with a young lady already in love with the result that he gets himself into a peck of trouble.

Further, Mack Sennett is seriously considering filming *William Tell*, *Romeo and Juliet*, and *The Barber of Seville*. They will be magnificent and spectacular productions. As a matter of fact, they will be creations of an artistic standard such as the motion picture and fan film world has never witnessed. The leading man role for all three pictures has already been filled. Ben will be the star. Don't get excited. They will be only satires, typically Sennettonian, but they promise a quality of entertainment for motion picture audiences and in the near future, these burlesque travesties will be unfolded on the screen.[176]

1923 August 19: The next Sennett Ben Turpin comedy special, *Sidetracked*, has been renamed *Asleep at the Switch*. The latter title was considered more appropriate in view of the type of story. Practically all of the story is laid in and about a rural railroad station where Ben is an all 'round combination passenger and ticket agent, soda water jerker, information clerk, and train announcer. Madeline Hurlock is again cast as Turpin's leading woman while Kewpie Morgan, Cameo, the almost-human dog, Billy Armstrong, and Bud Ross fill in and play the other characters. Roy Del Ruth is directing.[177]

Even Turpin's Wife Will Not Know Him (1923 August)

Ben Turpin is working on one of the fastest two-reelers he has ever appeared in called *The Stunt Man*. It is well-named, too. Ben said no one will ever know it is he when the picture comes to the screen, not even his own wife, who has been looking at him for over seventeen years. Del Lord, who is directing *The Stunt Man*, is putting Bennie through a rapid pace of slam-bang, yet sure-fire laugh action. In *The Stunt Man*, Turpin is thrown from a horse, gets drowned, beaten up by a giant, clawed by animals, thrown from a roof, and — well, if there is anything that could happen to a person, it happens to Ben Turpin in his next Mack Sennett comedy.[178]

Naming the Brainchild (1923 August 26)

It's true that a rose by any other name would smell as sweet, but the recently-completed Ben Turpin comedy special produced under the working title *The Stunt Man* would lack half its value if it had not been retitled *The Dare-Devil*. This new picture, directed by Del Lord, hits you with hurricane force and piles up laugh after laugh. It is, without doubt, one of the fastest two-reelers ever screened, showing the zigzag-orbed comedian in the role of a movie double at the receiving end of numerous hair-raising incidents and daredevil feats.

The Dare-Devil is Sennett's fourth of the series of Turpin comedies he contracted to produce for Pathé release and, not unlike the previous Turpin pictures, it is burlesque throughout, being a "take-off" on a serial company shooting scenes for a melodramatic thriller.

The Dare-Devil is really a picture within a picture. Del Lord and the Sennett cameramen under Blake Wagner directing and photographing the movements of what is presumed to be another company working with Harry Gribbon as director; Jack Richardson and Irene Lentz as the principles; Ben Turpin as the double for Richardson; Kewpie Morgan the heavy; Gordon Lewis as assistant director; and Bob Wagner as cameraman. Besides the thrills, there are numerous situations of genuine humor which, with the many original gags and funny titles, makes this new Turpin picture stand out as one of his best to date.[179]

Director Delmar Lord hailed from Hamilton, Ontario, Canada, finding his way to Los Angeles and Mack Sennett in 1914. Del's first job was as a stuntman and comedy cop and soon driver of the cop wagon. After a couple years with Keystone, Del went over to William Fox and evolved into a writer and director of a number of comedies, putting approximately twenty two-reelers under his belt. He next moved over to direct some comedies for Educational Pictures, where he added another fifteen titles to his resume. Sennett saw Del's comedies and hired him back to direct about May 1923. Some of Ben's best Pathécomedies were directed by Lord. Del went on to direct the Sennett comedies of Billy Bevan and was one of Mack's busiest employees. Years later, Del directed many of the best comedies of Andy Clyde and The Three Stooges.

Dominoes Double-Crossed (1923 September 4)

Ben Turpin, who is featured in *Pitfalls of a Big City*, gives the following rules for playing mah jongg:

"In the spring a jongg man's fancy lightly turns to chow and chop suey, which is perfectly natural, since this spring everyone is going in for everything Chinesey. These long evenings have been very interesting to me since I have mastered mah jongg.

"It is played with 144 ivory pieces. The kids will lose any one of them very easily. The game was invented about 4000 years ago and King Tut hasn't a thing to do with it. Chu Chin Chow was the greatest mah-jongger of his day, and the Chinese official mah jongg board is still making rules at its official headquarters in Shanghai.

"In playing it is well to have a Chinese band nearby. This will provide good atmosphere. The tune goes something like this:

"Mah jongg! Mah jongg! Mah! Inflection on the ong you get a very gongy effect.

"After each player has stacked his pile of ivories, it is best to refresh with a cup of Oolong.

"If you discover that you have too many pieces you can slyly drop one or more on the floor, where the kids will soon discover and annihilate them.

"After a while you speak of the pieces with familiarity. There are sprouts, bamboos, dragons, jozzes, pungs, punks, squabs, asparagus, bams, bums and hams.

"Speak in husky whispers and Oolong. This will add intenseness to the game.

"When you have dropped all your ivories on the floor you win the silk-lined chop suey bowl."[180]

Turpin supposed to star in the Sennett circus picture *Flip Flops*, which was turned over to newcomer Lewis Sargent in his first and only film for the King of Comedy. Another Sennett newcomer at this time was destined for better luck, Harry Langdon.

Turpin's Shoes Puzzle Repairer *(1923 September 13)*

A few days ago, Ben Turpin asked one of the property men on the Sennett lot to take his famous shoes to some shop to have the soles more securely fastened to the uppers. Said prop man took them to a little cobbler close by the studio and left them with instructions.

No sooner had the messenger left than did the cobbler throw the shoes into a corner, thinking someone was kidding him. He never imagined for a minute that such old, worn-out foot coverings as those Turpin wears in his pictures could ever be used, let alone have money spent on their repair. To make sure his shoes were fixed as he wanted them, Turpin found where they had been left and went after them himself. He frightened the shoemaker to death with his storming and ranting when he found his shoes had been practically thrown away.

The poor Greek, not being a picture fan, never heard of Turpin, but he soon found out when that worthy comique of the screen started to tell him and finally prove to him that without those shoes, he would be worth a thousand dollars less a week to Mack Sennett.[181]

News of Screenables Told in Paragraphs by Mildred Spain *(1923 September 30)*

Ben Turpin and the missus have left for the High Sierras to shoot wild game. Ben admits he's feeling wonderful and doesn't care where he shoots.[182]

1923 October 9: Closeups: Ben Turpin has been granted leave of absence from the Sennett studios on account of the serious illness of his wife, who for several weeks has been under the care of a trained nurse.[183]

Asleep at the Switch (re October 14, 1923):

Ben Turpin is a switchman at a little jerk water train station, where the lively scenes of life are few and far between. One day, a dramatic troupe is forced through circumstances to remain in the one-horse town and Ben is treated to the time of his life. A checker game is indulged in, in which Ben, shrewd player though he is, is forced to lose a lot of money because of the shrewd, keen eye of a sagacious dog, Cameo. Of course, a girl is mixed up in the affair and Ben, who would be the hero, tries a series of stunts and saves the girl from the villain, not knowing that the villain and the girl are old pals. He starts in pursuit and after a number of thrilling adventures, eventually rescues the girl, who undergoes a change of mind and weds the delighted Ben.

1923 November 7: Mrs. Ben Turpin is just about well again and she and her cross-eyed husband expect to leave Hot Springs, Arkansas, about November 10. After a visit to relatives in Michigan, the twain will return to Los Angeles.[184]

In late 1923, five years after their first article on Ben, *Photoplay*, possibly the largest-selling movie fan magazine at this time, was back to interview him. Herbert Howe penned *The Life Tragedy of a Sennett Beauty or How to Cultivate Sex Attraction:*

I pressed the door button. I pressed again. Not a stir, though a light shone through the tight-drawn shades. Then, as I turned to go, the lower corner of a window shade lifted furtively and I saw peering up at me two eyes that looked as one.

Need I add that I was at the portals of Chez Turpin? For several minutes, the eyes looked at me straight in both ears until the lobes tingled as though pierced for pearls. Then the curtain dropped. A pedal patter. A great clicking of locks and shifting of bolts. The door opened narrowly and out shot a head like a Jack in a Box.

"'Lo," it croaked, "'lo. Been waitin' up for you."

"What time is it?" I asked apologetically.

"Almost nine. C'm in." Stepping across the threshold, I was in the presence of Ben Turpin, the Mack Sennett beauty, famous as *The Shriek of Araby*. He towered to the romantic height of my top vest button with his neck fully stretched. His head juts up like a turkey gobbler's. It looks to me as though his neck had intended to stop and form a head at the Adam's apple, but, suddenly growing ambitious, had abandoned the original plan and shot on up to the present knobby eminence. As a result, there is an intense rivalry between the head and the apple, both for size and animation. Ben would make a lovely gargoyle for a cathedral except for his language. He grows extremely Biblical at times when things go wrong. Ordinarily he is good-natured. He feels he is too good-natured. They don't treat him with no respect. It grieves him. Ben is a serious comedian.

"They don't treat a comedian with no respect anymore," he deplores. "It hurts. I'm sensitive, I am. If they treated a five thousand dollar race horse like they do a comedian he'd go blooey. But they don't treat no five thousand dollar race horse like they do a comedian."

There was almost a sob in his croak. The sob of an artist unappreciated.

"They're always having me run and doing falls. I've done more falls than any acrobat alive. Falls! I've done so many falls I can't stand the sight of a sidewalk. I'm sensitive, I am. They don't treat a comedian with no respect.

"I can't stand falls like I used to. I'm fifty-four years old." His croak became emotionally husky again, though he tossed his white mane proudly — a mane on a knobby head, like the tassel on corn.

He had conducted me to his den, pattering ahead in his brown-stockinged feet. It is his custom, I take it, to remove his shoes promptly after the final dinner course. The den was what you might expect of a cross-eyed sheik. From the walls, the beautiful eyes of countless sirens focus fondly on Ben, each fancying, no doubt, that Ben's glance is for her alone. In reality, his gaze is fixed steadily, though circuitously, upon his wife.

When he entered the lists as a rival of Valentino and the theaters advertised "*The Shriek vs. The Sheik*," Ben haughtily called attention to the fact that he has held one woman for seventeen years, which was more than Valentino could say. You may think this a jest, but Ben doesn't. He's incredibly serious, as serious as *Merton*. When he stoops to jest, it is with obvious condescension; there's nothing funny about it.

When I referred to his competition with Valentino, he smiled deferentially. "Oh, I don't pretend to be no Valentino," he chortled modestly. "He does his stuff and I do mine. There's room for both of us, I figger. There's room for all of us in this bizness."

The women are crazy about him. He admits it. Ever and anon, he makes shy reference to his fan mail, "mostly from women." He accounts very simply for this: It's the old sex attraction.

"An actor's gotta have sex attraction these days," he croaks solemnly. "I don't claim to be no Valentino — I'm fifty-four — but I'm getting' just as big bizness in some places. That's what gets me. I make 'em the money, but they don't treat a comedian with no…"

I hastily interrupted to ask if his eyes had always been as sexy as they are at fifty-four. Ben bounded up, gestured for me to follow, and away we pattered to the front room. He switched on the front room lights. It was a regular front room with rose drapes, blue and rose shade on a gilt lamp, mahogany table, and a mantel adorned with objects d'art, including the photograph of a Young Man in a Wing Collar, not a bad-looking young man — quite a 'andsome 'Arry, in fact — with a slim neck arising like the Eiffel Tower from a highly-polished collar and crowned by a highly-pomaded dome.

"That's me," exhibited Ben with an attempt at modesty. "Taken in N'Orleans when I was nineteen." The dark eyes of the youth looked squarely at me.

"But them eyes, Ben!" I gasped. "Them eyes are straight."

"Sure," he croaked. "That was afore I crossed 'em."

I learned then of the sacrifice Ben had made on the altar of art. He was not born optically askew. He crossed 'em for art's sake while playing the character of *Happy Hooligan* on the vaudeville stage over twenty years ago. He made as many as ten crosses a day. One day, they didn't untwine. His fortune became permanent. Since Nature did not endow Ben with this baffling, enigmatic expression, as it did Rudolph, it seems to me he deserves a great deal more credit as a sex attraction.

Ben, like all our sheiks, admits he came of noble family, the very flower of French aristocracy in New Orleans.

"My grandfather," he says with a touch of old-world pride, "was the best auctioneer in Loozyana. And my old man kept a candy store 'til he went broke."

It was after his father's failure in trade that Ben, like many another scion of nobility, was forced to the stage. Then commenced the long series of falls that landed him in his present position and gave him his poignant aversion to sidewalks.

He's a rich man at fifty-four, a millionaire, perhaps. Next to his home in Hollywood, he is erecting an apartment house and he has many other property investments around Los Angeles that represent solid values. His fame is worldwide. Tributes to his genius pour in from everywhere. If you've seen *Where's My Wandering Boy This Evening?*, you will recall that, in carving a fowl, Ben dropped his bow tie in the soup. It was a tragic moment that touched the heart. A few days ago, Ben received a big card fastened with six brilliant Grip Bow ties from the Grip Bow Tie Co. of Omaha with an apologetic letter saying: "Several members of this firm who recently saw your excellent production were genuinely distressed over the fact that you lost your Grip Bow tie in the soup. We have therefore made up a selection of offerings, expressly for your own use, which we are enclosing herewith."

Such tokens of esteem make up somewhat for the respect a comedian don't get no more. But that which Ben desires above all else is denied him — a daughter. He offered to adopt his brother-in-law's child, to educate her in the best finishing school, and, at the age of twenty-one, to endow her with twenty-five thousand dollars. The offer was gently refused.

Sympathizing with Ben in his disappointment, his dog straightway brought two pups into the world. And to the inexpressible joy of the household, one of them actually was born cross-eyed. There's certainly something in prenatal suggestion. The dogs help to while away the long evenings from six until eight-thirty, when Ben precipitately retires. Occasionally, when he feels the desire for cutting up, Ben goes out on a busy corner of the boulevard near his home and acts as traffic cop while the regular officer is having dinner. Within ten minutes after taking his stand, he has worked havoc with his hands and eyes.

"You!" he'll croak belligerently, looking in two directions and pointing in another. "You! Drive on!" And six bewildered little Fords will leap at one another simultaneously. A frenzied melee ensues. Frightened Fords squeal and proud Pierces honk indignantly. When things seem as tangled as the European situation, Ben puts his hand over one eye, shakes his Lloyd-Georgian locks, and, with a lift of a hand, quells the riot. With such pastimes, he gets his mind off the indignities to which a comedian is subjected these days.

"I started wrong in this business," he sighs. "I ought to be upstage. But I can't. It ain't in me. They don't show no respect. And that hurts." I soothingly suggested that his Sennett contract would soon expire and he could seek more respectful quarters.

"Leave Sennett!" he barked fiercely. "I'll never leave Sennett. Every dollar I made I made through Sennett. I owe everything to Mr. Sennett and Mr. Chaplin — and the public. The public is the one I owe most to. Yes, sir, I owe everything to the public."

He'll never leave Sennett! They don't show him no respect, but he'll stick. He's fifty-four and he'll stick till he's eighty. Die in the harness, he will, unrespected. Before he dies, he craves just one thing. A dying wish. He wants to make a serious drama. He says serious dramas are funnier than comedies. In serious dramas, an actor is treated with… "Nowadays they don't treat a comedian with no…"

Photoplay, December 1923

Photoplay's interview with Turpin, surely read by millions of moviegoers and fans alike, may well have resulted in Sennett's posting the notice of a $100 fine "if anyone bribes, asks or demands a '108' from Ben Turpin," as well as his enforcing stuntmen such as Hubert Diltz. Authors Kalton Lahue and Sam Gill wrote, "Ben thought and acted comedy, both on and off the screen. He enjoyed having visitors on the sets and went out of his way to entertain them. 'I'm Ben Turpin, and I make a hell of a lot of money around here — in fact, I get paid first and what's left goes to the others' was inevitably followed by a backward somersault. Ben's compulsion to perform this stunt scared Sennett to death."[185]

Real and Unreel Ben Turpin and His Love for Children
(1923 December 4, in part)

There is something that we would like to arise and orate about this bird Ben Turpin. On the screen, he's a great comic and he doesn't seem to have very good sense, but if you think he hasn't got good sense, you ought to see the income tax he pays every March and try to count up all the apartment houses and things he owns around town. The cold fact is that he's a regular guy from his shoes up and he has a regular wife and he loves children, although he hasn't any of his own, and —

But say! There's a true story about Ben that hasn't ever been told before. It happened along about six months ago. It might give you some kind of a slant on him.

To start with, Ben is 56 years old. Oh, we admit he doesn't look it, but he is. And the great sorrow of his life is that he hasn't any kids to romp about the house. One day, he met a little schoolgirl and he fell in love with her right off the bat and so did Mrs. Turpin. She was the daughter of a poor family and Ben and Mrs. Turpin talked it over a long time.

And finally, one night Ben went to the girl's house and talked to her father. And he told him how much he and Mrs. Turpin loved the child and he made a cold flat proposition as follows: If the father would let them have the child to raise, he'd give the father $5000. He'd put her through all the schools there are and the day she was twenty-one, he would invest $25,000 in her name. And he didn't say so, but when he was all through and the final trumpet blew — well, he didn't have anybody else to leave his fortune to.

But the father wouldn't let the girl go and it nearly broke the Turpins' hearts.[186]

Stars Life No Bed of Roses, Says Ben Turpin
and Cites His Daily Routine To Prove Truth of Assertion (1923 December 30)

"Oh! For the life of a movie actor," sigh the aspiring youths who are desirous of showing the world how easy it is to improve on the work of matinee screen idols.

"Stay away from the screen if you are looking for a cinecure," says Ben Turpin. "It is an easy enough life if you are used to it but otherwise it is the bunk. I'll admit there isn't much to do when you get along as far as I have and become the rage among comedy stars. You see, when you become a star you can act independent and do what you want, for instance I never get to the studio in the morning until eight o'clock. I jump into my makeup, make a fool of myself for about three and a half hours, then they give me a chance to eat something so that I will not die during the afternoon work and will have something within me to help break the shock of falls and wallops. I have a few chairs and a piano or two bounced off my head; they throw me in the water, either from the deck of a burning yacht or the big studio tank; and then, when it gets too dark to do any more work outside, they take me into the night studio.

"After the director and other actors get so exhausted they can't stand it any longer, we change to our store clothes and spend an hour looking at what we shot the day before, on the studio screen. About nine o'clock I go home to my wife, wash up and have dinner about ten or ten-thirty. It is then time to give a little attention to my dogs and I run around the block and play with them for a while so they will know me and won't think I'm a burglar when I come home at night. About eleven o'clock I'm all through with my day's routine, and the rest of the evening is mine, provided I don't have to work on my next story in-between, which quite often takes up three or four nights of the week.

"But then, there is rest, even for the wicked, for every seven days, even in a studio life, there is a Sunday, and we don't have to work every Sunday. I got two Sundays off last year and had a great time with my dogs, after my relatives left for their homes. Somehow or other, the relatives always know when I am not going to work.

"Of course, I would not ask the maid to do anything for anyone not in the immediate family, so I prepared breakfast, made lunch for a bathing picnic, and drove them all over the highways, until we found a place to park the car; then I had a swim. I did all my swimming that day under water, because my sister-in-law could not stay up in the water, and whenever a big wave came along I had to hold her up and, naturally, when she was up — I was down.

"At any rate, after I had changed two tires on the way home and we get back to the house, they all admitted I was a good fellow to visit and that a good time was enjoyed by all. I could not see it, probably because I do not look at things the way other folks do.

Maybe I am mean. I hope I'm not; but I will say this: Stay out of pictures unless you can be a star. As for me, I want to work every Sunday."[187]

No Discord in Ranks Of The Turpin Family (1923 advertorial)

It seems to make little difference to Ben Turpin whether it is making cross-eyed fun for the motion picture fans, chasing a golf ball over the links, or discussing philosophy of marriage. He is an expert at all three sentences. Mrs. Turpin agrees with Ben that he is a fine golf player, but says he ought to be doing Hamlet instead of comedy.

They both agree that there is no such thing as single blessedness and claim that married happiness depends largely on whether you have a motorcar of a satisfactory make.

Both are golf enthusiasts. The winner gets the driver's seat in the sedan until the next one betters the score of the other. Driving the car is the prize. Sometimes when the lady of the house wants something, like a new hat or a fur or any of those little things dear to the feminine heart, she lets Ben drive when it is her turn. Ben is just as generous when he wants a favorite dish prepared for dinner. As the car will go in only one direction at a time and to only one place and as both of them love to drive it and ride around, the car puts them in each other's company a great deal. That is why they say that single blessedness is not in it with married happiness.

The only really important difference they have at home is as to which is the more expert driver. Ben claims that he gets more power out of the Big-Six Studebaker on a hill, but his wife says that it has more power than it needs and that Ben has nothing to brag about. She insists that Ben never keeps his eyes straight ahead on the road and that she does, which makes her the better driver of the two. Someday they are going down to the Studebaker store and ask Paul Hoffman to watch each of them drive and decide who is the more proficient. If they do, they'll probably own a car apiece.[188]

The Dare-Devil (re November 25, 1923)

Ben plays the part of a stagehand in a motion picture studio and when a particularly perilous stunt is to be performed, the director calls for a volunteer. Ben's histrionic soul is aroused and he attempts and successfully performs the stunt. From that time on, no thrill is too thrilling for Ben and he makes his career as a famous actor.

Ten Dollars or Ten Days (re January 6, 1924)

Ben is a clerk, soda jerk, and in love with the cashier of the same store, played by Irene Lentz. Of course, he has a rival, who by day is a salesman and by night is a burglar, Harry Gribbon. The burglar boldly attempts to rob the employer — he succeeds and the blame is placed on Ben. But fate takes a kindly hand — straightens out the tangle, the money is recovered, and Ben wins the girl.

Mack Sennett seems to have refreshed himself at some fountain of comedy or other; and his Ten Dollars or Ten Days, directed by Del Lord and starring Ben Turpin, is a laugh-getter every minute. It is a bit of a burlesque as well as being full of good gags, especially in the last half, and the fun runs high in the scenes where Ben is put in prison wrongfully for having killed a man, escapes, sees the supposed murderee in one dangerous escapade after another, and tries to rescue him in order to prove that the man isn't dead and, therefore, that he didn't kill him.[189]

All-Star Cast In This Two-Reel Comedy

A real all-star cast will appear in a two-reel comedy when Charlie Murray, Phyllis Haver, Ben Turpin, Marie Prevost, Billy Bevan, and Madeline Hurlock will be seen in Mack Sennett's latest production, *The Hollywood Kid*.

The story is a travesty on breaking into pictures, featuring a little boy, played by Jackie Lucas. Every phase of picture making is burlesqued. Mack Sennett himself plays the role of the motion picture producer that signs up the child actor. Three other stars have important roles in *The Hollywood Kid* — Teddy, the Sennett dog, Billy, the chimpanzee, and Numa, the 650-pound lion. As of this writing, Ben's appearance is unverified due to slightly incomplete extant prints, though it is believed Ben's part is of earlier Sennett footage.

Ben Turpin (1924 January 6)

He's all right, but he looks crooked.
If he goes where he's looking, he'll run into himself.
That guy is so cross-eyed that he dug a well so crooked he fell out of it.
More than that, he's so cross-eyed he has to lie on his back to look downstairs.

From these few ancient wheezes, it will be seen that there are any number of pleasant and encouraging things one may say about a cross-eyed man. Most cross-eyed men would resent them and they would be justified in doing so, but there is one such individual of our acquaintance who rejoices in the fact that his right eye gazes hopefully into the future while the left one contents itself with a glance over the immediate past. The man in question is Ben Turpin, than whom no more cross-eyed human being ever looked in two directions at one and the same time.

Now there's nothing at all inherently funny in crossed eyes, but a fractured glance from the Turpin soul lights has sent many a movie audience into convulsions of mirth. With his reckless Bohemian haircut, his defiantly up-tossed head, his giddy brush mustache, and his scattered eyes, Turpin is the very spirit of comedy, an optically defective genius.[190]

Stars Thrill Hero Fans — Hotel Lobby Thronged by Frenzied Crowd —
Ben Turpin Gives Solo Act (1924 January 20)

Who said the days of hero-worship are gone? Whoever it was, he should have been at the Palace Hotel yesterday noon when the Hollywood heroes and heroines arrived for the Wampas Ball. The Palace lobby and the sidewalks around the hotel were never so crowded before — not even at the President Harding funeral. Police Captain Charles Goff had to put in a last-minute hurry call for more men to handle the through and to clear the lanes for the stars and other dignitaries of the films to get into the hotel and through the lobby to the elevators. Every movie fan in San Francisco must have been there.

And when the stars came in — ! Ben Turpin got so happy over the reception that he put on a little impromptu act in the Palace lobby. The grand finale came when he tried to go out of two doors at once, not wanting to favor either eye.[191]

Spars With Seven At Once — Preparing to Box Ben Turpin (1924 January 18)

San Francisco, Jan. 18 — Boxing with seven different sparring partners at the same time, Benny Leonard, world champion lightweight, went through a strenuous workout here today in preparing himself for a bout tomorrow night with Ben Turpin.

The contest is on the program of the Western Advertisers Motion Picture Association's annual ball and frolic.

"Turpin is so cross-eyed I won't be able to tell where he's going to duck, so I'm working out with seven sparring mates in order to hit quickly in seven directions at the same time," Leonard explained today.

Bryant Washburn has been named to referee the bout. Jackie Coogan and Bull Montana will second Leonard and Baby Peggy and Tom Mix will swing towels for Turpin. Scores of actors are in San Francisco to attend the ball.[192]

The WAMPAS Ball, held recently in San Francisco, certainly did make history. Never was such an event staged in the bay city and more people turned out to see the parade of film stars when they got off the Lark in the morning than have ever lined San Francisco's streets, except for the funeral of President Harding. The Western Association of Motion Picture Advertisers — to give the Wampas their official name — after paying for special trains and hotel accommodations for the stars, cleared $20,000 on the ball. Everybody was there, including Ben Turpin, who boxed two rounds with Benny Leonard, world's champion.[193]

Ben Turpin at Work On Comedy (1924 January 20)

Ben Turpin has begun on a new comedy for Mack Sennett, entitled *North of 57*, the burlesque on Owen Wister's *The Virginian* having been postponed until later. *North of 57* (released as *Yukon Jake*) is a story of the Royal Northwest Mounted Police in which Ben rides the snowy wastes as an invincible arm of this strict law. The field is a new one for Turpin and offers him an abundance of opportunity for comic burlesque in his role as the defender of fair women and the cruel enemy of fur-trading rascals. Del Lord is directing Turpin in the new picture and has taken his company to Truckee, California, for the snow scenes. Natalie Kingston, a beautiful dancer on the coast, has been engaged by Sennett to play opposite Turpin.[194]

King of Comedy by Mack Sennett:

"Turpin was an emotional little man, especially under the influence of money or the bottle. Once when we had leased a special train to take a company to Lake Tahoe, scheduled to leave at seven in the evening, Del Lord found Mr. Turpin hitting crescendo in the throes of a crying jag. On such occasions Turpin demanded the attentions of his attorney, his business manager, and his priest.

"When Del arrived at the roaring Turpin establishment, Ben had decided that he was all right, but that for reasons obscure to everyone else, his wife was dying.

"Since Mrs. Turpin was blooming with health (Sennett wrongly remembered), Del dismissed the lawyer and business manager, took the priest home, and called up Tommy Lofthaus, chief of the Los Angeles Motor Patrol. Mr. Lofthaus was a good friend because we often gave his cops jobs on off-duty days.

"Turpin arrived at the station under full siren, delighted with his police escort. He dashed into his drawing room, belted down a scotch and soda, and went through the entire train announcing himself as Ben Turpin, $3000 a week. He performed a 108 in each car.

"We got him to Lake Tahoe in fancy fettle, but Turpin immediately became victim of a new terror. We had a scene in which the giant Kalla Pasha, wearing a black fur suit, worked interchangeably with a live bear which closely resembled him. The script called for Turpin to hop into bed with the fur-bearing Pasha. Ben winced and keened over this idea, said it was frightening enough to send a valuable actor to the looney bin just to think of getting into bed with Kalla Pasha, let alone a dangerous, man-eating critter.

Anyway, Turpin complained, he had no faith whatsoever in the integrity or the human kindness of anybody connected with Mack Sennett. He was dead sure he was being framed and would wind up in the embrace of the bear.

"During this tantrum our bear got his teeth into his trainer's arm, almost chawing it off. This upset all of us to some extent. It was particularly dismaying to Turpin.

"As things came out, we had to do away with that bear as a safety measure, but it seemed a shame to waste him. We put the warm corpse in Kalla Pasha's bed and inserted Mr. Turpin. Ben's histrionics made a notable scene for a few seconds.

He never forgave us.

"It is honorable to give credit where credit is due. It was Mabel Normand who connived the bedding of Ben Turpin and the bear."

Adela Rogers St. John elaborated on the latter, "Mabel Normand was in back of half the gags on the Sennett lot. It was Mabel who rigged Ben Turpin, the irresistible cross-eyed comic, and the bear.

"When the script called for Turpin to get into bed with a bear, it was Turpin who got into bed with the bear. But this time he balked. He said he would go back to being a janitor the way he was before Sennett found him. Everybody explained to him that the bear was old, toothless, without claws, and filled with a true love for humanity, especially cross-eyed comedians. But Ben was adamant.

"Finally, they compromised on a stuffed bear. Knowing well the studio motto — anything for a laugh — Turpin stuck (a long hatpin) right through the bear to be sure. When nothing happened, Turpin got in bed, the camera turned.

"A split second later came a yell that was probably heard in Kansas City. Turpin came out of bed running and they didn't find him for two days. Mabel had crawled in behind the bear and flung both the bear's furry arms around Turpin's neck and the camera got one of the funniest impromptu scenes ever filmed. Under the Sennett code, Turpin couldn't even protest because it got a laugh from spectators and film audiences for months to come."[195]

Stars Are Insulted When Identity Is Confused (1924 February 10)

James Finlayson, native of Scotland, pioneer film funster, and a familiar figure in many of Hal Roach's recent comedies, is now an American citizen, which is not the point of this story. He recently got his final naturalization papers in the Federal Court in Los Angeles. To conform with legal precedent, he had to have two citizens who had known him for five years appear in court and vouch for his moral character. Ben Turpin, an honest citizen despite the fact that he looks crooked, and Charles Chase, handsome and debonair actor, under contract with Hal Roach, officiated. The courtroom was crowded and Turpin and Chase were sitting at one side awaiting their turn.

"There's Ben Turpin!" somebody whispered. Ben got his admirer in fifty percent focus and smiled. Chase adjusted his tie and turned a classic profile. He was handsome, well-groomed. Turpin was just — well, he was Ben Turpin, not a matinee idol.

"Ben Turpin? Which one?" someone asked loudly.

Turpin and Chase each declared himself insulted.[196]

Film Comedian Directs Traffic *(1924 March 30)*

When Ben Turpin is not working on the Sennett lot, he may be found on one of the busy Hollywood corners directing traffic. He declares he is especially equipped for this work since he can see the traffic coming both ways. The invested authority and the experience gained as an arm of the law inspired Ben to have a police story written for him and is now at work under the direction of Del Lord in a Northwest mounted police role.

Ben Turpin Suffers From Snow Blindness

Ben Turpin, the Sennett comedian who was considered immune from all inflictions of the eye, fell a victim to a bad case of snow blindness while on location at Truckee, California's famous winter resort, for his latest two-reel Pathé comedy, *Yukon Jake*.

Ben has never even experienced the pain of "Kleig eye," which is a common ailment among movie stars caused by the blinding rays of the huge Kleig lamps. But after three weeks tramping the snowy wastes at Truckee, Ben came down with snow blindness and had to return to the Sennett studios in Hollywood with the crossed orbs swathed in bandages. For a while, Ben feared lest his condition might be serious, since the treatments for his novel affliction might have straightened the precious orbs. But after a week in a darkened room, the bandages were removed and the famous Turpin eyes came forth as good as new and still crossed.[197]

Real and Unreel Ben Turpin by Don H. Eddy *(1924 April 2)*

Ben Turpin dropped in the other afternoon to make his annual report. It seems he just got back from Truckee, where they have snow, and he made a few plain and fancy scenes while there. One day, he was remarking, they were shooting a snowy river scene and all at once something came floating down the river that didn't belong there and they had to stop the scene. It turned out to be the body of some poor unfortunate gent that had departed this vale of tears.

Natalie Kingston, Ben's leading woman, is a California girl that never was in snow before and Ben says she just ran wild. Finally, she tried to drive a dog team and the huskies tossed her into a bramble bush and she had to wear between nine and seventeen different bandages here and there.

They stopped off in Sacramento on the way home and went to see a movie and somebody pegged Ben Turpin in the house and he had to get up and make a speech. Otherwise, Ben said, the trip didn't amount to much and he didn't have much to report.

Flashes by Grace Kingsley: *Ben Turpin to Flit (1924 April 2)*

Immediately following the completion of *Yukon Jake*, a Mack Sennett comedy special burlesquing a popular drama of the North, Ben Turpin, cross-eyed hero of the screen, set the burglar alarms in his pretentious Hollywood home, locked all doors, and said good-bye to his studio friends for about six weeks.

Mrs. Turpin has not been in good health for the last few months and her condition has worried Ben exceedingly. Acting on the advice of his physicians, Turpin turned his caravan northward and he and Mrs. Turpin will enjoy a complete climatic change in the Canadian Province of Quebec.[198]

Rain Dampens Snow

The warm southern rains that have descended upon California caused havoc on one of the sets at the Mack Sennett studio. In *Yukon Jake*, Ben Turpin's current comedy, some of the action is laid in Eskimoland and a huge set containing some igloos was constructed on the open air stage. The long deferred rainy season set in suddenly and after one day's down-pour, the ice huts, icicles, and snowdrifts were a sorry-looking sight to behold. Fortunately, all the important action had been filmed, but the studio folk, some of whom had never seen snow, were loath to see the beautiful wintry scene go.[199]

1924 March 3: Billy Armstrong, comedian and character actor in dozens of comedies with Charles Chaplin and Ben Turpin, died Saturday, March 1, 1924, in Sunland, where he had gone only about a week earlier to combat an illness of long duration. The former comic had lived in Arizona for some time and was survived by his widow.[200]

No Comedy in Turpin's Visit — Famous Movie Comedian Making Pilgrimage to Ste. Anne de Beaupre With Wife. Paralysis Stroke Affected Her Hearing. (1924 March 31)

The name of Ben Turpin has become a byword for comedy, but Mr. Turpin's visit to Quebec has nothing of the comedy element about it and is in fact the exact antithesis of such. As announced in the Telegraph on Saturday, Mr. Turpin is at present in Quebec and is accompanied by his wife and it is primarily for the latter's benefit that the trip is being made. Some time ago, Mrs. Turpin suffered a paralytic stroke which left her slightly deaf.

After trying other means to cure this ailment, Mrs. Turpin decided to come to this province and invoke the aid of Ste. Anne. To this end, Mr. and Mrs. Turpin have been making a daily pilgrimage to the shrine at Ste. Anne de Beaupre and will continue the visits until a novena, or nine days pilgrimage, is completed. It is the hope of the couple that Mrs. Turpin's ailment will be cured by this means.

Mr. Turpin, as seen in the Chateau Frontenac, is the Ben Turpin of the pictures minus the exaggerated sartorial effects that aid him in his comedy pictures. He has just completed a picture in which the Canadian Northwest and the Mounted Police play a part and in a short time will leave for a sojourn in Europe.[201]

Joseph Gagnon of the Music Hall Theatre in Lewiston, Maine, met Ben Turpin and witnessed the miraculous recovery of her hearing by Mrs. Turpin at Ste. Anne de Beaupre, Canada, recently. Mr. Gagnon has just returned to Lewiston after a week's vacation. Mr. Gagnon said that Mrs. Turpin was seated two rows in front of him in the

Church of Ste. Anne and that after praying, she arose, quite able to hear again because she had had "faith."[206]

Wife of Comedian Regained Hearing (1924 April 10)

Quebec, April 9 — "Ben, I can hear a little and I really think that my hearing is gradually returning." Such was the statement made by Mrs. Turpin at the Chateau Frontenac to her husband, the comedian, shortly after the couple had returned to the city from Ste. Anne de Beaupre, where they had been making a novena at the shrine, the object healing to solicit the assistance of Ste. Anne in curing Mrs. Turpin's deafness, brought on in recent years by a stroke of paralysis.

In conversation with Mr. Turpin today, he said that there was no doubt about it that his wife's hearing had been miraculously cured in a partial manner through their pilgrimage to the famous shrine, twenty-one miles from this city, where they journeyed together in sunshine and in storm for the past nine days.

"You can imagine my feelings," said the comedian, "when shortly after we had returned to the hotel my wife calmly informed me that she was able to hear. Although hoping for the best, I could scarcely believe my own ears," he added, humorously, "but," growing serious again, "It was almost a physical impossibility to make Mrs. Turpin hear a single word, even when one stood as close as possible and shouted. Yes, her hearing has improved wonderfully and I am convinced that she is on the way to ultimate recovery."

"Do you attribute Mrs. Turpin's partial restoration of hearing to her visits to Ste. Anne de Beaupre?"

"There is not the least doubt about it," came the quick reply. "Anyone who has faith stands a good chance of being cured. My wife and I came to Quebec convinced that some good would be derived, and while she has not regained her hearing fully, she has benefited.

"I think that the Shrine of Ste. Anne is a wonderful blessing to mankind, and although this is our first pilgrimage, it will not be the last, and when we get home we will continue our prayers to Ste. Anne."

Mr. and Mrs. Turpin are leaving Quebec tomorrow afternoon for Montreal and Chicago. They will leave for the Western States shortly afterwards and then take an extended trip to Europe.[202]

Longs For Tragic Roles — Looks Lacking, Ben Turpin Admits (1924 April 12)

To the list of interesting theatrical and moving picture stars who have visited Montreal must be added Ben Turpin, the comedian, who was in the city yesterday. Mr. Turpin is on his way back to Los Angeles with Mrs. Turpin, who, it was stated yesterday, is a French-Canadian, following a visit to Quebec and the famous shrine of Ste. Anne de Beaupre. The trip has been in the nature of a pilgrimage from Los Angeles to the shrine, with which she has been long familiar, in hopes of a miraculous cure of Mrs. Turpin's extreme deafness.

The comedian is short, well-built, and elderly, an American of old stock. "No, I'm not a descendant of Dick Turpin, the famous English highwayman," Mr. Turpin said jokingly, "though I think I can trace my ancestors back that far." Incidentally, to answer a question frequently asked, he is permanently cross-eyed, though his feet are not the monstrosities they appear to be when made up for the screen. The manner in which Mr. Turpin has risen supremely over the handicap of those famous eyes is an example of the courageous turning of an impediment to good account. "I love serious acting," said Mr. Turpin, "and long to play tragic roles, but, of course, I haven't the looks. So I do the next best thing — I make people laugh. Moreover, it's a pretty hard job being funny all the time. Often when I go down to the studio I feel more like crying. But I've got to make 'em laugh or my head will be chopped off."[203]

RESTORED (1924 April 19)

Ben Turpin, movie comedian, and Mrs. Turpin rejoiced yesterday at restoration of her hearing following pilgrimage to Shrine of Ste. Anne de Beaupre in Canada.[204]

St. Anne's Visit Effects Cure of Mrs. Ben Turpin (1924 April 19)

Chicago, April 19 — Chicago friends today spoke reverently of the miraculous recovery from deafness of Mrs. Carrie Turpin, wife of Ben Turpin, the movie comedian, at a Canadian shrine. Ben, putting aside his comedian role, told a group of friends of Mrs. Mary Deusch, at whose home the Turpins stayed in Chicago, of the answer to their prayers for his wife's recovery.

"Prior to our nine daily pilgrimages to the shrine of St. Anne de Beaupre it was a physical impossibility to make Mrs. Turpin hear anything," Turpin told them. "On the day we completed the novena we came back to Quebec and prepared to leave Canada.

"Mrs. Turpin was silent on the way back to the hotel. While we were packing, forgetting, I spoke to her and she answered. I knew then our prayers were answered.

"I can now enjoy the laughter of the children as they watch Ben in his funny antics," Mrs. Turpin told friends.

According to writer Dorothy Donnell in her 1925 interview with Ben:

Money came presently and with it a fine car and a big house with several servants. Then, before they could enjoy their prosperity, Mrs. Turpin was hurt in an automobile accident which destroyed her hearing. She would never hear again, the doctors said, but Ben, a devout Catholic, believed differently. Together, he and his wife made the long journey to the shrine of Saint Anne de Beaupre near Quebec, where so many miracles are said to have taken place. Every day for the novena of nine days, Mrs. Turpin and Ben, on their knees, made the long toilsome ascent of the twenty-seven steps leading to the altar. And then one day in their hotel room he forgot and spoke to her in an ordinary tone and she answered him! The first thing she did was to go and see one of Ben's pictures so that she could hear the laughter and applause.

But the miracle did not last. Ben Turpin said little at the studio of his home life, but his directors knew that he must have an hour off every noon to go home to lunch in and that he would never work after four-thirty in the afternoon or on Sundays so that he could spend more time with his wife. They had always been a lonely little couple without children or the knack of making acquaintances. Now and then, the parish priest would come to dine at their big empty house. And there was Kate — the husky proprietress of Kate's Place, the studio lunch where Ben acted as guide, philosopher, and friend. Sometimes, Kate visited the Turpins and sat ill at ease while the servants waited on her. Now and then, the studio persuaded them to appear at a cafe opening or a preview. And that was their life. Perhaps their loneliness drew them closer together. It seems an odd trick of Fate that one who furnished so much merriment to the world and afforded so much amusement should find his greatest recreation in going, with Mrs. Turpin clinging to his arm with the timidity of the deaf, to the corner of Santa Monica Boulevard and Western. There for an hour at twilight, now and then he would take the place of his friend, the traffic cop, and direct the home-going automobiles while his wife sat on the car stop bench at the sidewalk, watching him in boundless admiration.

With his cap cocked comically over his mis-mated eyes, Turpin would clown the traffic signals while the passing autoists waved and shouted, "Hello, Ben!" But presently, the increasing poorness of his wife's health forbade this recreation. Mrs. Turpin could not bear, in her nervous state, to have the servants do anything for her and so they stood idle while Ben cooked the meals, tidied the room, and made beds.

The Lonely Clown.

Back at the Sennett Studio, writers Mel Brown, Al Martin, and Elmer Flohri having recently left, in April 1924, the remaining writers included Wallie Wallace, Carlton Andrews, and Charles Diltz and gagmen Jack Wagner and versatile Glen Cavender. Sennett soon added Jefferson Moffit, Arthur Ripley, Vernon Smith, Hal Conklin, Frank Capra, Tay Garnett, A. H. Giebler, Hal Yates, and Percy Heath in May 1925, who replaced the February 1925 loss of "Pinto" Colvig, who went to Century Comedies and later Disney.

Turpin, Tea Taster *(advertorial)*

Ben Turpin, bias-eyed Sennett comedian, has returned from a tour of adventure and achievement which led him through Canada and the Middle West. He discovered, among other strange phenomena of nature, English 5 o'-Clock Tea.

"Every day on the train," said Ben, "feller came around with a tray and some marmalade stuff.

"'Do you feel like a cup of tea?' he says to me. And I came right back at him with: 'No, do I look like a cup of tea?' But he never got it at all. He just kept coming around with the tea. I saw there was no way to get out of it, so I lapped up the tea, just to show there was no hard feelings."

Ben says that when he got to Detroit, he had a surprise. Who should be there at the same hotel but Mabel Normand. Mabel insisted that he should accompany her to the theater where she was giving a personal appearance. And when he got there, she suddenly seized him by the hand and dragged him out in front of all the folks.

"Ladies and gentleman," said Mabel to the audience, "this is my little son I brought along with me tonight." The audience yelled; Ben blushed and the orchestra played *Bright Eyes.* Ben's real purpose in making the trip, however, was a serious and reverential one. He took his wife to the famous Shrine of St. Anne de Beaupre near Montreal, where so many miracles have been vouchsafe to the sick and afflicted.

Mrs. Turpin feels that she was much benefited. Ben is about to begin work on a comedy which will be a burlesque on *Romeo and Juliet*. Natalie Kingston will play *Juliet*.[205]

Ben Turpin is scared — just plain scared. Recently, while the comedian and his wife were on vacation in Canada, they attended church in St. Anne de Beaupre and Mrs. Turpin's hearing was restored. They knelt for prayer and, arising, Mrs. Turpin declared she had regained her hearing. Now Ben's more than a trifle worried. He's afraid someone will have faith enough to set his eyes straight and that would never do.

Ben Turpin To Be At Bazaar (1924 May 2, in part)

Ben Turpin, with all his eyes, will be at the St. Francis de Sales Bazaar Saturday night in person. The Saturday night program will conclude the bazaar and a record crowd is expected, both for the opportunity to see the well-known Ben and to eat the delicious chicken dinner which will be served.[207]

Ben was present the final night program of the Catholic bazaar Saturday at the Elks clubhouse and did his part in raising a substantial sum for the fund for the new school building for St. Francis de Sales church. The bazaar proved a great success, financially and socially, and large crowds attended the afternoon and evening programs given.[208]

1924 May 25: Four companies are at work at the Mack Sennett Studio turning out two-reelers for Pathé under the new releasing contract signed by Sennett recently. Ben Turpin has begun a travesty on *Romeo and Juliet* under the direction of Harry Sweet. Natalie Kingston plays Juliet. Alice Day and Vernon Dent are also in the cast.

F. Richard Jones is directing *East of the Water Plug*, the first of a series of two-reel comedies starring Ralph Graves. Alice Day plays the feminine lead with Vernon Dent and Andy Clyde in the cast. Under the direction of Harry Edwards, Harry Langdon is working on the eighth of his series of two-reelers, tentatively called *The Night Watchman*. Marceline Day plays the feminine lead with Madeline Hurlock and Frank Coleman in support. Del Lord is working on an all-star comedy tentatively called *Five Gallons, Please* featuring Sid Smith, Billy Bevan, Jack Richardson. Barbara Pierce plays the feminine lead.[209]

Burlesque Is Popular In The Movies — Sennett (1924 June 1)

The Mack Sennett burlesque, *Where's My Wandering Boy This Evening?* with Ben Turpin and Madeline Hurlock, was received with such enthusiasm by comedy fans that the producer has followed this success with another series of burlesques. Ben Turpin is at work on a *Romeo and Juliet* travesty.[210]

Yukon Jake (re June 6, 1924)

Turpin is Cyclone Bill, a gum-shoeing sheriff with wriggly eyes and quick on the trigger. He is called in to quell the disturbances raised by Yukon Jake, an Eskimo bad man played by Kalla Pasha. Along with his henchmen, Kalla abducts the daughter of the Mayor of the town, Natalie Kingston in her leading lady debut, and Ben sets out in pursuit to rescue her. A chase takes them from one part of the country to Alaska (by clever split-screen technique) where Ben, after many heartbreaking struggles, succeeds in rescuing the girl and bringing back the bandit terrors in handcuffs.

A short time later, Sennett loses copyright infringement suit over *Yukon Jake*. Poet and author of *The Ballad of Yukon Jake*, E. E. Paramore, was awarded $2500 damages.

Alice Day Becomes Rapid Change Artist (1924 June 8)

Alice Day, dainty ingénue playing leads in Mack Sennett comedies, is doing a chic sale these days. Playing in two pictures simultaneously, Alice is learning all the tricks of the rapid change artist. When the director excuses her from the Ralph Graves set, in which she wears a riding habit, Alice makes a dash for her dressing room, emerging a moment later as a demure country lass to play with Ben Turpin in his current picture, *Romeo and Juliet*.

When not working on either set, Alice heads to the wardrobe to be fitted in an evening dress for the next Ralph Graves comedy. Being leading lady in two pictures at once has its disadvantages, particularly when one's lunch hour from one set has to be spent taking close-ups for the other picture.

Sioux City Sunday Journal

Sennett Busy On Four Big Films *(1924 June 15)*

To take care of the increased production called for under Mack Sennett's new contract with Pathé, four companies are working simultaneously on the Sennett "lot." Ben Turpin is finishing his travesty on *Romeo and Juliet* and getting ready to do a burlesque on *Three Weeks* with Madeline Hurlock as the queen. Ralph Graves is working on his second comedy for Sennett, supported by Alice Day, Vernon Dent, and Charlotte Mineau. Harry Edwards is directing Harry Langdon in the ninth of the comedian's series; Marceline Day plays opposite him with Madeline Hurlock and Frank Coleman in featured parts. Billy Bevan, Sid Smith, Madeline Hurlock, Barbara Pierce, and Kalla Pasha are being directed by Ralph Ceder in a new sea comedy.[212]

Cashing Checks Easy for Turpin *(1924 July 6)*

Ben Turpin had an amusing experience on his recent trip East. In Detroit, he ran short of cash and presented a check for a thousand dollars at one of the banks in the city. The teller looked at the amount, at the signature, and at the well-dressed, conventional-looking man on the other side of the counter. The bank's clerk was skeptical and called the cashier. After a lengthy discussion, which annoyed and then amused Ben, the efficient teller returned to the wicket and politely inquired if Mr. Turpin had any identification.[213]

Two Added to Sennett Staff *(1924 July 6)*

Reggie Morris and Edgar Kennedy are the newest additions to the Mack Sennett directorial staff. Both have been assigned to the Ben Turpin unit.

Fun — From the Seamy Side

"When slapstick events occur in real life they aren't so funny," groaned Ben Turpin, focusing his eyes on the tip of his nose.

"When I was a young fellow I earned a living pulling taffy at county fairs. Used to throw strings of taffy over a big hook outside a candy booth. Used to pretend to throw it at someone in the crowd, then yank it back just in time.

"One day when I made a swipe at a fat man in the crowd he mistook it and dodged the wrong way. I laid a big collar of red hot taffy around his neck. He let out a demoniacal yell.

"Someone whispered to me, 'Beat it, kid — that's the Chief of Police!' He was Chief of Police of Cincinnati. The next freight leaving town carried a badly scared taffy expert to far parts."[214]

Romeo and Juliet *(re August 3, 1924)*

Singer Rodney St. Clair (Turpin) and Bill Durham (Vernon Dent) compete for the love of Betty Baker, played by Alice Day. Ben, who thinks he has the prettiest girl in town engaged to him, is foiled by his prospective father-in-law when Betty's father chooses

Bill. Rodney sings a farewell song that moves everyone, including Bill. In revenge for his throw-down, Ben goes to the city to become an actor and incidentally meets Mlle. Midnight, a well-known vamp played by Natalie Kingston. He becomes engaged and, not knowing of the woman's past, he is confronted with some local gossip and photographs, determining him to break the engagement, but the vamp decides otherwise and Turpin proceeds to take the part of Romeo in a local amateur theatrical. All goes well until the second act when something goes wrong with the props and Turpin, in an attempt to scale the castle wall, is nearly drowned in an improvised moat. He is rescued, however, and the vamp turns him loose. Rodney then calls his mom, who tells him to pursue his love and not give up. Rodney eventually wins because he is smarter than Bill and he returns again to his old time sweetheart.

Moving Picture World thought: This subject joins a few thousand other burlesques on the story of adolescent love and at least earns a place near the head of the procession, though it doesn't get very far away from time-honored gags. But it is somewhat different from the rest in that Sennett has modernized it to the extent of a wallpapered home, the wax wreaths on the mantelpiece, and a dad who doesn't favor Romeo's subtle, slant-eyed suit. Only near the end does Sennett resort to the rustic stage presentation of *Romeo and Juliet* and it is well done. One of the most amusing bits is the result of some trick photography where Turpin wiggles his ears while he sings Tosti's *Goodbye Forever* at the family organ.

Are Cross-Eyes Bad Luck? Ask Ben Turpin

Ben Turpin says he knows a great many people who believe that cross-eyes are bad luck. He often sees people look at him and then quickly cross their fingers or count three. And an interviewer not long ago sat with Ben Turpin for an hour with the fingers of her left hand crossed while she took notes with her right.

"But," says Ben, "that's one superstition that's the bunk." And he can produce a bank book showing a more comfortable balance than a lot ever hope to enjoy to prove it. And it was all accumulated since his vision became scrambled. Before that fortunately unfortunate incident in his life, Ben was entirely satisfied to do his turn in burlesque and cheap vaudeville for a very modest wage.

Now he is engaged in such ambitious work as burlesquing the classics for Mack Sennett. He recently finished a travesty on *Romeo and Juliet* and will give a cross-eyed version of *Ben Hur* in the near future.[215]

Turpin, In Latest, Apes Von Stroheim by A.H. Frederick, NEA Service
(1924 August 2)

Hollywood, Aug 2 — Neither *Three Weeks* nor *Foolish Wives*, presenting as they do such ample opportunities for burlesque, should have escaped the hands of the funsters. They didn't. Mack Sennett recently completed the filming of *Three Foolish Weeks*, as the name suggests, a double-barreled burlesque.

Principal star is Ben Turpin, he of the misbehaving eyes and prankish nature, but otherwise a renovation. Not now the shabby suit and misfit neckwear; no, indeed. Turpin has modeled himself upon the person of Erich von Stroheim, due allowance being made for the different fields of their talents. Eyeglass, walking stick, uniform, and medals all complete.

To those who expect to laugh because of the dissimilar similarity between either of the serious pictures and the takeoff, perhaps Turpin's makeup will be the funniest thing in the picture. To those who enjoy Turpin and the Sennett studio humor, well, they may expect a two-reel treat in the near future.

Which all leads to the declaration — or hint to theatergoers — that the picture is much more a straightaway Sennett comedy than a burlesque. The title, Turpin's make-up, a tiger-skin rug, and a few scattered scenes are the principal connection between it and its serious predecessors.

Considered as a Sennett comedy only, it is good — with the exception of a few scenes which might much better have been left out. However, the fun moves fast. Turpin's courageousness, symbolized by his uniform, and the total lack of it gives him new opportunities for "gags" or incident development, of which he takes the fullest opportunity. Even the time-honored scene of the small man fearing physical violence from a larger threatener is given zest by Turpin's characterization.

Madeline Hurlock, the love-smitten queen, handles what part she has capably and, much more to the point, pulchritudinously, while Supervising Director F. Richard Jones has set the scenes with serious thought to the purpose for which the picture was planned. Perhaps you would wish *Three Foolish Weeks* was closer to the theme of *Three Weeks* and *Foolish Wives*. Perhaps not, depending upon individual inclination. But at the least, there is this: something new in Turpin's makeup and the picture's setting. At the best, there is an exceptionally good Sennett comedy with some new incidents.[216]

1924 August 6, *The Lowell Sun (Massachusetts, in part):*
Under the supervision of F. Richard Jones, Supervising Director, Mack Sennett has outlined a very definite schedule of production aims for his comedians, varying in degree from slapstick to the borderland of drama. Four distinct units are working each with a separate and definite field. First of these is the Ralph Graves unit, destined to produce "straight" comedies with a slight love theme interjected. To the Graves unit have been assigned the Sennett Bathing Beauties.

Second is the Ben Turpin unit, with the cross-eyed one programmed to make burlesque and satire — first of these, recently finished, being *Three Foolish Weeks* and with *The Virginian* being considered as the next object for Turpin's levity. The Sennett "All Star" group will continue much as formerly with slapstick. Harry Langdon, former vaudeville star, heads the fourth unit, which will produce the "situation" humor of the lot. These comedies will contain pathos and "straight" intermingled with some slapstick, slower moving than the Lloyd films, and comparable in tempo to those in which Mabel Normand starred prior to her eclipse — temporary or permanent, announcement not yet ready to be made.[217]

Turpin Breaks Ankle — X-Ray Discloses Fractured Bone as Result of Fall
(1924 August 4)
An X-ray examination yesterday disclosed that Ben Turpin had broken a small bone in his ankle when he slipped and fell on a greasy garage floor last Saturday. Turpin at first thought the pain only a slight sprain. His physician says he will be forced to discontinue work for three weeks and in the meantime, work on the production of his burlesque of

The Virginian will be stopped, it was stated. Harry Langdon, also working at the Mack Sennett studio, was forced to quit work when he developed a bad case of Kleig eyes.[218]

1924 August 16: Somehow or other, Ben Turpin seems to have all the luck when it comes to picking out real beauties for leading ladies. His latest, the statuesquely pulchritudinous Natalie Kingston, who makes her debut in Turpin's *Yukon Jake*, recently released by Mack Sennett for Pathé. Ben's eyes may look all wrong, but they do evidently see all right.

1924 August 31 *(in part):* Ben Turpin has just completed his new burlesque, which kids the main episodes of *Foolish Wives* and *Three Weeks* and is being released under the title of *Three Foolish Weeks*. Madeline Hurlock plays the Queen and Billy Bevan the King. Camera work begins this week on Turpin's burlesque on *The Virginian*, which will be called *The West Virginian* (released as *The Reel Virginian*). Alice Day will play the school teacher. Reggie Morris and Ed Kennedy are directing the new Turpin series. Ralph Graves is finishing his third two-reeler comedy, *Riders of the Purple Cows*, under the direction of Ralph Ceder. Under the direction of Harry Edwards, Harry Langdon is well into production of a war comedy, tentatively *Over Here* (released as *All Night Long*). Langdon is supported by Natalie Kingston, Vernon Dent, and Fanny Kelly.[219]

Ben Turpin Reported Recovering Rapidly (1924 August 21)

Ben Turpin, the motion picture comedian, yesterday was reported to be rapidly recovering following an operation performed Tuesday night by Dr. Carl E. Conn at the Hollywood Hospital. Although operated on for a small abscess on his back, Turpin also is receiving treatment for fracture of a small bone in his foot, received several days ago while working in a picture.[220]

Three Foolish Weeks (re September 14, 1924)

The Baron St. Clair (Ben Turpin) starts on a new conquest of hearts and selects as his victim the Queen of Anchovia, Madeline Hurlock. Fortune favors him when he rescues the Queen from a runaway accident. The chase is a long one and the pair seek shelter in the Witch's Inn. The gallant Baron, unable to restrain his wooing proclivities, attempts to make love to the innkeeper's daughter — a terrific battle ensues — and the luckless Baron is routed into the darkness.

Moving Picture World: Ben Turpin makes of the romantic the ridiculous in *Three Foolish Weeks*, a Mack Sennett comedy version of *Three Weeks*. Under the direction of Edgar Kennedy and Reggie Morris, Turpin is supported by Madeline Hurlock, Billy Bevan, William Lowery, and Judy King. This comedy is of the thriller type. Turpin as a Count is compelled through circumstance to rescue a restless princess from her runaway steeds. The timely arrival of night forces them to seek refuge in a house by the wayside. There the comedy supplies the most humor. Turpin, again through circumstance, is chased by the father of the house from one bedroom to the other. In each room, he compromises himself and one of the father's fair daughters. Eating breakfast in a bath of perfume and lashing himself amidships with a pair of corsets get the laughs right at the comedy's opening. This offering should prove a great success, especially with Turpin fans.[221]

"Old-Timer" in Ben Turpin's Latest Film

Sam Allen played the role of "Uncle Hughey" in the original stage production of *The Virginian* years ago. When Kenneth Harlan made the screen version, Allen was brought to the coast to work in the picture. Recently, Mack Sennett has completed a burlesque of this famous stage play, starring Ben Turpin, entitled *The Reel Virginian* and Allen was cast for the same role in the Pathé burlesque as he did in the legitimate stage performance.

On September 29, 1924, Sennett's Production Supervisor and longtime associate Dick Jones left for a similar position with Mack's biggest competitor, Hal Roach. In December, Arthur Ripley was bumped up to head the scenario department at Sennett.

The Reel Virginian (re October 26, 1924)

Ben as Rodney St. Clair, a cowpuncher of the Western plains, is violently in love with the newly-arrived schoolteacher played by Alice Day. Meanwhile, Rodney's Uncle Louie Larimore (Sam Allen) and his mail-order bride-to-be, Mademoseille Sans Souci (Fred Kovert), arrive in town. A double wedding is about to take place when Rodney is accused of being the head of a gang of cattle thieves. Just as he is about to be hung, the mail-order fiancée, who is in reality a male detective dressed in woman's clothes, arrives on the scene with a posse and arrests the real gang. All ends well for Rodney and his schoolteacher sweetheart.

One of Sennett's newer staff writers at this time was Tay Garnett, with whom Leonard Maltin had the privilege of discussing Ben Turpin. "I wrote a lot of stories for him, many in collaboration with Frank Capra, Hal Conklin, or Vernon Smith (the Sennett writers always worked in teams). In this area, I have some very definite opinions: Ben lacked a great deal of being a funny man. He was funny only when placed in a ludicrous position — particularly one of grave danger — then, playing it dead seriously (perhaps a bit over-seriously), which was the only thing he could do.

"Naturally, his material had to be prepared by someone who was familiar with his limitations. For purposes of illustration, take Stan Laurel or Harry Langdon. We used to say of Laurel (for whom I wrote many stories) that all one had to do was to put Stan in a set with a stepladder, turn the crank, and you were a cinch to come up with a beautiful hunk of very funny film. The same thing, in a lesser degree, was true of Harry Langdon. If you put a ladder in the same set with Turpin, he'd probably look at it, then say 'How 'n hell ya expect me to act? Get that goddamned thing outta here!'

"I guess what I'm trying to say is that in my opinion, Turpin was not a mental giant." Maltin added, "This is not to say that Turpin's films weren't funny — but those laughs were built in by the gagmen and directors, and not the star. Turpin was just one of many silent comics who depended almost entirely on their material; left to their own devices, they were lost."[333]

In one of Turpin's better interviews conducted by Neil M. Clark for *American* magazine, November 1924, Clark noted: "It is pleasant to hear Ben Turpin talk. He constantly surprises you with an accent all his own. He comes by it partly, I suspect, from the French of his people, partly from a long and intimate acquaintance with the vernacular of East Side New Yorkers, of tramps and vagabonds; and of actors, some of whom have a picturesque jargon. He is a small man, with features that have been roughened by a good deal of hardship and knocking about. But he is not at all bad-looking, as you might suppose him to be from his pictures. The crossed eyes so prominent on the screen are scarcely noticed when you are talking with him."

Turpin told Clark, "As for me on the screen, I'm just a goof. Everything I do is wrong, all wrong. That's why people laugh. I don't look right. I don't do right. I try to carve a roast and the dog gets most of it. I wear the wrong kind of tie, and it comes off in the peas. I try to propose to my best girl, and I say the wrong things. It isn't only comic looks that make a comedian. He's got to act comic too!

"I take my hat off to two men, and to one big bunch of men and women — Charlie Chaplin, Mack Sennett, and the public. Charlie brought me out here, and he gave me my start. He taught me a lot about the business. I'll always feel grateful to him for it.

"Mack Sennett put me over big. He never has broken his word about one single thing. That's the kind of man I tie to. I'll never work for anybody but him. He knows when I quit him, I'm through for good.

"And the public — every actor ought to take off his hat to the public! If they like you, you're good. If they don't, you're gone. If you make them cry, you're good. If you make them laugh, you're good.

"But if they sit out there and just look at you, and kind of yawn, you're through. You've got to move them, some way. You've got to get over or get out!"

"I'm fifty-seven years old — will be, my next birthday. I've taken all the hard knocks, but I don't regret them. Acting is hard work, but I like it. I take good care of myself now — I'm in bed by eight-thirty every night!

"Since I've been with Sennett I haven't missed a day, haven't been late to an appointment, and haven't had any spells of temperament. Just work — that's me!

"Money? Yes. It has come fast lately, even if it was a long time starting to come big. Money's nice to have, but I don't care so much for it. I'd just as soon start again tomorrow without a cent. I'd get along. I could eat soup bones now as well as I ever could, and they'd taste as good as porterhouse steaks. I could live in one room without the luxuries I've got here. I could live anywhere — as long as my wife was with me. That's what counts!"[3]

Author Don Ryan wrote of a day's visit to the Mack Sennett studio and his stops at the four working units one particular day, late 1924. Here Ryan witnessed the filming of Harry Langdon in *Boobs in the Wood*; Billy Bevan during *Giddap!*; Ralph Graves, Natalie Kingston, writer Felix Adler, and director Eddie Cline filming *Off His Trolley*; and Turpin in the midst of his latest production, *The Marriage Circus*.

On the first set, Ben Turpin, cross-eyed, naïve, religious, devoted to his art, which is himself, is working with Louise Carver, who, if one can believe her story, was the star of *Fifty Miles from Boston* when, nearly twenty years ago, Mae Murray danced as a chorus girl in that production. Miss Carver wears a cauliflower ear, the gift of Andy Clyde, who is called in as a specialist when inspired make-up is required.

Ben started out on the Sennett lot eight years ago. He was a comedian with Sennett and with Chaplin. Ben has not become a producer. He still lives in his make-up with a childish glee that animates his one-hundred-and-eight pounds of awkwardness, his crossed eyes, and his stubby mustache.

Directing traffic at Santa Monica Boulevard and Western Avenue near his Hollywood residence is Ben's recreation after work, a wish fulfillment carried over from his boyhood. The policeman on that corner is grateful for the opportunity to enjoy an hour's relaxation in Bernie's delicatessen and Ben is happy.

Ben is now fifty-six years old. But if he sees you looking at him, he will show off in the same manner as Tom Sawyer before his girl. Ben will do his "Fall 108."

He falls forward on his face, body rigid. Flops over on his back with a crash that makes you think he has broken every bone in his head — it is his hands and feet striking. Motionless he lies — a corpse for the time you could count ten. Then he raises his head at the end of his gosling neck and looks around like a bird. It is Ben Turpin's neck that is funny — funnier than his eyes.

"Ma!"

The squawk of a penguin pierces the din of the four comedy companies at work.

"Ma!" squawks Ben to his film mother of a cauliflower ear. "This collar's off, Ma!"

Rodney St. Clair is dressing for his wedding. His laundry arrived at the last minute — as in a Freudian nightmare. As his mother hurried to her son's chamber, bearing the necessary garments, she dropped the dickey — the starched shirt front that is the piece de resistance of any formal comedy make-up. The heavy — natural enemy of all heroes — was lurking in the hallway and the villain planted his foot with fell purpose on the virgin bosom. Rodney now stands under the chandelier in his chamber, equipped in the dickey marked by a sooty footprint, while his mother vainly strives to button the refractory wing collar about the gosling neck.

She nearly succeeds at last. Then, just as the stubborn wing is almost secured, the whole equipment gives way. The collar springs back and, imbued with life by wires, soars like a bird to the ceiling. At the same instant, a property man, lying at length on the floor, jiggles other wires and away comes the dickey, exposing the polka-dot underwear of the bedeviled bridegroom.

Bawling in a dismayed whiskey tenor, nevertheless, the resourceful Rodney removes a shoe and hurls it after the fleeing collar. It brings the collar down together with a globe from the chandelier, which crashes on the head of the devoted mother. In reality, the globe is dropped by a tousled young man wearing a green eyeshade who has seated himself astride a board laid across the stage above range of the camera. They were doing this scene at nine-thirty a.m. They will still be doing it at four-thirty p.m. At this hour, Ben always calls it a day. It is the only arbitrary piece of tyranny which this star inflicts. And he has a reason for it. At five o'clock, he is due to relieve his friend the traffic cop.[222]

In 1924, one movie fan in Bennington, Vermont wrote *Photoplay:*

Why do exhibitors show Mack Sennett comedies? In the well-known infancy of the industry, they were the best of their kind. But since then, other producers have made great strides. Sennett seems to stand still. Barring a few gags in Ben Turpin's pictures, I haven't gotten a healthy laugh from a Sennett comedy in years.

Having read about how funny Harry Langdon was, I saw three of his comedies. They created scarcely a ripple of laughter. We are not hard to please, either. Extraneous matters never did Mabel Normand half as much harm as the vehicles Sennett gave her. *The Extra*

Girl had a plot that was threadbare. *Suzanna* was totally devoid of humorous situations and *Molly O'* was extremely crude. No actress could survive such material.

— Elizabeth Kapitz

Ben Turpin Picked to Referee Fights (1924 December 9)

Ben Turpin will referee the fights at the Pasadena Armory Thursday night. Whether the cross-eyed comedian can please the fighters and the fans at the same time is in question. "Movie Night" will bring a crowd of film folk to the arena. Main Event: Phil Mata to meet Jimmie Powell.[223]

Ben Turpin May Leave Screen Soon by Jack Jungmeyer (1924 December 13)

Hollywood, Dec. 13 — Ben Turpin, the inimitable, is reported to be about to begin a slow process of voluntary retirement from the screen. He has one more contract picture to do for Mack Sennett. After that, the rumor is Ben will make a picture now and then as the mood hits him. He will retire and, when he does, full of honors and not without plenty of kale, for Ben concedes nothing to any man when it comes to saving his nickels.

Turpin, strange figure of the screen world, has left an indelible imprint of his personality. He will be remembered when many of the film's famous shall have passed the ken of fans. Queer combination of pomp and childlike simplicity is Ben. Most funny when serious. Funny to his studio mates because he is so deadly serious. Doing the wrong things at the right moment with the earnestness of an old-time Shakespearean actor. It was this proclivity of being unconsciously comic that paved the way to pictures for him.

An illustration is a Turpin classic of the old Essanay days in Chicago. He was employed as a roustabout, the butt of every practical joker on the lot. He was always trying to ingratiate himself. Flowers were needed for a scene. Resourceful Ben, eager to please, hopped a fence into a neighboring cemetery, plucked the required flowers from the graves, and after completion of the scene, as solemnly planted them on the grave again. Ben's idea of saving expenses.

At a critical moment on another occasion when a temperamental leading man wanted someone for the role of a cabby, Turpin volunteered. He was unconsciously so funny that hard-boiled eggs around the studio who hadn't cracked a grin for months screamed aloud. Shortly after that, he graduated from a $20-a-week porter to $25-a-week property boy, sent by the company to California.

He and Sennett eventually hit it off and Ben has been with the latter ever since. Turpin, whose "cocked" eyes resulted from constant deliberate crossing in a vaudeville act, is not at all sensitive about his affliction. It has indeed brought him a fortune. Life is all serious to Ben. That's why it's so funny to all his audiences. We hope that the reports of his impending retirement have been greatly exaggerated.[224]

1924 December 19: Ben and Carrie were among 40 Hollywood favorites who attended H. A. Snow's Jungle Movie Ball at Oakland Auditorium, Oakland, California. Arriving at the Southern Pacific station, First and Broadway, the stars were escorted by police motorcycle guard, six fire trucks, and a forty-piece band. They first toured Eastbay, ending at the Oakland Press Club, where they were entertained at luncheon. Following a banquet at the Hotel Oakland, the Ball was held that evening at the Auditorium, officiated and led by Mayor John Davie and actress Dorothy Devore.

The stars present also included Laura and Viola LaPlante, Ruth Roland, Clara Bow, Syd Chaplin, Lew Cody, Louise Fazenda, Willard Lewis, Otis Harlan, Irene Rich, Margaret Livingston, Charlotte Merriam, Neal Burns, Cecile Evans, Marguerite Snow, Carl Miller, Kathryn McGuire, Pricilla Dean, Joe Bonomo, Creighton Hale, and others.

Flashes by Grace Kingsley, **Stars in Their Orbits** *(1924 December 23)*
Lloyd Bacon starts a new comedy with Ben Turpin this week.[225]

Catholic Movie Actors' Guild Builds Church (1924 December 24)
Los Angeles — Hollywood Catholic motion picture actors will have a church of their own in which to worship Christmas Day.

The Church of the Good Shepherd, built through the efforts of the Catholic Motion Picture Actors Guild, is completed and the first mass will be celebrated in it Christmas morning at 5 o'clock. It is located in Beverly Hills.

Thomas Meighan is president of the actors' guild. May McAvoy donated the church organ, valued at $11,000. Jackie Coogan's father gave the three altars at a cost of $12,000 and Ben Turpin donated $8,000 for the pews.[226]

At Last! Ben Turpin Grants An Interview by Ben Turpin *(1924 December 28)*
Summer has gone and all the little buttercups have quit making butter and the bullfrogs have all stopped bulling.

The trees are even leaving while the old maids are dusting off the parlor sofa in hopes that the coming winter will bring better luck. I do love the call of winter as it softly coos to its fairy Godfather, old man Santa Claus. I love Santa Claus because he only comes around once a year — I couldn't afford to have him call any oftener. The only folks who can afford Santa Claus more than once a year, according to my boss, Mack Sennett, are chorus girls and bathing beauties. It's a poor year for them without nine birthdays and five Christmas celebrations. They don't call them that, but they amount to the same thing in the way of presents.

Sweet Christmas Cheer
There are other things I like about winter, but at the moment, I can't think of what they are. I could go on and on and on describing the snow-clad valleys with their virgin whiteness, but I don't recall having ever seen any. And winter girls, eh, how I love to see them in their bundled up loveliness; of course, you can see more of them in the summer on the beaches. Still, what you see in the winter ain't so bad, it ain't.

The department stores and their employees are about the strongest folks I know of for Christmas, especially the employees. Of course, the store hates to see Christmastime come around because it helps them clear their shelves of knick-knacks they have seen for years and have grown strongly fond of. The employees, like mailmen, are crazy at the chance of working 18 to 20 hours a day during the rush season.

Bootleggers' Delight

Bootleggers and their families admit that it's Christmas "spirit" that adds to their joy in life while snow shovelers find the season profitable everywhere but California.

Even motion picture folks are known to celebrate at least one Christmas each year. I can vouch for this statement as far as the Mack Sennett studios are concerned.

Every Christmas, the carpenters build a movie fireplace with a movie Christmas tree and then the fun begins. All the girls, before leaving the studio, hang up a stocking (an old one) and then come bounding in work the day after to see what they get. Some of them find Rolls Royce cars parked in the lisle hangar. Last year, I got a load of coal in mine.[227]

Sennett Cameraman Will Proffer New Trick Photography (1925 January 4)

Some trick photography will be seen shortly in a new Sennett comedy featuring Ben Turpin. Ernie Crockett, chief cameraman for Mack Sennett, has been specializing in this kind of work for many years and his new achievement has aroused the interest of a number of other camera experts. In the new comedy, Ben will appear to be exploring the depths of the ocean one minute and soaring through the clouds the next. Mr. Crockett believes his recent development marks a very important step ahead in this branch of motion picture photography.[228]

Carrie Turpin: *"I read in the magazines that comedians are always serious and thoughtful and tragic away from their work. Ben isn't. He is always carrying on at home. He has more pep than most men half his age…Maybe his good health is the reason for his good spirits. He is never sick and is always alive with energy. If Ben were the serious and tragic type of man, my illness of the past year would have been unbearable. His good humor and clowning have made me forget the hours. You might think I would get used to Ben's antics and cease to be amused by them. I don't. When he flits through my room doing a scarf dance with a bath towel, it is as funny to me today as it was fifteen years ago.*

"Ben's clowning at home mostly takes the form of dancing — any kind of dancing. And he is more graceful than many girls. He can kick high, and he loves to dance to the radio music. Ben's burlesque of Rudolph Valentino doing the tango is one of the funniest things I have ever seen. I wish Mack Sennett would put it into one of Ben's comedies.

"We have taken an apartment since I've been ill, and keep no servants. So Ben washes the dishes, and entertains me with the juggling act he used to do in the circus; only now it is my best Haviland ware he uses instead of the circus china.

"Ben is seldom serious before people. They always expect him to be funny and he never disappoints them. He likes to show off like a little boy, and loves an audience. I am the only one who probably sees him when he isn't cocking his eyes at somebody for a laugh, or doing his '108' fall. When we have guests Ben loves to startle them by suddenly doing this fall. To the onlooker it appears and looks as if he has cracked open his head as he strikes the floor. But the awful thud is made with the palms of his hands and heels of his shoes striking the floor as he falls prone. For a moment he lies there and you are convinced he is unconscious — then he pops up his head, cocks his eyes at you and grins.

"There is one hour of the day, however, in which Ben utterly relaxes. This is after dinner in the evening. He will go to the front porch of our apartment and sit in the twilight with his cigarette, watching the people thronging into the neighborhood theatre around the corner."[4]

1925 February 25, *Portsmouth Daily Times:*

Joseph Hergesheimer, James Branch Cabell, Theodore Dreiser, and George Jean Nathan have all written exhaustive and critical appreciations of Lillian Gish, the movie star. Yet at a theatre next door, Ben Turpin was playing and the box office receipts were higher than those where Miss Gish was displaying her subtle and elusive charms.

The Wild Goose Chaser (re January 18, 1925)

Because Rodney St. Clair is fonder of wild birds than his wife, she seeks a divorce. Her lawyer, who by chance was Rodney's college mate (Jack Cooper), plans to teach Rodney a lesson — but a movie show (taken in to kill time while waiting for a train) presents a picture based along the same lines. After reconsideration, the pair returns to Rodney's house and after a family mix-up, wherein the peacemaker gets the worst of it, the St. Clairs kiss and make up.

Moving Picture World: Ben Turpin fans will find that the comedian's latest for Mack Sennett to be replete with Turpin grimaces and Turpin stunts. It is about as funny a two-reeler as he has ever turned out. In this comedy, Turpin is a "great" hunter. He has guns ranging from a popper to a Springfield. One is a double-barrel affair, only the barrels separate when the comedian has "two birds to kill." Trilby Clark, in the role of the hunter's wife, follows Turpin through marshland and heather until a "friend" of her husband suggests that she flee with him. The flight includes a picture show and what they see makes them decide to return and tear up a note to the hunter. The hunter picks up the note and after shooting up the house in Turpin style, he and his wife agree to forget about hunting and estrangement.[229]

Turpin About to Retire (1925 March 1)

His strabismic excellency, Ben Turpin, is preparing to retire. The comedian of double outlook will not, it is said, renew his contract to star in Sennett pictures.

Wherefore Sennett has resolved to give special attention to the development of Harry Langdon as his ace. Ben is tired of the game and is not a little distracted by the continued illness of his wife. The devotion of the star to his wife is one of the proverbs of filmland. Last year, he gave up all work for several weeks and took Mrs. Turpin to the shrine of Ste. Anne Beaupre in Quebec. All efforts of doctors to alleviate her deafness having failed, the miraculous method of a novena was tried. It was a different Ben than the public knows who solemnly made nine pilgrimages to the Saint's shrine with his invalid wife. They returned happy in the belief that she had found partial healing, but the betterment was not permanent. Ben's contract now limits his daily work to six hours so that he may devote the remainder to Mrs. Turpin.[230]

A Raspberry Romance (re March 1, 1925)

Rodney St. Clair, an actor, is told to get a new act before night or leave town. A lawyer plans to marry his sweetheart in order to get her money. While Rodney is rehearsing a new act, the lawyer falsely tells him his sweetheart is locked in the home of Leo Mallet, the lawyer's partner. Leo catches Rodney in a room with his beautiful wife. He chases him into a bedroom, which turns out to be on the stage of a local theater. After a fight, Rodney wins his sweetheart and the audience, thinking it all a part of the show, applaud loudly.

Moving Picture World: Followers of Ben Turpin will like this Sennett subject featuring the cross-eyed hero. Ben is to marry Blanche, who is somewhat heftier than himself, and tries to make good as a singer on the old home Opera House stage, being greeted with vegetables.

Circumstantial evidence points to his having vamped a married woman and the husband pursues him onto the stage. There, the audience applauds Ben's frenzied attempts at escape and the husband's pistol shots, thinking them drama. Finally, Ben's gigantic wife-to-be effects a rescue. This is a good comedy.

Ben The Clown Is Scullion to Sick Mrs. Turpin (1925 April 9)

Los Angeles, CA, April 8 — (Special) — From grease paint and $2,500 a week as comedy king to elbow grease as sole dishwasher and manservant around his own little cottage is Ben Turpin's tale of chivalry. The happy married life of Ben and Mrs. Turpin in a comfortable dwelling in Hollywood had long been one of the idyllic bits of realism in a background of purple pasts and crimson presents in the movie colony. Last December, Mrs. Turpin fell ill. Her hearing became affected to the point of extreme deafness and in the last picture Ben made, he went through his ocular contortions more by force of will than from the love of it.

Doctors told Ben Mrs. Turpin's trouble was chiefly mental, but should not be aggravated. His wife's illness always became accentuated when the comedian was compelled to leave her side, so in December, he quit Mack Sennett's salary roll to stay home and cheer her up. Presence of anybody else irked Mrs. Turpin, so all the servants were dismissed and now Ben does the housework.[231]

Ben Turpin To Quit Work In Movies (1925 April 9)
Comedian's Action Due to Illness of Wife

Los Angeles, April 9 — (AP) — Ben Turpin, motion picture comedian, today announced that he has decided to quit the screen. His retirement was made imperative, he explained, by the serious illness of his wife, who recently suffered two strokes of apoplexy. The comedian said his contract with the Mack Sennett organization expired two months ago and that he had abandoned all plans for the future. "I have to take care of my wife. I think more of her than I do of pictures," he declared. According to friends of the comedian, Turpin is doing his own housework to be near his sick wife, who cannot stand his absence and becomes irritated at the servants.

Our Favorite Movie Star Quits (1925 April 10)

Press dispatches say that Ben Turpin has quit the screen so he can take care of his sick wife and is staying home with her doing the housework because his wife is so nervous servants exasperate her. Ben probably has no heart for doing funny stunts in the movies with his wife in that condition and we are to be deprived of our favorite screen comedian unless the story is just a clever scheme for press agenting Ben.[232]

The Marriage Circus (re April 12, 1925)

For a two-reeler, Mack Sennett has a knock-out in *The Marriage Circus*. Ben Turpin heads the cast of established screen comedians, among whom are Madeline Hurlock, Sunshine Hart, Louise Carver, and William C. Lawrence. Louise Carver as the aggressive mother and Ben as the dutiful and lovelorn son form a couple in this comedy that should weaken almost any audience with laughter. Madeline, the Pathe Vamp, "busts" Ben's heart when she turns him down at the church for another beau. Ben, in order to blot out the blighty past, does a "Ben Hur" with a couple of horses. The wedding party pursues him in several cars, during the course of which the bride is stolen by another admirer. It so happens that Ben's horses collide with the taxicab in which reposes the abducted damsel and he unconsciously effects her rescue. In our estimation, Turpin is at his best in *The Marriage Circus*. MPW

Ben Turpin Must Lay Off — Illness of Wife Requires His Constant Attention (1925 April 14 in part)

Turpin's contract with Sennett expired two months ago and he informed the producer that for the time being, at least, he would retire from the screen, but that he hoped to resume his work again and that if he did so it would be under the Sennett banner.[233]

Ben Turpin's Retirement (1925 April 15)

Ben Turpin, the eccentric comedian with the trick eyes who has made millions laugh, retires from the films. "I must take care of my sick wife," he explains. Mr. Turpin has discharged the servants and is doing the housework himself. This may strike motion picture fans as funny. They may laugh as they picture the whimsical Ben washing dishes, mopping floors, and making beds. There is no mirthfulness about the situation. Mrs. Turpin is very ill and can't endure having anyone around her but her husband and that housekeeping is a solemn business. So the clown of the films turns serious. Or possibly the clown shows his real nature more truly than he did when capering before the klieg lights. It has been observed that master clowns are usually sad when their masks are off. Perhaps it takes essential sadness to be funny.[234]

1925: Ben Turpin has retired. He has a comfortable fortune and his wife is now a chronic invalid, so he certainly has good reasons. But we'll miss him.

The Lonely Clown, The Greatest Love Story of Hollywood by Dorothy Donnell

Ben Turpin has retired. Or rather, Ben Turpin, the comedian with the toe-in eyes, the long stringy neck, and the trick mustache, is playing another role these days with an audience of one. And he is giving his best performance, though the only applause is a sick woman's voice calling in the flat accents of the deaf, "Ben, where are you? I want you, Ben."

Since last December, when his wife, an invalid for years, had grown so much worse that she could not bear him out of her sight, hardly out of her reach, the Sennett studio has caught only fleeting glimpses of Ben on such rare occasions as he could steal away from home for an hour or two to visit his old haunts. If there is wistfulness in his comic eyes as he watched his old friends, nobody knows it, for Ben speaks cheerily, "What's the good of all the money I got if it can't make my wife well? She's all that counts. As long as she needs me, the movies can go hang. I'm tired of acting anyhow."

They have had their last laugh at him now. Only one person has ever taken him seriously. When others saw only a grotesque little figure dressed as *Happy Hooligan* up on the stage going through ludicrous antics, the woman who played *Happy Hooligan's* wife saw a great actor, a Barrymore. Years later, when an audience shrieked with mirth over one of Ben Turpin's burlesque Romeos on the screen, there was one who did not laugh at the quaint little figure with thin legs in black tights and Adam's apple showing above the ruff as he rolled mis-mated eyes at the beauteous leading lady. To Ben Turpin's wife, he was a real Romeo, dashing, gallant.

Long before he left the studio, the Turpins had given up the big house and the servants and moved into a small apartment where Ben could do all the housekeeping after his day's work. It is a dramatic contrast, the slapstick comedian grimacing and taking comedy falls as a cross-eyed Lothario, a skinny sheik, a burlesque prince at the studio and then hurrying home to tie an apron around his waist and sweep the dust and cook supper for a sick woman lying on a couch. But those who know say that Ben Turpin was never so funny on the screen as he was at home, clowning the housework to win a smile.

But Mrs. Turpin wanted Ben where she could see him all the time and hear him with her deafened ears. So in December, Ben Turpin retired. He does not use that word.

"We're going to travel till we can find health for her," he told them at the studio.

"Maybe we'll go across to that place in France — Lourdes, where folks leave their crutches. If one novena isn't enough, we'll make two of them — three. Yes, sir, when she's well enough to take the trip, we'll go to France. And when she's better, I'll be back."

His last picture has just been released, but Ben Turpin has not seen it. He is playing cook and housemaid and nurse these days. When they are not wandering from Palm Springs to the mountains in search of health for his wife, they are spending their evenings in the little apartment, Mrs. Turpin lying always on her side, Ben listening to the radio, talking the scanty talk of the long-married. Off the screen, Ben Turpin is an insignificant, grey little man with cross-eyes. He doesn't look much like the Great Lover, perhaps, especially in Hollywood. But when I think of Romance in Hollywood, I don't think of Conway Tearle striding masterfully about or of Valentino dancing the minuet in white satin or of Ramon Novarro guiding his steeds in a chariot race; I think of a small, ungainly figure with bent shoulders, balancing a supper tray with clownish awkwardness that a smile may come to the lips of an invalid lying in the shadows.

Each Fault a Virtue by Helen Klumph *(1925 June)*

Everything he does in pictures is wrong and that makes him funny; everything he does in life is grotesque and that makes him the idol of girl interviewers.

Whenever I run into a group of serious thinkers who are talking about the intellectual development of movies and their truly great artists, I think of Ben Turpin.

Ben Turpin's work is the work of a master intellect. Of course, it may not be his intellect. Someone, you insist, may be responsible for his droll gags that inspire such shrieks of laughter. Yet would you deny Michelangelo the carving of his figure of Moses merely because some helper handed him a chisel and because the character was not his own invention? Dramatic acting is emotional; comedy is purely of the intellect. Intellect; ah! Yes, that brings us back to Ben.

I cannot recount to you any long and ponderous utterances of my hero. All that he said to me when I attempted to interview him was, "Where is that lady that has been waiting around and wanting to meet me? Pleased to meetcha. Well, I gotta run along now."

So saying, he pulled a large powder puff out of a grimy pocket and vigorously whacked his nose with it. But that succinct statement tells you a great deal about the man.

After fifty years or more of being pursued by the fair sex — I am sure that he always had the same fatal fascination for women that he has now — he still is too shy to be paraded before admiring interviewers. No luncheons a deux at the Ritz with Ben Turpin; no dreamy waltzes with him at the Annual Ball of Local No. 36 of the Los Angeles Motion Picture Operators Union — both traditional ways of stars' winning the favor of the press. No; in order to interview Ben, one has to sneak out on his set at the studio, hiding behind Mack Sennett himself and sending an emissary from the business office to fetch Ben. But from long experience, he knows that there is something amiss in Mr. Sennett's coming out this way. Ah — a woman! The ever-gallant Mr. Sennett has yielded to the pleading of one of his admirers and brought her out. Well then, he must submit for a moment to her admiring gaze.

He comes off the set with a mincing gait, the detached manner of a man of many affairs, and a distracted voice that proclaims he has yielded to the exigencies of the moment only after much coaxing.

But one can always admire him from a distance. Not at the Ambassador pool nor at one of the society polo matches does one look for Ben; it is at one of the busiest corners of Western Ave. in Los Angeles that one finds him every Sunday afternoon about four o'clock, taking the place of the traffic officer on duty. It is the one place where his ability to look due north and west at the same time stands him in good stead.

Nearby, he lives in a simple cottage with elegant garden walls of chicken wire. His one concession to the actors' policy of displaying temperament — or at least unusual tastes — in public is taking his parrot riding with him. This morose pet rides on the upper curve of the steering wheel and when the wheel must be turned, languidly moves a step or two to the side.

Riding in boxcars from coast to coast and begging handouts at back doors was Ben Turpin's primary and preparatory school; vaudeville was his Alma Mater; movies were the haven of refuge that beckoned him at twenty-five sure dollars every week after he had been playing *Happy Hooligan* on one-night stands and obscure vaudeville circuits for eleven years. It was during that time that his eyes became crossed.

Ben admits now that he is fifty-seven years old. Perhaps that allows for a vanity discount, too. What other hero has ever come into his prime — has ever reached the fine flowering of his art at such an age?

But of course. For our Ben — thus fondly do all the girl interviewers who have had the pleasure of grasping his hand refer to him — is like nothing and no one else in the world. If he weren't, he wouldn't be so funny. But he stands supreme in the field of utterly nonsensical comedy because he appears to be the sum total of everyone's faults and everyone's mistakes.[235]

Sennett Plans Many Pictures (1925 July 5)

With the recent retirement of Ben Turpin, Mack Sennett announces increased production activity at his studio with the addition of two more comedy troupes. Six companies are now at work at the Edendale plant making comedies for Pathé release.

New directors and players have been engaged and the administrative forces have been augmented to take care of the added activity. The scenario department, under the direct supervision of Mack Sennett, includes Percy Heath, Arthur Ripley, Jack Jevne, Gus Meins,

Frank Capra, Jefferson Moffitt, and Ewart Adamson. A research department has been added to the studio, in the charge of Leslie Gordon. Titles for Sennett comedies are being written by Felix Adler and A. H. Giebler under the supervision of J. A. Waldron, general manager.

Harry Langdon, having completed his first feature picture (*His First Flame*), is at work on a new two-reeler (*Lucky Stars*) under the direction of Harry Edwards. Del Lord is directing Billy Bevan, Madeline Hurlock, Andy Clyde, and Kewpie Morgan in a tramp story (possibly *From Rags to Britches*). Raymond McKee and Ruth Hiatt are being directed in a domestic comedy by Eddie Cline (*Isn't Love Cuckoo?*). Art Rosson is directing Alice Day, supported by Ernest Wood, Jack Richardson, and Alma Bennett, in her fourth starring film (*A Sweet Pickle*). Ralph Graves is about to begin a new comedy (*Don't Tell Dad*) under the direction of Gil Pratt, recently added to the directorial staff. Lloyd Bacon is preparing a new story to go into production soon. Other players in the Sennett company are Vernon Dent, Eugenia Gilbert, Ruth Taylor, Thelma Parr, Marvin Lobach, Natalie Kingston, William McCall, Joe Young, and Danny O'Shea.

1925 September 2: It was understood that when Ben Turpin quit Mack Sennett recently, it was because his invalid wife needed him more than the screen. He has signed a contract to play in a new picture, which Roy Del Ruth is making for Warner Brothers, *Hogan's Alley*. Turpin says that this is a personal favor to Del Ruth and that upon its completion, he will go into complete retirement.[236]

Ben Turpin And Charlie Murray in Same Film

James Hogan, director of *Steel Preferred*, at a luncheon one day in Hollywood, saw Ben. He suggested that Turpin come to the studio and see the production being filmed, as his old friend Charlie Murray was playing a part in the picture. When Turpin saw Murray, a sort of high jinks was had. Murray suggested that Ben be given a part in the production. When the picture was completed, Turpin was handed a large-size check for his services. "No, boys," said he, returning it, "I had more fun in this picture than I've had for years, and I've been well repaid by playing in the same cast with Charlie." *Pressbook publicity*

On September 22, 1925, newspapers announced that Carrie's condition had grown worse and that she was nearing death. Less than two weeks later on October 1, Carrie Turpin suffered a massive stroke at 3:55 pm at their bungalow at 1059 N. St. Andrews Place in Hollywood, bringing an end to her husband's ten-month vigil at her sickbed. She would have been 44 years old in three weeks. Friends, neighbors, motion picture folk, and the fans all expressed condolences. Other than her husband, Carrie was survived by a father and brother, both living in Michigan. Ben's sister, Ernestine Knies, spent the next few days comforting her brother at his Beverly Hills home. Funeral services were held at the Church of the Blessed Sacrament on October 2, burial at Forest Lawn Mausoleum the following morning.

Ben Turpin's Wife Dies After A Long Vigil Kept By Husband (1925 October 2)

Hollywood, CA, Oct 2 — (AP) — Ben Turpin's long vigil at the bedside of his invalid wife is at an end. The motion picture comedian abandoned his work at the studios when

Carrie LeMieux Turpin became seriously ill last December and the call of the camera was unheeded month after month as he cared for the woman who would accept no other ministrations but his. Yesterday death ended her suffering. The Turpins were married in Chicago about 18 years ago and Mrs. Turpin worked with her husband on the legitimate stage and later in pictures. They were brought to Hollywood ten years ago by Charlie Chaplin. Services will be held for Mrs. Turpin tomorrow at the Church of the Blessed Sacrament, after which her body will be taken to Forest Lawn cemetery.[237]

Cross-Eyed Ben Turpin a Tragic Figure, Sorrowing for Dead Wife
by John P. Miles, United News Staff Correspondent *(1925 October 3)*

Hollywood, CA, October 2 — He is a tragic, pitiful figure in his sorrow — Ben Turpin, the clown and comique, the booted, pathetic little hero of a thousand plays — mourning his lost wife. All day Friday, he sat by the side of his dead Carrie, rocking his body from side to side, his eyes moist with the tears that were being held back by force of will. His hands opened and closed jerkily, his lips quivered a silent requiem.

Ben Turpin, the cross-eyed clown — mocked and jeered at by an unthinking public, laughed at by the picture profession because of his physical handicaps — has brought a long vigil of love to an end. He met Carrie LeMieux, who was on the stage, and within a week they married.

Never Separated Long

For eighteen years, the couple lived together without a single disturbing incident and the pair never separated for more than a few days at a time. They attended each other's wants always with the same simple devotion of the first few days of marriage. The paralytic stroke, which caused Mrs. Turpin's death Thursday, had its cause in a serious illness more than a year ago. At that time, Turpin deliberately broke a starring contract with Mack Sennett and announced he would leave pictures until his wife was completely cured.

The Turpins journeyed to a shrine in Canada, where they knelt before an altar for days at a time. A partial cure was effected and they returned to Hollywood. Turpin still refused to resume work. His time, he said, was entirely taken up with the care of his wife. "She needs me, and I can't leave her now, even for a minute," he explained.

Up to the very moment of Mrs. Turpin's death, Ben, the clown who has made millions laugh, was nursing her back to what he thought was health.[238]

The Lonely Clown, The Greatest Love Story of Hollywood by Dorothy Donnell

You probably laughed uproariously when you saw Ben Turpin as Romeo in Mack Sennett's farce, *Romeo and Juliet.* You found it very amusing when that cross-eyed comedian looked mournfully toward the ceiling after his calico-clad girl had rejected him and began Tosti's *Good-Bye.* You wondered how he could make such realistic tears course down his cheeks.

"Great stuff!" you howled when they dropped him into a moat surrounding a castle where another of his Juliets lived.

"Look at that 'egg' getting cracked with the stick of firewood!" you chortled. "How does he keep from getting hurt?"

You shouted in glee when Juliet's dad and the successful suitor slammed Ben out of the house and you giggled when they dropped him onto a runaway mule. You hooted when he strummed a guitar and sang to his lady love.

"He's a sorrowful-looking boob, isn't he?" you remarked.

Yes, he is a sorrowful-looking boob and by this time, most of the world knows why. Ben Turpin's wife was marked for death when he made that picture. The doctors had just told him so. And behind his mask of buffoonery, as he went through scene after scene, his heart was bleeding. His nerves were on the ragged edge. He had known little sleep for weeks. His interest was not in the play. But he stuck to his role until the last shot was taken. Then he went home. His wife, with blindness and deafness creeping upon her, reached a feeble hand from the coverlets and said, "Ben, if the time is coming when I can't see you nor hear your voice, I don't want to live. I couldn't bear it. I want you now — all the time. Please don't leave me!" And because Ben never left her from that day until the day she died is the reason why you have not seen him on the screen for some time, except in old pictures. Ben Turpin told me the story a few days ago with tears in his eyes.

He told me how Carrie LeMieux had plighted her troth to him in Chicago in 1907 when he was earning twenty dollars a week. He told me how they had been married, had rented a little flat for nine dollars a month, and had to borrow fifty dollars from the manager of the old Essanay to help make the first payment on furniture. Five dollars a week, taken from Ben's salary, was to repay the loan.

"If they had taken any more, we wouldn't have been able to eat!" he declared.

"...And we did make it in California, just as she said we would. Then, after success had come, her health began failing. Nine years ago she was hurt in an automobile accident while returning from church. I believe that this indirectly brought on the deafness. Her eyesight began failing. A year ago she went to bed a hopeless invalid."

He cancelled all his motion picture engagements. He turned down offers from producers that would have brought him a quarter of a million dollars. He began a vigil at the bedside of the invalid. He carried her in his arms from room to room. When her strength was such that she could be taken outdoors, he placed her in a wheelchair and wheeled her about for blocks in the California sunshine. Sometimes, Turpin wheeled his wife up to the intersection of Santa Monica Boulevard and Western Avenue and there placed her comfortably in the shade. Then he used to go to the traffic button in the center of the street and ask Officer Schultz to let him relieve him for a while. For an hour or more, the comedian used to direct the movements of cars and people. It somehow helped to relax his tired nerves.

Tragedy Halts Ben Turpin's Comic Roles

To the world he is just a funmaker. The film comedy, even the popular song, have featured his eccentric, million dollar pair of eyes. The slapstick movie is scarcely complete without a close-up of Ben Turpin and his talented eyes meeting with all the rebuffs of a comedian's life on the screen.

Yet while thousands were laughing at the antics of his crossed eyes and his funny falls in movie houses throughout the country, few noted the little newspaper item recently telling of the death of Mrs. Carrie Turpin, wife of the comedian. While comedy smirked before the footlights, tragedy lurked in the wings for the famous Mack Sennett star.

To their friends, the married life of the Turpins was regarded as one of the few perfect examples of matrimony in Hollywood. At a time when stars acquired a new wife or husband almost with the seasons, the Turpins' marriage endured eighteen years. Their life together began in the cheap vaudeville theatres, where Turpin was struggling along with an act consisting in the main of his funny falls. In vain, he tried to remedy the accident of his crossed eyes and was content to drift along with the tide, careless and without ambition. In a Chicago theatre, he met Carrie LeMieux, who was playing on the same bill. It was evidently a case of love at first sight, for within a week the two troupers were married.

Then Ben chanced to try his luck before the camera and Sennett, realizing the comic possibilities in Turpin's crossed eyes, elevated him to a leading role in his galaxy of funmakers. The first few pictures justified Sennett's judgment and Turpin was made. The tramp comedian achieved a financial success beyond his wildest dreams and the Turpins were able to live in the utmost luxury. Riches, however, did not change the even tenor of their married life and they retained throughout the devotion that had characterized their life on the small town vaudeville circuits.

But just as their ambitions had been realized, the health of Mrs. Turpin began to fail. The best doctors were called in consultation, but all the resources of medicine seemed without avail. Mrs. Turpin grew steadily worse. During her illness, the only thing that brought temporary solace from pain was the presence of her husband at her bedside. In order to be continually with her, Turpin broke all his contracts at the studios. Without publicity or gesture, he relinquished his position as the premier funny man of filmdom. Together, the Turpins journeyed across the continent to the famous shrine in Canada just outside of Quebec. When medical science failed, they sought superhuman relief. At this little shrine, they remained for many days, praying for a cure. And for a time, it seemed that their prayers were to be answered. Mrs. Turpin began to regain her health and they returned to Hollywood again, anticipating that the return of her strength would be only a matter of time.

Still Turpin refused to appear again in pictures and devoted all his time to the needs of his wife, believing that eventually she would be fully restored to health. Their hopes, however, were not to be realized. Within a short time, Mrs. Turpin suffered a relapse. And soon a stroke of paralysis brought an end to her sufferings. Tragedy had driven comedy from the home of the great comedian.[239]

A Clown — And A Man (1925 October 5)

Mrs. Ben Turpin is dead. Few knew her or of her outside the theatrical and movie world, but all the world knows her husband. Ben Turpin, the cross-eyed, the inimitable, the farceur, the clown incomparable!

His antics, in the vernacular of the proscenium, are a wow. Comedy hokum of the broadest kind is his stock in trade. When the title of one of his pictures is first flashed on the silver screen, the kids in the gallery clap their hands with delight while the older ones downstairs settle themselves down in anticipation of twenty minutes of side-aches. For Ben Turpin, the clown, is about to "do his stuff."

Ben Turpin's life has not been a bed of roses. On the contrary, the Turpins have tasted little of the fruits of success until quite latterly. Then a far-seeing producer conceived the idea that Ben Turpin's face — or, rather, his cross-eye — was his fortune.

And so it proved to be. Money at last came in such generous quantity that all the comforts of life were available for Ben and his wife; but, alas, Mrs. Turpin was no longer able to enjoy the material results of her husband's new-found success. Ten months ago, she was forced to take to her bed, an incurable invalid, and Ben, accepting the inevitable, closed down his motion picture work and proceeded to devote the days — for as long as they might last — to ministering to the little woman who had been his mate through storm and stress for so many years. She became steadily worse and for months would only permit Ben to attend to her wants. This he did, day and night, while the world was screeching at his antics.

Ben Turpin, the clown, without a care in the world! What fun he must have making those pictures! So said the fans, forgetting that a clown is a man first and a clown afterwards. Last week, after ten months of constant care from her husband, Mrs. Turpin died in Ben's arms.

Ben Turpin probably will return to the screen. It would be a thousand pities were he to deny the world of laughter that it is within his power to give it. No doubt he will again fall upstairs and downstairs; shed crocodile tears from tubes concealed beside his cross eyes; send his audiences into shrieks by merely facing the camera and just looking at them.

He may not go down into movie history as a great artiste. Certain it is that his bust will never occupy a niche in any hall of the immortals. But he will have that which is beyond price or purchase — the good wishes of millions who have recognized his genius as a clown and his worth as a man.[240]

Funeral Service Conducted for Mrs. Ben Turpin (1925 October 5)

Funeral services were conducted yesterday morning from the Church of the Blessed Sacrament, 6657 Sunset Blvd, for Mrs. Carrie LeMieux Turpin, 44 years of age, wife of Ben Turpin. Following mass, interment was made in Forest Lawn Cemetery.

Mrs. Turpin died early Thursday morning after an illness of almost a year. On Easter Sunday, she suffered a stroke of paralysis and later had three similar attacks. She became seriously ill last December and since that time, her husband has been constantly with her, giving up all his film activities. Besides her husband, she leaves a father and brother in Michigan.[242]

A Hollywood Family (1925 October 5)

The death of Mrs. Carrie LeMieux Turpin brings to the reading public a picture of that delightful screen comedian with queer eyes, Ben Turpin, spending months at her bedside administering to her wants, neglecting his work and all things else for her comfort during her last months of life.

It is a story that would cause no comment were it not the story of a household in Hollywood. How can it be that this strange city that has earned a reputation for moral laxity, infidelity, frequent divorce, and marital divorce and marital disagreement can supply the story of loyalty and devotion worthy of a middle-western Babbitt.

The public will be interested in the fact that Hollywood has supplied the two extremes in family life and it will take little discernment to fill in the middle. The ordinary family that pursues unemphatic course is of little interest to the reading public and there are thousands in Hollywood who have never had the delight of wallowing in printers' ink. It requires something spectacular to win newspaper notice in a city like Hollywood, where the competition for publicity is so keen. Perhaps, after all, Hollywood is quite an ordinary community with a super-stratum of temperamental people that catches the public eye.[243]

The End of One Hollywood Romance (1925 October 7)

Not least among the stars that twinkle in our movie firmament is cock-eyed Ben Turpin. He is an amusing though certainly not a romantic figure, though if the truth were known, his salary is probably a good deal larger than that of some of the sheiks whose ardent eyes and faultless profiles set the hearts of girl fans to fluttering. But if true romance is related to the fidelity that endures between man and wife until death intervenes, Ben Turpin in his own life has furnished a better example of romance than most of the screen idols.

Ben hasn't been working for the past few months. He forsook the movie lot for the bedside of the invalid wife to whom he has been married for eighteen years. The newspapers made brief mention of this in connection the other day with a notice of Mrs. Turpin's death. Strange that some of those who write for the movie magazines haven't thought to exploit the Turpins as an illustration of Hollywood's delightful domesticity.[245]

Mrs. Ben Turpin Dies; Ben Devoted To Her — Film Comedian Spent Nearly Year at Bedside of Invalid — Left Studio for Home (1925 October 7)

Mrs. Carrie LeMieux Turpin, 44, former actress and wife of Ben Turpin, screen comedian, died at her home in Hollywood, California, Oct. 1. Mrs. Turpin had been an invalid for more than a year following a stroke of paralysis at that time, having had three others prior to her death. Turpin has been at her bedside constantly from early last December, forsaking his work at the Sennett studios. Mrs. Turpin was a native of Quebec. The couple were married in Chicago 18 years ago with Mrs. Turpin for some time afterward working on the stage and screen with her husband. Besides her husband, a father and brother living in Michigan survive. Funeral services were held at the Church of the Blessed Sacrament, Oct. 2, with burial in Forest Lawn.[244]

Ben Turpin's Affliction (1925 October 7)

When Ben Turpin, a favorite moving picture actor, was seen in a comedy on the screen last week at a Hartford theater, he was with his wife, Carrie LeMieux Turpin, who was dying at Hollywood, California. Mrs. Turpin's death occurred October 1. There are so many stories from the moving picture colony of Hollywood that are unpleasant that it seems worthwhile to take note of the devotion to his wife of Ben Turpin, who gave up his work at the studios last December when Mrs. Turpin became seriously ill and who gave her every attention during the months of sickness that followed. For ten months, the comedian forgot the call of the screen that the devoted husband might minister to the stricken wife. Perhaps he did no more than any man should have done, but it should not be forgotten that he was the faithful, loving husband first and the moving picture actor last. In the midst of the unique and sometimes questionable life of Hollywood, Ben Turpin was a true man and those who have enjoyed his roles will have a strong feeling of sympathy now for that man.[246]

1925 October 11: Ben Turpin enters Santa Monica Hospital, operated on the afternoon of the 12th for acute appendicitis. On the 13th, attending physicians announce that another 24 hours would determine if his recovery would be complete.

1925 October 14: Ben Turpin announced as the sole heir to late wife's estate, valued at $63,358.50 in cash and real estate, which was drawn February 1, 1924. It stated that her husband will receive the entire estate unconditionally and be made executive. Since Carrie's passing, Ben's sister, Mrs. Ernestine Knies, had been comforting him at his home in Beverly Hills. A month later, Ben wrote his will.

Despite Fabulous Wealth, Cross-Eyed Comedy Star Quit Studios So He Could Cook Meals For — and Nurse — Dying Wife. Sitting Alone in the Shadows of His Hollywood Home, Famous Clown of the Screen Sixty Years Old, Has No Desire to Resume Film Work — Started Career At Essanay at $20 Per Week — Wife Always Believed Him Great Actor, "Like Irving and Booth," and Wanted Him to Do Tragedies by Betty Morris

Hollywood, Oct. 17 — One by one, with final handclasps, those silent handclasps by which men speak with hearts, his friends went away and left Ben Turpin alone.

The house was quiet with that queer, awed stillness that follows the passing of a soul from its portals. The one to whom he had devoted years of tender care, the one for whom he had sacrificed money and fame in the movies, was gone.

Ben had given his all that his wife's last months might be as happy as he could make them, so he had nothing with which to reproach himself as he sat there in the familiar lounge chair beside the sofa in the living room. Loneliness must have crept over him, a vast loneliness, as his poor, crossed eyes rested upon that sofa where for so long she had lain. And who knows but what tears coursed down his lined cheeks?

You know from the newspapers that Mrs. Carrie Turpin, wife of the comedian, died recently, that she had suffered two strokes of apoplexy following an illness of many years' duration. But behind those few words is a story of a man's devotion that touches the heart.

It is difficult to picture funny, cross-eyed Ben as a Romeo, isn't it? Didn't the mere thought of it move you to hilarious laughter? Many a chuckle has rewarded Ben's absurd, grotesque attempts to make love to beauteous screen damsels.

Ben Turpin of the cross-eyes and scrawny neck? Little, undersized, funny Ben, a lover? The flappers will smile, for lovers these days must be stalwart specimens of manhood, flashing of eye, debonair of manner, skillful in the art of subtle romance.

The stolid, patient love which Ben lavished upon his invalid wife they may not understand. But the middle-aged people will.

The movie fans have probably wondered why Ben stopped making comedies.

Last December, he retired to stay at home and cook and keep house because the wasted form on the couch twinged with pain when other hands touched it and found tenderness and balm only in Ben's care. In hours of pain, his hands alone she could endure to touch her, from his only would she accept her food.

Ben Gives "All For Love"

She did not ask her husband to give up work and fame and money to brighten the light in her fading eyes with his constant devotion. Voluntarily, eagerly, Ben insisted, for he knew how much it meant to her and how unimportant, weighed in the balance, were the things he renounced.

"What's the good of all this money I got if it can't give her health again?" he replied to reminders that he was losing money by not continuing on the screen. "She's all that counts. The movies can go hang."

So Ben Turpin of the stringy neck and the mis-mated eyes said good-bye to the studio. His last visit was a pathetic one. He told everybody "S'long," and pretended to be very casual about it, but his voice was choky as he clasped Mack Sennett's hand. And the bluff, red-faced, good-natured Mack didn't say much. I suspected he was afraid his words would betray his feeling — the emotion that men try brusquely to hide.

It's an awful-looking old place, the Sennett studio, but it has charm. There's a tree grow-ing through one of the stages and a historic dressing room occupied at various times by Charlie Chaplin, Gloria Swanson, Mabel Normand, and other famous stars who began in the slapsticks and whose names are scrawled on its door.

There were dilapidated old seats that I know must have been used in the first custard-pie comedy, still standing, sprawling, rather, and cobwebbed. And the queerest collection of props, all odd things that have been used in comedy "gags."

"Wife Is All That Counts"

They have gorgeous new sets, of course, but they leave that clutter of old stuff around because of the sentimental memories that cling to every piece of rotted wood, to every bit of faded paper.

Ben Turpin has been longer associated with Sennett than any of the stars whom he started on the road to fame. I believe he loves every board of that ramshackle studio, though he insisted stoutly that "the movies don't mean a thing to me, the wife's all that counts."

Partly from himself, in interviews literally snatched, for Ben runs from a female ques-tioner, or any female for that matter, but mostly from old-time friends of his, I have learned the story of Ben's great romance.

Though as a boy his eyes were straight, he has always clowned. He was an inconspicuous, withdrawing little fellow, very meek and humble and never thinking he had any exceptional ability. Once upon a time, he traveled with a medicine show and when they let him beat the drum, he was in the height of his glory. People laughed at his antics and it pleased him that he could amuse them, though he had a way of apologizing for his success.

Never Clown To Sweetheart

While playing *Happy Hooligan* 18 years ago, he met the woman whom he loved imme-diately and whole-souledly. Timorously, he proposed and she accepted him. And for Ben, the rest of the weak gender ceased to exist.

To his wife, he never was a clown. He is a great actor, the finest of them all. She had heard of Irving and Booth and the thespic nobles, but none could hold a candle to her Ben.

Audiences chuckled at the "funny man" and later roared at the comic figure that he cut on the screen. One human being alone ever took him seriously — his wife.

Poverty was their companion during the early years of their marriage. Sometimes, they trouped together; again, when no bookings could be obtained, he would pull taffy at county fairs, his capers drawing a crowd to see the side-show wonders.

Always she was either by his side or waiting for him in their little home in Chicago.

"I never understood," he told me, awe in his voice, "what she could see in me."

Knew He Was Beautiful

The glory of a woman's love, to which his humility he had never aspired, was his, but it was incomprehensible to him that he, little sawed-off, skinny-necked funny man, could have evoked it when there were so many handsome fellows in the world.

His first movies were made for the Essanay Company at a salary of $20 a week, a fortune to meek Ben. Only Charlie Chaplin's constant goading nerved his courage to the point of asking for a raise and I don't think Ben has yet gotten over the shock of his success.

With fame came more money, which he invested so shrewdly — and their wants have been so few and so simple — that today, he is rated one of the wealthiest men in the motion picture colony.

Just when he was able to lavish upon her the luxuries that every woman, no matter how practical her nature, thrills at having, an automobile accident began to take toll on Mrs. Turpin's health. First, her hearing was impaired and she was not strong physically. All remedies resorted to failed.

But little Ben believed, in his simple child-heart, in miracles. Wasn't her very love for him a miracle? Surely the restoration of her hearing wouldn't be half as great a miracle as the fact that she, all that was fine and lovely in womanhood, should care for a "shrimp like himself."

So Ben reasoned and last year they made the pilgrimage to the shrine of Saint Anne de Beaupre near Quebec. A novena was made to the Saint, who is said to have wrought so many miraculous cures. For nine days, they ascended the 27 steps on their knees and knelt long hours in prayer at the altar.

"They Cried Together"

And then — oh, blessed day for Ben and his patient, suffering wife! She heard him when he spoke in a low voice. They cried together when they realized that such a sweet favor had been conferred upon them.

She felt so well that evening that they went to see one of Ben's comedies. She heard the people laughing.

She saw not the comic mask that he wore for the multitude's delight, but the talent beneath it — the big heart, the pathos of his life — and she wanted him to do tragic epics stirring dramatic scenes.

For long hours, she lay on the couch in the corner while he sat by her side in the big armchair. He kept in touch with what was going on in the world outside by radio and occasionally, when she drowsed into a comfortable sleep, would dash out to the studio to gossip with his cronies.

Played Traffic Cop For Wife

When she was able to walk the block or so, she would accompany him to the corner of Santa Monica Boulevard and Western Avenue. His good friend the policeman would obligingly — no doubt, willingly — give up his post and there Ben would glory in directing traffic. On a Sunday afternoon, one could almost always find him there, shrilling blasts on his whistle, halting the limousine of a millionaire star that a crippled child might cross, zipping the row of motors along with quick waves of his arms.

Oh, Ben got a great kick out of it and seemed mightily pleased with the friendly calls, "Hi, Ben, how's my boy?" that passersby yelled.

Mrs. Turpin would sit on a bench at the sidewalk and watch, proudly smiling back at him when he turned to her.

For the last couple of months, however, she was not strong enough to go out, so Ben has not been seen. Instead, he has stayed in the house, cooking their meals, cleaning and dusting and thinking up ways to amuse the patient invalid.

The heart that fluttered so faintly for long, weary months is now stilled. And a bowed, grief-stricken man cooks a meal for one instead of two.

Will Ben return to the movies? I doubt it. What he will do with his lonely life I don't know. Ben is close to 60. And the only reason for his existence, according to his viewpoint, is gone.

Besides, with a deep ache in his heart, how could Ben cavort and act the comic fool before the camera? Fame always frightened him and astounded him, for he has absolutely no vanity to be pampered, and the money will be useless to him now.

So Hollywood's Great Lover sits in the shadows, all alone. Day merges into night and becomes another stretch of light, but he seldom stirs far from the room where his sweetheart lay so long in suffering.[241] [318]

A Comedian's Sorrow (1925 October 21)

Ben Turpin's wife died the other day. The cross-eyed comedian's droll features and comical antics have made thousands roar with laughter in moving picture theaters from coast to coast. But there's no laughter in Ben's heart and he carries a load of grief these days. For marriage, esteemed altogether too lightly by many of his profession, meant something inexpressibly sacred in Ben Turpin's life. He and his wife had been married eighteen years and, in adversity and prosperity alike, she was his valued companion and trusted counselor. When the last illness came, Ben dropped his work, cancelled all engagements, and sat at her bedside until the end. Not for him was Hollywood then. Now she is gone and after a time, Turpin will go back to the familiar scenes, striving to find such balm as there may be for a bruised heart in the blessed boon of accustomed work. But though he may seem as funny as ever and cut capers that will make the masses hold their sides in mirth, Ben Turpin won't find life ever the same again. The comedian of the screen has come face to face with sorrow.[247]

Ben Turpin, the screen comedian who has made countless thousands laugh, is a tragic, pitiful figure in his sorrow over the death of his wife last Friday. Mrs. Turpin passed away nearly a year after suffering a paralytic stroke and, according to press reports, Turpin during that time rarely left her, even turning down attractive contracts.

At one time, he took his wife to the Shrine of St. Anne de Beaupre in Canada, where a partial cure was effected. It is said that from the days of Mrs. Turpin's final illness to her funeral in the Church of the Blessed Sacrament, Hollywood, California, Turpin kept a constant vigil at his wife's side, it being necessary to carry him away at the last services.

In his great devotion to his wife, Ben Turpin will certainly command the respect of all decent people, his case being an appealing one among hundreds of distasteful ones among the movie colony.

1925 October 25 *(in part):* Ben Turpin cried two or three times in his dressing room when he was in the State Theater more than a year ago. He wept over this and that — a bread line he had seen in Boston, the way Wallace Beery once treated him when they were making films in Chicago, and the condition of Mrs. Turpin.

At that time, the tears seemed to flow a little too easily. But that wasn't true.

Some months afterward, Mrs. Turpin became worse. Ben took her all over the country in search of health, even making a trip to Ste. Anne de Beaupre. But Mrs. Turpin grew steadily worse. Ben finally gave up his work and told Mack Sennett, to whom he was under contract, that never again would he work in a studio. That was at a time when Mrs. Turpin would have only Ben care for her. Then she died.

The other day, he was walking through the Metropolitan Studios, where Charlie Murray is working on *Steel Preferred*. Murray pleaded with Ben to come in and help out with a comedy scene. The old urge of the Kleigls caused Ben to succumb and he went through the scene "just for the fun of it," later refusing the customary cheque for his services. Being under contract to Sennett, he couldn't very well accept the money, but this does show that the funny fellow with the faithless eyes may be back with us again. Why not, Ben, there's nothing else for you to do?[248]

Ben Turpin (c November 1925)

Mite sorrow, buried romance, bewildering eyes, tender memories engross Ben Turpin of the screen and spell finis to Hollywood's most beautiful love story. Filmifornia has staged more than her share of gross lovemaking, untimely divorces, domestic mudslinging; and the tender sorrow of Ben Turpin will grow in that labyrinth of uncertain connubial bliss. We who have laughed at this clown with the cock-eyes and ostrich neck never realized he lived in the halo of a wistful romance.

That romance started with his marriage to a little French-Canadian girl, Carrie LeMieux. Eighteen years lasted their honeymoon; then the grim reaper appeared in the guise of illness. That was a year ago. Ben gave up his screen career immediately. For in her pain and weariness, his wife could not bear to have anyone around but the faithful old clown — her lover...

Then the fateful day came and the grim reaper took his toll — and left a little old clown to walk alone. Now he returns to Hollywood, to the movies, his second love — but the fire, the dash, that made his work interesting are absent. For love inspires — and his love is now a sacred memory.

1925: Old Clown Story Is To Be Revived Soon

The old, old story of the clown with the aching heart bringing guffaws to pleasure-seeking audiences will be revived next month when Ben Turpin once more dons the grease paint and steps into the glare of the Kleigs. Turpin will resume work at the Mack Sennett Studio on November 10 after an absence of a year. He voluntarily gave up the screen to care for his invalid wife, who recently died. When he speaks of her now, tears come to his eyes and his grief is poignant. A few weeks ago, the comedian visited his old friend, Charles Murray, at the Metropolitan Studio, where Murray is working in *Steel Preferred*.

"Ben, get into a costume and help out with the picture!"

Director James Hogan pleaded, "Just a few scenes. It won't take long."

Murray urged it, too. Turpin agreed — for his old friends' sake. At the end of the engagement, the business manager got the shock of his life when the comedian declined to accept a check. Studio officials then bought an expensive smoking set on which in a gold plate they inscribed a message of appreciation and thanks.

Turpin Rejoining Sennett Soon (1925 November 3)

Los Angeles — Ben Turpin will take a month's vacation and upon his return, start work again for Mack Sennett.[249]

Movies Make Yukon Jake Tough As Steak (1925 November 12)

Los Angeles — Yukon Jake, "tough as a steak," won a $2500 judgment for his author in federal court today. E. E. Paramore, Jr., of Carmel, California, sued Mack Sennett, film producer, for $25,000 damages, alleging infringement of copyright of a poem he wrote about Jake's life in the Yukon. Judge William James decided a Ben Turpin comedy released by Sennett under the title of Yukon Jake had spoiled Paramore's chance of gleaning $2500 in movie profits from his poem, but no more.[250]

Film Comedian's Genius Is Amusing Off Screen (1925 November 15, in part)

Since his wife's recent death, Ben Turpin's solace lies in his remarkable amusement of himself. Ben's greatest satisfaction is to stand at the corner of Western Avenue and Santa Monica Boulevard in Hollywood — one of our busiest intersections — and direct traffic. Ben is a "wow" as a traffic cop. Many a tie-up between south and westbound traffic results from the "wide-angled gaze" that issues from Ben's acutely separated orbs. But the cross-eyed comedian feverishly works with voice and arms to untangle his mischief and gets a great kick out of it.

Needless to say, the fun of the motorists is immense — when they get straightened out of the tangle.[251]

Ben Turpin Goes Under Knife at Santa Barbara (1925 November 13)

Ben Turpin, film comedian, was operated on in the Cottage Hospital at Santa Barbara for appendicitis at 6:30 o'clock last evening. He is reported resting well and not in dangerous condition, Drs. Benjamin Bakewell and Irving Willis announced immediately after the operation. Turpin was en route to Hollywood from San Francisco by automobile when seized with the attack Wednesday night. He went immediately to the Santa Barbara clinic and was rushed to the hospital. His sister, Mrs. Knies, was with him.[252] While here, Ben becomes acquainted with secretary Babette E. Dietz.

Ben Turpin Better (1925 November 17)

Santa Barbara, CA — Ben Turpin, who is in a serious condition after an operation for appendicitis, is reported resting well.[253]

Daily News Letter (1925 November 20)

Hollywood, Nov 20 — One of the most pathetic figures in Hollywood today is Ben Turpin. With the recent death of his wife, one of the only beautiful love stories in the film colony ended. The funny little cross-eyed clown quit pictures more than a year ago when he found his wife seriously ill and abandoned completely his screen career. He was constantly at Mrs. Turpin's bedside during her long illness, watching day and night. When she slept for a few minutes each day, Turpin was seen taking walks alone through Hollywood streets. Although he has been offered many contracts to come back to the films, Turpin has refused them all. He may never return to the screen.

Turpin Taking Sun Baths at Santa Barbara (1925 December 5)

(Exclusive Dispatch) Santa Barbara, Dec. 4 — Ben Turpin, the man whose crossed eyes have made him $1,000,000 in motion pictures, is taking a daily sunbath on the west porch of Cottage Hospital, Turpin was operated on recently at Cottage Hospital for appendicitis and is progressing so favorably that the nurses wheel him out into the sun every day. The comedy actor comments that the operation certainly did away with a cross disposition, but his star(dom) that it did not affect his eyes in the same way.[254]

Turpin Improving Rapidly — Back To Work Soon (1925 December 13)

Santa Barbara, CA — Ben Turpin, who was operated on recently in Cottage Hospital for appendicitis, is progressing favorably and says that he will be back at work on January 10.[255]

1925 December 14: The feature *Steel Preferred* released by Metropolitan Pictures. Photoplay thought the film fairly entertaining, writing in part: "Ben Turpin and Charlie Murray add a large quota of laughs to the picture, and Vera Reynolds and Walter Long help make it interesting."

1926 January 15: Ben returns to Sennett two months after originally expected and begins work on *When A Man's A Prince*, which is shelved until its release on August 15, 1926.

Ben Takes a Dare (1926)

It now comes out that it was trying to get gay with the old Sennett swimming tank that proved the undoing of Ben Turpin. The day he came back to work from his long retirement after his wife's death, one of the studio directors dared him to dive in. So in went Ben with all his clothes on. The next thing that happened to Ben was a hurry-up trip to the hospital, where his appendix was sawed off. He is well again and back at the studio, but he walks respectfully and widely around the swimming tank.

1926 c May: Ben Turpin, who has returned to the screen since the death of his wife last year, is working hard on his second comedy for Mack Sennett. Mrs. Turpin's long illness was the cause of Ben's temporary retirement from fun making and he stayed with her continually through her illness. His old contract with Sennett completed, he did not sign a new one — making $3,000 a week — until recently. The first picture now completed is titled with what Hollywood considers Ben's own title, *When A Man's A Prince*. The one he is doing now is with Madeline Hurlock, Thelma Hill, and Marvin "Fat" Loback, *The Prodigal Bridegroom*.

Ben Turpin Has Lucky Day at Bar — Judge Gives Film Actor Suspended Sentence for Speeding But Jails Others (1926 May 15)

Ben Turpin, the ocular-gifted film actor, was more fortunate than forty-five other motorists hailed into the court of Municipal Judge Chambers yesterday, all charged with navigating highways at too great a speed. Mr. Turpin appeared in court with an attorney and when he told the judge that since the death of his wife he had been in ill health — that he believed a jail sentence would be detrimental to his well-being — he was given a suspended two day sentence. And other less fortunate individuals drew jail sentences ranging from one to five days. Turpin was charged with having driven 28 miles an hour in a 20-mile zone. *At the time, Turpin's lucky day didn't sit well with the public.*

1926: Many were the typewriter ribbons used on sob stories about Ben Turpin and his devotion to his sick wife. Ben gave up his screen career to care for her and when she died, Ben was much written of as the sad little clown who made others laugh while stifling his own tears — you know the old line. Alas for those wasted typewriter ribbons! Ben has shown characteristic masculine resiliency and within a year after Mrs. Turpin's death has reestablished himself on the screen and — here's the point of the story — is planning to take unto himself a new wife! The lady's name is being kept a close secret by Mr. Turpin, but he states that they met at the California Lutheran Hospital during his wife's illness. No date for the wedding announced, but the bride-to-be is wearing a large diamond, so Ben evidently means it.

1926 May 25: These movie actors have a fatal fascination. Ben Turpin, who has been a widower for a little less than a year, has found a lady to share his lonely home. It is said that he met her at the sanitarium during his late wife's illness and her sympathy for Ben in his grief won the heart of the comedy sheik.

Ben Turpin Says Cupid Cross-Eyed
Actor Denies Little Love God Has Looked At Him, But Girl Not So Sure (1926 May 16)
While Ben Turpin, movie comedian, vigorously denied yesterday that he intends to wed anybody, Miss Babette Dietz, an office employee of the California Lutheran Hospital, to whom Turpin is reported to be engaged, was not so sure. The girl in question, who wears a large solitaire diamond ring on her engagement finger, showed confusion when questioned as to the widely-rumored engagement.

"Nothing can be given out now," she said, "because Mr. Turpin does not wish it. He has reasons of his own. But when the time comes I am sure he will be glad to give out all the details. The wedding will not be before the fall anyway. Maybe in a couple of months there will be a story."

Miss Dietz denied reports that she and Turpin met during the illness of the comedian's first wife, who died some time ago. She was not acquainted with the first Mrs. Turpin, she declared. Other employees at the hospital were fully aware of the engagement rumors and supplied Miss Dietz's name without hesitation as the person concerned. The comedian is said to have been her guest at the opening of the new hospital a short time ago. When questioned about this, Turpin declared that he had attended the opening because he contributed $500 for a room at the hospital and was interested in its future, but not in wedding any of its attaches.[256]

Ben Turpin Will Be There (1926 June 30)
Ben Turpin, Sennett comedian, will visit the Metropolitan Theater tonight at 8 o'clock and it is said that there will be some lively doings. Turpin is coming to see the preview of his latest Mack Sennett comedy, *When A Man's A Prince.*[257]

Turpin Joins Benedict Cast For Second Time — The Cross-Eyed Comedian's Bride Has No Connection With Movies

Hollywood, CA, July 8 — Ben Turpin, cross-eyed comedian, today zig-zagged to the altar with Miss Babette Elizabeth Dietz, formerly of Bismarck, North Dakota. When the comedian applied at the marriage license bureau, he wore black studio glasses. He gave his name as Bernard Turpin, 57, and had he not been forced to remove the "cheaters" to sign the application, he would have passed unrecognized. Asked when the ceremony would be held, the comedian said: "Well, try and follow me." The pair was married by Father Michael J. Mullins at the Church of the Good Shepherd in Beverly Hills late in the afternoon. Actor Andy Clyde appeared as best man and Miss Marie C. Schumacher attended Miss Dietz as bridesmaid. Turpin presented his bride with a diamond and platinum bracelet as a wedding gift. At the license bureau, it was revealed that is was the funny man's second matrimonial venture. His first wife died last fall. Turpin at that time became so grief-stricken he was taken ill. Only lately he has been seen in the company of Miss Dietz, who is 37. She declared that she had nothing whatsoever to do with motion pictures and that she was marrying for the first time.[258]

Babette Elizabeth Dietz was born in December 1886 in Wurttemberg, Germany and immigrated to the U.S. in 1892, settling with her family in North Dakota. As a young lady, Babette was sent with four other girls to St. Joseph's Academy in St. Paul and received excellent instruction. She was also taught piano and was later organist for the Evangelical Church in New Salem. She was employed by the Quain and Ramstad clinic in New Salem before leaving in 1916 to accept a job as secretary in the Bismarck Hospital before moving to Los Angeles in 1920.

1926 July 11 *(in part):* After a three week honeymoon motoring to San Francisco and in and about the Yosemite, Mr. and Mrs. Ben Turpin will return to Hollywood.[259]

Suit Contemplated Over Use of Name (1926 July 11)

Ben Turpin is getting pretty mad. Recently, there has appeared in Hollywood a young man calling himself Tommy Turpin and representing himself to be a nephew of the famous cross-eyed comedian. And Ben says there is no such person as Tommy Turpin, a nephew of his. H. L. Hughinin, assistant to the general manager of the studio where Turpin is working, is out with a statement which says, in part: "Mr. Turpin has only one nephew and his name is Julian Knies. Therefore the declaration that Tommy Turpin is a nephew of Ben Turpin is incorrect." A court order was issued last year restraining a screen player from using the name Art Mix because it tended to confuse the public in its thoughts of Tom Mix and a similar order restrained Charlie Aplin from appearing in the makeup of or impersonating Charlie Chaplin. It now appears that Tommy Turpin may soon be haled into court.[260]

In February 1927, Tommy Turpin was in trouble again, this time for owing actress Lita Cavalier $125 in unpaid salary for her promotion work to a film that didn't do so well.[261]

"Sammy" Gets New Movie Contract — To Be Featured In Series Of Comedies with Ben Turpin's Nephew — Has Toured T.O.B.A. Circuit Two Year — Received $250 Weekly Under Old Contract Before Leaving (1926)

Hollywood (PCNB) — Frederick Ernest Morrison, better known as *Sunshine Sammy*, will discontinue his vaudeville tour and return to Hollywood as the juvenile comedian in a series of 12 two-reel comedies. Jean Francis DeVillard, the Indian capitalist producer, has signed a contract for Sammy's services as the juvenile comedian in a series of Messenger Boy comedies starring Tommy Turpin, nephew of cross-eyed Ben.

Mira Adoree, sister of Renee of *The Big Parade,* who recently arrived in this country after starring in a French farce throughout the capitals of Europe, will be featured opposite Turpin. Walter Irving will handle the megaphone while Bill Thompson will grind the camera. The cast will include Eve Conrad, Sheldon Lewis, *Sunshine Sammy,* Spec O'Donnell, and Gibson Gowland, star of Von Stroheim's *Greed.* To a representative of this paper, it was announced that Sammy may later be starred in a series of comedies after the completion of the Messenger Boy series. Sammy's return to Hollywood ends his two-year tour of the colored vaudeville houses under the T.O.B.A. circuit.

1926 August 7: Annual vacation time begins at the Mack Sennett Studios.

Ben Got Huffy by Babette Turpin *(1926 July)*

Ben and I first met in a Los Angeles hospital. You get pretty lonesome in a hospital and when I learned my favorite comedian and I were under the same roof, I marshaled all my courage and called upon him. The result of my visit was a charming friendship and an autographed photograph on which he wrote "To My Little Fat Babette."

I still have that picture. It is one of my most cherished possessions. But I'm not so fat now. I won't deny that the autograph might have had an effect. Anyway, I've taken off a lot of weight since then. When Ben was stricken in Santa Barbara last year and went under the knife, he wired for me to come and I did. From then on, we saw a lot of each other, but it's hard for me to tell you just how he proposed. He tried it so many different ways before I understood.

I suppose one almost always thinks a professional comedian is joking. I know I did and Ben had to get downright angry to convince me he was serious. He seems to think he proposed a lot of times before he was accepted, but I assure you, I said yes the first time I knew he meant it. We might have been married weeks before if I hadn't always been looking for the laugh in the things Ben said and did.

So you see, being a comedian, even a high-salaried one, has its drawbacks, for it certainly made it hard for Ben to propose.[262]

Actress Peggy Hopkins Joyce says that Ben Turpin is the only man she has met in Hollywood and only met him because she came to inquire about renting a house.

Alf Goulding and Harry Connett completed Ben Turpin's newest comedy, also featuring Ruth Taylor, Thelma Hill, Marvin Lobach, Barney Hellum, and Andy Clyde. (possibly *The Pride of Pikeville*).[264]

Pie-Throwing Is Passing Out (1926 August 14)

"Public taste is rapidly frowning its disapproval of pie throwing and other forms of slapstick comedy," according to F. Richard "Dick" Jones, Director General of Hal Roach Studios, where short feature comedies are made for Pathé release. "And I must admit that I agree with the new idea. To me, there is nothing funny about the knock-about form of comic entertainment. To be sure, the public has liked it, and will probably continue to gets laughs, but the present trend is for more refined action, depending more upon ludicrous situations than upon buffoonery."[264]

When a Man's a Prince (re August 15, 1926)

Moving Picture World review: Ben Turpin's return to Sennett comedies is marked by a riot of fun, a burlesque of the mythical kingdom yarn, with the star as a Von Stroheim Austrian prince. The cross-eyed one is as funny as ever, the settings are of feature calibre, the gags are really funny. Madeline Hurlock is a stunning figure in a vamp part.

Louella Parsons column, The Milwaukee Sentinel (1926 August 25):

Ben Turpin is smiling again. He has a new and beautiful leading lady; a dark-eyed vamp will try her wiles on him in all forthcoming comedies to be made by the cross-eyed comedian for Mack Sennett. Turpin was inconsolable when Mack Sennett announced that Madeline Hurlock, who has been his leading lady for three years, would now be starred in her own picture. But now that he has a new leading lady, all is well and the goose hangs high. The new vamp is Alma Bennett.[265]

Ben Turpin Back in Movies Again (1926 August 28)

Hogan's Alley, the Warner picture, signalizes the return to pictures of Ben Turpin. The cross-eyed comedian had been out of pictures for nearly a year when the Warners nabbed him on his return to Hollywood. His absence had been caused by the illness of his wife. Turpin gave up all screen activities to watch at her bedside and he stayed with her to her death. He had no heart for comedy and it was thought he might retire. But, like all great comedians, there is pathos as well as laughter in his work and the new Ben Turpin is said to be more appealing than ever on that account.[266]

1926 September 29, *Variety:* They're speculating as to the future of Ben Turpin. Ben has been under contract to Mack Sennett, but with the latter scheduled to become supervising head of the Famous Players-Lasky comedy units, it is said there will be no place for the comedian with that organization. If such is the case, reports are current that Pathé will endeavor to get him to join the ranks of the Educational group of comics who release through that organization.[267]

A Prodigal Bridegroom (re September 26, 1926)

The second comedy of the new Mack Sennett series starring Ben Turpin shows him as a lad who returns from the city laden with money, is ensnared by a vamp, Madeline Hurlock, cooks up such a miraculous yarn about her so as to get rid of his village sweetheart, Thelma Hill, and is then thrown down by the vamp. It is a combination of slapstick and the burlesque on a youthful romance with a number of amusing moments and a novel climax showing Ben hanging on a water pipe, his golf trousers filled with water, which is being sprayed out in all directions. Madeline Hurlock is the vamp.

A Harem Knight (re November 7, 1926)

"In my latest picture I wear an elaborate harem gown of white lace trimmed with rhinestones and pearls, a long veil that covers the nose, mouth, and neck, and bracelets of graduated pearls and brass. Never have I found my clothes so attractive, so comfy, and so simple."

Danny O'Shea, an aviator, carries off the Rajah's Princess, Madeline Hurlock. He knocks Ben over the head and takes his clothes, dressing him in the Princess' gown. He is mistaken for the real princess and carried to the Palace. Later, the Princess hides in his apartment, where he finds her. She then tells him the sad story of her life and attempts to escape. He helps her to elope with the aviator. Later, what he takes for a nightmare is the real thing and he awakens to find himself married to the homeliest woman in the world, Louise Carver. *Moving Picture World* wrote: The picture has been produced on an elaborate scale and there are a number of amusing situations and it should generally please.

Ben Turpin (1926 December)

Salute the real discoverer of the fountain of youth — Ben Turpin, that veteran Mack Sennett comedy star. For 15 years, Ben has been a featured screen comedian. And to be successful, he has been the "goat" for many a screen bump, fall, and punch. He has been in the hospital no less than 20 times as the result of accidents which occurred during the filming of scenes. Just a few months ago, he broke his ankle. Life for him is just one mix-up after another, yet Ben smiles and makes others laugh with and at him and the years mean nothing. Although he is old enough to be granddaddy to most of the girls who have played with him on the Sennett lot, Ben doesn't look a day older than when he first cocked his eyes and looked soulfully into the eyes of his first movie sweetheart. Among Ben Turpin's current pictures are *The Prodigal Bridegroom*, *A Harem Knight* and *A Blonde's Revenge*. With additional films already in the can, about mid-December 1926, Turpin begins work under veteran director Harry Edwards on his last Sennett short, *Daddyboy*.

A Blonde's Revenge (re December 19, 1926)

Ben Turpin as Gerald Montague — handsome and a favorite with the ladies. He's also an aspiring-to-be Senator, who's backed by wealthy Peter Cody. One of Montague's opponents, Tim Hayes, seeking to put a crimp in Montague's campaign, induces his blonde stenographer to hamper his plans by getting her picture taken seated in Montague's lap. The plan is about to work — when Gerald's attempted love-making to the pretty blonde is hindered by the visit of Tim Hayes' wife. The little blonde is quickly hustled out of sight. Then, to add to Montague's troubles, along comes another candidate's wife — followed by her husband. Friend husband, not knowing of his wife's presence, has a cameraman ready to snap a flashbulb picture of the gallant Montague — which he does — but the picture never fulfilled its purpose, for in the melee that followed, the camera was smashed — the women made hasty exits and Montague fooled his foes.

The little blonde was played by Ruth Lee Taylor, a 102-pound, 5' 2" beauty with dark blue eyes born in Grand Rapids, Michigan on January 13, 1907. At two years old, her family moved to Portland Heights in Portland, Oregon, where she attended Rose City Park Grammar School and, later, Lincoln High, graduating in 1925. Having studied acting and dancing, she found work as an extra at Universal, then with Mack Sennett, who was looking for a blonde for his comedies. After two years at Sennett in comedies with Turpin, Billy Bevan, Ralph Graves, and Eddie Quillan, she left and starred in the film *Gentlemen Prefer Blondes*. Following that, Ruth soon married, dropped out of pictures, and was the mother of writer/actor Buck Henry.

Ben Turpin To Appear Screen Comedian to Preside at Liberty Show (1926 December 22)

Arrangements have been completed by Edwin G. Hitchcock, manager of the Liberty Theater, whereby Ben Turpin, world famous screen comedian, and a party from Hollywood will be in Portland soon.

Negotiations for Turpin's appearance at the Liberty have been pending for a week and it was only late yesterday that a telegram was received from Agnes O'Malley, publicity director for Mack Sennett studios, to which firm Turpin is under contract, permitting the funny man of the movies to make a personal appearance here.

Turpin will act as master of ceremonies at the Liberty Theater's New Year's midnight show. An announcement covering other big offerings for this occasion is expected soon. Tentative plans have been mapped out for Turpin. He will offer some funny bits of impromptu work in announcing the performers on the bill and will deliver a short talk on movie conditions in Hollywood.[268]

Band Meets Ben Turpin — Movie Comedian Welcomed to Portland
Star Will Be Taken Around Hood This Morning to See Movie Possibilities (1927 January 1)

They turned the band out for Ben Turpin yesterday. The city council was out, or part of it, in the person of City Commissioner Bigelow and the police force was there, represented by Chief Jenkins and a couple of traffic officers. Cameras clicked and Ben — he of the odd eyes — did a jig, and his wife smiled, and the crowd smiled, and then he led Herman Kenin's orchestra with Herman himself playing second fiddle — or was it a saxophone? — and everybody was happy.

Ben Turpin is known to thousands in Portland, but he knows very few of the same thousands. Anyway, he is going to stay here only until this afternoon, when he leaves for Seattle and Vancouver before returning to Hollywood. He was scheduled to act as master of ceremonies last night at the Liberty Theater's New Year's Eve Carnival.

Mr. Turpin will have few spare moments today, for a committee from the Portland Chamber of Commerce has arranged a motor trip over the Mount Hood loop highway with William P. Merry in charge, leaving this morning at 11 o'clock. It is the desire to show him the scenery available for motion picture features.

But on this point Ben admitted last night he was not qualified to speak, for he said he was not acquainted with Oregon weather or Oregon scenery. Beaverton citizens, too, were interested in getting Mr. Turpin as far as their large studio, idle for a long time, but he was not at all certain that time would permit the jaunt.[269]

Hood Draws Motorists — Record Weekend Expected at Government Camp
(1927 January 1)

Sandy, Oregon, January 1 — Although rain interfered to some extent, the weekend at Government Camp promises to set a record for crowds and entertainment. Friday night, motor parties began to arrive and they were still coming in tonight to spend Sunday. Sergeant Griffith and Patrolman McMahon of the state patrol handled traffic.

There were many skiing and snowshoeing parties and a contest was held this afternoon. Hotels were all filled. Among those present were Ben Turpin, motion picture comedian, and his wife. The road was in good condition.[270]

Ben Turpin Likes Snow — Comedian Visits Slopes of Mount Hood (1927 January 2)

Ben Turpin, cross-eyed movie comedian, frolicked on the snows of Mount Hood yesterday and enjoyed it as much as a youngster, he said. Mr. and Mrs. Turpin, who are visiting the city on a vacation trip, were guests of the Portland Advertising Club on a trip up the loop highway as far as Government Camp. William P. Merry, president of the club, and a party of members made up the group that accompanied them.

"Unlike many professional comedians Mr. Turpin provided amusement and entertainment for the party from the time we left until we returned," declared Ray Conway, one of the group. "He kept us in a continual uproar and proved to our satisfaction that he is as funny in real life as he is on the screen. He is simply a born clown. At the same time he was courteous and affable. When he was recognized he never refused to pose for a picture or autograph souvenirs."

Mr. Turpin declared that Mount Hood and the surrounding territory was a revelation to him. It would make, he thought, an ideal setting for a snow motion picture. He declared that such a picture could be filmed in three days with no difficulty in providing adequate "sets."

Both Mr. Turpin and his wife rode behind a dog team and donned snowshoes. The comedian engaged in a snowshoes race with Mr. Merry, coming off victor by a foot.

The Turpins leave Portland tonight for Seattle. They expect to visit Vancouver and Victoria, B.C., before returning to Los Angeles.[271]

Ben Turpin Hats Popular (1927 January 11)

New York, Monday, January 10 — The makers of carnival hats say that after Rudolph Valentino's death, public taste swung from sporting sheik turbans to Ben Turpin derbies for fancy dress parties.[272]

A Hollywood Hero (re January 30, 1927)

Mack Sennett's newest comedy starring Ben Turpin shows him in the role of a romantic screen idol who is a devil with the ladies. On board a train, he is recognized by a fan, played by Alma Bennett, who raves over him, but her matter-of-fact hubby objects seriously. Finally, when wifey invites the star to her home and hubby unexpectedly comes in, there is a full quota of excitement and amusing action with the star endeavoring to escape by posing as a waiter. There are some good gags and the situations are amusing. Bud Jamison does good work in the role of the irate husband and Harry Edwards capably directed this production.[273]

May Be Able To See A Joke, But Fails To Register Smile (1927 January 8)

Whether he maintains an immobile countenance by thinking of icebergs or other things elsewhere than in his immediate foreground or has an antipathy to slapstick comedy efforts of people who try to make him smile in the crowds which gather hourly before the show windows of Shepard & Co., 353 Central Ave., Thomas LaRose proves his ability to hold the frozen-faced stare of a mechanical man during the hours when he is aiding in advertising the sale being conducted by the clothing store. But then $100 is $100 and that is the amount of the forfeit he has agreed to pay to the person who can make him smile while posing.

After 26 years of posing as a mechanical mannequin in public, he has not been called upon once to pay the self-imposed fine for cracking a smile or winking an eyelash while on duty. And that last, according to physicians and professors of physiology, is the most difficult part of the feat, as anyone can test by trying to prevent their eyelids from moving even for a period as short as 60 seconds.

The nearest LaRose ever came to succumbing to the desire to laugh was some 10 years ago when he was appearing in a Los Angeles department store window, he says. Ben Turpin, not then as famous as he is now, entered the window with LaRose and just naturally made his life miserable with an exaggerated show of timing the posing act and giving an imitation of LaRose. However, he survived the ordeal and kept his hundred dollars intact. And that goes to show how much chance the amateur has.

LaRose will be in the Shepard & Co. window this evening from 3 until 8 o'clock after appearing in repeated poses throughout the greater part of the morning.[274]

1927 February 5: From Pathé comes the news that Lige Conley is to lay aside the grease paint and take up the direction of Mack Sennett comedies for them. His first effort will be the direction of Ben Turpin in a new two-reeler as yet unnamed.

The Jolly Jilter (re March 13, 1927)

Virgil Vancourt, Broadway playboy (Ben), becomes engaged to Myrtle (Madeline Hurlock), but she doesn't love him. He throws over his old flame, Alma (Alma Bennett), but she comes to his house while he is entertaining Myrtle and threatens to commit suicide. In the midst of the uproar, the cops move in and they are all taken to the police station.

Moving Picture World: Ben Turpin appears once again in the role of a heartbreaking debonair lady-killer in this Mack Sennett comedy with Alma Bennett and Madeline Hurlock as the objects of his affection. There are a number of clever and amusing gags that are good for laughter from the Turpin fans and audiences in general, centering around Ben's flirtations with a society dame (Madeline) and a lady of the footlights (Alma). He keeps getting into scrapes and skillfully getting out of them, keeps things in an uproar, and, of course, wins out in the end. J. A. Waldron supervised the production and Eddie Cline directed from a scenario by Phil Whitman and Harry McCoy. It is up to this star's usual amusing standard.[275]

Ben Turpin and Traffic Officer Play "Tag" in Street (1927 March 20, advertorial)

Ben Turpin may be a leading comedian on the screen, but to the traffic cop, he is just one more motorist — at least, that is what it looked like to the bystander when Ben parked his new Chrysler 70 Royal coupe in the yellow painted loading zone in front of a branch of the Greer-Robbins Company one day this week. Here is the conversation as reported by Floyd E. Manges, branch manager for Greer-Robbins:

Said Officer A.L. Moore, writing busily on a ticket, "You can't park there."

Said Ben, not yet able to get both eyes focused on the bit of paper in the officer's hand, "I can't, huh! I can park this car anywhere there is six inches to spare. Why she'll go in where no other — !!!! — (Both eyes finally coming to rest on the rapidly moving pencil in the officer's hand) — Is that a ticket I see?"

"Nothing else but."

Ben, climbing out of the Chrysler, his eyes speaking volumes, which the officer quite neglected to read: "Is this a loading zone? Is that a ticket? Am I breaking the law? Must I go to jail? Officer, what law am I breaking?"

"Ordinance 77,777 (that's what it sounded like). Forbidden parking in a loading zone."

"But, sergeant, doesn't that ordinance cover unloading as well as loading?"

"Sure."

"Ah, lieutenant, you can stop writing on that ticket anytime now, for I was using this zone for unloading and nothing else. You see, Captain, I have had this new Chrysler just a few days and am so full of enthusiasm about it that I pulled up here to unload some of it for the benefit of Mrs. Turpin. Yep, that's Mrs. Turpin in the car. Mother, meet the Captain! Captain, meet Mrs. Turpin!"

Manges, breaking into the conversation, while Turpin kept one eye on the motionless pencil and with the other did full duty as host: "Officer, we certainly have no objection to a Chrysler owner using our unloading zone to unload his praises of the Chrysler car. In fact, we would like to have greater unloading facilities to accommodate this kind of traffic."

"Chief," said Ben, one eye beginning to see hope, while the other continued to tend strictly to the urgent business of looking admiringly and supplicantly at the officer, "Chief, I want you to understand — "[276]

Good Short Stories from Everywhere — In Doubt

Ben Turpin took a taxi to the Southern Pacific depot to go on location. Spying a group of small boys, he said, "I'll give you a quarter to carry my bag to the train."

"Which one?" came the eager chorus.

"You," said Ben. There was a moment of silence.

Finally, one boy said: "Say, mister, close one eye and then look at the feller you want, will yuh?"[277]

Broke in China (re April 24, 1927)

Ben and his pal, both of them sailors, are in Shanghai. They are accosted by a couple of homely women in a waterfront dive. Neither Ben nor his pal has any money, but Ben accidentally wins a lot of money at roulette. Ben then tells the sad story of how his sweetie jilted him and her father threw him out in the street on the day of the wedding. It turns out that one of the homely women is his mother and his pal is his father, he having married her to win an election bet.

Moving Picture World: As a practically penniless American sailor who, with his companion, wanders into a Chinese cabaret, Ben Turpin has the leading role in an amusing burlesque produced by Mack Sennett. Ben unconsciously wins a fortune at roulette when some money wished on him lands on a lucky number and keeps repeating and piling up. Cornered by two flappers (Louise Carver and Alice Belcher) of the vintage of 1880, he is up against it. It finally develops that he is the long-lost child of one of them and that his sailor pal (Donald Maines) is really his father. The past is burlesqued by means of flashbacks, which are cleverly handled and should appeal to all who like this form of comedy.[278]

The Pride of Pikeville (re June 5, 1927)

Ben as Baron Bonamo, movie star and ladies' man, is traveling in a Pullman car — which has aboard a loving pair of about-to-be newlyweds. The prospective bride, a movie fan, catches sight of her hero and he, in turn, not averse to a new feminine conquest, horns in. The near-groom, jealously sizing up the situation, determines to let the flirtation proceed. When the parents of the girl have almost permitted the wedding to take place, the jealous one appears on scene, breaks up the party, routs the movie star, and has the last laugh — and wins out in the end.

Moving Picture World: Once more, Ben Turpin is pictured as a dashing breaker of feminine hearts in a Mack Sennett comedy. This time, we see him as a foreign nobleman on an enforced tour of the U.S. because of his affairs with the fair sex on the other side. In the town of Pikeville, he unwillingly gets mixed up with an unattractive country girl and is about to be the hero in a shotgun wedding when he escapes and almost duplicates the performance when he flirts with a pretty girl. Finally, he manages to escape and boards his private car only to find that the homely girl is already there ahead of him. An improbable combination of farcical situations with plenty of slapstick and several humorous twists should please this star's fans and the majority of patrons.

— Ben Turpin Here, Jests On His Cave of the Winds Trip — Famous Screen Comedian of Crossed Eyes Says He Was "Cock-Eyed" Down and Up (1927 June 24)

Ben Turpin, movie comedian, and his wife, accompanied by another couple on their way back to Hollywood from the Shriners' Convention in Atlantic City, were guests of Niagara Falls today. They came to this city from Buffalo by auto shortly before noon and immediately embarked on a sightseeing tour through Prospect Park and around Goat Island before crossing to the Canadian side.

After descending to the Cave of the Winds on a special tour conducted by Harold Wright, the cross-eyed wonder of the screen wrote in Mr. Wrights' guest register, "I went down cock-eyed and came back the same way."

The party crossed over to the Canadian side about noon and remained there until late today, when they again returned to Buffalo to resume their journey to the west coast to begin work on Mr. Turpin's latest picture.[279]

Daily Movie Service by Dan Thomas

Atlantic City, July 6 — Hollywood's cinema colony, or at least a goodly portion of it, is making its headquarters in this Atlantic seaboard resort for the time being.

As a rule, Atlantic City's claim to fame is its annual bathing beauty contest for the selection of a "Miss America." Recently, it boasted of being the home of celluloid notables, for more than 50 members of the movie crowd made the jump across the continent aboard a special "Screenland Limited" to participate in the Shrine conclave.

When the sun was up, the gang either slept or swam. At night, they rode on glorious floats, representing all of Hollywood's studios, in the huge electrical pageants staged by Harry D. Brown. It's easy to see who the popular players are in small towns around the country.

When the special train stopped in Needles, California — only a few hundred miles from the film capital — only a mild interest was shown in the big dramatic stars. But when Ben Turpin and Jack Hoxie appeared, the natives nearly went wild. Jack's ten-gallon Stetson attracted most attention, so Ben took a dive into his drawing room and reappeared with a flock of autographed pictures of himself. When he started passing them out, Hoxie's admirers left him flat, so he pulled a disappearing act, came back with photos, and a mad scramble was enjoyed by all.[280]

Love's Languid Lure (re August 28, 1927)

Ben, a simple country boob, is engaged (to Peggy Montgomery). A city slicker (Jack Cooper) comes to town and tries to persuade Peggy to run away to the big city with him and study for grand opera. Peggy's mother tells Ben that Jack is making love to Peggy and to surprise them. But Jack is wise and when Ben bursts in, he is playing solitaire. He gets Ben into a game of poker and takes all of Ben's savings away from him. Peggy decides to run away with Jack and Ben is only consoled when his mother promises to make him some animal crackers.

Comedian Turns Director

From now on, you will look in vain for Lige Conley to be cutting up didoes on the screen. Nevertheless, paradoxical as it may sound, you will still see some of Lige's antics on the screen. You see it is this way. The comedian has long cherished a want to be a full-fledged director-comedy writer. Mack Sennett has given him his chance. He has just finished writing and directing a story starring Ben Turpin, known as Love's Languid Lure. That picture turned out to be so good that Sennett at once signed him on a long-term contract and Conley is now engaged in writing a story for the celebrated Smith Family.

Daddyboy (re October 23, 1927)

Ben, engaged to Alma Bennett, tells her it is all off when three pretty high school girls come into his office. He then realizes how old Alma is. However, Alma's mother is determined, so she makes her put on a blonde curly wig and walk down the street, swinging some school books. Ben sees her and falls for her. At dinner, Alma says she is going to bed, as it is nine o'clock. She gets a telephone call from the boy she loves telling her to skip out and run away with him. She goes up and gets into her regular clothes and tries to get away, but Ben sees her. When he sees that she is his former fiancée, he tells her to hurry on out, not knowing his new love is the same person. As Ben goes to kiss her good night, Ben finds only a dummy and this brings on a severe attack of indigestion as the picture ends.

The King of Comedy

Mack Sennett later remembered Ben in his autobiography with Cameron Shipp: "Ben Turpin could fall, tumble and prank with the best of my roughnecks, but his special and universal appeal was, of course, like Langdon's and Chaplin's, the appeal of all undersized gents who stand up against Fate anyway. Ridiculous to everyone yes, but never to himself. In Von Stroheim breeches and monocle Turpin reduced Von Stroheim and all domineering Prussians to absurdity. With cross-eyes batting he could lie on a tiger-skin rug and make the heaving sultriness of Theda Bara (or all pretentious love-making) a silly joke.

"The thing was, he seemed to take himself with utter seriousness. You never felt sorry for him no matter how you laughed. You had to see that Mr. Turpin was very, very brave.

"Ben Turpin died rich and having fun. After his retirement it was his hobby to direct traffic at the intersection of Santa Monica Boulevard and Western Avenue. With his eyes crossed and arms flailing he engineered some of the most outrageous automotive jams in the history of congested Los Angeles.

"He yelled to every motorist, 'I'm Ben Turpin, three thousand dollars a week!'"

After ten long and hard years with Mack Sennett, Ben Turpin had called it quits. He made a fortune for both himself and his employer. Worldwide fame was now his, as were the ups and downs of both business and life itself. Shrewd investments in real estate allowed Turpin to live quite comfortably and allowed him the opportunity to retire at any time. By March 1927, when he left Sennett for the last time — although only to return once more a few years later — it looked as if Turpin at last would truly retire in his 57th year. But never one to sit down nor sit still, once word of his leaving Sennett reached all the studios, Ben's phone never stopped ringing.

The College Hero with Rex Lease and Bobby Agnew.

Ben Turpin
At Liberty/ Freelancing

After ten long, hard, and successful years with Mack Sennett, Ben Turpin chose to take the plunge as a freelancer in the movies as well as returning to making public appearances over the next several years.

1927 April 26: Ben signs contract with Marion Mack Productions, Louis Lewyn, General Manager, to work for $500 a day on one of their first films, *Alice in Movieland*.

1927 June 27: Turpin makes 3 performances at the Senate Theatre for Lubliner & Trinz, earning $200 for the day. The following day, Ben next does 3 more appearances for Lubliner & Trinz, earning another $200 for a day's work at the Harding Theatre, both Los Angeles. About this time, Ben shared the bill with newcomer Baby Nan, soon known as Nanette Fabray.

Ben Turpin Rose from Janitor's Job (1927 August 7, in part):
One day, a comedian failed to appear for the filming of a script. The director was desperate. As he was pacing the floor in desperation, Turpin popped into the room with his broom. The assembled actors burst into laughter. That was enough for the director and Mr. Ben Turpin became a screen actor. Later, he became a $3000 a week star. Few of his public saw Mr. Turpin on his New York visit. Despite his affluence, he stayed at an unpretentious hotel in the Forties with his wife (his third), chose the subways instead of taxis, and his biggest party was a trip around the island on a sightseeing steamer. He also took in Chinatown and the Bowery.[281]

Turpin Signs Contract (1927 September 18)
Ben Turpin, the wavy-eyed comedian who has been with Mack Sennett for many years, has been signed on a contract by the Columbia Pictures Corporation for the comedy relief in *The College Hero.* Ben should be a good foil for Pauline Garon and Bobby Agnew, the other principals.[282]

328   FOR ART'S SAKE: THE BIOGRAPHY & FILMOGRAPHY OF BEN TURPIN

One Time When No Laughs Come From Studio (1928 January 31)

Hollywood, Jan 31 — The dirty, cracked gates of the old Mack Sennett studio — through which scores stepped from obscurity to motion picture stardom — have been closed.

In line with an announcement earlier in the week, the home of the famous Sennett comedies, the oldest standing studio of the film colony, has been closed, not to reopen.

Suspension of the comedy release through Pathé was given as the immediate reason, but the basic cause is "newer and cheaper quarters."

The ancient sets, stages, and dressing rooms on Glendale Blvd., some erected in 1910, will be torn down. The sub-dividers will supplant the property man and when Sennett continues production, presumably April 1st, it will be in a new plant in San Fernando Valley, just north of Hollywood. It was in Sennett comedies that Charlie Chaplin, then a little-known dance hall performer, first displayed the baggy trousers and trick feet that carried him to stardom.

Ben Turpin Now In Vaudeville (1928 May 2)

Ben Turpin, having finished the last of a number of comedies, has forsaken the screen for vaudeville. He was given a leave of absence of about eight weeks and will return to the Weiss Brothers after filling his vaudeville engagement.

On the first of May, it was announced that Ben and Snub Pollard were returning to pictures. "Both comedians are to make an individual series of ten two-reelers each for Artclass," as was a third comic as yet unsigned (Poodles Hannaford).[283]

Ben later told author Harry T. Brundidge, "I'm with a small company now (Weiss Brothers) and only work one week a month." Nearly all of these comedies have circulated among film collectors over the years and all are enjoyable, fast-moving two-reelers featuring capable casts and Turpin's comic acting is as funny as ever.

Ben Turpin Plans Film Return by Louella O. Parsons *(1928 June 24)*

I understand Ben Turpin is considering a return to pictures. He and his wife are living very happily and quietly these days with Ben indulging his favorite hobby — raising dogs.

He gave Doris Arbuckle a bit of a dog, which she reckoned to be a Chihuahua. The Lilliputian animal became ill, so Doris rushed him to the hospital. Much to her surprise, she learned the critter wasn't a Chihuahua at all, but a Manchester.

"I never heard of the breed," I admitted to Doris.

"Oh, yes," she returned proudly, "you must have heard of the Manchesters of Mexico." But then, one's fate is to live and learn.[284]

1928 July 14, Waterloo, IA: Ben Turpin, acrobatic-eyed film comic, has been signed as master of ceremonies for eight weeks, opening a tour of the Interstate Circuit at Dallas, Texas, August 1.

On Looking Ben Turpin In The Eye (1928 August, in part)

By this time, talking pictures were the rage. While on tour in Kansas City, Turpin told a reporter for *The Star:* "I'm not worried about talking movies. Listen, I have a voice. The other actors go to speaking classes. Not me. I took lessons on a huckster wagon. Listen, you have to talk plain in selling ve-ge-ta-bles; just like this: bah-nan-no! I'm going to practice up on a banana wagon when I get home."[287]

Turpin Is In Court — X-Eyed Movie Actor Called Before Grand Jury (1928 August 30)

Fort Worth, August 29 (AP) — Ben Turpin, film comedian, went before a Tarrant County grand jury today. The comedian, here for a vaudeville contract, sat across the table from the 12 probers with his cross-eyes flashing.

Ben Turpin, Cross-Eyes N'All Coming to San Antonio Majestic (1928 September 2)

Grown-ups as well as the kiddies have a real treat in store for them at the Majestic Theater next Saturday. Ben Turpin, the cross-eyed comedian of film fame, is coming in person. He has an exceptionally funny act of gags and talk. Many years ago, this comedian worked for the first time before the camera and later with Charles Chaplin in a two-reel picture called *His New Job*. Chaplin refused to use the funny fellow with the cross-eyes again. Mack Sennett figured if Turpin in a small part could make such a hit that he was worth featuring; hence his quick rise to stardom. A reception for the kiddies is planned and the place will be announced at a later date.

Ben Turpin Will Sell Keys to State Fair (1928 September 5)

Ben Turpin, he of the crossed eyes and solemn mien, in person will take a hand Thursday in helping set a new record for opening day at the State Fair October 6. Mr. Turpin, who is appearing at the Majestic Theater this week, will offer for sale State Fair keys in front of the Baker Hotel to the noon crowds.

The Junior Chamber of Commerce has arranged for the comedian's appearance. Cooperating with service clubs and business houses of the city as well as a number of other organizations, these young businessmen are distributing 40,000 keys, which will admit the bearer to the fairgrounds on opening day as often as he wants with automobile and also carries admittance to the grandstand attractions.[285]

Ben Turpin At Majestic — Heads Strong Bill of Vodvil (1928 September 9)

Ben Turpin, who with his crossed eyes and eccentric antics on the screen made himself one of the biggest comedy favorites of the theater, is at the Majestic this week, entertaining in a personal appearance. Turpin and his awry eyes are the chief attraction of the new program that opened Saturday afternoon. Turpin is doing a "single" working up comedy chatter with dance and fall interpolations. Turpin's chatter and dance steps on the stage are as they were on the screen — of the eccentric variety. He is making the personal appearances over the Interstate circuit "between pictures" and returns to the flicker lots again next month.[286]

Turpin's Eyes Rest As He Inspects San Antonio Park System (1928 September 11)

"This is restful to my eyes," remarked Ben Turpin, cock-eyed comedian, as he drove through Brackenridge Park as the guest of Commissioner Jacob Rubiola on Tuesday morning. Then Ben Turpin hastened to explain that he was not joking. "I'm serious," he said. "San Antonio has the prettiest parks in the country." Commissioner Rubiola took Turpin through all of the major parks. Turpin is on the Majestic Theater stage this week.[288]

Screen Comedian Tops Martini Bill
Ben Turpin Heads Current Majestic Vaudeville Offering (1928 September 30)

Keeping pace with the standard set by the opening bill, the second vaudeville offering of the season at the Martini Theater affords much in the way of entertainment and diversion. Sharing headline honors with Ben Turpin, king of slapstick comedians, are Harry Anger and Mary Fair, old-timers on the Interstate circuit, and the Rigoletto Brothers in a potpourri of music and song. Turpin, whose crossed eyes have beguiled movie fans for a number of years, is present in person. By way of preliminaries, there are several snaps of Ben in his various roles, after which he is personally introduced. Handicapped by a severe cold, his antics were somewhat curtailed, but his versatility is easily recognized on the stage as on the screen.

Eye and Ear Enjoyment (1928 October 6)

Alice in Movieland is a short trip behind the scenes at Hollywood linked up with a light comedy plot. It shows many movie stars in short parts in the film. Among them are Gloria Swanson, Ricardo Cortez, Eugene O'Brien, Ben Turpin, and others. There is a story woven into the novelty production upon which the glimpses of the various stars is built.[289]

Ben Turpin at Orpheum, New Orleans (1928 October 8, in part) review:

A good bill of vaudeville and a fairly good screen farce are at the Orpheum this week with Ben Turpin headlining rather ineffectually in person. Turpin, one of the funniest men on the screen, actually a satirist, apparently was suffering from severe hoarseness Saturday. Still, he had a few clever gags, a few clever falls, and a burlesque of an esthetic dance that was amusing. And it was good to see the little man in the flesh. He was born in New Orleans in 1869, by the way.[290]

Ben Turpin Is Given Memento of Noted Uncle
As He Presents Candy to Children at Hospital (1928 October 11)

A copy of the Charity Hospital journal issued in 1854 in which Dr. C. C. Turpin, uncle of the famous Ben, was named as one of the hospital board was given Ben Turpin Thursday morning after he had visited the children in the Milliken Memorial building and had distributed packages of candy among them.

Ben Turpin was welcomed into an honorary fellowship with the present directors of the hospital for his own sake and that of his distinguished uncle and the fifty children in wheelchairs who looked up in eager hero-worship to him unanimously named him a great fellow, uncle or no uncle. They sympathized with his bad cold, which prevented him from doing any of his stunts.

"I don't feel like cutting up," apologized Ben when the youngsters begged for tricks. "I just came to see you. You see, I've got a pernicious cold."

"Oh — I'm so sorry!" they said. "Do you feel very bad?"

Ben looked down the line of wheelchairs, bandaged legs, and thin, twisted bodies.

"Not very," he said.

Then he took out boxes of candy from a big bundle he had brought.

"These are for you," he said. "Hope you like them."

While the older children hugged their candy, Ben picked up several of the babies in his arms and had his picture taken.

"Ain't this grand, sister?" said one of the little boys to a nun who stood supervising the party.

"Wonderful," nodded the sister. "How's your leg?"

"All right," he said. "Ben's got a bad cold."

Turpin grinned and waved at the children. They plunged into their boxes of candy. Before he left, Ben visited the ward for Negro children and distributed more candy.[291]

Ben Turpin Lands On Top of World by Falling Down (1928 October 14, in part)
Cross-Eyed Comedian from New Orleans Has Own Success Recipe by K.T. Knoblock

"You gotta land on your spine if you want to get a laugh. Talking ain't going to mean much in comedies, they're mostly running around and falling down."

These are the pearls of wisdom culled last week from under the Fuller brush mustache of Ben Turpin, screen comic and native of New Orleans, as he sat in his dressing room at the Orpheum Theater. The sheik of screenland was in the checked suit and brown derby he wears at the beginning of his act, looking like a successful plumber. (At that, he's almost as successful; he gets $3000 a week for his celluloid efforts.)

"I'm sixty years old, but I can do flops with the youngest of 'em. It's all in knowing how to light; if you ain't careful you're going to bust on your spine and cripple yourself all up. There's many a man going around Hollywood now, all busted up and hump-backed, who was a youngster with me in the Keystone police force. It's all in keeping in condition and living regular. When I'm home I'm up at 5 every morning, doing road work. Then I work from 8 to 4, go home, maybe read a book or once in a while go to a show, and I'm in bed every night by 10.

"I don't know why they laugh when you sit down hard — neither do they. But they do. I laugh myself when I sneak into the back of some theater with dark glasses on and look at myself. But when I'm seeing the daily 'rushes,' all I can think of is what a silly guy I'm being."

Ben talks in a rough voice with fluid, pungent idiom. He rises frequently to pantomime a word or an idea, the one about the hump-backed down-and-outers, for instance. The famous cross-eyes are much in evidence; when he's looking at you, he seems to be looking at your reflection in the makeup mirrors that line the wall. When he points at you, his eyes are at a diagonal. They made his fortune; he wouldn't have 'em fixed for a million dollars.

Turpin dons an evening gown and dashes out of his dressing room to appear in another act; he's helping them all out, he says. A burst of applause echoes back. He bustles in, beaming.

"I think they like me," he says naively. "They sure are nice to me, and don't think I don't appreciate it. I feel just like this was home to me, even if I did leave when I was a kid. It's just like coming back home and me, I've sure been having me a good time. I mean I've been eating me some oysters and fish."

And so, with a cordial farewell, a gallant figure passes, a great comedian, neither a giant intelligence nor an actor with a consciousness of art, but a trouper who had natural gifts and got the breaks. He may not know why his falls are funny. But they are. They express the satire of the ages.[292]

The Meaning of Comedy (in part)

Mr. Roark Bradford relates that once when working for a newspaper, he was assigned to interview Ben Turpin. The interview took place in the wings of a vaudeville theatre where Turpin was playing. Bradford asked Ben what, in his opinion, was the essence of comedy. "I will show you," replied Turpin, whereupon he strutted onto the stage with many gestures and grimaces — before a silent and unresponsive audience. Returning to Bradford in the wings, he said, "Now, watch again." This time he ran onto the stage and fell with great force on his seat. There was a roar of applause from the audience. "That," said Ben when he returned to where the reporter was waiting, "is the essence of comedy." Of course, Turpin was quite right; for that, too, is comedy, though not of a very high order. Satires on the dignity of man and the awkwardness of walking with the gingerly balance of the upright position have their place just as much as any other type of comedy. Low comedy as well as high comedy is comedy.

Ben Turpin Heads Good Card at Keith's Georgia by Ben Cooper *(1928 October 30)*

They've got a cock-eyed man at Keith's Georgia Theater this week. You're right, it's Ben Turpin. The world's champion cross-eyed man of the silver screen divides honors this week at the Georgia with a pair of harmonizing fellows billed as Hewett and Hall and with another pair entitled Anger and Fair. The show also included The Rigoletto Brothers and The Agemos.[293]

1928 Nov: Ben playing the Ritz Theater, Birmingham, Alabama to excellent business

1928 Nov. 24: The Cincinnati chapter of the Stage and Screen Scribes of America held a midnight frolic at Hotel Gibson Roof Garden last week drawing an attendance of more than 500. Ben Turpin, playing the Palace Theater, was Master of Ceremonies.

Motion Picture News, pg 1603

Santa Fe Notes (1928 December 13)

Ben Turpin, noted film comedian, was a passenger on Number 19, the westbound Chief, Friday morning. Mrs. Turpin accompanied him.

August Lemieux, Aged 82, Dies
Aged Tradesman Stricken by Pneumonia 10 Days Ago (1929 January 7, in part)

August LeMieux, aged 82 years, died this morning at 3:45 at his home at 324 Sable Street of pneumonia, with which he had been suffering the past ten days. Mr. LeMieux, although not very strong, had been in apparent good health, ailing only at times, until stricken with pneumonia. His daughter, Mrs. Ben Turpin, died October 1, 1925. His was the sixth death due to pneumonia in the last two weeks in Alpena, Michigan.

Alpena News, pg 1

Ben Turpin Company Use Van Nuys as Background (1929 January 18)

Ben Turpin and his company were here for a time yesterday taking scenes in the Valley for one of the coming productions. Vanowen Street near Van Nuys Boulevard will appear in the movie.[294]

Before completing ten two-reel comedies for Weiss Brothers-Artclass, production on the films were now and again interrupted by Ben's personal appearance tours throughout America. Unfortunately for Weiss Brothers-Artclass, their ten Ben Turpin comedies saw minimal exhibition due to most theaters having recently wired for sound film projection. Fortunately, the films enjoyed a good life among those few last silent theaters and a better life to the audiences abroad. These films have a much better survival rate thanks to the Weiss family's having saved most prints and negatives over the years.

1929 February 7-9: Turpin personal appearances at Yost Broadway Theater, Santa Ana, CA. Ben to receive $300 for his 3 days' work and 35% of the gross proceeds over and above $3,000 for the 3-day period.

Film Comics Booked for Keith Dates (1929 July 15)
Charles Murray and Ben Turpin Will Appear In Person by Chester B. Bahn
Two screen comedians will make personal appearances in Syracuse via the B.F. Keith rostrum during August, bookings announced today by John J. Burns. Turpin will headline the Keith bill opening on August 21 while on August 24, Charles Murray will make his bow in the flesh here.[295]

1929 August 10: State-Lake Theater, Chicago, Aug 10, review *(in part)*
Ben Turpin met with a reception on his entrance and answered with a nip-up. Turpin's material, using a straight man for cross-fire gags, is not so choice. Too many time-worn gags. But Turpin can take falls that are funny and that's something.[296]

1929 August 13: Ben in Akron, Ohio on Radio-Keith-Orpheum theaters tour.

The Big Thrill Due to Mistake — Billy Oetzel Finds Greetings Were Meant for Movie Star (1929 August 16)
"Billy" Oetzel, son of Paul Oetzel, county superintendent of highways, received a huge jolt when he alighted from a train at the Union depot, Chicago, while on a vacation trip last week.
"When I reached the steps of the car I heard everyone on the platform cheering and rushing toward me. I wondered just what I had done for my country when I happened to glance around and just behind me were Ben Turpin and some other celebrity. It was clear to me then but I surely felt funny for a while." Friends of Billy who received news of his experience enjoyed a big laugh.[297]

1929 August 29: Ben Turpin has refused Keith time offers at his current salary of $1,250, asking $2,500 for a continuation. Turpin is playing the Interstate Circuit at present.[298]

Ben Turpin Plays Bit In New Talkie and Retires Again (1929 August 31)
Hollywood — Credit to Ben Turpin the most original and shortest comeback in screen history. After a retirement lasting almost three years, the gentleman with the trick eyes popped before the camera for one-half a day and then retired again. There was no especial ballyhoo or promotion to his comeback.

Paramount asked him to take a small part in *The Love Parade*. He accepted terms without hesitation or without objections or dickering. He played his part and then left the studio. He didn't mention any desire to get back on the screen for good and he made no effort to arrange for more work.

Trenton Evening Times, Sept 1, 1929

According to studio hype at the time, director Ernst Lubitsch insisted that no other actor would do for the scene and Turpin performed the part just to please his staunch friend, Lubitsch. Ben appeared very briefly as a lackey in a castle scene and recalled, "Old Man Lubitsch offered me $300 just to say 'Hello' in one of his productions. But I held out for a grand and got it."[363]

Turpin Brings Crowds Into Keith's by Franklin H. Chase *(1929 August 22, in part)*

Ben Turpin, the man who made crossed eyes an asset, simply jammed the crowds into Keith's (Syracuse) right from the very first performance yesterday. Hundreds were turned away. That was a big thing. When the marker went up on the side to show Turpin was about to arrive, the audience was right on edge to see the man who had pulled a million or more laughs. He jumped in, flopped around, and then began wisecracking. Candidly, they liked him. Even after his act was over, they tried to tease more out of him. But the big thing was just to have seen him. If there was any doubt as to the comedy cult in pictures, it must have been settled yesterday.[363]

Asked about his famous mustache while in Syracuse, Ben quipped, "It's made from the eyebrows of little fishies they catch in the Ohio River. Each fish has only one hair in an eyebrow. It keeps five men busy with a net catching enough to keep me supplied."

1929 September 14: Turpin took part in E. F. Albee's Palestine Relief Fund held in Brooklyn along with Charlie Murray, Bert Lahr, Fred Allen, Ted Healy, John Bowers, Marguerite de la Motte, Harry Hershfield, Irene Rich, Bill Robinson, and many others.

Tom Sims Says (1929 September 23, syndicated column)

Now that practically everyone else has written an autobiography, maybe Ben Turpin will write his and give us a new slant on things.[300]

1929 September 29: Ben and Arnold Johnson and his orchestra are the headline stage attractions this week at Brooklyn's Kenmore Theater (RKO).

1929 October 9: 6th Street Theater, New York, appearance review *(in part):*

Ben Turpin, away from Hollywood on a sightseeing tour, has been caught several times, but still has the same answer. Outside of isolated Turpin-tined spots where the erstwhile screen comic's fascinating orbs may arouse curiosity, he means little. Turpin's material is slapped together with no head or tail. He probably switches gags and situations as he goes along, but it makes no difference. Here Ben wound up by having himself supposedly canceled by the manager with the curtain closing down on him.[301]

1929 October 9, 10 and 11, Ben playing Proctor's 58th Street Theater, New York.

1929 October 19-22, Ben playing an R-K-O theater in Queens, New York.

A year later, while on yet another tour and again back in New Orleans, Turpin told their newspaper, The Times-Picayune, "People got more action for their money," in reference to silent versus sound film. "The pictures were funnier.

"Nowadays we just say what they tell us to say and do what they tell us to do. There was more real acting in silent pictures.

"But the silent pictures are done." There was a solemn expression on the face of the little man who has occupied the spotlight in screenland for more than twenty years; as he spoke these words, the tone of his voice bespoke regret.

But Ben Turpin has by no means given up. He is an actor. Acting is his profession and he plans to go on doing his best to provide laughs for the public. Asked if after 23 years he had not tired of the movies, he promptly replied: "Never."

"The trouble with this world is a lack of good, deep laughs and the trouble with the motion picture industry today is that the producers, in the mad scramble to grind out pictures that sing and dance and which, after all, are nothing but canned musicals or melodrama, have forgotten all about the good, old-fashioned comedies.

"Don't get me wrong — I'm not crying for work. I didn't drag down my $3,000 a week for three years for nothing. I've got mine and plenty of it. But what is going to happen to this old world if the comedies are forgotten? All the wise-cracking writers and alleged humorists in the world never caused half the laughs that resulted from the antics of the slapstick comedians on the screen. They're forgetting all about us."

New Orleans Times-Picayune

Following the completion of his ten Artclass comedies, Ben "retired" in the early days of the talkies, reputedly worth a fortune, and invested his movie earnings in real estate at a time when more people were gambling with the stock market. Ben always had the last laugh. From then on, he took only occasional talking parts, always demanding a thousand dollars a week for his services. If a producer thought it too much to pay, Ben's answer was that he didn't have to work — "Take it or leave it," or "Well, I guess I'll go and collect some rents."

Ben told writer Harry T. Brundidge in 1929, "I get up every morning at 5 o'clock, exercise the dogs, take a two-mile walk, look after the cars and then eat breakfast. If you want to be happy and healthy, don't worry, and take a lot of good, deep laughs every day. I'd be the same Ben Turpin if I lost every dime I own — but I won't.

"You ought to see that nice house out in Beverly Hills. And my Great Dane dogs. And Mrs. Turpin. Come down to the bank and take a look at the money I've made with these eyes; then write your own answer."

Turpin's first talkie between vaudeville dates and his personal appearances was a small walk-on in director Ernst Lubitsch's extravagant feature for Paramount, *The Love Parade* with Maurice Chevalier and Jeanette MacDonald. Ben's friend Lupino Lane helped him get the job (according to Lane's autobiography), Turpin signing a contract on July 26, 1929, his work beginning almost immediately. Nearly all of Turpin's film appearances over the next ten years were quickies or cameos like this.

Ben next made a surprise appearance in a star-studded fifteen-reel Warner Brothers-Vitaphone feature, *Show of Shows*, in a musical number along with other comedy favorites Lupino Lane, Lloyd Hamilton, Lee Moran, and old Sennett co-stars Bert Roach and Heinie Conklin, singing the old stage hit *Flora Dora*. Ben played a waiter and actually took turns singing one of six verses with the other comics before hitting the floor with a nice smacking 108.

R.K.O. Stars at Lunch (1929 November 2)

The R.K.O. officials gave a luncheon yesterday at the Hotel Astor to the prominent stars of the screen now appearing, or about to appear, in the R.K.O. theaters in Greater New York and in R.K.O. productions. Leatrice Joy, Helen Kane, Baclanova, Claire Windsor, Carmel Myers, Viola Dana, Irene Rich, Mr. and Mrs. Morton Downey, Charles Murray, George K. Arthur, Rudy Vallee, Glenn Hunter, Theda Bara, Ben Turpin, Alice Joyce, Sally Rand, and Robert Woolsey were among the guests.

Haywire Optics to Take Tour — Turpin Will See Cock-Eyed World (1930 February 25)

Ben Turpin, whose haywire eyes and comic antics have tickled millions in America, will leave his Beverly Hills home with Mrs. Turpin in May for a tour of Europe, his attorney, Harold E. Sacklin, announced yesterday. He signed a contract in Sacklin's office under which Frank G. Mollenhauer of Elizabeth, NJ, will manage a tour of England, France, Italy, Germany, and possibly Russia and Palestine for "one or maybe two years," Sacklin said. Mollenhauer has written a comedy skit for the comedian and they will begin the tour with it. Later, Turpin may engage in motion picture work in Europe.[302]

Turpin Fears Europe (1930 February 26)
Hears of "Robbing" Americans, But All Looked Crooked to Ben

Hollywood, Feb. 26 — No matter how honest European tradesmen may be, Ben Turpin is sure that they will all look crooked to him when he goes abroad in May.

The comedian has signed a contract with Frank C. Mollenhauer, German impresario, calling for a two-year tour of the continent.

"I'm almost afraid to go to Europe after all I've heard of how Europeans 'rob' Americans!" Turpin said with a sigh. "But then, everyone looks crooked to me!"[315]

Hollywood Sights and Sounds by Robbin Coons (1930 March 27)

Hollywood — The cross-eyed countenance which brought fame to Ben Turpin has been utilized by others whom the comedian has never seen. Mr. Gene Howe, otherwise known as "Eramus R. Tack," the "Tactless Texan" columnist of the *Amarillo Globe* who recently broke into national news reports by labeling E. H. Sothern the noted Shakespearean "the king of high hatters" because Sothern refused a newspaper interview, has a small cut, unmistakably of Turpin, adorning his column heading.

Turpin, of course, makes no pretense at columning and says he did not know his cock-eyed grin was greeting *Globe* readers daily, but he does not mind.

Price of Fame

The comedian, naturally not sensitive about an affliction that has compensated him so well, seldom objects to exploitation of his name by others unless the exploiter is reaping large gains thereby, in which case Ben naturally, too, wants a "cut."

After all, it's publicity and no little compliment.

Once an oculist used pictures of Turpin before and after his optical trouble — but in reverse order — as an advertisement of his own curative powers. Turpin became irate and threatened to sue.[303]

Turpin Returns To Pictures In Speaking Role (1930 April 13)

Hollywood, April 12 — Ben Turpin speaks his lines from the screen as the cross-eyed bartender in *Swing High*, Pathé's circus romance featuring Helen Twelvetrees and Fred Scott. Turpin has been in motion pictures 23 years. Born in New Orleans, Louisiana and raised in New York, he came to Los Angeles in 1908 and got a job as prop boy with Essanay.

After various positions as grip, script clerk, bookkeeper, and whatnot, he got his first opportunity to act. It was only the advent of talking pictures and a restless nature that caused him to come back before the public in *Swing High*, directed by Joseph Santley.[304]

Turpin Is About Through — Salary Too Big & He Is Too Funny, So Producers Are Afraid He Will Make Their Stars Look Like Chumps by Hubbard Keavy (1930 April 20)

Hollywood, April 19 — One of the first remarks of visitors from "back east" usually is, "I suppose Ben Turpin is about through." And Ben, unfortunately for those who like to laugh, seems to be.

Ben just about grew up with the movies. The antics of this cross-eyed comedian made him an ace among cinema clowns and his salary grew in proportion to his popularity. I've heard that he was paid $3,500 a week before he left the Sennett lot.

Turpin was Mack Sennett's shining star for a long time. He worked almost exclusively for nearly 10 years for the Irishman, whose real name is Michael Sinnott. Three years ago, Sennett told Ben he couldn't continue paying him the salary he was worth because he was making fewer comedies for fewer theaters.

With the exception of "bits" in three or four pictures recently and a try at vaudeville, Turpin has been "at liberty" since.

Ben's Reasons

"This'll give you a laugh," Turpin told me the other day. "I was up for a part in a picture, a good part, too. Salary okayed and everything. Just getting ready to go to work and they called me up to say the part was cut. Why? I asked, 'You're too funny,' they said. Now is that a scream or is it?

"Just between you and me," Ben went on in more or less confidence, mostly less. "I'm not in pictures for two reasons. My salary's too big and I'm too funny. Even if I have only a very small role, the producers are afraid I'll make their stars look like chumps."

Pioneer

Turpin is thinking about accepting an offer to make a vaudeville tour in Europe. If he does accept, he will use a different act than the one he tried recently. Ben admits with a sigh that it was a flop.

Turpin, recently turned 60, but still as agile as ever, is credited with being the movies' first slapstick comedian. He came to Los Angeles sometime before 1910 to make outdoor scenes for a split-reel comedy.[305]

In 1930, Ben was "the greatest cock-eyed radio announcer in the world!" for radio station S-T-A-R in the eighth episode of *The Voice of Hollywood*, an entertaining series of little one-reel varieties from Tec-Art Studio, featuring many of Hollywood's best and newest faces. This particular Turpin episode also featured Madge Bellamy, Mickey Rooney, Alberta Vaughn, and Al Cooke and included some of Ben's favorite "eye" jokes such as: "I'm so cockeyed that when I was a young fellow I spent five years in the South East trying to join the Northwest Mounted Police."

The Voice of Hollywood — Tiffany — one reel *(Motion Picture News)*
"Number Eight and another of these entertaining series of Tiffany broadcasts from Station S-T-A-R. Ben Turpin is the master of ceremonies, and gets off some good laughs on his cross-eyes. He introduces Madge Bellamy, Alberta Vaughn, Kit Guard and Mickey McGuire. Running time, 11 minutes. Good for any bill."[306]

1930 June 30-July 1: Ben back in New Orleans for a visit, staying at the Roosevelt Hotel then returning home to Beverly Hills on July 2.

1930 July 8: Ben Turpin is now working with one of the famous Colonel W. L. Swain's famous tent shows. We understand the ingenious and resourceful colonel is figuring on a novelty wire act with Ben using two wires while he does a crossword puzzle. The act will be called *The Cock-Eyed Whirl*. *The Film Daily*, pg 3: Turpin signed to do a four-week tour for Swain as part of the *Hollywood Follies of 1930*, which began on June 3 in Wewoka, Oklahoma and wrapped up in New Orleans. Turpin was hired to help cover for the Colonel's recent loss of Jimmie Rodgers, the famous Singing Brakeman, who had other obligations, both personal and professional.

Turpin for RKO Short (1930 July 15, The Film Daily, West Coast Bureau)
Hollywood — RKO has signed Ben Turpin for a short subject entitled *Pure and Simple*.

Turpin Out of Pure And Simple (1930 July 23, The Film Daily, West Coast Bureau, page 4)
Hollywood — Ben Turpin has been replaced in *Pure and Simple*, RKO-Darmour comedy in which Louise Fazenda is being starred. Unfortunately, the film, intended for director and former Sennett associate Phil Whitman (but turned over to Lewis R. Foster), never happened for Ben. Nor did a then-rumored series. Production was actually slated to begin in June; however, Ben had already signed to tour with Colonel Swain. Louise did make the film and five other shorts for RKO, but how good it might have been if Turpin made comedies for the same company responsible for the great shorts of Benny Rubin, Edgar Kennedy, Walter Catlett, Mickey (Rooney) McGuire, Karl Dane and George K. Arthur, and Clark and McCullough.

1930 December 29: Another anonymous writer for the *Rochester Evening Journal* noted: The Christmas Holidays just wouldn't be complete without Ben Turpin. I have been hearing and writing about Ben for eighteen years and the other day someone asked me what had happened to him. Imagine my embarrassment when I had to admit ignorance. However, Ben is coming back to the screen in *Assorted Nuts* (released as *Cracked Nuts*), a Radio picture, starring Bert Wheeler and Robert Woolsey. Eddie Cline will direct.[307]

Cock-Eyed Ben's Return Suggests A Brighter Day by W. Ward Marsh (1931 April 23)

The chief reason why Ben Turpin has been kept from the talkies is because there has been little or no demand for him.

Back in the old silent days before people decided that heavy lovin' was to be preferred to a good old laugh, cock-eyed Ben could give 'em their money's worth.

Then there came the period when the pictures found their voices and as with all new mediums of expression, it began to take itself with deadly (literally) seriousness.

Another Reason

Ben suffered what once seemed to be an insurmountable handicap. His voice was rotten — from any chair you occupied in the theater.

It was guttural. It grated like a dentist's drill against a molar. It sounded as if Ben was talking from his shoes and half the eyelets stuck in his throat.

No, Ben wouldn't do. And he didn't "do." He quit.

I've heard Ben talk when you could swear that not only was his voice bad but his tongue was thick with liquor — and he was as sober as the traditional judge.

Surprise! Surprise!

Ben is given his first bit playing an airplane mechanic in *Cracked Nuts*. Wotta voice compared to what it once was!

Why, that old nutmeg grater of his functions like a lyric soprano's voice fighting for the high C's. You don't get much of Ben in this film, but his good old cock-eyes are just as sparkling as ever and his voice is literally marvelous.

Of course, he won't ever run Tibbett a second in the "Home, Sweet, Home" numbers, nor will he ever knock the spots from Robert Montgomery in deft comedy roles, but Ben's return is an encouraging sign.

Wheeler and Woolsey and plenty others are forerunners of the big laughs to come. Ben seems to prophesy that happy days are here again.[316]

Ben Turpin, Actor, Has An Operation (1931 April 25)

Hollywood, CA, April 25 — (UP) — The condition of Ben Turpin, motion picture comedian, following an operation was reported favorable today by attendants at the Hollywood Hospital. The actor was operated upon by Dr. Carl E. Conn for an intestinal ailment.

Knife Employed On Ben Turpin (1931 April 26)
Comedian's Condition Said to Be Satisfactory Following New Major Operation

Ben Turpin, screen comedian, underwent a major abdominal operation yesterday at Hollywood Hospital and his condition was reported as "satisfactory" by Dr. Carl E. Conn, the attending physician. About three years ago, Turpin was operated on for a similar ailment, but the results were not all that had been anticipated, friends said. A rapid recovery is expected now.[308]

Turpin Improves (1931 April 28)

Los Angeles — Ben Turpin, crooked-eyed film comedian who underwent a major operation yesterday, was reported recovering tonight. "His condition is good," physicians said. The operation was performed to relieve an intestinal disorder.

Ben's next appearance was in one of the popular team of Bert Wheeler and Robert Woolsey's early features for RKO, *Cracked Nuts*, directed by old associate Eddie Cline. Ben played an enemy bombardier ordered to drop destruction upon a mythical country, though naturally his criss-cross orbs seem to miss their mark.

In late March, Ben went over to Hal Roach Studios to appear in the two-reeler *Our Wife*, with two of his favorite screen comics, Stan Laurel and Oliver Hardy. Babe London added to the fun and old friends, Jimmy Finlayson and Blanche Payson, were there too.

The publication *Film Daily* wrote: "The Laurel & Hardy combination put on some hilarious pranks for the benefit of this Hal Roach subject, which is a pip. Oliver undergoes a lot of grief in eloping with his fat sweetie (Babe London) principally through the stupidities of his pal. Finally they reach the home of the justice of the peace, played by Ben Turpin, and that cross-eyed individual marries the femme to the wrong man. Entertainment deluxe for any audience."

Following that, Ben appears in a surprise cameo in the Sennett-Educational short *Movie-Town*, which looks more like candid footage than acting as Ben and his dancing partner whiz past the camera to the music of George Olsen and His Orchestra.

Film Actors Now Woo Fame By Playing 'Bit' Parts Well
(1931 September 19, in part)

Hollywood, Sept. 19 — Once upon a time, a picture actor thought he was lost for the future unless he had an important role. Now he goes looking for "bit" parts. In these days of stress, many an actor who hadn't held down a screen job for a long while now has as much work as he can do because he made a big hit in a tiny bit. Ben Turpin is the talk of the studios for the bit he did with Lena Malena, who also did her bit, in *Ambassador Bill*. At the very end of his good friend Will Rogers' feature, *Ambassador Bill*, Turpin shows up with a large ax in hand and severs the handcuffs from Will's arrest and sets him free.[309]

Sennett Plans a Super Comedy (1931 December 9)

Hollywood — Plans for a fifteen-reel comedy with a cast of at least a dozen stars was announced today by the veteran producer-director, Mack Sennett. Sennett said he was negotiating for the services of Clara Bow, Lupe Velez, Jean Harlow, Dorothy Burgess, Edmund Lowe, Roscoe Ates, and W. C. Fields. He has made arrangements for Moran and Mack, Andy Clyde, Mack Swain, Ben Turpin, and Lloyd Hamilton to appear in his "Super Spectacle."

All-Star Cast (1932 January 4)

A trend, prominent now as producers group their big box office stars into pictures together, would attain a new peak if Sennett is successful in negotiations for the headliners he wants, some of whom he has already. Clara Bow, Lupe Velez, Jean Harlow, and Dorothy Burgess are mentioned along with Edmund Lowe, Roscoe Ates, W. C. Fields, Andy Clyde, and the blackface team of Moran and Mack. Also, there are Mack Swain, Ben Turpin, and Lloyd Hamilton, all Sennett stand-bys. *Unfortunately, the film with this cast never saw production.*

Ben Turpin To Play On Stage (1932 January 20)

As an added attraction, Ben Turpin, comedian, will appear as guest star in *The Wager*, vaudeville farce, tomorrow at all shows at the Hillstreet Theater, Los Angeles.[310]

1932 March 5: Ben Turpin will stage a comeback with a series of comedies while Wallace McDonald is to be presented in a series of features. Both players have been inactive for a long time, with Ben in vaudeville for at least four years.[311] *This announced "series of comedies" starring Turpin unfortunately never reached the public.*

In the spring of 1932, Ben was back working for Mack Sennett to knock off a small part in the two-reeler *Lighthouse Love* with Arthur Stone, Franklin Pangborn, Dorothy Granger, Mack Swain, Tom Kennedy, Barney Hellum, and Heinie Conklin. Ben pops up at the very end of this film in full white Von Stroheim uniform and, after a kiss from sexy Dorothy, does a 108 and falls into a state of unconscious ecstasy.

Ben Turpin Himself (1932 May 11)

Ben Turpin signed with Paramount yesterday for a film characterization based on his own life. He will play this role in the forthcoming *Gates of Hollywood* (work title of *Make Me A Star*), adapted as a talking picture from Harry Leon Wilson's novel of Hollywood. Wilson is said to have modeled one of the principal characters along Turpin lines and ever since the work was published, the comedian has been anxious to play the role.[312]

Make Me A Star (1932 July 10)

"Ben Turpin furnishes the laughter as the successful comedian who looks very suspiciously like Ben Turpin himself. This is the first time he has played the role of Ben Turpin imitating Ben Turpin, and he outdoes himself!"

San Antonio Review

1932 c August: Paramount's latest *Hollywood On Parade* reel, issue A-1, featured Ben marching in full Von Stroheim regalia along with the stars Fredric March, Jack Oakie, Mitzi Green, Ginger Rogers, and Eddie Peabody, among others.

Question & Answer Man Column (1932 September 22):
Q: Is Ben Turpin, the cross-eyed comedian, living?
A: He recently appeared in the photoplay *Million Dollar Legs* and is to be featured in a forthcoming Fanchon and Marco stage presentation.
Historian Kalton C. Lahue, in his book *World of Laughter*, tells "Ben seldom got along with his directors. He was always at odds with them and always had his own ideas how a scene should be played. W.C. Fields discovered how to keep him quiet. Ben's greatest asset was his crossed eyes, and he lived in mortal fear of their becoming normal again. He was also deeply religious. Utilizing these two factors, Fields came up with the perfect squelch: Whenever Ben began to vent his spleen on a director, all the director had to say was, 'Ben, if you don't see it my way, I'll go home tonight and pray to St. Joseph to uncross your eyes,' and Turpin became as easy to work with as a contented housecat for as long as three weeks at a stretch."

Stars Fall Hard In Fanlike Ways — Telling On Hollywood by Robert Grandon *(in part):*
Hollywood — Pass along the streets before the Brown Derby…and attend one of the famous first nights…and what a gang of fans you'll find, lined with camera and albums, seeking autographs and snapshots of the stars…No wonder the screenic star's gun shy! In face of which, it's a trifle amusing to find them going in for the same things themselves. Ben Turpin has the finest collection of autographs of any fan, professional or otherwise. He started it back in his old Essanay days and it makes a library. Ben always has a volume handy for emergencies.

Cross-Eyed Children Not For The Screen (1932 November 6)
It is nice to know that the parents of children with crossed eyes are reluctant to capitalize on that affliction. This information developed after Jack Hayes, producer of a series of children's pictures, advertised for a junior Ben Turpin. Only one mother brought her three-year-old child to his studio and she explained she only wanted to earn enough money to pay for an operation to have her boy's eyes corrected. Then Hayes decided a child so affected, unlike Ben Turpin, might be an object of pity and sympathy instead of comedy. But he didn't have to worry about refusals because no other cross-eyed children applied for work.[313]

Ben Turpin Just Itching To Show World A Hamlet (1932 November 11)
"Cock-Eyed" One Laughs at the Wise Guys — Made His "Dough" and Has It — 64 Years Of Age
Ben Turpin, the only man in the world to make a fortune because he was cock-eyed, ogled his way into Toronto today with ideas on this and that.
"This here election," he said, "you heard about that, eh?"
"Sure did."
"You know Roosevelt was elected, eh?"

"Sure did."

"Yes, well he takes office on the fourth of March, doesn't he?"

"Yes."

"Well, I'm telling you that in four months there won't be a bank open in the United States. Not one bank. Laugh that off."

The reporter obediently laughed. "You mean it will be the Fourth of July and that's a holiday anyhow."

"Sure you catch on. Smart guys up here."

"Well, about this fortune for being cock-eyed; did you really make a fortune?"

"I did and I've got it yet — and there are mighty few of the Hollywood crowd who can say that. Well, I hung on to my dough and I'm laughing at some of those other wise guys."

Eyes Insured for $25,000

"And I suppose like the other comedians, cock-eyed or otherwise, you'd like to do heavy serious parts. *Hamlet* or something?"

"Yes, I really would. That's acting, that is. Listen, I'm 64 years old. I've never weighed over 130 in my life. I've been taking falls and getting laughs since 1890. That's 42 years of bumping and clowning around. I think the real actors are those slow-spoken English fellows we're just beginning to get into pictures now. You know, those guys who never jump when the phone rings or never stop what they're saying if somebody happens to knock at the door. They're smooth. Of course that's not for me. I have to get laughed at, on stage or off, because I'm a sort of freak. Well, that's okay by me. I like it. I got my eyes insured for $25,000 but if I ever happened to be built that way I'd go in for heavy dramatic stuff and boy I'd wow 'em. I'd wow 'em because I'd study the parts."

"Well the stage has pretty well gone to the dogs since you started in 1890; how do you account for that?"

"Well, I'll tell you; it's become too doggoned serious and efficient. There's no more ad libbing. A man comes on stage now and gives his act. No more, no less. He can't change a line. If he tries shouting out something new, you know, like Will Rogers or Ed Wynn or some of them, he's jerked and the manager gives him the devil. Probably writes a report about the thing and sends it to the head office. Can you imagine an old-time showman writing a report? Half of 'em couldn't write — but they did the business."

Chaplin the Greatest

"And who, in your opinion, is the greatest of the film funny men?"

"Chaplin. He never had an equal. Probably never will have. He's got something. He outlasted all his imitators. I never had any imitators. They got to have eyes to do my stuff." Turpin rolled those roly-poly eyes of his and the reporter simply had to laugh.

"And I suppose you're quite a gay lad with the girls — all you film star heroes are!"

"Now wait a minute," Turpin put in. "Get this thing right. I am popular with the girls. No kidding. But not in that sex-appeal good-looking-guy-in-the-moonlight sort of way. If I'm Clark Gable or Bill Powell or one of those lover guys and I meet a girl, she's liable to have ideas about me doing my stuff. I mean loving her. Well I'm not. I'm the buffoon, the funny guy. But by golly the girls do like me. My eyes now, they look like the very old Nick, I suppose, but do you think they are friendless or cruel? No boy, they're warm eyes."[314]

Speaking Very Candidly (1932 November 13, in part)

Ben to writer Chester B. Bahn, syndicated Hollywood columnist:

"I'm not through with pictures and I never was. They still know me. And some day when those writers get busy and put in parts that a cross-eyed actor can play I'll prove to the world that Turpin can do a come-back.

"Why, just walk into a movie today when I play a small part. Do they recognize me? And do they howl like they used to? Of course they do! All I need, pally, is a break — and believe me I'm on my way to get it. Pantomime is not dead; neither am I. I'm 63 years old, but I've got just as much pep as ever."

Turpin, Cock-Eyed Comedian, Asserts World Is Cock-Eyed (1932 November 18)

Detroit, Nov. 18 — Ben Turpin believes the world of today is just as cock-eyed as he is. The Hollywood comedian discussed world affairs on a recent visit here.

"What the world needs most, aside from a good five-cent cigar," he said, "is to settle its war debt problems."

In Turpin's opinion, the United States should lend Europe the money to pay its war debts through the Reconstruction Finance Corporation.

"We need the money," he said. "Europe can't pay. We should loan it to them so they could. Then all the vice presidents of banks could go back to work. That would solve the unemployment problem."

America needs an overproduction amendment, according to the comedian. He believes the Democrats are right — that the Eighteenth Amendment will be out of work by next summer. As for balancing the budget, Turpin is convinced the country needs a good football coach.

"Look at Michigan!" he said. "Also look at Northwestern and Purdue! What do they do to balance the budgets? Why, the coach shifts tackles and plays with an unbalanced budget."

The Navy could be turned into a fleet of showboats, thereby merging disarmament with the problem of paying off the soldiers' bonus, Turpin said.[319]

c December 1932: "the latest issue of *Screen Souvenirs* shows an early drammer with Ben Turpin as a gangster of 1909." Surely featuring a rare Essanay clip.

1933: Ben (Intersecting Orbs) Turpin announced over the microphone at the Santa Monica Dance Marathon that he was "cock-eyed as usual." Ben goes on tour shortly for Fanchon and Marco.

1933 February 27: Walter Hiers dies of pneumonia after a short illness at the home of his father-in-law. He was only 40 years old. Turpin was bumped up earlier to replace Hiers in the act when the rotund comic was first stricken with influenza.

1933 May 4: Ben Turpin, comedian with the trademark squint, arrives in San Francisco today to prove that the whole world is cock-eyed. The famous comedian will complete his plans for a brand-new and unique nightclub and restaurant to be opened in San Francisco — unique to the extent that doormen, waiters, cashiers, cooks, and entertainers all will be looking at the world with a squint. Even the customers will be cock-eyed on 3.2 beer.

1933 May 4: Another item in the county news concerns Ben Turpin, who disported himself in Niles the other day by invading a gasoline station and serving as a window wiper and man-of-all-work. By interjecting comedy into his work, he soon had traffic congested at the lower end of First Street, Jack Williamson begs to report. Turpin, by the way, is soon to blossom forth as a nightclub proprietor in San Francisco. For a time, he dallied with the idea of entering the restaurant business in Oakland. Apparently, he has decided that the screen is no longer his for the asking.

Oakland Tribune

Small Town Idol Just An Antique (1933 May 24, a trimmed two reel re-release)

Dusted off from the studio files, *A Small Town Idol* is still a relic despite the monkey-gland treatment attempted through sound effects. It carries a number of laughs and interests one in the manner of an old daguerreotype. The laughs are all at it rather than with it. It is unfair to use the names of Marie Prevost, Ramon Novarro, and Andy Clyde in billing this featurette. They are stuck in and have no place in it. The others play legitimate parts, but it is nothing to be proud of and since this picture was made, all, excepting Turpin, have changed radically.[320]

Ben Turpin's Cafe (1933 May 30)

San Francisco, May 29 — Ben Turpin has quit double-eyeing the camera and by June 15 will have his own cafe opened here. Turpin has taken over a large basement space in the location of former Coffee Dan's and has spent considerable dough to fix up the slot as "Tropical Town."[321]

Ben Turpin's Error Opens New Nite Joint in Frisco With $5 Dinner (1933 June 20)

San Francisco, June 19 — Ben Turpin opened his "Hollywood Jungle" night spot Friday (June 16) with a $5 plate that was much too much for this burg. The comic has a floor show with Earl Sapiro's band, 10 Peggy O'Neill girls, the Alfredo and Maxine dance team, and The Harmonizers, male trio. Talent will be changed weekly. Turpin has a pair of local backers.[322]

Ben Turpin Sued Over Club Opening (1933 June 23)

San Francisco, June 23 — Ben Turpin, former motion picture comedian, was named in a suit for $11,500 in damages on file in superior court today as a result of the opening of his new nightclub here. The suit, filed by Grover C. Reinkens, Oakland candy manufacturer, and Harold Morris, charges Turpin, Louis Rose, blues singer, and Joseph Franks failed to keep an agreement to incorporate the Ben Turpin Inn Company. The plaintiffs asserted Turpin and the others incorporated under the name of the "Ben Turpin Hollywood Jungle Company." They claim they were to receive 29 percent interest under the original agreement and were not mentioned in the new company.[323]

Oakland Man Sues Ben Turpin of Films (1933 June 23)

San Francisco, June 23 — Those famous cross-eyes of Ben Turpin, movie comedian and more recently San Francisco restaurant man, have got him into $11,500 worth of trouble.

He looked at two partners — and did business with two entirely different ones, according to Grover C. Reinkens, Oakland candy manufacturer, and Harold Morris, who have filed the $11,500 damage suit against him.

Turpin Nitery Folds In Quick Order with Wage Troubles Next (1933 July 18)

San Francisco, July 17 — Ben Turpin's Hollywood Jungle cafe took it on the button in short order and went down for the count Sunday night, July 9. On Monday, the employees went before the State Labor Commission and asked for back salaries, including some $800 that was due Earl Sapiro's band for nine days' work.

Charles Eisenberg and a man named Louis Rose were operators of the spot, which had Ben Turpin in as MC on a percentage. The spot started in haphazard fashion a month ago with a $5-plate opening night. Before the evening was over, one or two bucks looked pretty good to the management. Had a big floor show and so many entertainers and waiters the customers were a bit hard to find. Also a jam over musicians' salaries has caused Musicians' Union to lay down an ultimatum that requires all new spots, unless posting a bond, to pay salaries every night until the spot has established itself as reliable pay.[324]

Ben Turpin's Cafe in San Francisco Is Burned (1933 November 27)

San Francisco, Nov. 27 — Fire of unknown origin swept through the closed Hollywood Jungle Cafe on the top floor of a two-story building at 1456 Market Street late yesterday and destroyed furniture and fixtures worth $10,000. Water seeping through the floor destroyed stocks in the Offenbach Electric Co., 1452 Market Street, and Radio Owners' Service Co., 1446 Market Street. Three alarms were turned in to battle the flames, which threatened the Grand Central Hotel adjoining. The cafe is a beer parlor which had been operated by Ben Turpin, film comedian.[325]

On December 18, 1933, Turpin took part in a benefit performance sponsored by a Los Angeles newspaper to raise funds for Christmas relief work. Notables of both stage and screen made personal appearances to aid the benefit, which was held at the Shrine Auditorium, Los Angeles.

Two months later, February 13, 1934, the Lowe's Theater on Salina Street in Syracuse, New York presented "Hollywood Stars In Person On Stage" that night at 8:30 One Performance Only. 20th Century Pictures sponsored a galaxy of stars, including Mary Carlisle, Roscoe Ates, Anna Q. Nilsson, Jack Mulhall, Dorothy Dunbar (Mrs. Max Baer), Ben Turpin, Nancy Welford, Antonio Moreno, Creighton Hale, John Huntley, and the Moulin Rouge Starlets, live on stage in combination with the showing of the Constance Bennett feature *Moulin Rouge,* the troupe known as the *Moulin Rouge Caravan.* Others in the Caravan included Eddie Quillan, Sally Blane, Mr. and Mrs. James and Lucille Gleason, Russell Gleason, Raymond Hatton, Johnnie Mack Brown, Mary Brian, Sally O'Neill, Arlene Judge, and Patsy Ruth Miller.

Leo Carillo, also part of the *Caravan,* told *The Syracuse,* "A trip like this is something that every motion picture actor in Hollywood ought to take at least once a year. We talk, think, dream, eat and sleep movies month after month, and become so immersed in shop-talk that we lose touch with the public that it is our business to please." According to report, only 17 of the largest cities in America would be visited as most of the stars had to return to Hollywood to fulfill film contracts.

1934 February 16: Ben playing the Hanna Theater, Cleveland, Ohio this night, part of the *Moulin Rouge Caravan*, which included Mary Brian, Anna Q. Nilsson, Dorothy Dunbar, Mary Carlisle, Hoot Gibson, Antonio Moreno, James and Lucille Gleason, Russell Gleason, Roscoe Ates, Nancy Welford, Jack Mulhall, Eddie Quillan, Doris Hill, and Creighton Hale. The stars were to also appear live over radio station WHK before hitting the stage that night.

While in Cleveland, Ben dropped by to talk with old friend, writer W. Ward Marsh, who told how Ben wept again in Carter's Rainbow Room for fear someone would list him among the has-beens:

"I can talk for the screen, too," Ben told me in that horse-rasping voice, which must give the jitters to studio microphones. "I've proved I can talk. I'm just as cock-eyed as ever, and I can memorize my lines. I dunno what the 'ell ails 'em…maybe when I get back somethin'll break."

Turpin isn't particularly worried if he ever works again. He declared he had lived a comparatively frugal life.

The last time he was here, back in the early part of the last decade, he was worried about his wife's health. She was taken fatally ill shortly after they left Cleveland. Ben refused to work in studios all during the time she was ill. He would not leave her. He turned down better than $1,000 a week just to be with her. After she died, he said: "Anyway, I've no regrets now. I did all I could. I've saved my money," he told me the other night, "and I've enough to see me through now."[317]

Ben Turpin Invests Film Earnings in Property And Laughs at Movie Producers
by Inez Wallace *(1934 March 18, in part):*

Too much sun makes the desert and, with so many old timers broke and out of work, it is as refreshing as a day in June to meet one who doesn't give a whoop about Hollywood producers. Such a person is the cock-eyed Ben Turpin.

I can't remember the time when Ben wasn't in pictures — it seems as though he started in when Edison invented them and I told him so the other day.

"I wasn't with Edison," he said, looking over my shoulder with one eye and into my face with the other, "but I was with Essanay — which started about the same time. Let's see, it was in 1907 — that's 27 years ago. I started with them as a property man at $20 a week. After two years I asked for $40. Didn't get it but I did get $26. We only made one-reelers then — but I watched the other actors to see how they did and decided I'd go into vaudeville. I did eight shows for the sum of $3 a night.

"Then Chaplin came to the screen in a film called *His New Job* and he gave me a new job. I really owe all my success to Charlie Chaplin and Mack Sennett. The name of the next company was the Vogue Film Co. and they gave me $100 a week. You see, they just asked me what I wanted and I named the figure (never dreaming I'd get it) but they took me on and very soon I got myself a business manager and all the trappings that now befitted my position."

Raised to $3,000 Weekly

"Let me tell you, it paid to have all that extra front because, when Mack Sennett phoned me and asked if I'd come to work for him, I knew I could get even more money. My manager and I talked it over and decided to ask for $200 a week. We did — and again we got it without any argument. It was unbelievable. There seemed to be no end to what these movie men would pay. My salary kept going up and up until I was getting $3,000 a week for ten years!"

"Ben," I said, "if you haven't saved money with that record, you ought to be shot."

"I've saved it," he replied. "I've put it into Hollywood real estate where it can't run away. I own lots more real estate in Hollywood than anybody dreams of," he went on proudly. "It won't matter if I never work another day. I'm independent — but of course, I want to work. I mean, I won't retire. Why should I? But I'll not ask those producers for a job — no sir. I've got some pride. They'll have to send for me if they want me."

"What do you think of the Hollywood producers and their attitude about new talent?"

"I think they're crazy. Can you imagine any intelligent person paying big salaries to the Barrymores, Jack Oakie and others — paying because of their faces — and then covering those same faces up with masks, as they did in *Alice in Wonderland*? I can't. I think it shows a weak mind. They could have hired extras or even property men at $5 a day to walk around with a mask. What good are those famous faces if nobody can see them?"

Cleveland Makes Him Sad

"Is this your first visit to Cleveland, Ben?" I went on.

"No, I've been here before and this town always makes me sad. You see, it was just nineteen years now that I was here in vaudeville and my wife had her first stroke at a Cleveland hotel. I walked through that same hotel today, walked to the very place we used to sit, and it made me feel so badly I wanted to cry. So finally I did, and then I felt better. It seems, looking back, that I was happier then than I am now, though, I didn't have so much money."

"Money doesn't make happiness, Ben," I said.

"Maybe not," he replied doubtfully. "But one sees so much grief from the lack of it in this business, that one soon learns to respect it. Take me, for instance. I married a little over a year ago and do you know what business my wife was in before that marriage?"

"No — what?"

"Don't laugh now. She was an expert accountant."

Wife Is Economic, Too

"Don't tell me you married her to take care of your money. I couldn't bear it."

But he never cracked a smile. "I wouldn't say I married her just for that; but it did occur to me that it would be nice to have my money in such expert hands — and can she handle it? You asked me a minute ago, about other old timers out of work in Hollywood. Well, I don't care for myself, see, because I'm independent, but it does make me feel awfully bad for those who didn't save their money. Probably Tony Moreno and myself are the only two who are really independent. Of course, I'm not talking now about Ruth Roland, who owns more real estate than any other person in Hollywood — that woman's awful rich — but, I mean those others, who played all day and spent their money while they had it. It's very pathetic."

"I'm wondering, Ben," I said thoughtfully, "just how you happened to save your money. I mean, how could you, in Hollywood where it is so easy to spend?"

He smiled then, for the first time during the interview — a wise little smile that seemed somehow quite foreign to him as we know him.

"Maybe I didn't have the same temptations as the others," he said slyly. And I let it go at that. "The old law of compensation," I said to myself as I picked up my purse and gloves. And then, as I walked out through the crowded theater, "I wonder if it's worth it?"[326]

Ben Turpin's Strabismus Cost of Fame by David W. Hazen *(1934 April 21, in part)*

The man who has made so many millions laugh many millions of times is now living quietly in Beverly Hills. He isn't crashing into the neon signs as he did, but still plays now and then to keep the wolf a safe distance from the kitchen door.

"I just worked in a picture, *Hollywood on Parade*, but I'm practically retired," Mr. Turpin explained yesterday after having been greeted by the committee from the Portland, Oregon Chamber of Commerce as he alighted from the Southern Pacific. "I work when they ask me to, but as a rule I live calmly in my home watching the world go by. I've seen a lot of it pass.

"Say, you've got a wonderful city here; do you know it?"[327]

1934 c May: Turpin appears in one of the *Hollywood on Parade* shorts with Rudy Vallee, Ted Healy, Polly Moran, Chic Sale, Jimmy Durante, and other recent additions to the screen, including The Three Stooges, Moe, Larry, and Curly, at the beginning of their successful motion picture careers.

1934 June 4: About Celebrities *(in part):* Ben Turpin will celebrate his 27th anniversary in pictures by emerging from cross-eyed retirement. He'll do serial comedy roles.

Syracuse (anon)

On May 25, Ben signs with Mascot Pictures serial *Law of the Wild*, at $100 per day, work to begin June 5, 1934.

Director William Whitney worked with Turpin during the making of the serial *Law of the Wild* and years later recalled, "Ben Turpin was cross-eyed, and somehow Sennett thought that was funny. He had starred Ben in comedies of his own and as a Keystone Kop.

"Actually, Ben was nearly blind. Ben was a small man and had a lot of experience in front of the camera. Now he was getting old, and I imagine he was put in the cast because (producer Nat) Levine thought he still brought some name value to the people who bought the serials.

"Breezy (Eason) was explaining the scene to Ben and acting out the part as he showed Ben what to do. The scene was set on the outside of a stall in the middle of a long runway of stalls. All the stalls had Dutch doors — you could open and close either the top or bottom door separately. On this particular stall, the top door was open and the bottom one was closed. The hasp on the door had a pin through it that locked it and Rex could be seen standing in the back of the stall. Breezy said, 'You're sneaking up to the stall so no one can see you,' Breezy hugged the wall and inched toward the open door. 'You reach for the pin to unlock the stall door." Breezy reached for the pin, Rex lunged for Breezy, and his teeth snapped together inches from Breezy's face. The big horse's chest slammed into the locked door. It stopped his charge and made a noise like a clap of thunder. Breezy never even flinched. He turned to Turpin and said, 'That's all there is to it.' Ben hadn't moved. He said to Breezy, 'Do you want me to pull the pin?' Breezy smiled at him and put a hand on his shoulder. 'No,' he said, 'I'll let the double pull the pin!'

"Ben had been in the business a long time, and he was a real trouper. The camera rolled, Ben slid along the wall, reached at arm's length toward the pin and Rex lunged at him with his teeth bared. Rex hit the stall door again, only this time the hasp flew off and the door crashed open. Ben turned and ran. With his poor eyesight, he didn't see the reflector that was set up at a low angle. He ran right up to the reflector and flew into the air over the top. His legs were still running when he hit the ground on his belly. It was a scene straight out of a Keystone Kop slapstick comedy, but no one laughed.

"If Ben had waited a second longer he would have seen Swede step into the stall opening and drive Rex back into the stall with the whip. Breezy ran to Ben and picked him up. Ben was shaken but not hurt. Ben said, 'Breezy, if you need another take on that, call the double!' Then he laughed, and Breezy laughed, and then the whole crew laughed. I learned something from that scene that helped me when I later became a director: never put an actor at risk if you can use a stuntman."[328]

Old Comedians No Longer In Demand (1934 July 15)

Hollywood soon forgets. The film city has difficulty in recalling the comedy stars of yesteryear. Harry Langdon, Buster Keaton, Ben Turpin, Ford Sterling, and Kate Price are seldom heard of today. Douglas MacLean, now a producer at Paramount, is about the only one of the old crowd who turned to more lucrative fields when his acting days were over.

On the set of George Bancroft's *Elmer and Elsie* at the Paramount studios are 12 persons whose names meant something in comedies a decade ago. Gil Pratt, who recently got his chance at directing features and who is the director of this film, was a leading director at the Sennett plant. With him as gag constructionist is Bobby Vernon, a comedy star not long ago. The others who were somebodies in the old Sennett and Christie comedies include: Jack Duffy, Vera Steadman, Jimmie Harrison, Nick Cogley, Bobby Dunn, Eddie Baker, Bess Nagel, Ford West, Gus Leonard, and Neal Burns.

"Casting offices don't have much use for funny actors anymore," sighed one old timer. "We were lucky to land a job in this picture. Usually all we get from them now is a polite smile that means no."[329]

1934 December 24, *The Evening Independent:*
Ben Turpin, to be featured in Educational Pictures' new *Frolics of Youth* comedy, titled *The Little Big Top*, comes back to the screen following his 65th birthday. The veteran comic is financially independent and is working now principally for the love of it. Appearing with Turpin in *The Little Big Top* are Junior Coghlan and the entire Hanneford family, the famous circus troupe.

1935 March 4, Amarillo, Texas (AP) — The much-maligned mother-in-law — Gene Howe calls her a "mother who has made good" — will be honored tomorrow in festivities fit for a conquering hero. About 4,000 mothers-in-law are expected here for the second annual Mother-In-Law Day sponsored by Howe, editor of the *Amarillo Globe and News.* Governor James V. Allred will make two addresses. Ben Turpin, film comedian whose likeness appears at the head of Howe's column, "The Tactless Texan," will be master of ceremonies (side note: On Howe's desk sat a particularly cross-eyed statuette of Ben Turpin). There will be a 5-mile parade with 17 bands, two National Guard units, and cowboys and cowgirls.

1935 March 5, Amarillo, Texas: Ben Turpin was in Amarillo today to lead a parade of three thousand mothers-in-law from eighteen states whom were accorded honors enough to compensate for years of serving as the butt of a nation's jokes. Dressed in cowboy regalia, Turpin acted as master of ceremonies and parade marshal: "There is no more misrepresented human being than the mother-in-law. She has been the butt of jokes through the centuries, due mostly to human ignorance and perversity of sons-in-law. Slowly and surely, however, the human family improves. With this improvement and a more intelligent appreciation, we have come to see the value of mothers-in-law." Fox Movietone News was there to capture the festivities.

1935 April 7: from the syndicated newspaper column of Walter Winchell: "Ben Turpin, the one-time movie comedian, is completing his life yarn to be christened; *My Cock-Eyed Past.* Willis Gordon Brown reported it for him. Ben wishes you'd give it a mention, he will appreciate it. He's 66, you know." *Unfortunately, Turpin never found a publisher or perhaps never finished his autobiography. Ben's book would have made some interesting reading and could have been a great source in the compilation of my biography. When the unpublished manuscript turned up at auction several years ago, the reserve price was never met. The book went back to its private owner. Here's hoping Ben's autobiography will resurface and finally see publication.*

Pie Throwing To Be Revived — Old Slapstick Comedies Will Be Tried Again on Screen
by Robbin Coons *(1935)*

Mack Sennett's departure from the Hollywood scene, where once he was king of comedy, was preceded by several years, during which he tried making what he called "sophisticated" funny pictures instead of his old reliable slapstick. The sophistication, to whatever degree it was achieved, did not keep Sennett on his throne. And now there is a producer who is deliberately going back, as an experiment, to the very things that Mack Sennett tossed overboard for the sake of the talkie.

Old-Timers To Play

Ralph Staub, who is quite a figure in the field of "shorts," used to work for Sennett. He also had a father in the movie exhibiting business in the early days of Sennett glory, and he remembered what raucous response always greeted the throwing of a pie, a chase by the Keystone Kops, or the breaking of a heavy vase over a comedian's pate. One of his successes in "shorts" was the series of *Hollywood Memories* and the amount of fan mail he received from these minute revivals showing old favorite stars set Staub to wondering…"We're going to make one picture on the old Keystone Kop order," says Staub, "just to see how it goes. We're going to get as many of the old-timers as possible to work in it. We're going to have pies, chases, and fast action. It may be a hit — if it is we'll make a series — and it may be a terrific flop. A lot of exhibitors have shown interest in the idea."

Turpin In Cast

Chester Conklin, Ford Sterling, and Ben Turpin already have been lined up (as of May 1st) as actors for *Good Old Days*. And some who were not in Sennett comedies, but were old-timers in fun films, are being sought for or seeking places in the comedy. Al St. John — remember his bicycle? — Snub Pollard, Victor Potel, Heine Conklin, Billy Franey, Eddie Gribbon, and several others will probably be seen. Staub wanted Mack Swain, but Swain has been ill *(soon dying on August 25, 1935)*. Bobby Vernon, now a writer at Paramount but once a comedian, and Mervyn LeRoy, now a director, once a "gag-man," have said they wanted to help.

Charlie Murray, who is kept busier than some of the old-timers, might work a day or two "for old times' sake," says Staub.

"It's going to be a real old-time comedy — so fast we'll have to shoot most of it 'wild,' that is silently, and dub in the sound later," according to Staub. "We have on the lot now Hans Koenenkamp, who used to shoot Larry Semon's pictures, and he's going to do it for us. And just as they used to do, we're not having a script, but merely an outline. On the set one thing always led to another, and that's how we'll work."

1935 May 19. Louella Parsons: Not in days has anything made me as happy as the word that Marie Prevost will play the lead in a Warner Brothers short, *Keystone Hotel*, with a cast of the old Keystone actors. Director Ralph Staub has done a grand job in lining up Ben Turpin, Chester Conklin, Ford Sterling, Hank Mann, and Eddie Gribbon, all former Keystone comics, for this short.

Turpin Returns To Films (1935 May 24)
Finds Pies Improved Old-Time Actors Making Reunion Comedy by George Shaffer
Hollywood, CA, May 23 — (Special) — "They have improved the pies since the early days." It is Ben Turpin talking. Ben, now 66, is one of a group of old-time Keystone comedy players who have been gathered for an old home week movie comedy, full of pie throwing, breakaway chairs, bathing beauties, heavies with ripped trousers, and such stock-in-trade gags and appurtenances of the old Sennett, Christie, Keystone, Kalem, and Essanay days.

Ben was reminiscing between scenes of *Keystone Hotel*, in which he, Chester Conklin, Hank Mann, Ford Sterling, Neal Burns, Heinie Conklin, Marie Prevost, Alice Lake, Vivian Oakland, and Juanita Hansen are appearing at Warner studio. "Now take the pies in the old days," said Ben, wiping a bit of blackberry jam from his ear, "in those days we thought white of egg and a bit of wet flour was good enough to get hit in the face with. But this pie we are throwing now is really high-class pie. It breaks faster and smears better. You can get a grip on it for handling and I'm telling you that last night it took me three hours to get genuine strawberry stain off my bald spot."

Keystone Hotel is a modernized version of the old movie slapstick. They have the cops, the patrol wagon, the buxom lady who chases her hubby down the hotel corridor, the girl who kneels to tie her shoe while her eyes rove a little, and you almost have the feeling that if you peer very sharply into the shadowy corners of the sound stage, you will see the wraiths of John Bunny, Fatty Arbuckle, Mabel Normand, Max Linder, Larry Semon, and Mary Thurman hovering over the rack of pies. Ralph Staub is directing.[330]

Back Come The Keystone Cops — and Up Goes The Pie Market by Jeanette Meehan
(1935 July 28, in part)

"These pies are from a different family tree than the ones I used to know," remarked Ben Turpin, "and I was personally acquainted with them all. In the good old days we thought white of egg and a lump of damp flour was the 'top.' But this is what I call high-class pie. It breaks more easily, smears more smoothly, and last night it took me an hour to get a genuine blackberry stain off my bald spot. I think they're wonderful."[331]

Hollywood In Review by George Shaffer *(1935 August 2, in part)*

Aug. 1 — One of the most hilarious previews seen in months was *Keystone Hotel*, made with eight of the old-time Sennett and Keystone comedy top-notchers featured. A short reeler, it was full of custard pies, awkward cops, beautiful girls in lingerie, and wives finding husbands in hotel corridors. To trim it up, Warners inserted some of the old police patrol chases made in the silents nearly two decades ago.

The way a Hollywood Boulevard audience, filled with present-day talkie notables, reacted, guffawing so loudly one couldn't hear the dialogue and rocking the theater with mirth, proved something, although it is hard to tell what; possibly that custard pies still are funny or else that the old, broad slapstick struck a reminiscent chord for an audience that was juvenile when these last pies were thrown.[332]

1935 August 20: When he was in New York, *The Schenectady Gazette* asked Ben: "Are the good old slapstick days over?"

Turpin replied, "No, sir. The public will accept them with relish as there are too many now living who like to recall those pictures made in the early days.

"The roundup of the veteran Keystone Cops included Ford Sterling, Chester Conklin, Hank Mann, myself and others, recently, and the filming of *Keystone Hotel* will bring memories to the thousands of theater fans when they see the comic antics of the players." The first slapstick comedian in motion pictures tells the world that the work is not all a bed of roses. However, the actor, born 66 years ago in New Orleans, still can go through his comedy falls like he did 40 years ago. The fall which draws the most laughs is the one where he literally kicks one of his feet from beneath himself, falls forward, makes a somersault without the use of his hands, and then lies stiffly on his back while his feet perk convulsively like those of an animal during the last throes of death. Because of his lifetime of falls, practically every tooth in his mouth had been knocked out, his body is covered with scars, and many of his bones have been broken. "Anything for a laugh," is Turpin's motto.

1935 *(anon):* Whether those brothers Warner know it or not, *Keystone Hotel* justifies the faith of cross-eyed Ben Turpin. When Ben was in Syracuse more than a year ago with the *Moulin Rouge Caravan,* he told me, "You wait, slapstick's coming back someday." Others in the party smiled, but the last laugh bids fair to be Turpin's after all. As a footnote, this:

Warners, sensing the possibilities in "names" of the silent era, postpone further to produce a series of short subjects in which the old favorites will again attain stellar dignity. For the first of these pictures, Helene Chadwick and Charles Ray are under consideration. Both were popular idols more than a decade ago.

In his *The Great Movie Shorts,* author Leonard Maltin later interviewed Ralph Staub and asked him about *Keystone Hotel:* "The picture, including all the chases, was made in seven days. I personally knew Ford Sterling, Ben Turpin, Chester Conklin and others appearing in the film. I sold them on starting a new slapstick series. Jack Warner would only permit me to contract with the players for one picture. After the preview at Warner's Hollywood theater, Warner said 'sign them up for a series,' but this was not possible. Their agents were there at the preview and when I approached them, they wanted triple the salary they received in *Keystone Hotel.* Jack Warner wouldn't go for the hike in salary (I couldn't blame him)."[333]

1935 October 10: A screen version of the old-time melodrama *The Drunkard* will be routed through the Midwest and possibly the East this fall with a number of old-time film stars tagging along for personal appearances. Among the stars will be Leo White, Ben Turpin, Mildred Harris Chaplin, Rex Lease, Clara Kimball Young, and Franklyn Farnum. They're all in the picture, too.[334] The cast debuted their show at the Roxy in Salt Lake City that night.

Ben Turpin Back — Of the Butcher Counter (1935 November 29)
Hollywood, Nov. 29 (AP) — Ben Turpin, cross-eyed victim of custard pies in the Keystone comedy days, finds time heavy on his hands since his screen retirement. Today, that was his explanation for his Thanksgiving appearance behind a meat market counter.

"When my friend, Joe, who runs the place, asked me to come down and help him sell, I took him up on it," said Turpin.[335]

Ben Turpin Sues on Rent (1936 February 12)
Ben Turpin yesterday filed suit in municipal court for recovery of two months' rent asserted owed by tenants of property owned by comic. He is asking for $110.33.

Ben Turpin Accepts Invitation to Niles (1936 March 19)
Niles — Ben Turpin plans to come to Niles on May 2 and 3 as guest of honor during the annual Wild Flower Show. At the invitation of Sam Kerns, president of the Niles Junior Chamber of Commerce, which is sponsoring the event, Mr. Turpin wrote the following letter:

"Dear Mr. Kerns:
I greatly appreciate your kind invitation to be your guest of honor at your first annual flower show. I assure you it will be a great pleasure for me to appear and meet all my good old friends in Niles. I have a very warm spot in my heart for that community and sincerely hope to be able to come. However, there may be just one possible occasion to prevent my being present: I may happen to be tied up working on a picture. In that case, I should notify you in plenty of time. Thanking you kindly, I remain, Ben Turpin, Ex-Mayor of Niles."[337]

Favorites Featured (1936 March 29)

More former stars are being used in *Preview Murder Mystery* than in any picture of recent years. They include Chester Conklin, Hank Mann, Ben Turpin, Conway Tearle, Reginald Denny, Jack Mulhall, Rod LaRocque, George Barbier, Ian Keith, and Bryant Washburn. *In this author's recent screening of this film, Conklin and Mann appear; Turpin does not.*

Turpin Thinks He Would Be Colossal As Gateman (1936 December 22)

Hollywood, Dec 21 (AP) — Ben Turpin winked one of his zigzag eyes today and offered to tend the gate at any of the movie studios.

"I'd be terrific as a gatekeeper," said the former $3000-a-week slapstick comedian. "Imagine it! The only guy in the business who could see 'em going and coming. No, I'm not broke," he hurriedly explained. "I'm merely tired of having nothing to do and they don't call me to act, anymore."

The little cross-eyed hurler of custard pies was 67 last September, but he counts the hours lost since he last wore grease paint. Baldish, spry, he strolls about Beverly Hills, collecting rent from a dozen pieces of real estate which he bought with his film earnings. He's crazy about Mickey Mouse, the little cartoon creature, and Laurel and Hardy. He occasionally wears dark glasses to hide his off-center optics from the curious. In his own two-story home, he spurns the luxury of a butler, answering the doorbell himself. "I'm better fixed than most stars who were at the top when I was, 12 years ago," Turpin said. "But we're all alike in our feelings when the casting director doesn't ring.

"If they only tried, it seems to me, the studios could salvage a lot of favorites from the scrap pile — big names that drew big money at the box office only yesterday. They'd be welcomed back by the public.

"In my case, I've got a face that's just as funny looking as the day it got permanently cock-eyed. I was impersonating *Happy Hooligan* in vaudeville, at $20 a week, when it happened.

"It's the same face that got a laugh when I spilled potatoes down Marie Prevost's back in *A Small Town Idol*, a Sennett five-reeler, years ago.

"Since the talkies came in, I've seen plenty that needed laughs. Even the serious drama could have a humorous break once in a while. And that's just the spot for a cross-eyed waiter, or a cross-eyed professor to walk into view.

"Well, I haven't worked much in the last twelve years, but I'll do all right, even if producers keep forgetting me.

"I've kept my scrapbooks and my cancelled checks. I'll be colossal as a studio gateman."[338]

Turpin Announced As Ringmaster Of Antlers' Circus (1937 April 16)

Ben Turpin, cross-eyed film comedian, will be ringmaster of the 1937 Antlers' circus, DeWitt Mytinger, exalted antler-elect, said last night.

The circus will be presented in the Elks clubhouse next Thursday, Friday, and Saturday to raise funds to send the Antlers' music organizations to the Elks' grand lodge convention in Denver, July 11. The circus acts will be comprised of Jack Storey & Co., bicycle riders; Billy Joy, acrobat; Steve Clements, knife thrower; Jack Razier and his trained dogs; Sonny and the Wonder Horse; Reri and His Hawaiian Troupe; the Flying Kitchens, trapeze artists; Jack Thomas, escape artist; and the Rhythm Rogues, comedians.[339]

Turpin Forgotten By Studio Guard (1938 February 2)

Hollywood, Feb 2 — AP — Fame is fleeting — as Ben Turpin, the once-famous cross-eyed comic, can tell you. Turpin, who was at the height of his popularity 15 years ago, tried to get past the gateman at Universal studios, where he once starred, to visit Director Leo McCarey. The watchman would not admit Turpin, so McCarey's secretary sent out a pass.[340] Leo's name may have been erroneous in this article, intended for brother Raymond McCarey, who was directing for Universal at this time. It is this author's assumption that Ray may have considered Turpin for a part in the film, *Goodbye Broadway*.

Cock-Eyed Comic, Ben Turpin, Here (1938 May 6, in part)
Film Funster Stops Briefly On Way To Spokane by David W. Hazen

Ben Turpin was asked the big difference between movies now and when he was a screen star. He thought about it a minute, then began to talk…

"Today everything is set before they start taking the picture," he explained. "In my days, Sennett would go to the writers, and say:

"'Write a story around Turpin. Make Turpin a hero. He's in love with a girl. There's a pearl necklace in the story, too.'

"That's all the orders Sennett would give them. Then the writers would get together and write up something. Mack would then go to the head carpenter and tell him to put up a big cafe set, with four or five hallways for chasing, and a couple of bedrooms.

"Then we actors would get around and talk gags over. Mr. Sennett would come in and help us. We would do this four or five days, and then we would all go to work and make a picture in three weeks."

One of Mr. Turpin's earliest pictures was *Breaking Into Society*, which he made for the Essanay Film company in 1909. "Speaking of breaks recalls wrecks," said the non-twinkling star, "I've been in several bank wrecks. But I still own plenty of houses down in Beverly Hills and Los Angeles, and they are all rented, too."

Ben confessed that his favorite lady star today is Joan Crawford and that Robert Taylor is the male hero he likes to see best on the screen.

The Oregonian

Ben Turpin Tops Orpheum Billing (1938 May 6)

Ben Turpin, the cock-eyed comedian of silent picture days, may be seen in person at the Orpheum, where the road show *Fads and Fancies of 1938* opened an engagement today. Also included: Ted Claire, America's Number One Gloom Chaser; Ray Parker and Porthole, The Truly Human Dummy; Miss Billy Joy, Formerly with Mickey McGuire Comedies; Miss Betty Castle, dancing star of *Fifty Million Frenchmen;* Jack Raye, The Asbestos Boy. Comedy, singing, dancing, ventriloquism, and fire-eating are found in the various acts.[342]

Ben Turpin Star of Palomar Bill (1938 May 31)

Ben has the same old expression he always had and still capitalizes the fact that his eyes don't track; still wears funny clothes, a trick mustache and a little hat. This time, he is doing a comedy monologue with the ample assistance of Jerry Ross and for an encore, he tells about being in pictures since 1908, saying what is true, that in these thirty years he had made a lot of persons happy and made a lot of them laugh. It is nice to see Ben again.[344]

Turpin Applauded on Palomar's Bill by J.R.R. *(1938 May 31)*

Nearly three decades ago, when movies cost a nickel and the stage still reigned supreme, a droll little man with a brown derby and eyes that multiplied everything they saw by two began to entertain theater fans with his sly humor and what was then perhaps the favorite sort of comedy, slapstick. Now that little man is 68 years old. He's Ben Turpin, still being encored before the footlights, still wearing his mustache and brown derby, still cross-eyed. Yesterday, he came to the Palomar Theatre, where he is headlining the new vaudeville show this week and the capacity holiday audiences proved to him that genuine old troupers will always be received with warm affection. His wisecracks and banter are presented much the same quiet way they used to be, but it is the romantic glow that surrounds an old favorite comeback that makes his appearance at The Palomar successful — it is.[345]

1939 April 30 *(in part):* Six stores fronting on San Fernando Blvd. and Tujunga Ave., Burbank, have been purchased by Ben Turpin, comedy star of silent films.[343]

Historical Review of Hollywood To Be Made by Louella O. Parsons *(1939 June 7)*

Ben Turpin and Chester Conklin will do one of their "Keystone" specialties with Mal St. Clair directing under Mack Sennett's supervision. Ben will do one of his old-time back flops and that certainly reminds me of the days when Ben did bits on the Essanay lot and acted as sort of general messenger boy when he wasn't working. Guess I'd better stop or you'll soon find out how old I am.

Harrison Carroll column (1939 July 14)

Seventy-year-old Ben Turpin is burned up about a sob story depicting him as broke. Truth is, the cross-eyed comedian doesn't need the salary Zanuck is paying him for *Hollywood Cavalcade.* Ben Turpin saved his money. Only recently, he bought two business buildings in Burbank and paid for them with cash — $60,000.

Turpin Signed (1939 July 24)

Ben Turpin, the grand old-time comedy star of the screen's silent era, has been signed by Warner Brothers for a small role in *Kid Nightingale.* He plays an orchestra leader with a yen for the clarinet and I'm laughing already. The picture, an original screenplay, is now in production with a cast headed by John Payne, Jane Wyman, and Walter Catlett. *This author's recent screening failed to notice Turpin in the film. The part of the orchestra leader was played by comedian Jerry Mandy.*

1939 September 14: Talk about odd hobbies! Ben Turpin's is to raise and plant gourds. The cross-eyed star of Sennett days just presented one to director Irving Cummings as a souvenir of their association in *Hollywood Cavalcade.* [346]

The World Needs Laughs by Ben Turpin *(1939 October 22)*

The other day, I was sitting at home brooding about (not working) and wondering why some producer didn't step out and make another picture with rip-roaring slapstick filled with belly laughs. For the first time in several years, my brooding was interrupted by a telephone ring. Darryl F. Zanuck, Twentieth Century-Fox production chief, was on the line to ask me if I would play a role in *Hollywood Cavalcade*.

Zanuck explained that the film would be a dramatized history of Hollywood's silent screen days from 1913 'til the advent of talkies in 1927. The first two reels of the production would deal with the old Mack Sennett Keystone Comedy days. Never was I so happy to get back to work. When I was making $3,000 a week, I saved my money until today I have all I need, but I have discovered that an idle man is the most miserable creature on earth. I was glad to get a chance to hit myself over the head again with a hammer.

There are many topnotch slapstick comics in Hollywood who are ready and anxious to make the world laugh if just given the chance. Hank Mann, Chester Conklin, Jimmy Finlayson, Snub Pollard, Jack Cooper, Heinie Conklin, and many, many others are on deck.

There is Charlie Chaplin, the finest of them all, making only an occasional film. He's been planning another picture, but he doesn't make enough movies to even touch the world demand for this type of entertainment.

The only comics comparatively active in slapstick are Laurel and Hardy and they're funny.

There is nothing like comedy to teach fundamentals of acting. Careful preparation, rehearsals, and timing, three of the cornerstones of all thespian efforts, are drilled into you day after day in comedy.

I had the advantage of starting early. In my boyhood in New Orleans, where I was born in 1869, a mere 70 years ago (I say "mere" because I can still do a backflip, leap over a piano, and cross my eyes with the best of them), I gained a reputation as a sidewalk comedian.

Sennett was given to tricks. Let me tell you about this one, which I will never forget. We were making *A Small Town Idol* with Phyllis Haver and others. Sennett wanted a startled, funny expression from me. When I looked in one direction and was busy throwing things, Sennett got a lion he had secreted in the next room and put him on a bench beside me. When I turned around, I saw that lion for the first time in my life. My look was startled all right; I was never so scared in my life. Sennett roared with laughter. He said it was one of the funniest sights he ever saw in his life.

For the first time, I got my father's point of view on my lassoing customers with taffy candy. I didn't think there was anything funny about that lion. But comedy depends so much on point of view. And I have tried to give you mine.

I think the world has been missing a lot of needed laughs.

— (signed) Ben Turpin.[348]

"COMEBACK"

1939 December 5: Oldsters whose memories go back to the salad days of the silents may be pleased to hear that Ben Turpin, the cockeyed comedian of some years ago, is making a comeback.

Turpin was recalled from retirement for a silent scene in *Hollywood Cavalcade*. Now Laurel and Hardy have given him a speaking role in their Roach comedy feature *Two's Company* and Mr. Charlie Chaplin has hired him for a part in his *The Great Dictator*.

In *Two's Company*, Turpin will be the plumber who is responsible for the erratic plumbing in the Laurel and Hardy apartment; in *The Great Dictator* he will be the executioner who purges the wrong spies. Retired since 1925 and 70 years of age, Turpin was sought out by reporters the other day for his opinion on new production methods.

Confessing himself nervous at his debut, he said, "I heard there were a lot of changes in pictures, but I had no idea it was anything like this. We never used to have so many lights, and when we made a picture in the old days, all we had for a story was a general idea of a stolen neckless or a kidnapped heroine. We used to make 90 scenes a day and somehow all the water scenes were shot in winter. And no stand-ins or doubles!"[347]

Turpin Shines Again (1939 December 7)

Ben Turpin, veteran screen comic, will have a top part in the Stan Laurel and Oliver Hardy picture for Hal E. Roach, *Two's Company* (released as *Saps at Sea*). Ben was last seen in the full-length film *Hollywood Cavalcade*.

Turpin in Sea Farce (1940 March 4)

Ben Turpin, cross-eyed comedian of the silent days, heads the supporting cast in the Hal Roach comedy, *Saps at Sea*.[349]

Old Mack Sennett Police Team Will Tour The Country (1940 March 29)

(AP) The Keystone Kops, hot on the comeback trail, went through a final rehearsal with the same enthusiasm as of old. But they confessed to feelings of anxiety and hope over the reception to their forthcoming tour, matters of no concern in the carefree days of one-reelers.[350] Ben was listed among the recruits along with Chester Conklin, Al St. John, Hank Mann, and Snub Pollard, first stop, Portland, Oregon, March 31.

On or about June 21, 1940, Ben suffered a stroke paralyzing the right side of his body. After a few days in the Cedars of Lebanon hospital, his physician, Dr. Rudolph Marx, allowed him to return to his home at 602 N. Cannon Drive, Beverly Hills. A week later, early Sunday June 30, Ben was apparently feeling fine, but later that day was rushed to Santa Monica Hospital complaining of chest pains. On the early morning of July 1 at 1:50 am, Ben died of a massive heart attack. Dr. Marx, on Turpin's death certificate, listed Ben's fatal heart attack as being due, in part, to ten years of arteriosclerosis, two years of coronary sclerosis, and several years of asthma. Turpin would have been 71 years old on September 19.

Ben Turpin Of Films Is Dead (1940 July 1)

Hollywood, July 1 — (UP) — Ben Turpin, famous cross-eyed comedian of the silent films, died today of heart disease. The comedian, who won his greatest fame in the Mack Sennett comedies, had been in retirement for many years, although a year ago, he played a brief role in a film based on the early days of the picture industry.

Turpin had been slightly ill for about a week, but his condition was not believed serious. During the night, he suffered a severe heart attack and died almost immediately.

Death Ends Long Career of Ben Turpin, Star Comedian (1940 July 2)

Hollywood — (AP) — *(in part)* Ben appeared in good health last year when he was in Hollywood Cavalcade, but his physician said yesterday he had been suffering from asthma for several years. He suffered a stroke last Sunday afternoon and died early yesterday.[351]

Clown, Memories of Days When Turpin Was in Flower (1940 July 2)

The passing of Ben Turpin reminds us that we are growing older. There are people now grown to whom his name will mean nothing but a vague and somehow disappointing little old man who popped up briefly in a picture called *Hollywood Cavalcade*.

But in the teens and twenties, he was a great American institution. Maybe there was a little cruelty in our convulsed laughter as we looked at his goofy, sad eyes while the custard pies rained upon him or as his advances to the Mack Sennett bathing girls met with the inevitable slap. The natural human cruelty which finds pleasure in the spectacle of incompetence and defeat.

But there was also some dim sympathy — perhaps some dim perception that in this strutting, ugly little man whose schemes for self-assertion always came to grief, all of us were ultimately pictured to some extent. As well as Charlie Chaplin, he somehow summed up the case of the pathetic, ill-favored underdog in the world.

And now he is dead. And, horrid thought, the bathing girls with whom he played are themselves getting on to forty, fat, matronly, their charms almost as faded as those of Villon's old woman of the helmet. And Adolf Hitler is in the world and there is not much left of the old hearty laughter which even in the World War the dead little man could somehow still command.[352]

Ben Turpin (1940 July 2)

The fellow who wrote the "better mousetrap" formula for success overlooked the "108" and crossed eyes. But Ben Turpin didn't. He used them to extract laughs from movie patrons over a period of more than three decades.

The "108" is a somersault from a standing-still start. But Turpin's "108" followed by a close-up of his crossed eyes — that was Ben Turpin's successful technique.

Fathers who were convulsed at Ben Turpin's antics in Mack Sennett's Keystone comedies of World War days took their sons to see him last year in *Hollywood Cavalcade*. In the earlier days, the comedians were the butts of real custard pies and two-by-fours. But Turpin's specialties, the "108" and the crossed eyes, weren't altered by what Hollywood calls progress. His comedy underwent no change.

The average movie comedian of today recites the lines written for him by the studio's punsters. If he can ad lib a little, so much the better. But emphasis is no longer placed on grotesque costumes and what the producers call "slapstick." And yet Ben Turpin's career, which came to an untimely end Monday, attests to the fact that a great many movie fans still like that kind of fare.[353]

Cross-Eyed Entertainer of Custard-Pie Days Given Last Tribute (1940 July 3)
A little cross-eyed man was consigned to his Maker today.

Beverly Hills, CA, July 3 — And veterans of the custard pie days of silent pictures gathered in the Church of the Good Shepard in Beverly Hills to pay tribute to one of the greatest of them all — Ben Turpin, who turned an affliction into a fortune. Fans and friends who had laughed at and loved the comedian who turned an affliction into rollicking entertainment and a fortune in the days when the movies were young came to say good-bye.

Masses of floral tributes banked the casket in the dimly lit, fragrant precincts of the Catholic church where requiem high mass was said.

Big Wreath from Chaplin

A seven-foot-tall wreath of red roses, sweet peas, and Easter lilies was from Charlie Chaplin, who brought Turpin to California a quarter of a century ago. The people in the church remembered the Ben Turpin whose cock-eyed comedy made him a star in the era of Keystone Kops, Mack Sennett Bathing Beauties, and slapstick fun. He had been in retirement for ten years, returning only occasionally to play "himself" as he was in his heyday. He died Monday of a heart ailment at the Santa Monica Hospital. He was nearly 71.

In a brief sermon, Father J. P. Concannon praised the actor as a "fine member of his church, strong in his faith."

The men who bore the casket were the comedian's associates on the Sennett lot years ago — Charlie Murray, Andy Clyde, Jimmy Finlayson, Billy Bevan, Del Lord, and John Waldron.

Honorary Pallbearers

Among the honorary pallbearers were Sennett, Chaplin, Otto Kirscher, Theodore Van de Kamp, Lawrence Frank, H. A. Dunn, Carl Blank, Charles Scruble, George Campbell, M.D. Sales, Fred L. Cook, O. R. Maddux, Sid Grauman, and Paul Guerin.

Familiar names at the service included Dot Farley, often Turpin's leading lady; Joe Murphy, the Andy Gump of old-time comedies; Louise Carver and Ruth Renick, old-time stars; Raymond Griffith, the comedy producer; Verne Day, who was manager of the Essanay studio in Chicago, where Turpin made early films; Billy Franey, Buster Keaton, Mr. and Mrs. Victor Potel, Vernon Dent, Hank Mann, Snub Pollard, Al St. John, Tiny Ward, "Dad" Quillan and his son, Eddie. His widow, Mrs. Babette Turpin, on the verge of a collapse, attended the funeral with Mr. and Mrs. Theodore Van de Kamp and other friends. At the request of the widow, interment was private.

On July 3, Ben was interred in his family crypt at the Great Mausoleum, Begonia Corridor of Forest Lawn Memorial Park in Glendale, returning to his dear wife Carrie, who died fifteen years earlier.

Hollywood by Louella Parsons (syndicated column, 1940 July 3)

What a host of memories the passing of Ben Turpin brings to this writer. I knew Ben long before he became a Mack Sennett comic. He did odd jobs on the old Essanay lot in Chicago. One day, a comedy director decided Ben was so funny, he put him in a picture. Ben stole the show and from then on, his fame mounted. His crossed eyes were one of his great assets and just to look at him made people laugh. I wish we had comedies today as good as those Mack Sennett made with Ben and the other Keystoners. Ben always used to reminisce about those old days with me and about the time he delivered some flowers at my house from an actor whom he called an unknown admirer.

Ben Turpin (1940 July 3)

And now Ben Turpin is gone, he who made an asset of what most people regard as an affliction. With a start, we read that he was 71 years old, although kindly biographers had always listed him as some six years younger. But it is hard to think of him as in his sixties, even, for it seems only yesterday that audiences were howling with delight at his antics.

Would today's moviegoers enjoy him as much as those earlier audiences? We will never know. We only know that we laughed at him and with him, that he helped brighten the days that are gone. He was in the grand old tradition of comics, the zanies who have lightened the human load since crowds first gathered in the marketplace to be entertained by visiting monte-banks.[354]

1940 July 3: Ben Turpin, whose crossed eyes were insured for $100,000 against becoming uncrossed, did not belong to any classical tradition of actors. In the films, he made his own tradition. So long as any memory of the old silent pictures remains, his name will be good for a smile. That is, at least, a sort of immortality — part payment for having made millions laugh.[355]

Turpin's Death Ends an Era by John DeMeyer, Whirligig staffwriter *(1940 July 4)*

Well, old Ben Turpin has passed along. And we've lost an old friend. Some of the youngsters today probably don't know who he was and some of us have almost forgotten. Ben wasn't what you could call a great comedian. Ben was more than that. Ben was an age all by himself. Ben was and that would go for the youngsters if they knew what it meant. Ben stood for the time when it was easy to laugh, the time when crossed eyes and custard pies were all we needed to make us laugh. Some folks call those the horse and buggy days. But we know they weren't. They were the days when it didn't take so much to make us laugh today because we knew we could always laugh tomorrow. Today, it takes a seven thousand dollar a week comedian to make us laugh because we're not so sure we can laugh tomorrow.[356]

Ben Turpin Laughed Back At Life *(1940 July 6)*

Relatively little attention was paid last week to the announcement that Ben Turpin had died. To the great company of moviegoers who belong of the era after his retirement, it was just a routine announcement.

Yet here was no mere gathering in of mortal by time, striding by. Here was the passing of a man who was great because of his humility. He capitalized on a handicap. He made people laugh and forget their troubles. He pioneered in a field of entertainment that numbered among its exponents the Keystone Cops, the slapstick bathing beauties, and the great Charlie Chaplin.

Ben Turpin did not feel sorry for himself because of the prank which fate had played with his countenance. He made his living with it. He out-laughed life and turned back a cruel jest with better ones. Eyes of millions that once sparkled with enjoyment of his funmaking were downcast at the news that his laughing days are over.[357]

The Sound Track: Ben Turpin, Cross-Eyed Comic, Lived a Real-Life Romance That Was Cherished by Hollywood by Herbert Cohn *(1940 July 7)*

There is, in the *Brooklyn Eagle*'s files, a yellowed one-inch clipping. It is dated April 9, 1925. Its headline reads "Turpin Quits Screen to Aid Sick Wife" and under a Los Angeles dateline, it says: "Ben Turpin, motion picture comedian, announced today that he had decided to quit the screen. His decision was made because of the illness of his wife…"

Behind that little clipping there is an extraordinary story, extraordinary because one wouldn't expect to hear it told about the cross-eyed little man with the paintbrush mustache who clowned in baggy pants and derby hat for Hollywood cameras during the Keystone era. It is a love story. On the Coast it is famous. I heard it first a couple of years ago from a studio publicity man who thought I was ribbing him when I admitted I knew nothing about Ben Turpin.

Turpin used to be a taffy puller back at the beginning of the century. He used to travel with county fairs, amusing the audience that invariably gathered around taffy pullers — so the story goes — by pretending to throw his hot, gummy taffy at a spectator. Usually a twist of the wrist would bring it back safely to his hand with no damage done. But Turpin wasn't an expert taffy puller. Or maybe, as he used to explain not too scientifically, it was his crossed eyes that were to blame. Anyway, his accident record was rather bad. Too often the taffy got out of control and gummed up a spectator's face. It happened once in Cincinnati and the victim was the town's chief of police, a fastidious man who complained strenuously to the fair officials and insisted that Turpin be sacked. He was and it was probably the luckiest thing that happened to Ben in his life, which ended last week.

Turpin became an actor. Not a player of important roles, for his eyes were really crossed. When they became his fortune in the slapstick days, he had them insured against straightening. But while he was touring in vaudeville and stock, they were his greatest handicap. They didn't prevent him from falling in love, though. And they didn't prevent pretty Carrie LeMieux, a French actress in his traveling company, from falling right back in love with him. They were married in Chicago in 1907 and for the next few years, they played the country together, he in bit parts, she in more important roles.

Stranded in Chicago

But show business petered out for a time and the Turpins were stranded in Chicago. The Windy City was almost as important as Hollywood in the movie industry in those days and Ben got a job in one of the Lake Michigan studios. He wasn't an actor; he was a janitor. But one day, he marched onto a set with his broom over his shoulder, a dustpan swinging at his side. He spoiled the scene, but even a tough director, who couldn't have been too happy about a ruined "take," had to laugh. He hired Turpin to clown in one-reelers. Ben didn't last long in Chicago. Charlie Chaplin saw one of his shorts and brought him and his wife on to Hollywood. That was in 1915. A few years later, Turpin was drawing down $3,000 a week, one of the few big salary checks that Hollywood producers signed in those days.

Turpin didn't care much for money. He gave a lot of it away, they say. And he was happy living a simple life with Carrie. But in 1924, Carrie became ill with influenza. She never fully recovered and within a few months, she had suffered several paralytic strokes. Ben took a few months' leave from the studios so that he could take his wife to Canada, where she had once lived. She wanted to pray at the shrine of St. Anne de Beaupre. She was sure that St. Anne could cure her just as others had been cured. She seemed to be improved after a few months, so the couple returned to their California home.

Why He Quit The Screen

But Carrie wasn't well for long. She suffered another stroke, worse than any she had suffered before. The last one left her helpless. It was then that Ben Turpin announced that he was quitting the screen. What he didn't announce was that he planned to devote his time entirely to his wife, tending her because she wouldn't have a nurse — preparing her meals and sitting by her bed because, in her illness, she was disturbed by household help and was comfortable only when her husband was waiting on her.

Turpin was her nurse for almost a year. His friends vouch for the fact that he was in constant attendance, cooking for her, doing the household work in the rooms that she used, trying to make her as happy as he could. They will also tell you that after she died, he was never again as gay as he had been in the few years when Carrie LeMieux was able to share in his success. He soon remarried and went back into pictures, but stayed only a few years. He had nothing to work for, he used to say. He remained in retirement, practically hiding in an inconspicuous house in North Hollywood, until Darryl Zanuck lured him back to the screen last year for a few brief scenes in *Hollywood Cavalcade.*

I saw some of the old Ben Turpin comedies the other night at the 48th Street Music Hall. Sid Lubin, the hall's imaginative pianist and sound-effects man, helped bring them up to date with his ratchets, his horns, and his assortment of noisemakers. But it seemed to me that it was primarily the Turpin brand of clowning that had the crowd in stitches at the tent-like music hall in W. 48th St. Like Chaplin, his mentor, Ben Turpin's art was pantomime. With Chaplin, he will stand as one of the screen's ablest comics.[358]

Timely Editorial — Ben Laughs Last (1940 July 13)

Ben Turpin, at whose crossed eyes the world laughed for more than 30 years, is dead. But then, laughter itself is dead over most of the world.

They laughed at Ben in the old Sam T. Jack's burlesque theater on Madison Street in the days when Edison's kinetoscope was still a scientific curiosity. They laughed at Ben in vaudeville in the days when vaudeville was still a thriving institution. They laughed at him in the medicine shows in the days when the medicine show brought flesh and blood entertainment to the sticks. They rolled in the aisles when Ben rolled his strangely twisted eyes.

But it wasn't until he got into the movies by way of Chicago's Essanay studios and achieved a worldwide audience that the world really appreciated how funny he was. Ben didn't have to do anything or say anything to put the world in stitches — one glimpse of those aberrant orbs and the world howled.

But Ben got the last laugh. In recent months, he must have laughed continually at the effrontery of a cock-eyed world that dared call Ben Turpin cock-eyed.[359]

Afterword

"He may not go down into movie history as a great artiste. Certain it is that his bust will never occupy a niche in any hall of the immortals. But he will have that which is beyond price or purchase — the good wishes of millions who have recognized his genius as a clown, and his worth as a man."

Anonymous writer on Ben Turpin,
Olean Evening Times, New York, October 5, 1925

Turpin's Estate of $100–200G To Widow

Los Angeles, August 20: The Estate of Ben Turpin, who died July 1st, goes to his widow, Babette Turpin, under terms of his will, which was admitted to probate in Superior Court. Veteran film comic named only one other beneficiary, Mrs. E. E. Knies, a sister who receives a "satisfaction" gift of $5. Turpin is believed to have left between $100,000 and $200,000, most of which was in business property and securities.[361]

On July 24, 1940, three weeks after Ben was laid to rest, his widow, with the help of attorney Earl J. Opsahl, posted a Notice of Hearing of Petition for Probate of Will and for Letters Testamentary in the *Los Angeles Daily Journal*, a copy of which was supposedly also sent to Ernestine Knies, Ben's sister, by then living in Los Angeles.

To the Superior Court, Babette presented the holographic, supposed last will and testament of her late husband, written exactly and only three weeks after their marriage. She was determined to follow through the dictates of the will, including Ben's wish that she be made Executrix of the estate and receive everything as well. Mrs. Turpin proved herself to the court to their satisfaction as the widow of Ben Turpin and asked of the court that all joint tenancy, both real and personal, be terminated and that she alone be granted sole ownership.

This included, to Babette's calculations, a $5400.94 savings account, $910.59 checking account, a promissory note of $3220.16, several pieces of real estate in Beverly Hills, Burbank, and in or around Los Angeles. Babette's initial rough estimate of stocks, bonds, and real and personal property valued at "over $10,000."

Three weeks later on August 14, Babette was indeed appointed Executrix by the Superior Court and swore to carry out the will and the wishes of her late husband. Inheritance tax appraiser William F. Daggett, Jr. was appointed by the court to appraise the property. A few days later, the Turpin savings account had somehow now dwindled down to $237.91 with no mention this time of a checking account; a 1937 Chevy sedan was valued at $330 and a 1939 Chevy coupe valued at $490. Household furniture was valued at $1850, fifty shares of stock with General Motors worth $2150, and $11,000 in Bonds. Only two real estate properties in Burbank *(those Ben bought just a year ago for $60,000)* valued at $1900 were claimed; a promissory note for property in the County of Gregory, South Dakota; Ben's life insurance policy for $2500, of which Babette already received $893; and two watches once belonging to Ben, worth but $35, totaling $22,305.

Babette soon sold the '39 coupe and much more after advertising her estate sale in the late August-early September *Los Angeles Daily Journal* every day for two weeks as well as posting notices in "three conspicuous places," City Hall, the Hall of Justice, and the Hall of Records. Almost immediately, the two properties in Burbank listing for $1900 were sold for $1600 cash to Mr. Emanuel Peterson. The promissory note for the property in South Dakota was considered "unimproved grass pasture" and worth, according to the president of the Burke State Bank, Burke, South Dakota, but only "$2.00 to $3.00 per acre." To settle the note, Babette gladly accepted $500 from Elmer E. and Dorothy Smith and handed them the deed.

However, Inheritance Tax Appraiser records interestingly indicate that, when he died, Ben had but $237.91 cash at hand; but through joint tenancy, he and Babette had $6,311.53 cash at hand. Turpin was said to have had $17,662.25 in intangible personal property, $2,705 in tangible property, and, surprisingly only $1700 in real estate. In comparison, both Ben and Babette had, again in joint tenancy, $6,311.53 in cash, intangible personal property valued at $3,201.26, and now suddenly a whopping $89,800 in real estate, totaling: $121,617.95. Of course, Babette had to pay taxes on this amount and pay her attorney and her appraiser $2,997.33. Ben's medical bills, funeral expenses, and miscellaneous bills tacked on an additional $4,525.71. Believed to be a millionaire by many, on January 7, 1941, the clear market value on the Ben Turpin estate as presented to the Superior Court of California was given as $114,094.91 and Babette prepared to collect every cent but a portion of the inheritance for Ben's sister Ernestine, five dollars.

After Babette had finished almost everything in her role as executrix and was ready to move on with her life, Ernestine at last caught wind of what was going on and immediately hired the law firm of Dempster, Dempster and Brown to petition and revoke the will.

On March 10, 1941, in the Superior Court of California was filed an amended petition for the Revocation of Probate of Will, contested by Mrs. Ernestine Knies and her lawyer, Michael F. Brown, against Babette Turpin. It alleged that on or about August 14, 1940, the court made its order admitting to probate a document purporting to be the last will and testament of Ben Turpin and at the same time appointing Babette as executrix. Ernestine tried to have the will revoked on grounds that Ben, at the time of the alleged execution of this will, was not of sound and disposing mind, nor was the will executed in the manner or form required by law.

Ernestine asserted that Ben, for several years and up to the time of his death, was mentally and physically weak, infirm, and was afflicted with disease of body and mind. Which by reason of said diseased condition and infirmity and credulity, he was unable to properly take care of himself. He became so weak and infirm of mind and body and reasoning faculties that he was so easily influenced by those under whose custody he came and was easily influenced by artful and designing persons and that Babette was, during said time, his companion. She kept constant company with Ben and, during a great deal of the time, secluded herself with her husband from his sister.

Ernestine also claimed that Ben, prior to his death, consulted Babette constantly about his business affairs and followed her advice explicitly in all matters. That Ben reposed confidence and trust in Babette and that she did control and influence his mind and actions to such an extent that he did whatever she suggested and instructed him to do.

Also, that upon numerous occasions during the time, Ben expressed a desire to give presents to the natural object of his bounty, his sister, but at the suggestion of Babette, he would suddenly and strangely refuse to carry out such intentions. And that during such period and up to the time of his death, Babette succeeded in substituting her will for the original will of Ben Turpin. That at the time of the execution of this purported Last Will and Testament, Ben wasn't following the dictates of his own will, which would have naturally led him to have devised and bequeathed his estate to his only heir and sister, Ernestine E. Knies, whom he had at all times loved as a sister, but he was acting wholly under the said influence of Babette Turpin, who suggested and dictated to him the terms of said will; that the decedent had, prior to the execution of purported Will, stated to his sister that she was to receive all of his property as his heir and sister and had theretofore and on November 12, 1925, executed a will leaving all his property to Ernestine.

That this said purported Will was not the free and voluntary act of decedent, but the making and execution thereof was procured by the undue influence of Babette Turpin. Ernestine petitioned and prayed that the probate of this document, purporting to be the last will and testament of Ben Turpin, be revoked.

But by the time Ernestine caught wind of the settlement and tried to contest the court's decision, the case was over and done and her attempts to reopen the case went nowhere.

One of the first things Babette the heir did was to treat herself to some cosmetic surgery and the results were amazing. Her late husband would never have recognized her.

Ernestine's grandson (Ben's grandnephew), Richard Knies, recently told me, "My grandmother was Ben's housekeeper at the end of his marriage (to Carrie). When Ben married Babette there was an armed truce between her and Babette. This continued through the rest of Ben's life. She, as you know, contested Ben's will. Ernestine and Babette kept it in the courts for a few years. What Babette Turpin didn't get, the lawyers did.

"(Later) at Ernestine's passing, her estate was settled by a lawyer named Kristovich, a Public Guardian for the County of Los Angeles in 1969. How this came about is a long story. My grandmother's estate was settled and liquidated with final hearings held two days prior to my being notified in Illinois!

"My first remembrance of Ben was in 1926/1927. We were living on his property in a small cottage. I was allowed free run. My father did not go into the house if Grandma was there! He spoke to me in passing; patted me on the head or told me to get out of the way.

"Ben Turpin was one of the pioneers! Although his persona was one of an inept but charming clown, in his personal life he was an astute businessman.

"There were many parties and I got to see or meet many show biz people. Ernie Adams, Sunshine Hart, Jack Mulhall, Tyrone Power, Sr., Gary Cooper, frequent visitor Hoot Gibson, Kenneth Harlan, and Bob Bradbury who became Bob Steele. Ben was a cowboy fan.

"Through Ben's influence my father (Julian Knies) made several short films as Tommy Turpin. None of which were with Ben and, the only film I recall was *The Patent Leather Kid*.

"My father and his mother (Ernestine) did not talk, write or phone each other during my lifetime. She out-lived my father and did not respond to many overtures on my part at the time of his passing. I got a birthday card each year with a five-dollar bill in it — likewise Christmas."

Ernestine (Turpin) Knies died May 18, 1969, in Los Angeles, five months shy of reaching her 102nd birthday.

Beverly Hills Jewel Theft Suspect Held (1944 May 30)

Santa Monica, May 30 — Accused of having stolen several hundred dollars' worth of jewelry from Mrs. Ben Turpin's home in Beverly Hills, Charles Lee, 22, of 3013-1/2 Ocean Front, today was held by police on burglary charges. Held for questioning were Bernard Powers and Paul Magierowski, living at the same address.

Detectives Frank Warren and Vern Hodges said Lee had given some of the loot taken from the Turpin residence to Magierowski with instruction to "throw it into the ocean" because it was "too hot to handle." Lee told police he had recently been released from a Federal reformatory, where he spent three years. He is to be questioned further by Los Angeles and Beverly Hills police.[362]

Ben's third wife Babette lived nearly forty years after the passing of her husband. She never remarried and at age 91 died at St. John's Hospital, Santa Monica, on Saturday, February 11, 1978. She was the last of the original A. F. Dietz family.

1949 September 5 — Ben appears on the cover of *Life* magazine to accompany the article Comedy's Greatest Era by James Agee who wrote of Turpin, "he remains a particularly friendly memory to those who like comedy broad and low. He was a fine acrobat."

Early on, Ben told one writer of his life in movies, "I was doing it for art's sake."[20]

Filmography

Unfortunately, the earliest of Turpin's Essanay comedies, many directed by Gilbert M. Anderson, may never be completely and correctly documented until the films themselves are rediscovered or a very rare reference is made to Ben's participation in particular film titles. All Essanay titles are one reel (approximately 1000 feet in 35mm) or less (often half reels or split reels) unless noted. It is this author's opinion that Ben appeared in — or was involved in — nearly all of Essanay's pre-May 1909 productions, but are documenting only those verified or questionable titles.

All filmography titles marked with a bullet (•) are extant and housed at archives mentioned in parentheses, and are or were available via DVD, video, or film through distributors such as Blackhawk Films, Unknown Video, VtVideoClassics, Looser Than Loose, and others.

Essanay 1907-1917
(A work in progress)

•*An Awful Skate* or *The Hobo on Rollers* — released July 27, 1907 *(683 ft.)*
(George Eastman House)

Slow But Sure — released August 10, 1907 *(647 ft.)*

Mr. Inquisitive — released August 24, 1907 *(647 ft.)*
A man with well-developed butting-in proclivities gets into all kinds of trouble as a result
of this weakness.

Life of a Bootblack — released September 7, 1907 *(Half Reel)*

The Street Urchin — released September 7, 1907 *(Half Reel)*
Shows every incident of the little street merchant's career. Shows his struggle for existence — his squalid surroundings — his final rise in life — owns automobile, etc.

The Dancing Nig — released September 21, 1907 *(390 ft.)*

99 in the Shade — released September 28, 1907 *(300 ft.)*

Hey There! Look Out! — released October 19, 1907 *(400 ft.)*

The Vagabond — released October 26, 1907 *(770 ft.)*

A Free Lunch — released November 2, 1907 *(Half Reel)*

The Street Fakir — released November 2, 1907 *(Half Reel)*

Where is My Hair? — released December 14, 1907 *(400 ft.)*

The Bell Boy's Revenge — released December 28, 1907 *(Half Reel)*

The Football Craze — released January 4, 1908 *(650 ft.)*

A Jack of All Trades — released January 11, 1908 *(650 ft.)*

A Novice on Stilts — released January 18, 1908 *(400 ft.)*

A Home at Last — released January 18, 1908 *(250 ft.)*

The Hoosier Fighter — released February 1, 1908 *(800 ft.)*

Babies Will Play — released February 8, 1908 *(750 ft.)*

Louder Please — released February 15, 1908 *(350 ft.)*

The Dog Cop — released February 22, 1908 *(585 ft.)*

All is Fair in Love and War — released March 4, 1908 *(823 ft.)*

Well-Thy Water — released March 11, 1908 *(310 ft.)*

The Juggler Juggles — released March 11, 1908 *(418 ft.)*

Hypnotizing Mother-In-Law — released March 18, 1908 *(552 ft.)*

A Lord for a Day — released March 25, 1908 *(889 ft.)*

James Boys in Missouri — released April 8, 1908 *(One Reel)*

Don't Pull My Leg — released May 6, 1908 *(425 ft.)*
The owner of an artificial limb store searches the town for a stolen limb, pulling at every suspicious leg and getting in trouble along the way.

Ker-Choo — released May 6, 1908 *(400 ft.)*

Just Like a Woman — released May 20, 1908 *(500 ft.)*

I Can't Read English — released May 20, 1908 *(400 ft.)*

An Animated Doll — released May 27, 1908 *(One Reel)*

The Gentle Sex — released June 10, 1908 *(750 ft.)*

The Little Mad-Cap — released June 17, 1908

Oh, Splash! — released June 17, 1908 *(600 ft.)*

The Tragedian — released June 17, 1908 *(400 ft.)*

The Younger Brothers — released June 20, 1908 *(400 ft.)*
Directed by E. Lawrence Lee **Camera by** Gilbert P. Hamilton. Harry Clifton, Jack Jesperson, (Ben Turpin?).

Oh! What Lungs — released July 1, 1908 *(One Reel)*

Wouldn't That Tire You? — released July 1, 1908 *(One Reel)*

Checker Fiends — released July 8, 1908 *(One Reel)*

An Enterprising Florist — released July 8, 1908 *(One Reel)*

Stung! Or Who Can It Bee? — released July 15, 1908 *(428 ft.)*

•*A Disastrous Flirtation* — released August, 1908 *(Half Reel)*
(Filmoteca de Catalunya, Barcelona)
"This is a story devoid of plot, but full of well-executed comedy. A youth who winked a roving eye and breathed a non-connubial sigh at every damsel he saw, gets his, and that is a plenty. The Essanay Co. has a splendid pantomimist, whoever he is."
                                   Frank Wiesberg, *Variety,* August. 29, 1908, pg 11a

Beg Pardon — released September 30, 1908 *(450 ft.)*
"How often have you had somebody step on your corn, sit on your hat, bump into you, drop water on you, and various other things and then say to you in a very apologetic manner, 'Beg pardon.' But our victims in this picture do not accept the apology of our comedian, who happens to be a very clumsy and awkward fellow. He gets into all kinds of scraps and is lucky to come out alive after causing much damage by his indifferent ways. We feel we have an excellent comedy subject in this feature and judging from our former success and our style of comedies, we do not hesitate to state positively this picture is a real winner."
Essanay publicity

Soul Kiss — released September 30, 1908 *(450 ft.)*

Breaking Into Society — released October 3, 1908 *(Half Reel)*

The Impersonator's Jokes — released November 25, 1908 *(550 ft.)*
Ejected from his flat for not paying the rent, the impersonator packs his bags with clothes, beards, wigs, etc., the tools of his profession. He disguises himself as a wealthy man and has his chauffeur take him for a ride. He soon impersonates a foreign nobleman at a party in his honor with everything going well until a telegram arrives from the real nobleman stating he's unable to attend. Immediately, everyone pounces on the fraud, tearing him to shreds before making a hasty exit.

An All Wool Garment — released November 25, 1908 *(400 ft.)*
After changing into his woolen union suit, our comic develops a scratching fever. At work, his scratching begins and soon the clerks are afflicted. He enters a street car and soon, all the passengers are scratching, resulting in his ejection. Everywhere he goes, everyone starts scratching. So, desperate to get out of his all wool garment, he steals some cotton underwear only to be caught by the storekeeper, who gives chase.

The Obstinate Tooth — released December 2, 1908 *(165 ft.)*
Showing the ingenious methods of one in pain trying to rid himself of his troubles.

The Somnambulist — released December 8, 1908 *(225 ft.)*
The tale of an overworked bank teller who misplaces a large sum of money while asleep and who is unable to satisfactorily explain what has become of it. The money is found and the teller forgiven.

A Christmas Carol — released December 9, 1908 *(1000 ft.)*
Serio-comic story in ten elaborate scenes based on Charles Dickens' famous story, starring Henry Dixey.

The Installment Collector — released December 16, 1908 *(550 ft.)*
A comedy based upon the "purchased by installment" theory. Twelve payments give the story twelve humorous settings.

A Battle Royal — released December 16, 1908 *(396 ft.)*
A comedy involving a prize fight with much realism.

Who Is Smoking That Rope? — released December 23, 1908 *(400 ft.)*
A comedy involving bargain-counter cigars purchased by the lady of the house, who presents them to her husband with dreadful results.

Bill Jones' New Year's Resolutions — released December 23, 1908 *(600 ft.)*
Comedy of a married man who has an exacting wife and a troublesome mother-in-law, who insists upon the regulation New Year's pledge, which is promptly broken.

• *The Haunted Lounge* — released January 6, 1909 *(370 ft.)*
(Library of Congress)
The adventures of a tramp who, in order to escape the clutches of the law, hides in a folding lounge.

• *The Neighbor's Kids* — released January 6, 1909 *(550 ft.)*
(Library of Congress)
A film illustrating the mischievous pranks of two little girls.

An Actor's Baby Carriage — released January 13, 1909 *(467 ft.)*
An actor deciding to paint the baby carriage dons a cast-off convict suit. He is taken for an escaped prisoner, pursued, and many humorous scenes follow until the real convict is caught.

The Professor's Love Tonic — released January 13, 1909 *(490 ft.)*
Depicts the funny situations of a professor who, after experimenting to obtain a love tonic, becomes the victim of his own discovery.

Too Much Dog Biscuit — released January 27, 1909 *(400 ft.)*
A cook mistakenly serves her late ariser dog biscuits instead of the breakfast he ordered. The unsuspecting one devours the breakfast and at once assumes all the canine characteristics and ends up in a dog catcher's wagon.

A Cure for Gout — released January 27, 1909 *(540 ft.)*
A comedy in which the daughter, being refused attendance at a ball by a gouty parent, escapes and attends, whereupon he goes to bring her home. Many strange and wonderful things happen.

Educated Abroad — released February 10, 1909 *(970 ft.)*
A comedy showing the tendency of Americans of wealth to imitate foreign manners.

Tag Day — released February 17, 1909 *(560 ft.)*
First Essanay film produced in Los Angeles.
A comedy portraying the experiences of a tramp who, observing how easily victims are trapped on tag day, disguises himself as an old lady and proceeds to observe the day for his own benefit.

Bring Me Some Ice — released February 17, 1909 *(350 ft.)*
A housewife sends her son for some ice and this comic story graphically depicts his many adventures, each one funnier than the previous one.

An Expensive Sky Piece — released March 10, 1909 *(500 ft.)*
A man sitting on a bench puts his money in his hat, placing it beside him. A tramp takes the hat and disappears, starting a wild search for the hat. When a policeman finds the tramp, the angry crowd who have lost their hats take it out on the tramp. "An Essanay comic which is really funny. The situations are unusually funny and the audience is kept in laughter." *MPW*

The Crazy Barber — released March 10, 1909 *(500 ft.)*
An offer of a $100 prize to the fastest worker interests a crazy barber. He registers and immediately starts training for the contest. He shaves and cuts the hair of everyone he passes, including a dog, a girl in a hammock, and more. But when he tries trimming a tree in a public park, he is nabbed by a policeman whose face is lathered in the tussle. "It is an Essanay and has the merit of being more original than the average humorous picture, and the acting is funny throughout. It created considerable laughter." *MPW*

A Midnight Disturbance — released March 24, 1909 *(525 ft.)*

The Energetic Street Cleaner — released March 24, 1909 *(450 ft.)*
Finding work as a street-sweep, a White Wing covers everyone with dust or mud, upsetting everyone in his path. He soaks two women with mud and water, upsets a man helping a woman tie her shoe, overturns the suitcase of a man waiting for a car, scattering its contents into the street, upsets a grocery boy carrying a sack of flour, and also a waiter carrying a tray of food. He then sweeps the street debris into a manhole as a worker is ascending. The upset crowd secures the help of a policeman and all pounce on the sweep and see to his termination. "Few films are greeted with more laughter than this. It is lively and the sport is clean." *MPW*

The Rubes and the Bunco Men — released April 14, 1909 *(430 ft.)*
A rube and his wife land in the city and are immediately spotted by two con men. The first thing they do is sell the rube a stolen wagon and two horses for $25. Soon, the crooks offer the rube a house for his horses and wagon plus $200. The troubles of the rube begin when the real owner of the home has his butler roll the rubes down the steps.

The Chaperone — released April 14, 1909 *(550 ft.)*
A father orders a young man out of the house who is calling on his daughter. The young man ascertains that the only objection to him is that the father insists a chaperone must be present. Accordingly, he induces a friend to make up as the chaperone and accompany him to the woman's home. The father immediately falls for the chaperone, who then induces him to sign a paper permitting the marriage of his daughter to her lover. When the father next tries to kiss the supposed chaperone, the wig falls off and his identity disclosed. "Very funny and gets not only hearty laughs, but vigorous applause." *MPW*

A Pair of Garters — released April 21, 1909 *(225 ft.)*

A Mexican's Gratitude — released May 5, 1909 *(One Reel)*
G. M. Anderson, Ben Turpin

•*Mr. Flip* — released May 12, 1909 *(450 ft.)*
Currently the earliest known instance on film of a pie in the face.

The Bachelor's Wife — released May 12, 1909 *(550 ft.)*

The Sleeping Tonic — released June 2, 1909 *(625 ft.)*
A young man is troubled with insomnia. A doctor prescribes the remedy. The result is he sleeps everywhere and everyplace he finds, at last on the concrete wall of a fountain. In his slumber, he rolls over into the water. The situations are rapid and amusing.
                                              Fred Weisberg, *Variety*, June 19, 1909, pg 9

The Dog and the Sausage — released June 2, 1909 *(350 ft.)*
A great deal of difficulty caused by two errand boys changing baskets. In one is a dog and in the other some sausage. They get to the wrong places and all kinds of trouble ensue. The comic features are emphasized and the film is rewarded with hearty laughs.

A Hustling Advertiser — released June 16, 1909 *(550 ft.)*
While it might not be safe or desirable to undertake a repetition of this outdoor man's methods, it will be generally admitted that if an advertiser really did as this picture represents, he would get a class of advertising he might not like. The acting is grand and, as most of the action occurs outdoors, the staging has plenty of room. The photography alone could be improved. *MPW*

The Little Peacemaker — released June 16, 1909 *(450 ft.)*

The New Cop — released July 14, 1909 *(Half Reel)*

Which is Which? — released July 14, 1909 *(Half Reel)*

•*A Case of Seltzer* — released July 28, 1909 *(Half Reel)*
(George Eastman House)

A Tramp Story — released July 28, 1909 *(Half Reel)*

Turpin leaves Essanay in May 1909, returning to vaudeville and odd jobs and finds some movie work with the American Flying A and also the Independent Motion Picture Company (IMP), including unidentified stunt work for *America's Sweetheart*, Mary Pickford, while in Cuba.

IMP
(A work in progress)

•*The Hobble Skirt* — released October 27, 1910 *(500 ft.)*
(UCLA Film and Television Archive)

Pictureland — released March 4, 1911
Pictureland is unique in its way and really two stories are photographed. The arrival of the IMP Company in Cuba, prepared to pose for films and the reception of the company, are in the opening pictures. All the well-known IMP stars appear in traveling costume, which is their first formal introduction in proper persona, an innovation which will be welcomed by their many admirers.
                    Moving Picture World, February 11, 1911, pg 17 (with Turpin?)

The Fisher Maid — released March 16, 1911 *(One Reel)*
Mary Pickford, Owen Moore, (Ben Turpin?)

American
(A work in progress)

•*The Hidden Treasure* — released November 30, 1912 *(Split Reel)*
Directed by Gilbert Hamilton (or W.D. Emerson?).
On same reel as *On Board the S.S. Dubuque*.

Mrs. Brown's Baby — released December 21, 1912 *(Split Reel)*
Directed by Gilbert Hamilton (or W.D. Emerson?).
On same reel as *Saving the Innocents*.

Turpin returns to Essanay, winter of 1913.

Essanay
(All one-reelers unless noted)

The Usual Way — November 19, 1913
Wallace Beery, Charlotte Mineau, Ben Turpin

The Fable of the Brash Drummer and the Nectarine — June 17, 1914
Director & Story: George Ade(?)
Wallace Beery, Beverly Bayne, Ben Turpin, Leo White
The first of Essanay's George Ade Fables.

Sweedie the Swatter — July 13, 1914
Wallace Beery, Ben Turpin, Leo White

Sweedie and the Lord — July 27, 1914
Wallace Beery, Harry Dunkinson, Charlotte Mineau, Alfred Gronell, Ben Turpin

The Fable of the Busy Business Boy and the Droppers-In — August 5, 1914
Director & Story: George Ade(?)
Wallace Beery, Robert Bolder, Mildred Considine, Leo White, Ben Turpin, Harry Dunkinson, Kitty Robinson

Sweedie Springs a Surprise — August 24, 1914
Wallace Beery, Betty Brown, Ben Turpin

The Joblot Recruits — September 14, 1914
Ben Turpin *(Captain of the Police)*

Sweedie and the Double Exposure — September 21, 1914
Wallace Beery, Harry Dunkinson, Sadie Pearl, Frank Hamilton, Ben Turpin

Sweedie's Skate — September 21, 1914
Wallace Beery, Charles Wright, Leo White, Ben Turpin, (Gloria Swanson?)

Sweedie's Clean-Up — September 28, 1914
Wallace Beery, Leo White, Ben Turpin, Robert Bolder, Frank Hamilton, Frank Owen

• *Golf Champion "Chick" Evans Links with Sweedie* — October 2, 1914
(clip possibly extant)
Wallace Beery, Chick Evans, Ruth Hennessy, Leo White, Charlotte Mineau, Ben Turpin

The Fickleness of Sweedie (#1663) — October 5, 1914
Wallace Beery, Leo White, Robert Bolder, Ben Turpin
Much footage is given to drills and adventures of the police.

• *Sweedie Learns to Swim* — October 12, 1914
Directed by Wallace Beery *Story by* Joseph Anthony Roach
Wallace Beery, Betty Brown, Ben Turpin *(Captain of Lifesavers)*, Leo White, Charlotte Mineau

• *She Landed a Big One* — October 19, 1914
Wallace Beery *(Sweedie)*, Robert Bolder *(Her Father)*, Harry Dunkinson *(Her Best Beau)*, Leo White *(A Stranger)*, Alfred Gronell *(The Fisherman)*, Ben Turpin *(Captain of the Police)*

• *Sweedie, the Laundress* — November 2, 1914
Wallace Beery *(Sweedie)*, Robert Bolder *(The Tailor)*, Charlotte Mineau, Leo White, Ben Turpin
Numerous complications keep the interest in this film alive throughout. Wallace Beery as Sweedie is the central character and is supported by Robert Bolder, Ben Turpin, Charlotte Mineau, and Leo White. It is sure to draw laughs from the class that enjoys slapstick comedy. Bessie and her hairdresser quarrel, so she writes a note to the tailor, telling him that she will dine with him that evening. Sweedie, the laundress, who is desperately in love with the tailor, hears of the dinner engagement and writes a letter to him saying that she is going to drown herself in the dye vat. After rigging up a dummy resembling her, she sticks it head first into the vat. She then leaves, but returns shortly after in a man's attire, telling the tailor she is Sweedie's brother. He weeps and wails, declaring that if Sweedie were only alive, he would marry her in a minute. Sweedie then pulls off her disguise and the tailor falls in a dead faint.

Sweedie the Troublemaker — November 9, 1914
Wallace Beery, Leo White, Robert Bolder, Ben Turpin

Countess Sweedie — November 16, 1914
Sweedie again gets in wrong in this picture and furnishes considerable amusement thereby. A large ballroom set, which is quite exceptional for this style of comedy, is used for the climax scenes. Wallace Beery and Ben Turpin have the leads. Countess Von Swatt goes on a slumming party and loses one of her calling cards in the hash house where Sweedie works. Sweedie finds the card. Next day, an invitation to a ball to be given by Mr. Wealth is delivered by mistake to Sweedie. She has an idea; she will go to the ball and pretend to be the countess. The night of the party, Sweedie arrives at the Wealth home, accompanied by a waiter from her place of employment. She is introduced to the waiting guests as Countess Von Swatt and in the middle of the introduction, stubs her toe and rolls down the stairs. She is paid great attention by all present and they insist upon her demonstrating the modern dances. Sweedie and the waiter are in the midst of the Swedish tango when the real countess arrives. Upon seeing her, the pair makes a rush for the door, but is captured and spend the night in jail, but Sweedie is happy that she was a countess for a while.

Sweedie at the Fair — November 23, 1914
Wallace Beery, Charlotte Mineau, Ben Turpin

Sweedie and the Hypnotist — December 7, 1914
Wallace Beery, Harry Dunkinson, Ben Turpin

Madame Double X — December 14, 1914
Wallace Beery, Robert Bolder, Ben Turpin, Leo White

Their Cheap Vacation — December 21, 1914
Wallace Beery, Betty Brown, Ben Turpin

Sweedie Collects for Charity — December 28, 1914
Wallace Beery, Charlotte Mineau, Ben Turpin

Sweedie and the Sultan's Present — January 4, 1915
Wallace Beery, Ben Turpin
Wallace Beery and Ben Turpin have the leads in this farce. While the action at times is humorous, it drags in some places, but will be popular in houses where others of this series have "gone big." In the opening scenes, Sweedie's domestic difficulties are illustrated, ending with pitching her husband from the house. She falls asleep and dreams that the Sultan of Puff-Puff sent a servant to her as a present and forces her to accept by threatening her life. When her husband objects, there is a strenuous argument with the result that the sultan orders her to behead him. Just as she is about to wield the butcher knife, she wakes up and finds her husband at her side and again handles him in anything but a gentle manner and heads him for the sidewalk.

Sweedie's Suicide — January 11, 1915
Wallace Beery, Robert Bolder, Leo White, Charlotte Mineau, Ben Turpin
Jilted by her sweetheart, Sweedie determines to commit suicide and writes a note to her lover explaining all about it. Meanwhile, some tricksters dope Sweedie and, while she is asleep, erect a tombstone beside her. On waking, Sweedie does not know whether she is alive or a ghost, but when she beholds her lover mourning at her grave, she determines to make sure and so sails in and all but annihilates the mourners, thus proving conclusively to herself that she is alive.

American
(A work in progress)

The Clubmen's Wager — January 15, 1915
American-Mutual *(Split Reel)* comedy *(wt: A Thousand Dollar Bill)*
William Bowman, William Morse, James Hamilton, Harry Devere, Herman Frank, Ben Turpin *(a tramp)*

Essanay

Sweedie and Her Dog — January 18, 1915
Wallace Beery, Betty Brown, Leo White, Ben Turpin *(dog catcher)*
Sweedie, her dog, a band of dogcatchers, and a timid employer form the elements which the comedy incidents in this production are built. Mr. Dingby engages Sweedie as cook and she insists on taking her dog, "Skinny," with her. The dogcatchers capture Skinny and Sweedie forces her new employer to help her recover him. When they arrive at home, her antics cause a great deal of trouble, some of the incidents at this point proving real laugh-getters. Her best friend calls and takes her for a ride in his cab and the incidents during this affair are also humorous. Upon her return, Sweedie finds that her dog has been abused and the film ends with a general riot in the household. Wallace Beery, Betty Brown, Leo White, and Ben Turpin do excellent work in the four laugh-getting roles.

Two Hearts That Beat as Ten — January 25, 1915
Wallace Beery, Robert Bolder, Betty Brown, Charlotte Mineau, Ben Turpin

•*His New Job* — February 1, 1915 *(Two Reels)*
Director: Charles Chaplin
Charlie Chaplin, Ben Turpin, Leo White, Charlotte Mineau, Robert Bolder, Charles Stine, Agnes Ayers, Gloria Swanson

Sweedie Goes to College — February 8, 1915 *(Two Reels)*
Director: Richard F. Baker
Wallace Beery, Ben Turpin, Charlotte Mineau, Gloria Swanson

•*A Night Out* — February 15, 1915 *(Two Reels)*
Director: Charles Chaplin
Charlie Chaplin, Ben Turpin, Leo White, Edna Purviance, Bud Jamison, Charlotte Mineau

Sweedie's Hopeless Love — March 1, 1915
Wallace Beery, Betty Brown, Ben Turpin
A typical Sweedie comedy in which Wallace Beery and Ben Turpin are the chief fun-makers. The story deals with the attempts of Sweedie to gain the love of a grocery boy. The latter, however, cannot exactly enjoy her attentions and makes many comical attempts to avoid delivering groceries to the home in which she is employed as cook. When he is forced to make the delivery by his employer, Sweedie insists on embracing him. He hides in a closet and when the husband of Sweedie's mistress returns home and discovers him, he thinks him a suitor for his wife's affections. The delivery boy escapes and secures another position, but again Sweedie gets on his trail. The limit is reached when the loving miss secures a position as cook in his boarding house. A fire breaks out and Sweedie offers to save her Romeo, but he prefers death. There are many incidents which will draw real laughs.

•*The Champion* — March 11, 1915 *(Two Reels)*
Director: Charles Chaplin
Charlie Chaplin, Edna Purviance, Leo White, Bud Jamison, Charlotte Mineau, Broncho Billy Anderson, Lloyd Bacon, Ernest Van Pelt, Billy Armstrong, Ben Turpin (cameo as crowd vendor).

Love and Trouble — March 15, 1915
Wallace Beery, Ben Turpin

Sweedie Learns to Ride — March 22, 1915
Wallace Beery, Betty Brown, Ben Turpin

Two Bold, Bad Men — March 25, 1915
Victor Potel, Harry Todd, Margaret Joslin, Leo White, Ben Turpin, Carrie Turpin (WIFE)
Ben Turpin and Leo White, now at the Essanay western studio, are featured in this single-reel release as two bold bad men who come into town ready for any criminal act. When they find the village constable asleep, they enter the home of a nagging husband just as his wife turns on him and throws him out. The husband then assists them in stealing everything in the place, which they hide in a trunk. Later, the constable, following them, removes the silverware from the trunk and hides therein himself. Unconscious of the charge, they carry the trunk to the barnyard and bury it, but the constable emerges from the ground to overpower and capture them.

Curiosity — March 29, 1915
Ruth Hennessey, Robert Bolder, Florida Kingsley, Ben Turpin, Leo White
A pleasing little comedy in which Ruth Hennessy, Robert Bolder, Leo White, and Ben Turpin will draw many laughs from almost every audience. It deals with the curiosity of a number of persons to know who mailed a note to the girl in the case, asking her to come to a certain bench in a certain park. Both the girl's aunt and uncle visit the bench, the former to spy on the girl and the latter to spy upon his wife and the man he believes to be her lover. A lunatic escapes from the asylum and gets into the affair and, for several hundred feet, the girl's lover, the uncle, and the lunatic are scarcely able, to themselves, tell which is which, but in the end, all is straightened out.

•*A Coat Tale* — April 1, 1915
(BFI — as *The Wrong Coat*)
Ben Turpin, Margie Reiger, Snub Pollard, Victor Potel, Harry Todd
The wife insists on purchasing a coat worth $100, but hubby refuses to buy it and he sends home a $6.95 coat with a $100 bill tucked in one of the pockets. Wifey is satisfied until she learns that the lady across the hall has a coat just like it for $6.95. She throws the coat out of the window and a negro street cleaner picks it up and takes it home to his wife. Later, when hubby tells wifey about the $100 bill tucked in the pocket, they both start out in search of the coat. Hubby gets arrested while the wife, who has found the colored woman, starts a fight with her that results in both being brought to the station. The $100 bill finally pays the fines of all.

The Undertaker's Uncle — April 29, 1915
Harry Todd, Ben Turpin, Margaret Joslin, Victor Potel

How Slippery Slim Saw the Show — May 6, 1915
Director: Roy Clements
Victor Potel, Margaret Joslin, Harry Todd, Ben Turpin

•*His Regeneration* — May 7, 1915
Director: G. M. Anderson
Broncho Billy Anderson, Marguerite Clayton, Lee Willard, Hazel Applegate, Charlie
Chaplin, Lloyd Bacon, Ben Turpin

Sweedie in Vaudeville — May 13, 1915
Wallace Beery, Edmund Thompson, Arthur Bates, Ben Turpin

Sweedie's Hero — May 20, 1915
Wallace Beery, Ben Turpin, Charlotte Mineau, Leo White

A Bunch of Matches — May 27, 1915
Bob McKenzie, Margie Reiger, Florence Cato, Hazel Applegate, Ben Turpin, Victor Potel,
Snub Pollard

Sophie and the Fakir — June 3, 1915
Director: Roy Clements
Margaret Joslin, Ben Turpin, Harry Todd, Victor Potel

Sweedie's Finish — June 10, 1915
Wallace Beery, Betty Brown, Arthur Bates, Ben Turpin

Others Started But Sophie Finished — July 22, 1915
Director: Roy Clements
Margaret Joslin, Harry Todd, Victor Potel, Ben Turpin, Carrie Turpin

Snakeville's Twins — July 29, 1915
Director: Roy Clements
Victor Potel, Harry Todd, Ben Turpin, Margaret Joslin

The Bellhop — August 12, 1915
Ben Turpin, Victor Potel, Robert McKenzie, Harry Todd

•*Broncho Billy Steps In* — August 13, 1915
(EYE Film Institute)
Director: G. M. Anderson
G. M. Anderson, Marguerite Clayton, Lee Willard, Lloyd Bacon, Ben Turpin, Harry Todd,
Victor Potel, Bob McKenzie

•*Love Versus Sledge Hammers (aka Versus Sledge Hammers)* — September 2, 1915
Director: Roy Clements
Victor Potel, Harry Todd, Margaret Joslin, Bob MacKenzie, Ben Turpin

A Quiet Little Game — September 9, 1915
Director: Roy Clements
Harry Todd, Lloyd Bacon, Margaret Joslin, Ben Turpin, Bob and Eva McKenzie

Broncho Billy and the Card Shark — September 17, 1915
Director: G.M. Anderson
Broncho Billy Anderson, Lloyd Bacon, Lee Willard, Florence Cato, Harry Todd, Victor Potel, Ben Turpin, Bob McKenzie

Snakeville's Hen Medic — September 23, 1915
Director: Roy Clements
Margaret Joslin, Harry Todd, Victor Potel, Ben Turpin, Carrie Turpin, Robert McKenzie

The Convict's Threat — September 28, 1915
Director: G. M. Anderson
Broncho Billy Anderson, Marguerite Clayton, Lee Willard, Harry Todd, Lloyd Bacon, Ben Turpin, Victor Potel, Robert McKenzie

When Snakeville Struck Oil — October 21, 1915
Director: Roy Clements
Harry Todd, Victor Potel, Margaret Joslin, Ben Turpin, Robert McKenzie, Lloyd Bacon

Too Much Turkey — November 19, 1915
Director: G. M. Anderson
Broncho Billy Anderson, Ruth Saville, Ben Turpin, Carrie Turpin, Robert McKenzie, Eva McKenzie

It Happened in Snakeville — November 25, 1915
Director: Roy Clements
Margaret Joslin *(Sophie)*, Harry Todd *(Pete)*, Ben Turpin *(Bloggie)*, Lloyd Bacon, Marguerite Clayton, Carrie Turpin, Robert McKenzie
"Mustang Pete and Bloggie are rivals for the hand of Sophie Clutts. One day, after she has witnessed a fight between the two, Sophie sits down to read the newspaper. She sees an ad for a movie actress and decides to go to the big city to apply. Several months later finds her a stunning leading actress and living in great luxury. She is longing for their company when both Bloggie and Mustang appear. She has an arm around each of them when she awakes to find herself caressing two dogs." *MPW*

Broncho Billy's Love Affair — November 26, 1915
Director: G. M. Anderson
Broncho Billy Anderson, Ruth Saville, Lee Willard, Ben Turpin, Harry Todd, Robert McKenzie, Lloyd Bacon, Belle Mitchell

The Merry Models — December 9, 1915
Director: Wallace Beery
Ben Turpin *(Bloggie)*, Margaret Joslin *(His Wife)*, Harry Todd *(Mustang Pete)*, Carrie Turpin *(His Wife)*, Ruth Saville, Robert McKenzie, Belle Mitchell
"When the manager of a café receives a telegram informing him that the marble statues he ordered were destroyed by fire, he employs Bloggie and Mustang to pose as statues in his café. The patrons are deceived and compliment the manager for his fine taste in statuary. All goes well until both the wives of Bloggie and Mustang enter the café and recognize their husbands. A riot ensues in which the place is completely wrecked and the two statues are chased home by the angry wives." *MPW*

The Escape of Broncho Billy — December 10, 1915
Director: G. M. Anderson
Broncho Billy Anderson, Ruth Saville, Rodney Hildebrand, Ben Turpin, Lloyd Bacon, Lee Willard

•*Snakeville's Champion* — December 16, 1915
Director: Wallace Beery
Ben Turpin, Lloyd Bacon, Margaret Joslin, Harry Todd, Victor Potel, Robert McKenzie
Hotch *(Lloyd Bacon)*, world's greatest wrestler, arrives in Snakeville and stands ready to defend his title against all comers. Bloggie *(Turpin)* meets him on the street and, not knowing who he is, starts a fight. The result is that the champ sends Bloggie a challenge. Bloggie immediately starts training for the match. In the ring, he wins the first fall and Hotch the second. Bloggie wins the third and deciding fall by tickling the bottom of his opponent's feet and, amid cheers, is carried away on the shoulders of his admirers.

A Christmas Revenge — December 18, 1915 *(Two Reels)*
Director: G. M. Anderson
Broncho Billy Anderson, Marguerite Clayton *(His Sweetheart)*, Lloyd Bacon *(His Rival)*, Ben Turpin, Harry Todd, Robert McKenzie.
"Mr. Anderson repeats his familiar impersonation of Broncho Billy, and Ben Turpin and Harry Todd introduce several minutes of their always welcome comedy." *MPW*

In the Spring of 1916, Turpin joins Vogue Comedy Company while Essanay continued to release a backlog of his comedies, some new and some reissues.

•*A Safe Proposition* — November 8, 1916
Director: Roy Clements
Ben Turpin *(Burglar)*, Harry Todd *(His Accomplice)*, Victor Potel *(Policeman)*, Belle Mitchell
Ben decides to become a burglar. First thing is to find a place to rob until he notices a homeowner installing a safe. The movers go from house to yard, back and forth, as the man's wife, who doesn't want the safe, drives them out with bribes. The man raises the tip each time and the movers continue their trips with increasing profit. That night, Ben and his accomplice break into the house, only to find the safe empty. So they fill it with cigars, wines, tapestry, and everything else available. Before a squad of police captures the burglars, the lady of the house presents Ben and Harry with a load of cash for removing the safe.

Some Bravery — November 22, 1916
Director: Roy Clements
Ben Turpin *(The Brave Bellhop)*
The bellhop gets a job in an eccentric family hotel, where every guest seems to have a penchant for ice water. Amid numerous other experiences, he manages to saturate everyone with ice water. Then a fire breaks out and the bellhop sees his chance to deliver his water in wholesale lots to the guests with a hose. Instead of winning their indignation, however, he is acclaimed a hero.

A Waiting Game — December 6, 1916
Director: Roy Clements
Ben Turpin *(The Waiter)*, Lloyd Bacon, Ruth Saville, Belle Mitchell
Ben, attired none too elegantly, enters a high class café and orders everything on the menu. He cannot pay for it and a riot ensues. The manager thinks he has solved the affair by letting Turpin work out his check as a waiter, but several costly errors prove this an unwise decision.

Taking the Count — December 20 or 21, 1916
Ben Turpin *(The Cabin Steward)*, Harry Todd, Eva McKenzie, Robert McKenzie, Lloyd Bacon, Belle Mitchell, Carrie Turpin, Leo White, Margaret Joslin
A crowd of society women come to the wharf to get the Count on his arrival. Ben and another cabin steward are the only men to be seen in dress clothes, so they are promptly mistaken for the Count and his companion. The pair is entertained extensively and society tolerates their wild antics and believes them highly amusing. However, the police locate them and the two find themselves back on the ship waiting at the captain's table after their one plunge into the whirl of society.

•*A Burlesque on Carmen* — April 22, 1916 *(Four Reels)*
Director: Charles Chaplin
Charlie Chaplin, Edna Purviance, John Rand, Wesley Ruggles, Ben Turpin, Leo White, Bud Jamison, May White
Originally scheduled as a two-reeler for December 1915, but pulled & padded by Essanay with added footage of Turpin and others directed by Leo White.

Two Laughs — July 21, 1917 *(Two Reels)*
Director: Roy Clements/Wallace Beery
Ben Turpin, Lloyd Bacon, Ruth Saville, Victor Potel, Bob McKenzie, Eva McKenzie, Belle Mitchell. Two earlier one-reelers tied together to appear as one film.

Pete's Pants — July 28, 1917 *(Two Reels)*
Director: Roy Clements/Wallace Beery
Harry Todd, Margaret Joslin, Ben Turpin, Victor Potel
Two earlier one-reelers tied together to appear as one film.

Vogue-Mutual
(One Reel each unless noted)

National Nuts — May 28, 1916
Director: Jack Dillon
Ben Turpin, Paddy McQuire, Rena Rogers, Arthur Moon, Jack Gaines, Ed Sedgwick

Nailing a Lie — June 4, 1916
Director: Jack Dillon
Ben Turpin, Paddy McQuire, Rena Rogers, Arthur Moon, Jack Gaines

His Blowout — June 11, 1916 (rereleased circa 1921/22 as *The Plumbers)*
Director: Jack Dillon
Ben Turpin *(Bloggie)*, Paddy McQuire *(Bungling Bill)*, Rena Rogers *(Dora)*, Arthur Moon *(The Crook)*, Jack Connelly, Ed Sedgwick, Louise Owens
Bungling Bill and Bloggie read that a rich plumber is willing to let two men conduct his business while he is on his honeymoon. They apply, interest Murphy, and he gives them the business. Murphy, seeing he has been buncoed, tries to follow the girl, but Slim knocks him off the running board of the car. Arriving home, Slim and Dora find that a pipe is leaking. The janitor phones for Bloggie and Bill. Bill's efforts to stop the water prove unavailing. He sees the stolen necklace and purloins it and starts out with Slim following him. From now on, the complicated action is fast and furious. The picture closes in a gale of fun. (Working title: *Doctor the Leak)*

•*The Delinquent Bridegrooms* — June 18, 1916
(EYE Film Institute)
Director: Jack Dillon
Ben Turpin, Paddy McQuire, Rena Rogers, Arthur Moon, Jack Gaines, Ed Laurie, Louise Owens, Margaret Templeton

The Iron Mitt — June 25, 1916
Director: Jack Dillon
Ben Turpin *(Bloggie)*, Paddy McQuire *(Bungling Bill)*, Jack Gaines *(The Iron Saw)*, Ed Laurie *(A Multi-Billionaire)*, Rena Rogers *(His Daughter)*, Arthur Moon *(The Detective)*

Just for a Kid — July 2, 1916 (rereleased circa 1921/22 as *The Leading Man*)
Director: Jack Dillon
Ben Turpin *(Bloggie)*, Paddy McQuire *(Bungling Bill)*, Rena Rogers *(Rena)*, Arthur Moon *(Her Husband)*, Jack Gaines *(Joshua Elliot)*, Ed Laurie *(The Doctor)*
Bill and Bloggie read in the paper that a "Better Babies Contest" is going to be held and that $50,000 will be offered to the mother of the prize infant. The rogues steal the offspring of Mr. and Mrs. Moon and, after many complications, Bloggie, dressed in women's clothes, pushes a perambulator to the contest. Bloggie wins the prize with his "son Oscar," only to find that the money is offered to encourage the birth of babies in China and for this reason the $50,000 is paid in coin of that realm, equal in America to about 17 cents.

Hired and Fired — July 9, 1916
Director: Jack Dillon
Ben Turpin *(Bloggie)*, Paddy McQuire *(Bungling Bill)*, Arthur Moon *(The Director)*, Rena Rogers *(The Leading Lady)*, Jack Gaines *(The Manager)*, Ed Laurie *(Prop Man)*
Bungling Bill and Bloggie, youths out of work, through the advertising columns of a newspaper secure employment at the Vogue Studio. There they steal one of the property men's lunch and the theft is blamed on the tragedian, who is always complaining of hunger. The director calls Bloggie to play his part. He has a long wavy mustache, which Bill ties to one of the scene supporters after hitting him with a dumbbell without satisfactory results. As the director calls for action, Bloggie enters the set, but falls, tearing off his mustache, and the scene is marred. After many trials, he is discharged and for his revenge, he turns the fire hose loose in the studio with disastrous effects on everybody.

A Deep Sea Liar — July 16, 1916 (rereleased circa 1921/22 as *The Landlubber*)
Director: Jack Dillon *Story:* Robert A. Dillon
Ben Turpin *(Bloggie)*, Paddy McQuire *(Bungling Bill)*, Rena Rogers *(Rena)*, Arthur Moon *(the Agent)*, Jack Gaines *(Admiral Shimsky)*
Admiral Shimsky comes to confer with Murray Sinclair, the Moth Ball Magnate, regarding the latter's invention, which borders on the submarine. At the hotel, the head of the Limburger Navy is quite a social favorite. Moon, a government agent in love with Rena, the inventor's daughter, has unsuccessfully tried to buy the invention. He employs two men to answer an ad which the hotel has inserted, stating that they need the services of two ex-sailors to act in ship-shape order while attending the wants of the Admiral. Events move rapidly to an uproariously funny ending.
   "The scenes are short and jerky, giving much of the action a meaningless character. The plot, which might have shown up to better advantage, is lost in the abrupt change of scenes. This is a rapid fire, slapstick comedy, in which the complications are too involved to detail." *MPW*

Bungling Bill's Dress Suit — July 30, 1916
Director: Jack Dillon
Paddy McQuire, Ben Turpin, Gypsy Abbott, Arthur Moon, Elsie Greeson, Jack Gaines

Vogue-Mutual
(Two Reels each unless noted)

For Ten Thousand Bucks — July 23, 1916 (rereleased circa 1921/22 as *Forced to Work*)
Director: Jack Dillon
Ben Turpin *(Bloggie)*, Paddy McQuire *(Bungling Bill)*, Arthur Moon *(Jack Braveheart)*, Gypsy Abbott *(His Sweetheart)*, Jack Gaines *(Malcolm Valentine)*, Nell Farrin *(Carmen)*, Ed Laurie *(Ignatz Daschundsky)*
After Bill and Bloggie steal a flivver, they are pursued by the police and take refuge in the apartment of Carmen Sapho, an adventuress, who hires them to steal a shipment of $10,000 from the Limited Express for her. They jump on the train and are arrested for trespassing and forced to take jobs as strike breakers. Dressed as brakemen, they collect the tickets from the passengers with disastrous results. Carmen is determined to get the money and trails the owner to his house. She notices a bag he carries and suspects it contains the money. She substitutes another bag for it, going to his office and making the exchange. As she is about to leave Valentine, the villain enters and snatches the wrong bag after knocking out the owner. Both Carmen and Valentine board the train and a fight for the bag ensues. Adventures galore befall the pair until finally the bag is returned to its owner and Bloggie and Bungling Bill are rewarded for their efforts.

Lost and Found — August 6, 1916
Director: Rube Miller
Ben Turpin, Rube Miller, Paddy McQuire, Lillian Hamilton
Two crooks see Rube and Ben, who have just arrived in town with a bag of money. The crooks follow them and steal their bag, taking it with them to their rendezvous. The rubes are unable to locate the crooks and finally land in a park bemoaning their loss. While in the park, they read an advertisement for shoe clerks. They apply for the positions and are employed. Rube is given the women's department and Ben the men's. Ben complains to the manager, demands the women's side, but is refused. A girl whom they had met in the park happens along and comes in to purchase a pair of shoes. Ben insists upon waiting on her and Rube, refusing to let him, starts an argument while the girl intercedes. The girl's sweetheart comes into the store and recognizes Rube and Ben as the two men he saw making love to his girl in the park. Thinking they are still trying to make love, he becomes angry and starts an argument. The manager, hearing the uproar, comes in in time to see them start a fight that tears up his store. He goes for the police and returns with three large officers, who mix up in the fighting. Unable to win against those odds, Ben and Rube flee and a chase ensues. The chase leads Rube and Ben to a barroom, where they discover the two crooks with their bag of money. They seize the bag and start a struggle. Meantime, the manager of the shoe store, lover, and girl reach the exterior of the saloon; Rube and Ben are thrown against the brick wall, going through upon their pursuers amidst a falling of bricks and dust.

Some Liars — August 13, 1916 (rereleased circa 1921/22 as *Why Men Leave Home*)
Director: Rube Miller
Ben Turpin, Rube Miller, Gypsy Abbott, Eva Thatcher, Owen Evans

•*The Stolen Booking* — September 3, 1916 (rereleased circa 1921/22 as *Brainstorming)* (BFI)
Director: Rube Miller
Ben Turpin, Rube Miller, Ed Laurie, Larry Bowes

•*Doctoring a Leak* — September 17, 1916 (rereleased circa 1921/22 as *A Total Loss)*
Director: Rube Miller
Ben Turpin, Rube Miller, Lillian Hamilton

•*Poultry a la Mode* — October 1, 1916
(rereleased circa 1921/22 as *The Harem*, also simply known as *Poultry)*
Director: Rube Miller
Ben Turpin, Rube Miller, Lillian Hamilton *(Omaho)*, Walter Rogers *(Mohammed Alo)*
Rube and Ben are neighbors; one raises ducks on one side of their fence and the other raises geese on his side. They are caught flirting with a pretty girl by their wives and are warned to attend to their fowl. Rube and Ben get into a quarrel and dump their water buckets on each other. Meanwhile, a duck and goose waddle off and find the perfect watering hole in the home of a Sultan. They hasten back to tell the rest of their flocks, but not until Rube and Ben have followed them and behold a wonderful sight. The water in the pool had been treated with a magic liquid that turns the fowl into beautiful maidens. At the sight of this and after a rough ejection by the home owner Turk, the boys hurry home to bring all their ducks and geese, which are magically changed into a multitude of laughing girls. After the Turk breaks out of a trunk the boys had locked him in, chaos abounds. Then the police arrive and it's a rude awakening for the boys by their wives. Clips from this title have circulated as *The Harem* and *Magic Pool.*

Ducking a Discord — October 15, 1916 (rereleased circa 1921/22 as *The Hero)*
Director: Rube Miller
Ben Turpin, Rube Miller, Lillian Hamilton
Rube's wife is an expert at the Dutch Inn and Out. The house is filled with the music of the old accordion from dawn to dark. He decides to get rid of her, puts her in a bag, and throws her in the river. She is rescued by Ben, who loves her devotedly. Together, they plan to give Rube a scare. They cover their faces with flour and she walks in on her husband in the midst of his lovemaking with Lillian. He thinks she is a spirit. Another time, when the pickpocket gang to which Rube belongs meets at their rendezvous, she appears again and succeeds in crabbing the game forever for her erring husband.

He Died and He Didn't — October 29, 1916
Director: Rube Miller
Ben Turpin *(The Gambler)*, Rube Miller *(The Prospector)*, Lillian Hamilton *(The Girl)*
The prospector enters the western dance hall and, upon seeing the gambler, takes a mallet and apparently kills the man. He is captured by the posse and, as he is dangling from a tree, tells the story of how, years before, he and Ben had been in Texas together. Ben fleeced Rube of all his savings, robbed him of his girl, and disappeared. As Rube is about to breathe his last word, a message is heard that Ben has recovered. The posse cuts Rube

down and takes him back. He discovers that the girl is still with Ben and is the mother of seven urchins. Ben tries to rid himself of this domestic burden, but Rube flees on his trick mule and has the last laugh on the gambler. (Working title: *Revenge Is Sweet*)

•*Picture Pirates (#38)* — November 12, 1916 (rereleased circa 1921/22 as *High Art*)
Director: Rube Miller
(BFI)
Ben Turpin, Rube Miller *(The Ne'er-Do-Wells)*, Lillian Hamilton, Rosie Rosee *(Their Wives)*, Larry Bowes *(The Picture Pirate)*, (Paddy McQuire?)
Rube and Ben's wives are waitresses. An art collector purchases a rare picture and the "picture pirate," representing himself as another collector, calls on the first collector. As he is leaving the place, Rube and Ben try to pick his pockets and, admonishing them as amateurs, he tells them to join in with him and try to steal the picture. They take the art collector's wife with them to the same café wherein their wives are waitresses. Ben and Rube leave her there and hasten to her home to steal a copy of the picture, the owner having hid the original. They also drink some poisoned whiskey left for them and fall into a fit. Later, the "picture pirate" pays Rube and Ben for the picture, thinking it is the original. *MPW*: The action is in burlesque style and does not get up much humor. Some of the knockabout scenes are fairly amusing, but as a whole, the number is not strong.

The Wicked City — December 3, 1916 (rereleased circa 1921/22 as *The Porter*)
Director: Robin Williamson
Ben Turpin *(The Proprietor)*, Gypsy Abbott *(The Waitress)*, Paddy McQuire *(The Cook)*, Margaret Templeton *(His Wife)*, Arthur Moon *(The Drummer)*
Ben, proprietor of a small town restaurant and in love with his waitress, presents her with an engagement ring. About this time, the waitress goes to the city to buy her trousseau. The cook receives word that a fortune awaits him in the city and he and his wife leave. When the waitress arrives, she finds that her aunt is not in town, so puts up at the Chargealot Hotel. A drummer also decides to stay at the same place, but his room is given by mistake to the waitress. The cook and his wife get the rooms adjoining the waitress' and the night after, Ben comes to the hotel, having just sold his restaurant. While there, things happen that keep everyone jumping and finally a wild chase ensues, which results in the drummer and waitress bungling into the home of a preacher, where they are married.

Shot in the Fracas (#76) — December 10, 1916 (rereleased circa 1921/22 as *The Janitor*)
Director: Rube Miller
Ben Turpin *(The Janitor)*, Margaret Templeton *(His Wife)*, Paddy McQuire *(The Peddler)*, Arthur Moon *(The Husband)*, Gypsy Abbott *(His Wife)*
Arthur Moon, a champion archer who has a medal that he values highly, lives in a fashionable apartment with his wife, Gypsy. Ben, the janitor of the building who believes in letting his wife do all the work, is in the hall sweeping when all of the trouble over the medal takes place. Paddy, the peddler, seeing the curtains in Arthur's window swaying and, thinking someone is flirting with him, climbs up the fire escape and enters Moon's apartment. Here he spies the medal and pockets it just before Moon's wife comes in. Paddy hides behind a screen and furtively watches Gypsy practice archery. One of her arrows hits Ben, who

is brought into her room to recover. Arthur comes home and, finding Ben in the house, becomes jealous. He misses the medal and begins searching. Paddy manages to slip it into Ben's pocket and it is found. The medal falls into the hands of all concerned and finally to its rightful owners, but not before a two-story brick factory building is destroyed and Paddy takes a sail through the clouds.

Treed — December 17, 1916
Director: Rube Miller
Rube Miller, Harry Huckins, Owen Evans, (Ben Turpin?)

Jealous Jolts — December 31, 1916 (rereleased circa 1921/22 as *A Country Lover)*
Director: Rube Miller
Ben Turpin, Paddy McQuire, Gypsy Abbott, Margaret Templeton, Arthur Moon

A Lisle Bank — January 14, 1917
Director: Rube Miller
Paddy McQuire, Gypsy Abbott Arthur Moon, Edward Laurie, Margaret Templeton, (Ben Turpin?)

A Circus Cyclone (#97) — January 28, 1917
Director: Rube Miller
Ben Turpin, Paddy McQuire, Gypsy Abbott, Margaret Templeton, Arthur Moon

• *The Musical Marvel (#105)* — February 11, 1917 (rereleased circa 1921/22 as *Some Jazz Baby)*
Director: Robin Williamson
Ben Turpin, Gypsy Abbott, Ed Laurie, Arthur Moon

• *The Butcher's Nightmare (#115)* — February 25, 1917 (rereleased circa 1921/22 as *Ben's Wild Dream)*
Director: Robin Williamson
Ben Turpin, Gypsy Abbott, Ed Laurie, Arthur Moon, Margaret Templeton, Fred J. Woodward

• *His Bogus Boast (#159)* — March 10, 1917 (rereleased circa 1921/22 as *A Cheerful Liar)*
Director: Robin Williamson
Ben Turpin, Gypsy Abbott, Ed Laurie, Arthur Moon, Margaret Templeton. Ben in a dual role.

• *A Studio Stampede* — March 24, 1917 (rereleased circa 1921/22 as *Out of Control)*
Director: Robin Williamson
Ben Turpin, Gypsy Abbott *(Dora Darling)*, Ed Laurie *(movie director)*, Arthur Currier, Russell Powell *(gateman)*

• *Why Ben Bolted* — April 7, 1917 (rereleased circa 1921/22 as *He Looked Crooked)*
Director: Robin Williamson
Ben Turpin, Gypsy Abbott, Ed Laurie, Lillian Hamilton (Working title: *Frightened Flirts)*

•*Masked Mirth* — April 21, 1917 (rereleased circa 1921/22 as *The Skyrocket*)
Director: Robin Williamson
(BFI)
Ben Turpin, Lillian Hamilton, Ed Laurie, Arthur Currier, Margaret Templeton, Eugene Shaw

•*Bucking the Tiger* — May 5, 1917
Director: Robin Williamson
(BFI)
Ben Turpin, Lillian Hamilton, Arthur Currier, Ed Laurie, Margaret Templeton

•*Caught in the End (#243)* — May 19, 1917 (rereleased circa 1921/22 as *After the Ball*)
(Library of Congress)
Director: Robin Williamson
Ben Turpin, Lillian Hamilton, Arthur Currier, Ed Laurie, Margaret Templeton

Mack Sennett Keystone-Triangle
(Two Reels each unless noted)

Oriental Love (released 5/27/17)
Director: Walter Wright and/or Clarence Badger
Ora Carew, Joseph Belmont, Joseph Callahan, Nick Cogley, Andy Anderson, Blanche Payson, Edgar Kennedy, Sid Smith, (Ben Turpin?)

Cactus Nell (6/3/17)
Director: Fred Fishback *Assistant Director:* Whitey Sovern *Camera:* J.R. Lockwood
Polly Moran, Wayland Trask, Wallace Beery, Dora Rodgers, Cliff Bowes, Joey Jacobs, Robert Kortman(?), (Ben Turpin?)

Sole Mates (6/4/17, One Reel)
Triangle Komedy
Director: Herman Raymaker *Camera:* Roger Dale Armstrong
Ben Turpin, Florence Clarke, Vivian Edwards, Alfred Gronell

•*A Clever Dummy (6/15/17)*
Director: Herman Raymaker *Assistant Directors:* Robert Kerr & Ferris Hartman
Cinematographer: Elgin Lessley
Ben Turpin *(a janitor)*, James Donnelly *(an inventor)*, Claire Anderson *(his daughter)*, James Delano *(the partner)*, Juanita Hansen *(showgirl)*, Chester Conklin *(stagehand)*, Wallace Beery *(theater owner)*, Joseph Belmont, Eva Thatcher *(in audience)*
(Working title: *The Automaton Figure*)

•*Lost — A Cook (8/12/17)*
Director: Fred Fishback(?)
Mack Swain, Ethel Teare, Joey Jacobs, Maude Wayne, Cliff Bowes, Sylvia Ashton, Mal St. Clair, Ben Turpin

•*The Pawnbroker's Heart (8/19/17)*
(UCLA Film and Television Archive)
Director: Eddie Cline(?)
Chester Conklin, Glen Cavender, Caroline Rankin, Peggy Pearce, Ben Turpin, Alice Maison (Working title: *A Safe Arrangement*)

Mack Sennett-Paramount
(Two Reels each unless noted)

•*A Bedroom Blunder* MS1 *(10/7/17)* (rereleased in 1923 as *Room 23*)
Director: Eddie Cline *Camera:* Phil Whitman
Charlie Murray, Mary Thurman, Wayland Trask, Pat Forde *(aka Frank Terry)*, Eva Thatcher, Glen Cavender, James Donnelly, Wallace Beery, Tom Kennedy, Gonda Durand, Phyllis Haver, Roxanna McGowan, Vera Steadman, Marvel Rea, Eddie Cline. Ben Turpin in small role as desk clerk at the Sea Shell Inn, second reel.

•*Roping Her Romeo* MS2 *(10/21/17)*
Director: Fred Fishback *Assistant Director:* Whitey Sovern *Camera:* Hans Koenekamp
Polly Moran, Ben Turpin *(Honest Eyed Jack, A Poor Butterfly)*, Slim Summerville, Ethel Teare, Eva Thatcher, Wayland Trask, James Donnelly, Gonda Durand, Eleanor Field, Phyllis Haver, Pat Kelly, Roxana McGowan, Marvel Rea, Edith Valk, Vera Steadman (Working title: *A Lovesick Bandit*)

•*Are Waitresses Safe?* MS4 *(11/18/17)*
Director: Victor Heerman *Camera:* Fred Jackman
Louise Fazenda, Ben Turpin *(Who Loved Her So)*, Slim Summerville, Glen Cavender, Tony O'Sullivan, Cliff Bowes, Wayland Trask, Jack Cooper, Grover Ligon, Al McKinnon, Wallace Beery, Tom Kennedy, Phyllis Haver, Gonda Durand, Laura LaVarnie, Roxanna McGowan, Gene Rogers, Hal Prieste

That Night MS6 *(12/16/17)*
Director: Eddie Cline *Camera:* Fred Jackman
Charles Murray, Mary Thurman, Wayland Trask, Wallace Beery, Vera Steadman, Phyllis Haver, Gene Rogers, Roxanna McGowan, Marvel Rea, Eva Thatcher, Glen Cavender, Tom Kennedy, Pat Kelly, (Ben Turpin?)

Taming Target Center MS7 *(12/30/17)*
Director: William S. Campbell *Camera:* Fred Jackman
Polly Moran *(the new sheriff)*, Ben Turpin *(the sheriff)*, Gonda Durand *(his leading vampire)*, Tom Kennedy *(cafe proprietor)*, Larry McGrath *(the parson)*, Gene Rogers, George Binns, Marvel Rea, Grover Ligon, Frank J. Coleman

Watch Your Neighbor MS10 *(2/10/18)*
Director: Victor Heerman *Camera:* Fred Jackman
Charles Murray, Mary Thurman, Wayland Trask, Gene Rogers, Edgar Kennedy, Frank J. Coleman, Harry Booker, Cliff Bowes, Billy Armstrong, Albert Gillespie, Marvel Rea, Vera Steadman, Roxanna McGowan, (Ben Turpin?)

•*Sheriff Nell's Tussle* MS12 *(2/24/1918)*
(UCLA Film and Television Archive)
Director: William S. Campbell *Camera:* Fred Jackman & Kenneth MacLean
Polly Moran, Ben Turpin *(Still After Her)*, Billy Armstrong, Gonda Durand, Frank J. Coleman, Al McKinnon, Gene Rogers, Pat Kelly

Saucy Madeline MS15 *(4/21/1918)*
Director: F. Richard Jones *Camera:* Fred Jackman & J. R. Lockwood
Polly Moran, Ben Turpin *(A Rolling Stone Out of Work)*, Charles Lynn, Jack Cooper, Frank J. Coleman, Harry Gribbon, Wayland Trask, George Jeske, Gonda Durand, Alice Maison, Sloppy Gray

•*His Smothered Love* MS16 *(5/5/1918)*
(Museum of Modern Art)
Director: Eddie Cline *Camera:* Fred Jackman & Phil Whitman
Chester Conklin, Harry Gribbon, Marie Prevost, Jack Cooper, Laura LaVarnie, Alice Maison, Paddy McQuire, Wayland Trask, Marvel Rea, Phyllis Haver, Vera Steadman, Frank J. Coleman, Slim Summerville, Erle Kenton, Gonda Durand, Billy Gilbert. Turpin in small role as Conklin's messenger boy.

The Battle Royal MS17 *(5/19/1918)*
Director: F. Richard Jones *Camera:* Fred Jackman & J. R. Lockwood
Ben Turpin *(After a Wife)*, Charles Lynn, Polly Moran, Wayland Trask, Fanny Kelly, Al McKinnon, George Jeske, Glen Cavender, Abdul Maljan, Teddy, Pat Kelly, Billy Gilbert, Eva Thatcher, Hal Haig Prieste

•*Love Loops the Loop* MS18 *(6/2/1918)*
(Museum of Modern Art)
Director: Walter Wright *Camera:* Fred Jackman & Hans Koenekamp
Charlie Murray, Mary Thurman, Wayland Trask, Harry Booker, Laura LaVarnie, Abdul, Paddy McQuire, Gene Rogers, Al McKinnon, Bert Gillespie, Roxanna McGowan, Phyllis Haver, Vera Steadman. Ben in small role as cafe bandleader.

Two Tough Tenderfeet MS19 *(6/16/1918)*
Director: F. Richard Jones **Camera:** Fred Jackman & J. R. Lockwood
Ben Turpin *(a crooked tenderfoot)*, Charles Lynn *(his pal)*, Polly Moran *(the sheriff of Crooked Bend)*, Bert Roach *(owns the town & wants to own the sheriff)*, Laura LaVarnie *(the sheriff's mother)*, Jack Cooper, Wayland Trask, Hank Mann, Paddy McQuire, Roxanna McGowan, Billy Gilbert, Ed Kennedy

Her Screen Idol MS20 *(7/1/18)*
Director: Eddie Cline **Camera:** Fred Jackman & J. R. Lockwood
Louise Fazenda, Ford Sterling, Jack Cooper, Edgar Kennedy, Glen Cavender, Gene Rogers, Laura LaVarnie, Marvel Rea, Roxanna McGowan, Marie Prevost, Teddy, (Ben Turpin?)

She Loved Him Plenty MS23 *(8/11/1918)*
Director: F. Richard Jones **Camera:** Fred Jackman & J. R. Lockwood
Ben Turpin *(A Fickle Youth)*, Charles Lynn, Polly Moran, Marie Prevost, Edgar Kennedy, Al McKinnon, Gonda Durand, Harriet Hammond, Phyllis Haver, Pat Kelly, Roxanna McGowan, Eva Thatcher, George Gray

– *Sleuths!* MS26 *(9/22/18)*
Director: F. Richard Jones **Camera:** Fred Jackman & J. R. Lockwood
Ben Turpin *(Eagle Eye Jack, Detective)*, Charles Lynn, Marie Prevost, Tom Kennedy, Chester Conklin, Bert Roach, Al McKinnon, Eva Thatcher, Pat Kelly

It's A Cinch (circa 9/10/1918, One Reel)
Liberty Loan Special
Director: ?
Louise Fazenda, Ford Sterling, Chester Conklin, Ben Turpin *(selling bonds)*, Charlie Lynn, Phyllis Haver, Tom Kennedy, Pat Kelly, Mal St. Clair, Dave Anderson

Whose Little Wife Are You? MS28 *(11/17/1918)*
Director: Eddie Cline **Camera:** Fred & Floyd Jackman
Charlie Murray, Eva Thatcher, Joseph "Baldy" Belmont, Alice Lake, Wayland Trask, Mary Thurman, Paddy McQuire, Tom Kennedy, Teddy, Pepper, Harriet Hammond, Phyllis Haver, Laura LaVarnie, Marie Prevost, Vera Steadman; Ben & Charles Lynn in a surprise appearance, floating on raft through Murray's flooded pharmacy.

Hide and Seek, Detectives MS31 *(12/15/1918)*
Director: Eddie Cline **Camera:** Fred Jackman and Phil Whitman
Ben Turpin *(A Detective)*, Charles Lynn, Marie Prevost, Gene Rogers, Tom Kennedy, Al McKinnon, Paddy McQuire, Charles Murray
"It is not expected that the ingenuity and fun-making ability of Sennett will always flow in a torrent, though the font has seemed inexhaustible at times, but he manages to introduce some new features in each release, even if compelled to rely on older situations for his rough-and-tumble style of production. A farcical presentation of Turpin and Lynn as detectives, very swift in action, but lacking in true humorous situations. Exaggeration that

it is, there is some humor and it is to be hoped that the human element, that of characterization, will broaden in future releases. There is not enough of it and almost too much activity by trick work with the camera for a modern audience. There is, however, plenty of material in the farce for good laughs." *MPW*

Cupid's Day Off MS35 *(1/12/19)*
Director: Eddie Cline *Camera:* Fred Jackman & Hans Koenekamp
Ben Turpin & Charles Lynn *(A Couple of Shoe Men)*, Alice Lake, Tom Kennedy, Eva Thatcher, Bothwell Browne, Bert Roach, Hughie Mack, Abdul Maljan, Harriet Hammond

•*Photoplay Magazine Screen Supplement* #2 *(2/5/19, One Reel)*
(EYE Film Institute)
Director & Story: Julian Johnson *Producer:* James R. Quirk for Educational Films
Ben Turpin and Paddy McQuire take their morning ride to the studio on the cowcatcher of a trolley. We also view them warming themselves in the rays of the shivering sun in the studio. Also, Wm. S. Hart on Broadway; Thomas Ince directing Charles Ray; Bessie Love; Cleo Ridgely and husband James Horne with their twins; Paul Powell, Eddie Dillon; Helen Holmes and husband J.P. McGowan and their adopted daughter, Dorothy. Photos of Doug Fairbanks and Geraldine Farrar at age five are also shown.

•*East Lynne with Variations* MS37 *(2/23/19)*
(EYE Film Institute)
Director: Eddie Cline
Ben Turpin *(A Matinee Idol)*, Charles Lynn *(the villain)*, Marie Prevost *(the girl)*, Tom Kennedy, Bobby Dunn, Alice Lake, Bert Roach, Ford Sterling, Marvel Rea, Billy Armstrong, James Finlayson

•*The Village Smithy* MS38 *(3/9/19)*
(Filmoteca Espanola)
Director: F. Richard Jones *Camera:* Fred Jackman & J. R. Lockwood
Louise Fazenda, Chester Conklin, James Finlayson, Kalla Pasha, Paddy McQuire, Billy Armstrong, Al McKinnon, Fanny Kelly, Ben Turpin (cameo)

The Foolish Age MS42 *(4/13/19)*
Director: F. Richard Jones *Camera:* Fred Jackman & J. R. Lockwood
Louise Fazenda, Chester Conklin, James Finlayson, Phyllis Haver, Kalla Pasha, Paddy McQuire, Garry Odell. Ben Turpin & Charles Lynn in a small role as a couple sour musicians

When Love Is Blind MS40 *(5/11/19)*
Director: Eddie Cline *Camera:* Fred Jackman & Phil Whitman
Ben Turpin & Charles Lynn *(Men About Town)*, Alfred McKinnon *(a detective)*, Marvel Rea *(his wife)*, Phyllis Haver *(a blonde)*, Marie Prevost *(a brunette)*, Erle C. Kenton, Gene Rogers, Kalla Pasha, John Rand, Charlie Murray, Pepper

Love's False Faces MS41 *(5/25/19)*
Director: F. Richard Jones *Camera:* Fred Jackman & J. R. Lockwood
Chester Conklin, Marie Prevost, James Finlayson, Kalla Pasha, Billy Armstrong, Charlotte
Mineau, Edgar Kennedy, Eddie Gribbon. Ben & Charles Lynn in a small role as a couple
of freeloading drinkers.

No Mother to Guide Him MS45 *(6/8/19 or 6/22/19)*
Director: Erle Kenton & Mal St. Clair *Camera:* Fred Jackman & Hans Koenekamp
Ben Turpin *(A Happy Married Man)*, Myrtle Lind *(his wife)*, Charles Lynn *(the other man)*,
Baldy Belmont *(a true friend)*, Isabelle Keep, Billy Armstrong, Fanny Kelly, Edgar Kennedy

Trying to Get Along MS46 *(7/6/19)*
Director: F. Richard Jones *Camera:* Fred Jackman & J. R. Lockwood
Charlie Murray, Charlotte Mineau, Kalla Pasha, James Finlayson, Fanny Kelly, Ford
Sterling, Eva Thatcher, Eddie Gribbon, Baldy Belmont, Harriet Hammond, Teddy, Harry
Gribbon, Isabelle Keep, Kathryn McGuire, Gladys Whitfield. Turpin & Charlie Lynn in
a small role as a couple of diners.

Mack Sennett for Sol Lesser

•*Yankee Doodle in Berlin* #31 *(7/28/19, Five Reels)*
Director: F. Richard Jones
Bothwell Browne, Ford Sterling, Marie Prevost, Mal St. Clair, Bert Roach, Ben Turpin
(German Soldier), Charlie Murray, Chester Conklin, Edgar Kennedy, Kalla Pasha, Frank
Hayes, Joseph Belmont, Fanny Kelly, Eva Thatcher, Wayland Trask, Al McKinnon, Jim
Finlayson, Charles Lynn (Working title: *The Kaiser's Last Squeal*)

Mack Sennett-Paramount
(Continued; Two Reels each unless noted)

Treating 'em Rough MS49? *(8/3/19)*
Director: Fred Jackman *Camera:* Fred & George Jackman
Louise Fazenda, Baldy Belmont, Pat Kelly, Edgar Kennedy, Billy Bevan, Ford Sterling,
Jack Ackroyd, Jimmy Finlayson. Ben Turpin cameo as a drunk.

•*The Dentist* MS50? *(8/17/19)*
(Filmarchiv Austria)
Director: F. Richard Jones *Camera:* Fred Jackman & J. R. Lockwood
Charlie Murray *(the dentist)*, Charlotte Mineau *(his wife)*, Eddie Gribbon, Kalla Pasha *(her
disreputable brothers)*, James Finlayson *(a real estate agent)*, Marie Prevost *(his stenographer)*,
Fanny Kelly *(his wife)*, Hughie Mack, Baldy Belmont, Phyllis Haver, Pat Kelly, Garry Odell,
Pepper the cat. Turpin cameo as an eccentric dental patient.

Uncle Tom Without a Cabin MS48 *(8/31/19)*
Director: Ray Hunt *Camera:* Fred Jackman & Perry Evans
Ben Turpin *(A man of many parts)*, Charles Conklin *(the villain)*, Marie Prevost *(the leading lady)*, Ford Sterling *(a complimentary audience)*, Eva Thatcher *(a critic)*, James Finlayson *(a stage-door Johnnie)*, Teddy *(a bloodhound)*, Billy Bevan, Eddie Gribbon, Kalla Pasha, John Rand, Isabelle Keep, Kathryn McGuire, Dave Anderson, Gladys Whitfield

•*Up in Alf's Place* MS53 *(10/12/19)*
(UCLA Film and Television Archive)
Director: F. Richard Jones *Camera:* Fred Jackman & J. R. Lockwood
Charlie Murray, Harriet Hammond, Charlotte Mineau, Kalla Pasha, Jim Finlayson, Fanny Kelly, Billy Armstrong, Gordon Lewis, Marvin Lobach, John Rand, Grover Ligon, Edgar Kennedy, Dave Anderson, Mildred June, Thelma Hill, Kathryn McGuire

•*Salome Vs. Shenandoah* MS54 *(10/26/19)*
(Filmoteca Espanola, Madrid)
Directors: Erle Kenton & Ray Grey
Ben Turpin *(John the Baptist & A Confederate Spy)*, Charlie Lynn, Phyllis Haver, Charlie Murray, Marie Prevost, Eddie Gribbon, Ford Sterling, Eva Thatcher, Harry Gribbon, Billy Bevan, Al Cooke, Elva Diltz, Fanny Kelly, Alice Maison, Kathryn McGuire, Bert Roach, Charles Murray, Annette DeGandis, Sibye Trevilla, Gladys Whitfield

A Lady's Tailor MS51 *(12/7/19)*
Directors: Erle Kenton & Ray Grey *Camera:* Fred Jackman & Vic Scheurich
Ford Sterling, Bert Roach, Harriet Hammond, Eva Thatcher, Billy Bevan, Kathryn McGuire, Phyllis Haver, John Rand, Myrtle Lind, Ben Turpin cameo.

The Speak-Easy MS58 *(12/21/19)*
Director: F. Richard Jones *Camera:* Fred Jackman & J.R. Lockwood
Charlie Murray, Fanny Kelly, Marie Prevost, Eddie Gribbon, Garry Odell, Pat Kelly, Baldy Belmont, Al Cooke, James Finlayson, Bert Roach, George O'Hara, Ben Turpin cameo as a drunk in speak-easy.

The Star Boarder MS59 *(1/4/20)*
Director: James Davis *Camera:* Fred Jackman & Perry Evans
Louise Fazenda *(a kitchen slavey)*, Billy Armstrong *(a gentleman crook)*, Bert Roach *(a boarding housekeeper/barber)*, Harriet Hammond *(a manicurist/Bert's wife)*, John Henry, Jr. *(their baby)*, Billy Bevan *(Armstrong's accomplice)*, Baldy Belmont *(Louise's sweetheart)*, Teddy, Marvin Loback, Kalla Pasha. Ben Turpin cameo as cigar salesman/customer in barbershop.

Movie Stars at Home (released circa April 1920)
Paramount
Ben Turpin, William S. Hart, Charles Ray, and others when not at work. Note: Possibly the same film as *Paramount Screen Supplement #2*

Mack Sennett for United Artists

•*Down on the Farm* #56 *(4/25/20, Five Reels)*
Directors: Erle Kenton & Ray Grey
Camera: Fred Jackman, Perry Evans & Victor Scheurich
Louise Fazenda, Harry Gribbon, James Finlayson, Bert Roach, Marie Prevost, Billy Armstrong, John Henry, Jr., Ben Turpin *(as Marie's husband)*, Eva Thatcher, Phyllis Haver, Mildred June, Harriet Hammond, Teddy, Pepper, Baldy Belmont, Elva Diltz, Fanny Kelly, Pat Kelly, Charles Murray, Kalla Pasha, Virginia Fox, Kathryn McGuire, Jane Allen, Thelma Bates

Mack Sennett for First National

•*Married Life* #57 *(6/15/20, Five Reels)*
Directors: Erle Kenton, Reggie Morris & Ray Griffith *Camera:* Fred Jackman
Ben Turpin *(Rodney St. Clair, A Man's Man)*, Phyllis Haver, James Finlayson, Heinie Conklin, Ford Sterling, Charlotte Mineau, Kalla Pasha, Charlie Murray, Louise Fazenda, Baldy Belmont, Billy Bevan, Al Cooke, Eddie Gribbon, John Henry, Jr, Harriet Hammond, Pat Kelly, Bert Roach, Eva Thatcher. Some footage extant.

Mack Sennett-Paramount
(and others, Two Reels each, unless noted)

You Wouldn't Believe It! MS64? *(6/27/20)*
Director: Erle Kenton *Camera:* Fred Jackman & Victor Scheurich
Heinie Conklin, Marie Prevost, Bert Roach, James Finlayson, Charlotte Mineau, Eddie Gribbon, (Ben Turpin?)

•*The Quack Doctor* MS67 *(7/4/20)*
Directors: George Gray & Billy Bevan *Camera:* Fred Jackman & Perry Evans
Louise Fazenda, Billy Bevan, Gordon Lewis, Gladys Ballard, Dave Anderson, Kalla Pasha, Billy Armstrong, John Henry Jr., Fanny Kelly. Ben Turpin cameo as Justice of the Peace.

Screen Snapshots #7 *(released circa September 1920, One Reel)*
Produced and Distributed by Federated Film Exchange
Ben Turpin with the Sennett Girls, J. Warren Kerrigan, Mabel Normand, Jack Hoxie, Anna Little, Creighton Hale, Mary Hay, Ben Wilson

Screen Snapshots #10 *(released circa October 1920, One Reel)*
Produced and Distributed by Federated Film Exchange
Ben Turpin, Charlie Murray, Fred Niblo and wife Enid Bennett, Omar Locklear, Louise Glaum, Kate Price, Sheldon Lewis, Norma and Constance Talmadge, Virginia Faire, Carter DeHaven, Bobby Vernon, Mildred Harris Chaplin, George Beban

Mack Sennett for First National

•*A Small Town Idol* #75 *(2/20/21, Six reels)*
(Originally scheduled for release *1/16/21*)
Director: Erle C. Kenton *Story:* Ray Griffith & John Grey *Continuity:* Tom Regan
Camera: Fred Jackman, Perry Evans, & Ernie Crockett *Editor:* Allen McNeil
Costumes: Violet Schofield
Ben Turpin, Phyllis Haver, Marie Prevost, Charlie Murray, James Finlayson, Dot Farley, Bert Roach, Billy Bevan, George O'Hara, Lige Conley, Kalla Pasha, Eddie Gribbon, Charles "Heinie" Conklin, Al Cooke, Fanny Kelly, Pat Kelly, Bud Ross, Andy Clyde, Gordon Lewis, John Rand, Gary Odell, Harriet Hammond, Mildred June, Marvin Lobach, Kewpie Morgan, Ramon Novarro, Derelys Perdue, Gladys Whitfield. Rereleased in 1930 and again by Vitaphone in 1939 in two reels.

Associated Producers-First National
(and others, Two Reels each unless noted)

•*She Sighed by the Seaside* MS69 *(5/22/21)*
(Lobster Films, France)
Director: Erle C. Kenton *Camera:* Fred Jackman, C.G. Crane, & Victor Scheurich
Ben Turpin *(A Saver of Lives)*, Marie Prevost, James Finlayson, Heinie Conklin, Bert Roach, Charlotte Mineau, Tiny Ward, Lige Conley, Jack Ackroyd, Al Cooke, Jane Allen, Thelma Bates, Elva Diltz, Virginia Fox, Isabelle Keep, Kathryn McGuire, Gladys Whitfield, Irene Tiver.

PG 181

•*Home Talent* #91 *(6/19/21, Five Reels)*
Director: Mack Sennett *Camera:* Fred Jackman & Perry Evans
Roman Sequences Camera: James Abbe
Ben Turpin *(A Stranded Actor)*, Phyllis Haver, Charles Murray, James Finlayson, Dot Farley, Eddie Gribbon, Kalla Pasha, Kathryn McGuire, Harriet Hammond, Billy Bevan, Joseph Belmont, Jane Allen, Virginia Fox, Mildred June, Pat Kelly, Kathryn McGuire, Irene Tiver. Some footage extant. (Working title: *Furnished Rooms*)

•*Love's Outcast* #88 *(7/3/21)*
Director: Raymond Griffith *Camera:* Fred Jackman & Perry Evans
Ben Turpin, Dot Farley, Kathryn McGuire, James Finlayson, Billy Bevan, Mildred June, Kalla Pasha, Al Cooke, Bud Ross, Jack Richardson. Some footage extant.

Behind the Scenes at the Mack Sennett Studios (released circa September, 1921)
"Interesting and informal glimpses of the Sennett Company, Bathing Girls, Teddy, Pepper, and Ben Turpin," Marie Prevost, Phyllis Haver, Mildred June. A special publicity film not to be confused with the similarly titled *Behind the Scenes* (circa November 1921).

•*Love and Doughnuts* #95 *(9/15/21)*
Director: Roy Del Ruth
Ben Turpin, Phyllis Haver, Billy Bevan, Mildred June, Kewpie Morgan, Franklyn Bond, Al Cooke, Billy Armstrong. Some footage extant.

Screen Snapshots #10 *(released circa October 1921, One Reel)*
Produced and Distributed by Federated Film Exchange
Ben and Ora Carew do a little skit. Others include Charles Chaplin, Mary Pickford, & Doug Fairbanks; Gloria Swanson & Marcus Lowe; Gilda Grey, Dorothy Phillips, and Erich Von Stroheim at work on *Foolish Wives*.

Screen Snapshots #11 *(released circa October 1921, One Reel)*
Produced and Distributed by Federated Film Exchange
Ben & Carrie's appearance in New York is filmed, among other things.

Behind the Scenes (released circa November 1921, One Reel)
Glimpses of the home lives of Marie Prevost, Pauline Frederick, Lois Wilson, Daniel Frohman, Betty Blythe, Ben Turpin, and other popular motion picture stars.

•*Molly O'* #81*(12/1/21, Six Reels)*
Director: F. Richard Jones
Mabel Normand, George Nichols, Anna Hernandez, Albert Hackett, Jack Mulhall, Jacqueline Logan, Ben Deeley, (Turpin not in extant footage, small appearance unverified).

•*Bright Eyes* #92 *(12/24/21)*
Directors: Mal St. Clair & Roy Del Ruth *Camera:* Fred Jackman & George Jackman
Ben Turpin *(A Rural Romeo)*, Phyllis Haver, Billy Bevan, Harriet Hammond, Dot Farley, Bud Ross, George O'Hara, Gordon Lewis, Kalla Pasha, Jack Richardson, Louise Fazenda (Working title: *Tripped at the Altar*)

The Border Line #97 *(1922, never produced)*
Ben Turpin, Phyllis Haver, Billy Bevan, Kewpie Morgan, Al Cooke, Franklyn Bond

Screen Snapshots #17 *(released circa February 1922, One Reel)*
Produced and Distributed by Federated Film Exchange
Shows Ben & Charlie Murray writing a world-beating scenario.

•*Seeing Stars (released 1922, One Reel)*
(Lobster Films)
Produced and Distributed by First National
Features Turpin and other First National stars Buster Keaton, Charlie Chaplin, Jackie Coogan, Charles Ray, and more.

• *Step Forward* #100 *(4/13/22)*
Director: Gus Meins *Camera:* Perry Evans & Ernie Crockett
Ben Turpin *(A Motorman)*, Phyllis Haver, Heinie Conklin, Kewpie Morgan, George
Nichols, Jack Richardson, Dorothy Vernon, Andy Clyde, Kalla Pasha, Fanny Kelly, Andy
Clyde, Pat Kelly, Gordon Lewis, Joe Bordeaux (Working title: *The Robins Nest)*

• *Home Made Movies* #102 *(7/15/22)*
Directors: Ray Grey & Gus Meins *Camera:* Homer Scott & Bob Walters
Editor: Allen McNeil
Ben Turpin, Phyllis Haver, Dot Farley, James Finlayson, George Cooper, Al Cooke, Andy
Clyde, Cecile Evans, Joe Bordeaux. Some footage extant. (Working title: *The Frozen Trail)*

Allied Producers and Distributors

• *The Shriek of Araby* #108 *(4/24/23, Five Reels)*
Director: F. Richard Jones *Camera:* Homer Scott & Bob Walters
Editor: Allen McNeil *Story:* John Grey
Ben Turpin *(The Shriek)*, Kathryn McGuire, Ray Grey, George Cooper, Louis Fronde,
Charles Stevenson, Dick Sutherland, Walter Perry, Kewpie Morgan, Marion Nixon
(Working title: *The Shriek)*

Screen Snapshots #25 *(released circa April 1923, One Reel)*
Produced and Distributed by Federated Film Exchange
Ben and Phyllis Haver appear, among others.

Paramount

Hollywood (8/19/23, Eight Reels)
Director: James Cruze *Story:* Frank Condon *Scenario*: Tom Geraghty
Hope Drown, Luke Cosgrave, George K. Arthur, Harris Gordon, Ruby Lafayette, Bess
Flowers, Eleanor Lawson, King Zany, Charles Chaplin, Fatty Arbuckle, Baby Peggy, Ben
Turpin, Jim Finlayson, Kalla Pasha, Ford Sterling, Doug Fairbanks, Wm. S. Hart, Walter
Hiers, William Boyd, Bebe Daniels, Cecil B. DeMille, Lloyd Hamilton, etc.

Mack Sennett for Pathe
(Two Reels each)

Where's My Wandering Boy This Evening? #113 *(7/8/23)*
Director: J.A. Waldron *Camera:* Blake Wagner & Ernie Crockett *Editor*: Ray Enright
Ben Turpin, Pricilla Bonner, Dot Farley, James Finlayson, Madeline Hurlock, Billy
Armstrong, Wheeler Dryden, Fanny Kelly, Pat Kelly, Teddy, Billy Gilbert, Jack Duffy,
Gordon Lewis. (Working title: *Deserted at the Church)*

•*Pitfalls of a Big City* #114 *(9/2/23)*
Director: John A. Waldron *Camera:* Blake Wagner & Ernie Crockett
Supervisor: F. Richard Jones
Ben Turpin, Pricilla Bonner, Dot Farley, Madeline Hurlock, Jimmy Finlayson, Mack Swain, Bud Ross, Billy Bevan, Billy Armstrong, Andy Clyde, Kewpie Morgan. Short clip extant. Herman Raymaker supposed to direct.

•*Asleep at the Switch* #116 *(10/14/23)*
Director: Roy Del Ruth *Camera:* Ernie Crockett & Bob Walters *Editor:* Ray Enright
Supervisor: F. Richard Jones
Ben Turpin, Kewpie Morgan, Madeline Hurlock, Bud Ross, Billy Armstrong, Fanny Kelly, Cameo *(the dog)*, Cecile Evans, Margaret Cloud, Andy Clyde, Gordon Lewis. (Working title: *Sidetracked)* Clip used in Robert Youngson's *Days of Thrills and Laughter.*

•*The Dare-Devil* #118 *(11/25/23)*
Director: Del Lord *Camera:* Blake Wagner *Story:* Al Martin
Supervisor: F. Richard Jones
Ben Turpin *(Joe Magee)*, Irene Lentz, Harry Gribbon, Kewpie Morgan, Jack Richardson, Madeline Hurlock, Arthur Rowlands, Gordon Lewis, Bob Wagner (Working title: *The Stunt Man)*

•*Ten Dollars or Ten Days* #120 *(1/6/24)*
Director: Del Lord *Camera:* Blake Wagner *Special Camera:* Ernie Crockett
Titles: J.A. Waldron *Supervisor:* F. Richard Jones
Ben Turpin *(A Soda Jerk)*, Irene Lentz, Harry Gribbon, Bud Ross, Louise Carver, Spencer Bell, Silas Wilcox, Ernie Adams, Billy Gilbert, Fred Spencer. Clip used in Robert Youngson's *The Golden Age of Comedy.*

•*The Hollywood Kid* #117 and/or #133 *(3/30/24)*
Director: Roy Del Ruth *Camera:* Bob Ladd & E. B. DuPar
Special Camera: Ernie Crockett
Editor: Wm. Hornbeck *Titles:* J. A. Waldron *Supervisor:* F. Richard Jones
Jackie Lucas, Charlie Murray, Louise Carver, Vernon Dent, Andy Clyde, Jack Cooper, Madeline Hurlock, Bud Ross, Ray Grey, Alice Belcher, Cameo *(the dog)*, Billy Bevan, Elsie Tarron, Sunshine Hart, Cecile Evans, Thelma Hill, Marvin Lobach, Margaret Cloud, Evelyn Francisco, Gladys Tennyson, Dorothy Dore, Billy *(the chimp)*, Ben Turpin cameo.

•*Yukon Jake* #128 *(6/6/24)*
Director: Del Lord *Camera:* Ernie Crockett & George Spear
Editor: Wm. Hornbeck *Titles:* J. A. Waldron *Supervisor:* F. Richard Jones
Ben Turpin *(Sheriff Cyclone Bill)*, Natalie Kingston, Kalla Pasha, Jack Richardson, Leo Sulky, Bud Ross, Eli Stanton, Thelma Hill, Lois Boyd, Tiny Ward, Gladys Tennyson, Fanny Kelly, Elsie Tarron, Joe Young, Hazel Williams. Clip used in Robert Youngson's *When Comedy Was King.* (Working title: *North of '57)*

•*Romeo and Juliet* #140 *(8/3/24)*
(EYE Film Institute)
Directors: Harry Sweet & Reggie Morris *Camera:* George Crocker & George Unholz
Special Camera: Ernie Crockett *Editor:* Wm. Hornbeck
Titles: J. A. Waldron *Supervisor:* F. Richard Jones
Ben Turpin, Alice Day, Natalie Kingston, Vernon Dent, Jack Curtis, Billy Bevan, Fanny
Kelly, Sunshine Hart, Andy Clyde, Dot Farley, Leo Sulky, Louise Carver, Marvin Lobach

•*Three Foolish Weeks* #144 *(9/14/24)*
Directors: Reggie Morris & Ed Kennedy *Camera:* Billy Williams & Leland Davis
Special Camera: Ernie Crockett *Editor:* Wm. Hornbeck *Supervisor:* F. Richard Jones
Ben Turpin, Madeline Hurlock, Christian J. Frank, Judy King, William Lowery, Billy Bevan,
Tiny Ward, Jack Duffy, Fanny Kelly, Eli Stanton (Working title: *Three and a Half Weeks)*

•*The Reel Virginian* #148 *(10/26/24)*
Directors: Reggie Morris & Ed Kennedy *Camera:* George Crocker & Bob Ladd
Special Camera: Ernie Crockett *Editor:* Wm. Hornbeck *Titles:* J. A. Waldron
Supervisor: Dick Jones
Ben Turpin *(Sheriff Rodney St. Clair)*, Alice Day, Christian J. Frank, Sam Allen, Fred
KoVert, Alice Belcher, Coy Watson (Working title: *A West Virginian)*

•*The Wild Goose Chaser* #166 *(1/18/25)*
Director: Lloyd Bacon *Camera:* George Crocker & Sam Moran *Story:* Frank Capra
Titles: Felix Adler & A. H. Giebler *Special Camera:* Ernie Crockett
Editor: Wm. Hornbeck *Supervised by:* J. A. Waldron
Ben Turpin *(Rodney St. Clair)*, Trilby Clark, Jack Cooper, Eugenia Gilbert, Leo Sulky,
Blanche Payson, Evelyn Francisco, Barney Hellum, Louise Carver, Thelma Hill

•*A Raspberry Romance* #161 *(3/1/25)*
(EYE Film Institute)
Director: Lloyd Bacon *Camera:* George Crocker & Sam Moran
Story: Jefferson Moffitt & Hal Yates *Titles:* Felix Adler & A. H. Giebler
Special Camera: Ernie Crockett *Editor:* Wm. Hornbeck *Supervisor:* J. A. Waldron
Ben Turpin *(Rodney St. Clair)*, Blanche Payson, Jack Cooper, Madeline Hurlock, Thelma
Parr, Leo Sulky, Barney Hellum, William McCall, Silas Wilcox, Alice Belcher, Irving
Bacon, Evelyn Francisco, Thelma Hill, Eli Stanton, Evelyn Sherman

•*The Marriage Circus* #155 *(4/12/25)*
(Museum of Modern Art)
Directors: Reggie Morris & Ed Kennedy *Camera:* George Spear & Leland Davis
Story: Vernon Smith & Frank Capra *Titles:* Felix Adler & A. H. Giebler
Special Camera: Ernie Crockett *Editor:* Wm. Hornbeck *Supervisor:* J. A. Waldron
Ben Turpin, Madeline Hurlock, Louise Carver, Christian J. Frank, Sunshine Hart, Ford
West, Bud Ross, Pat Kelly, Andre Bailey, Claire Cushman, Thelma Hill, Evelyn Sherman,
Heinie Conklin (Working title: *Monsieur Don't Care)*

The Squawk Man #173? *(1925, never produced)*
Story: Al Martin
A parody of *The Covered Wagon* intended for production after completion of *The Wild Goose Chaser*, but never realized due to Turpin's sudden retirement

Ben Turpin — Freelancing

Hogan's Alley (12/12/25, Feature)
Warner Bros.
Director: Roy Del Ruth *Story:* Darryl F. Zanuck *Camera:* Charles Van Enger
Monte Blue, Patsy Ruth Miller, Louise Fazenda, Willard Louis, Ben Turpin, Charles Conklin, Max Davidson, Frank Hagney, Herbert Spencer Griswold, Mary Carr, Nigel Barrie, Franklyn Bond

Steel Preferred (1/3/26, Seven Reels)
Metropolitan Pictures of California, Distributed by Producers Distributing Corp.
Directed by James P. Hogan *Story:* Hershell S. Hall *Adaption:* Elliot Clawson
Vera Reynolds, William Boyd, Hobart Bosworth, Walter Long, Charlie Murray, William V. Mong, Nigel Barrie, Helen Sullivan, Ben Turpin in small role as the Bartender.

Mack Sennett for Pathé
Ben Turpin's Return *(Two Reels each)*

•*When a Man's a Prince* #220 *(8/15/26)*
Director: Eddie Cline *Camera:* Vernon Walker
Story: Vernon Smith, Clarence Hennecke, Harry McCoy, Jefferson Moffit, George Green
Special Camera: Ernie Crockett *Editor:* Wm. Hornbeck
Titles: A. H. Giebler & Reed Heustis *Supervisor:* J. A. Waldron
Turpin's return to Sennett, starring Madeline Hurlock, Blanche Payson, Danny O'Shea, Dave Morris, George Gray, Bud Ross, Sunshine Hart, Leo Sulky, James Donnelly, Arthur Rowlands

•*A Prodigal Bridegroom* #236 *(9/26/26)*
Director: Lloyd Bacon *Camera:* Earl Stafford *Special Camera:* K. G. MacLean
Story: Jefferson Moffitt, Clarence Hennecke, Harry McCoy
Editor: Wm. Hornbeck *Supervisor:* J. A. Waldron
Ben Turpin *(Rodney St. Clair)*, Thelma Hill, Madeline Hurlock, Andy Clyde, William McCall, Irving Bacon, Louise Carver, Marvin Lobach, Dave Morris, Vernon Dent, Patsy O'Byrne, Barney Hellum, Joe Young. Clip used in Robert Youngson's *The Golden Age of Comedy*.

•*A Harem Knight* #243 *(11/7/26)*
Director: Gil Pratt *Camera:* Harry Fowler & Wallace Fish *Special Camera:* K. G. MacLean
Editor: Wm. Hornbeck *Supervisor:* J. A. Waldron
Ben Turpin *(Rodney St. Clair)*, Madeline Hurlock, Danny O'Shea, Andy Clyde, Marvin Loback, Dave Morris, Arthur Rowlands, Louise Carver, Joe Young, George Gray, Billy Gilbert, Irving Bacon, Barney Hellum. Clip used in Youngson's *The Golden Age of Comedy*.

•*A Blonde's Revenge* #256 *(12/19/26)*
Director: Del Lord(?) *Story:* P. Whitman, H. McCoy, J. Moffitt
Supervisor: J. A. Waldron
Ben Turpin *(Gerald Montague, A Live Politician)*, Ruth Taylor, Vernon Dent, Johnny Burke, Alice Belcher, Barbara Tennant, Barney Hellum, Irving Bacon, Mary Ann Jackson, Thelma Parr, Dave Morris, William McCall, Alma Bennett, Mary Mayberry, Johnny Burke, Arthur Rowlands

•*A Hollywood Hero* #264 *(12/30/26) (Eastman House)*
Director: Harry Edwards *Camera:* Billy Williams *Editor:* Wm. Hornbeck
Story: C. Harbaugh, P. Whitman, H. Edwards & G. Jeske
Titles: A. H. Giebler & Jimmy Starr *Supervisor:* J. A. Waldron
Ben Turpin, Alma Bennett, Bud Jamison, Irving Bacon, Marvin Lobach, William McCall, Bobby Dunn, Eleanor Hibbard (Working title: *Montague the Magnetic*)

•*Broke in China* #241 *(4/24/27)*
Director: Eddie Cline *Assistant Director:* Glen DeVol
Story: Vernon Smith, Harry McCoy, Jefferson Moffitt, and George Jeske
Camera: Harry Fowler *Special Camera:* Earl Stafford *Editor:* Wm. Hornbeck
Titles: A. H. Giebler & David Weissman *Supervisor:* J. A. Waldron
Ben Turpin *(An American Sailor)*, Louise Carver, Alice Belcher, Donald Maines, Ruth Taylor, William McCall, Dave Morris, Andy Clyde, Joe Young, Tiny Ward, Bud Ross, Marvin Lobach

•*The Pride of Pikeville* #251 *(6/5/27)*
Director: Alf Goulding *Assistant Directors:* Glen DeVol & Ray McCarey
Camera: St. Elmo Boyce *Special Camera:* K. G. MacLean
Editor: Wm. Hornbeck *Supervisor:* J. A. Waldron
Story: Earle Rodney, Jefferson Moffitt, Clarence Hennecke, Phil Whitman, Harry McCoy, Grover Jones, Randall Faye, and Lex Neal *Titles:* A. H. Giebler
Ben Turpin *(Baron Bonamo)*, Thelma Hill, Andy Clyde, Wm. McCall, Stanley Blystone, Barney Hellum, Vernon Dent

•*The Jolly Jilter* #261 *(3/13/27)*
Director: Eddie Cline(?) *Editor:* Wm. Hornbeck *Supervisor:* J. A. Waldron
Story: Arthur Ripley, Clarence Hennecke, Grover Jones, Harry McCoy, & Phil Whitman
Ben Turpin *(Virgil Vancourt)*, Madeline Hurlock, Sunshine Hart, Alma Bennett, Billy Gilbert. Clip used in Youngson's *The Golden Age of Comedy*.

Love's Languid Lure #268 *(8/28/27)*
Director: Lige Conley *Camera:* Vernon Walker *Editor:* Wm. Hornbeck
Story: Phil Whitman, Harry McCoy, Harry Edwards, Vernon Smith, and Ralph Cedar
Titles: A. H. Giebler & Jimmy Starr *Supervisor:* J. A. Waldron
Ben Turpin, Peggy Montgomery, Jack Cooper, Irving Bacon, Sunshine Hart

•*Daddyboy* #276 *(10/23/27) (Lobster Films)*
Director: Harry Edwards *Camera:* Lee Davis & Lewis Jennings
Story: Phil Whitman & Jefferson Moffitt
Titles: A. H.Giebler & Jimmy Starr *Editor:* Wm. Hornbeck *Supervisor:* J. A. Waldron
Ben Turpin, Alma Bennett, Johnny Burke, Bill Searby, Alice Ward, William McCall. Ben's last starring Sennett two-reeler.

Ben Turpin — Freelancing

•*Screen Snapshots (Series 9, #4, One Reel)*
Federated Film Exchange
Ben Turpin, Buster Collier, Jobyna Ralston, Wallace Beery, Lois Wilson, Pat O'Malley, Edmund Lowe, Bessie Love, George Archainbaud, May MacAvoy, Ruth Roland, Carmel Myers, Marion Nixon, Lilyan Tashman

•*The College Hero (October 9, 1927, Six Reels)*
A Columbia Picture
Director: Walter Lang *Story:* Harry R. Symonds *Editor:* Arthur Roberts
Pauline Garon, Rex Lease, Bobby Agnew, Ben Turpin *(the Janitor)*, Churchill Ross, Joan Standing, Charles Paddock

The Wife's Relations (Jan 13, 1928, Six Reels)
A Columbia Picture
Director: Maurice Marshall *Story:* Adolph Unger *Adaption:* Stephen Cooper
Editor: Arthur Roberts
Shirley Mason, Gaston Glass, Ben Turpin *(Rodney St. Clair)*, Armand Kaliz, Arthur Rankin, Flora Finch, Lionel Belmore, Maurice Ryan, James Harrison (Working title: *A Woman's Way)*

Alice in Movieland (June 23, 1928, One Reel)
Distributed by Paramount
Marion Mack, Gloria Swanson, Ricardo Cortez, Eugene O'Brien, Ben Turpin, Creighton Hale, Hank Mann, Blanche Payson

Weiss Brothers-Artclass
(Two reels each unless noted)

• *Taking the Count (1928)*
Director: ?
Ben Turpin *(A Streetsweep)*, Leo White, Addie McPhail, Joe Bonner, Alfred Hewston

• *Why Babies Leave Home (1928)*
Director: Jess Robbins
Ben Turpin, Jack Lloyd

• *She Said No (1928)*
Director: ?
Ben Turpin, Addie McPhail, Edwin Argus

• *Holding His Own (1929)*
Director: ?
Ben Turpin, Marvin Lobach, Harry Martell

• *The Cock-Eyed Family (March 1929)*
Director: ?
Ben Turpin *(Amos Gettig)*, Vera White, Billy Barty, Sherwood Bailey, Arthur Rowlands, William McCall

• *Seeing Things (1929)*
Director: ?
Ben Turpin *(Joe Grubb)*, Molly Malone, Alice Belcher

• *Idle Eyes (June 1929)*
Director: ?
Ben Turpin *(Benjamin Turps)*, Alice Belcher, William McCall, Billy Barty, Leo White, Bud Ross, Josephine Borio

• *The Cock-Eyed Hero (1929)*
Director: ?
Ben Turpin, Josephine Borio, Charles Dorety, Alice Belcher

• *Two Lonely Knights (1929)*
Director: Charles Dillon
(Library of Congress)
Ben Turpin, Charles Dorety, Marvin Lobach, Ruby McCoy

• *The Eyes Have It (1929)*
Director: Leslie Goodwins
Ben Turpin, Helen Gilmore, Georgia O'Dell, Jack Lipson, William McCall

The Hollywood Dressmaker (1929)
Director: Leslie Goodwins
Ben Turpin, Jimmy Aubrey. Originally intended as a feature, possibly released as a short.

Ben Turpin — Freelancing (Sound Era)

•*The Show of Shows (December 29, 1929, Feature)*
Warner Brothers-Vitaphone
Director: John G. Adolfi *Supervisor:* Darryl F. Zanuck
Many stars as themselves, including Ben Turpin as a waiter in a little song and dance skit, *Flora Dora*, along with veteran comics Lloyd Hamilton, Lupino Lane, Bert Roach, Charles Conklin, & Lee Moran

•*The Love Parade (1929, Feature)*
Paramount-Famous Players-Lasky
Director: Ernst Lubitsch
Story: Ernest Vajda and Guy Bolton from the play *The Prince Consort* by Leon Xanrof & Jules Chance *Camera:* Victor Milner Music: Victor Schertzinger
Maurice Chavalier, Jeanette MacDonald, Lillian Roth, Lupino Lane, Eugene Pallette, Lionel Belmore, Virginia Bruce, E.H. Calvert, Edgar Norton, Ben Turpin in a cameo appearance.

•*The Voice of Hollywood #8 (April 26, 1930, One Reel)*
Tec-Art Studios
Ben Turpin *(Guest Announcer)*, Madge Bellamy, Myrna Loy, Mickey Rooney, Alberta Vaughn, Al Cooke

•*A Royal Romance (March 17, 1930, Feature)*
Columbia Pictures
Director: Erle C. Kenton *Producer:* Harry Cohn
Story & Dialogue: Norman Houston *Camera:* Ted Tetzlaff
William Collier, Jr., Pauline Starke, Clarence Muse, Ann Brody, Eugenia Besserer, Walter P. Lewis, Betty Boyd, Ullrich Haupt, Bert Sprotte, Dorothy DeBorba, Ethan Laidlaw, Ben Turpin *(as a Cossack guard)*

•*Swing High (May 4, 1930, Feature)*
Pathe Pictures
Director: Joseph Santley *Story:* Seymore and Joseph Santley
Dorothy Burgess, Chester Conklin, Ben Turpin *(the bartender)*, Stepin Fetchit, Helen Twelvetrees, Fred Scott, John Sheehan, Daphne Pollard, George Fawcett

A Hollywood Theme Song (December 7, 1930, Two Reels)
Mack Sennett for Educational
Director: William Beaudine **Story & Dialogue:** Jack Jevne, Arthur Ripley, Earle Rodney, Harry McCoy, Andrew Bennison, Walter Weems, & John A. Waldron
Camera: George Unholz, Paul Perry, & Mack Stengler **Editor:** William Hornbeck
Harry Gribbon, Yola d'Avril, Patsy O'Leary, Billy Barty, Ben Turpin, Charles Conklin, William McCall, Gus Leonard

•*Cracked Nuts (April 18, 1931, Feature)*
RKO
Director: Eddie Cline **Story:** Douglas MacLean & Al Boasberg
Screenplay: Al Boasberg
Bert Wheeler & Robert Woolsey, Dorothy Lee, Boris Karloff, Edna May Oliver, Leni Stengel, Stanley Fields, Harvey Clark, Frank Thorton, Frank Lackteen, Wilfred Lucas, Roscoe Ates, Edward Piel, Sr., Ben Turpin *(as the cross-eyed enemy bombardier)*

•*Our Wife (May 16, 1931, Two Reels)*
Hal Roach for MGM
Director: James Horne **Dialogue:** H.M. Walker **Camera:** Art Lloyd
Editor: Richard Currier **Sound:** Elmer Raguse
Stan Laurel & Oliver Hardy, Babe London, James Finlayson, Charles Rogers, Ben Turpin *(Justice of the Peace, William Gladding)*, Blanche Payson
(Working title: *Wanted — A Wife*)

•*Movie-Town (July 5, 1931, Two Reels)*
Mack Sennett for Educational
Director: Mack Sennett **Story & Dialogue:** J. A.Waldron, Earle Rodney, & Harry McCoy
Marjorie Beebe, Luis Alberni, Mack Sennett, Frank Eastman, Virginia Whiting, Marion Sayers, Buster Crabbe, George Olsen & His Orchestra, George Gray, Barney Hellum.
Ben Turpin, in cameo, dances past Sennett's table.

•*Ambassador Bill (November 22, 1931, Feature)*
Fox
Director: Sam Taylor **Screenplay:** Guy Bolton
Story: Vincent Sheean, Ambassador from the United States
Will Rogers, Marguerita Churchill, Greta Nissen, Tad Alexander, Ray Milland, Gustav von Seyfferitz, Arnold Korff, Ferdinand Munier, Edwin Maxwell, Ben Turpin *(ax-wielding butcher)*

•*Running Hollywood (January 27, 1932, Two Reels)*
Thalian's Club short for Universal
Director: Charles Lamont **Producer:** Bryan Foy
Story: William Halligan & Harry Sauber
Buddy Rogers, Arthur Lake, Sally Blane, Benny Rubin, John Wayne, Sessue Hayakawa, Louise Fazenda, Charles Murray, George Sidney, Noah Beery, Vivien Oakland, Leo Carillo,

Gertrude Astor, Ralph Ince, Little Billy, Mary Carr, Claude Gillingwater, Virginia Sale, Florence Lake, Ben Turpin *(traffic cop)*, Guinn "Big Boy" Williams, John T. Murray, Monte Collins, Eddie Kane, Kit Guard, Marion Byron, Ginger Rogers, George E. Stone, Nancy Dover

•*Lighthouse Love (May 6, 1932, Two Reels)*
Mack Sennett-Paramount Publix
Director: Michael Delmer
Arthur Stone, Franklin Pangborn, Tom Kennedy, Mack Swain, Dorothy Granger, Heinie Conklin, Ben Turpin *(the Prince)*

•*Make Me A Star (July 1, 1932, Feature)*
Paramount
Director: William Beaudine *Screenplay:* Sam Mintz, Walter DeLeon, & Arthur Kober
Based on *Merton of the Movies* by Harry Leon Wilson
Stuart Erwin, Joan Blondell, Zasu Pitts, Ben Turpin, Charles Sellon, Florence Roberts, Arthur Hoyt, Helen Jerome Eddy, George Templeton, Sam Hardy, Ruth Donnelly, Oscar Apfel, Bobby Vernon, Bud Jamison, Victor Potel, Snub Pollard. (Working title: *Gates of Hollywood)*

•*Million Dollar Legs (July 8, 1932, Feature)*
Paramount
Director: Eddie Cline *Story:* Joseph Mankiewicz & Henry Myers
Camera: Arthur Todd
Jack Oakie, W. C. Fields, Lyda Roberti, Andy Clyde, Susan Fleming, Hugh Herbert, Dickie Moore, George Barbier, Billy Gilbert, Vernon Dent, Ben as a silent lurking secret spy

•*Hollywood on Parade (circa August 1932, One Reel)*
Paramount
Frederic March, Jack Oakie, Mitzi Green, Ginger Rogers, Eddie Peabody; Ben opens this short marching in full prince regalia.

•*Hollywood on Parade (1934, One Reel)*
Paramount
Jimmy Durante, Mack Gordon & Harry Revel, Ben Turpin, Polly Moran, Chic Sale, Ted Healy & The Three Stooges, Rudy Vallee, John Boles, Benny Rubin

•*Law of the Wild (release starting September 5, 1934)*
A Mascot Serial in 12 two-reel episodes

Chapter 1: *The Man Killer!*	Chapter 7: *The Death Stampede*
Chapter 2: *The Battle of the Strong*	Chapter 8: *The Canyon of Calamity*
Chapter 3: *The Cross-Eyed Goony*	Chapter 9: *Robbers Roost*
Chapter 4: *Avenging Fangs*	Chapter 10: *King of the Range*
Chapter 5: *A Dead Mans Hand*	Chapter 11: *Winner Take All!*
Chapter 6: *Horse Thief Justice*	Chapter 12: *The Grand Sweepstakes*

Produced by Nat Levine
Directors: Armand Schaefer & Breezy Eason *Supervising Editor:* Wyndham Gittens
Writers: Ford Beebe, John Rathmell, Al Martin
Screenplay: Sherman Lowell & Breezy Eason *Camera:* Ernest Miller & William Nobles
Editor: Earl Turner *Sound Engineer:* Terry Kelly
Rex, the King of Wild Horses, Rin Tin Tin, Jr., Bob Custer, Lucille Brown, Ben Turpin *(Henry, the Ingram hired hand)*, Rychard Cramer, Ernie Adams, Ed Cobb, Charles Whittaker, Dick Alexander

The Little Big Top (February 1, 1935, Two Reels)
Educational Pictures (#8 in the *Frolics of Youth* series)
Director: Alf Goulding *Story:* Glen Lambert
Poodles Hanneford, Junior Coghlan, Dorthea Kent, Ben Turpin

•*Fox Movietone News (March, 1935, One Reel)*
Footage of Ben at Mother-In-Law's Day Parade, San Antonio, Texas

•*Bring 'em Back a Lie (July 1, 1935, Two Reels)*
Universal
Director: Alf Goulding *Story:* Raymond Cannon
Sterling Holloway, Ben Turpin

•*Keystone Hotel (August 24, 1935, Two Reels)*
Warner Bros.
Director: Ralph Staub *Story:* Joe Traub *Camera:* Hans Konenkamp (?)
Ben Turpin, Ford Sterling, Chester Conklin, Hank Mann, Bert Roach, Marie Prevost, Vivien Oakland, Joseph "Baldy" Belmont, Jack Duffy, Glen Cavender, Dewey Robinson, Bobby Dunn, George Gray, Billy Engle, Jack Richardson, Patsy O'Byrne, Joseph Bordeaux (Working title: *Good Old Days*)

•*Starlit Days at the Lido (September 28, 1935, Two Reels, Full Color)*
Louis Lewyn for MGM
Constance Bennett, Buster Crabbe, Clark Gable, Reginald Denny, Robert Montgomery, Baby LeRoy, Cliff Edwards. Ben Turpin in a skit with the Tic-Toc Girls.

•*Cinema Circus (January 23, 1937, Two Reels, Full Color)*
Louis Lewyn for MGM
Director: Roy Rowland
Lee Tracy, Cliff Edwards, Leo Carrillo, Boris Karloff, Baby LeRoy, William S. Hart, Mickey Rooney, Ole Olsen, and Chic Johnson. Chester Conklin, Charles Murray, Hank Mann, and Ben in a skit and song medley, *She Was An Acrobat's Daughter/Man on the Flying Trapeze.*

•*Hollywood Cavalcade (October 13, 1939, Feature, Full Color)*
Twentieth Century
Director: Irving Cummings, Mal St. Clair
Story: Lou Breslow, Hillary Lynn, & Brown Holmes *Screenplay:* Ernest Pascal
Camera: Allen M. Davey and Ernest Palmer
Alice Fay, Don Ameche, J. Edward Bromberg, Stuart Erwin, Alan Curtis, Jed Prouty, Buster Keaton, Al Jolson, Donald Meek, Ben Turpin, Dave Morris, Chester Conklin, Eddie Collins, James Finlayson, Hank Mann, Snub Pollard

•*Fox Movietone News (circa October 1939, One Reel)*
Fox
Turpin among the stars at premiere of *Hollywood Cavalcade.*

•*Saps at Sea (May 3, 1940, Feature)*
Hal Roach, United Artists
Director: Gordon Douglas
Story: Charley Rogers, Felix Adler, Gil Pratt, & Harry Langdon *Camera:* Art Lloyd
Stan Laurel and Oliver Hardy, Richard Cramer, Mary Gordon, James Finlayson, Bob McKenzie, Patsy Moran, Ben as cross-eyed maintenance man (Working title: *Two's Company)*

•*The Great Dictator (March 7, 1941, Feature)*
United Artists
Director: Charles Chaplin *Writer:* Charles Chaplin
Charlie Chaplin, Paulette Goddard, Jack Oakie, Reginald Gardiner, Billy Gilbert
Turpin's death put an end to what would have been his last film appearance. (Working title: *The Dictator)*

In his last film, Saps at Sea, *released May 3, 1940.*

Bibliography

Every attempt was made at noting all reference sources used in the making of this book. However, some clippings had slipped through the cracks and are presently unknown or unidentified at my time of writing, for which I apologize.

1. *Twinkle, Twinkle, Movie Star!* by Harry T. Brundidge, E.P. Dutton & Co., Inc., 1930.

2. *My Cock-Eyed Past* by Ben Turpin (in part, unpublished).

3. "The First Fifty Years Were the Hardest for Ben Turpin" by Neil M. Clark, American magazine, November 1924.

4. *Keystone. The Life and Clowns of Mack Sennett* by Simon Louvish, Faber and Faber, Inc., 2003 (pgs 147, 148) via Academy of Motion Picture Arts & Sciences, Mack Sennett Collection, Ben Turpin Files.

5. "The World Needs Laughs" by Ben Turpin, Screen and Radio Weekly, October 22, 1939.

6. "Don't Let Your Left Eye Know What Your Left is Doing" by Fritzi Remont (source unidentified).

7. "Turpin Tribulations" by Kenneth McGaffey (unidentified).

8. *New Orleans Times-Picayune* Jan. 1899 Ernest Turpin obituary.

9. "Ben Turpin's Strabismus Cost of Fame" by David W. Hazen, *The Oregonian*, April 21, 1934, pg 10.

10. "The Expressions of Ben Turpin, Crossed His Eyes Once Too Often" (anonymous) *The Picture Show*, August 4, 1923, pg 21.

11. "See Comedian in Pictures & Real Life," *The Film Index*, October 30, 1909, pg 2.

12. "Why Ben Turpin Left the Screen" by Dorothy Wooldridge, *Picture Play*, February 1926, pgs 23 & 106.

13. "The Lonely Clown" by Dorothy Donnell, 1925, pgs 24, 25 & 80.

14. *Broncho Billy and the Essanay Film Company* by David Kiehn, Farwell Books, 2003, excerpt from an interview conducted by Columbia University with G.M. Anderson.

15. "Turpin Recalls Early Days of Film Comedy, Veteran Comedian Tells of Experiences as He Reviews His Long Career Started Around 1907," (syndicated) *Schenectady Gazette*, August 20, 1935, page 8.

16. *Ben Turpin, Little Movie Mirror Books* series, Ross Publishing, circa 1920/21.

17. Ben Turpin Greets Movie Fans, Comedy Star Recalls Days When He Lived in Cincinnati by Manuel Rosenberg, *The Cincinnati Post*, August 9, 1921, pg 5

18. *The Daily Inter-Ocean*, August 18, 1892

19. "Flickers of the Past Make a Clear Picture to Essanays' Mr. S" by Louis M. Starr, *The Chicago Sun*, February 2, 1947.

20. "Looking Backward with Ben" by Harry C. Carr, *Photoplay*, December 1918.

21. (unidentified)

22. (unidentified)

23. *History of the Motion Picture Industry* by Beatriz Michelina, The Binghamton Press, NY, c1917.

24. "My First Film" by Ben Turpin, Oxnard Daily Courier, July 12, 1922.

25. "Ben Turpin's Charms," anon via *The New Yorker*, Brooklyn (NY) *Daily Eagle*, July 31, 1927.

26. (unidentified)

27. *The Movies Are: Carl Sandburg's Film Reviews and Essays*, 1920-1928 by Carl Sandburg, Arnie Bernstein & Roger Ebert, Lake Claremont Press, 2000, page 77.

28. "Ben Turpin Invests Film Earnings in Property and Laughs at Movie Producers" by Inez Wallace, *Cleveland Plain Dealer*, March 18, 1934.

29. "Ben Is Almost As Funny Off Screen As He Is On" by W. Ward Marsh, *Cleveland Plain Dealer*, October 19, 1921.

30. *New Orleans Courier* (LA) July 11, 1860.

31. *Gaillard's Medical Journal*, Vol. 42; published by M. E. Gaillard, 1886, page 231 (Dr. Chas. Turpin info).

32. *New York Herald* (LA) February 28, 1870.

33. *The Queens Daily Star* (NY) October 19, 1929.

34. *The Daily Inter-Ocean* (IN) August 18, 1892.

35. *Oshkosh Daily Northwestern* (WI) May 16, 1896.

36. *The Omaha Bee* (NE) Jan. 10, 1899.

37. *New York Clipper*, September 17, 1899.

38. *Motography*, November 20, 1915, p1093.

39. *Philadelphia Inquirer* (PA) March 28, 1922.

40. *St. Mary's Oracle* (WV), June 12, 1975, Letter from Nick Riggs.

41. *National Police Gazette,* June 14, 1902, p2.

42. *San Diego Evening Tribune* (CA) September 16, 1902.

43. *Niagara Falls Gazette* (NY), September 16, 1903, p4.

44. *New York Clipper*, December 23, 1903.

45. "How Turpin's Eyes Went Awry" by Francis Orlando Starz, September 2, 1928.

46. *National Police Gazette*, November 18, 1905, p2.

47. *Variety*, June 30, 1906, p10.

48. *Variety*, September 1, 1906.

49. *New Orleans Item*, August 23, 1906.

50. *New Orleans Times-Picayune*, September 3, 1906.

51. *Goodwin's Weekly*, October 27, 1906.

52. *Salt Lake Telegram*, (UT) October 23, 1906.

53. *A Chicago Firehouse; Stories of Wriggleyville's Engine #78* by Karen Kruse.

54. *Variety*, May 29, 1909, p25.

55. *The Evening Independent* (Massillion, Ohio), Jan. 6, 1910.

56. *Moving Picture World*, Jan 14, 1911, p93.

57. *The Oxnard Daily Courier*, July 12, 1922.

58. *The Cleveland Plain Dealer*, all by author W. Ward Marsh: "A Sob-Story As Told by Turpin," August 4, 1923; "Old Ironsides Reminds Fan That Wallace Beery is a Great Photo Player," November 5, 1927; "One Moment, Please! Notes on Ben Turpin, Charley Chase and Others," July 6, 1940.

59. *The Seattle Daily Times*, November 22, 1913.

60. *The Seattle Daily Times*, April 2, 1914.

61. *The Springfield News* (MO), August 6, 1914.

62. *The Gay Illiterate* by Louella Parsons, 1944.

62. *Movies Demand* by Louella Parsons, 1916.

63. *Motography,* December 5, 1914.

64. Motography, December 26, 1914, p918.

65. *The Cleveland Plain Dealer*, March 18, 1934, "Ben Turpin" by Inez Wallace.

66. *Waterloo Times Tribune*, March 28, 1915.

67. *My Autobiography* by Charles Chaplin.

68. *Photoplay*, October 1915, "Charlie Chaplin's Own Story" by Harry C. Carr.

69. *Daily Alaska Dispatch*, May 19, 1915.

70. *Niles Washington Press*, July 5, 1915.

71. *Chicago Daily Tribune*, August 13, 1915, "Flickerings from Film Land" by Kitty Kelly.

72. *The Riverside Independent*, April 9, 1915.

73. *The Riverside Independent*, September 14, 1915.

74. *Janesville Daily Gazette*, September 24, 1915.

75. *The Idaho Statesman*, Jan. 23, 1916.

76. Source unknown; however, author Donald Parkhurst.

77. *The Film Daily*, June 2, 1924, by Louella Parsons.

78. *The Film Daily*, June 3, 1923, p43 "How I Broke Into the Movies" by Ben Turpin.

79. *Pictures and the Picturegoer*, February 12, 1916, by Louella Parsons.

80. *Janesville Daily Gazette*, June 13, 1916, p1200.

81. *Motography,* July 8, 1916, p82.

82. *Janesville Daily Gazette*, September 30, 1916.

83. *Seattle Daily Times*, December 10, 1916.

84. *The Salt Lake Telegram*, November 22, 1916.

85. *The New Orleans States*, March 4, 1917.

86. *New Orleans Times-Picayune*, April 15, 1917.

87. *New Orleans Times-Picayune*, April 29, 1917.

88. *New Orleans Times-Picayune*, April 14, 1917.

89. *Perrysburg Journal* (Ohio), May 10, 1917.

90. *Motography*, July 21, 1917, p134.

91. *The Oakland Tribune*, August 26, 1917.

92. *Janesville Daily Gazette*, December 18, 1917.

93. *The Oakland Tribune*, May 5, 1918, p18.

94. *The Augusta Chronicle*, April 8, 1919.

95. *The Smart Set*, 1929, by Harry Carr.

96. *Moving Picture World*, November 2, 1918, p597-598.

97. *Moving Picture World*, November 9, 1918, p671.

98. *Motion Picture*, April 1919, "The Sad Business of Being Funny" by Emma Lindsay Squire.

99. "Ben Turpin, A Falling Star" by Eddie Cline, 1938.

100. *Fort Wayne News-Sentinel* (IN), May 24, 1919, "The Saddest Spot in Los Angeles" by Karl K. Kitchen.

101. *The Atlanta Constitution*, November 4, 1919, p6 "Ben Turpin's Careless Optics."

102. *Moving Picture World*, March 6, 1920, p1574 & 1641 "Six Ben Turpin Comedies Now Being State-Righted."

103. *New Orleans States*, March 7, 1920, "Ben Turpin On Way Here."

104. *The Billings Gazette* (MT), March 28, 1920.

105. *The Bulletin* (San Francisco), July 20, 1920, "Neilan and Stars Arrive In Oakland."

106. *Los Angeles Times*, August 7, 1920, "Turpin As Orator."

107. *San Diego Union*, October 3, 1920.

108. *Modesto Evening News* (CA), August 30, 1920, "Married Life Scores Success at the Star."

109. *Ironwood Daily Globe*, February 10, 1921, "May Get Chance To Rest Eyes."

110. *Moving Picture World*, December 11, 1920, p741, "Warner Bros. Will Re-Issue Ten Essanay-Charlie Chaplin Comedies."

111. *The Oakland Tribune*, December 17, 1920.

112. *The Oakland Tribune*, December 19, 1920, "Stars Laugh at Scheme to Lower Salaries by Ben Turpin."

113. *Lima News & Times-Democrat* (Ohio), February 21, 1921, "A Small Town Idol Goes Over Big" by Esther Wagner.

114. *The Lowell Sun*, February 23, 1921, "A Small Town Idol review" (anon).

115. *Olean Evening Herald* (NY), March 22, 1921, "Newsy Notes from Movieland" by Daisy Dean.

116. *New Orleans Times-Picayune*, April 1, 1921, "Ben Turpin Buys A Tomb."

117. *Variety*, April 1, 1921, p34, "New Orleans" by O. M. Samuel.

118. *Los Angeles Times*, May 22, 1921, pII9 "Orphans in Joy Riot" by Grace Kingsley.

119. *Chicago Daily Tribune*, July 8, 1921, p14, "Mr. Turpin Enchants His Many Fans" by Mac Tinee.

120. *Fort Wayne Journal-Gazette* (TX), April 6, 1921, "Alas Girls! Handsome Ben Is As Married As He Looks."

121. *Los Angeles Times*, May 11, 1921, pII12, "To Sell Signatures of Harding Cabinet" (unid, in part).

122. *Moving Picture World*, May 28, 1921, "Ben Turpin Series Planned for Associated Producers."

123. *Fort Worth Star-Telegram* (TX), July 24, 1921, "Sycophants Bow Before Riches of 'Cross-Eyed Ben.'"

124. *Fort Wayne Journal-Gazette* (TX), August 6, 1921, "Turpin Visits Chicago."

125. *Variety*, August 5, 1921.

GOOD WRITING PG 104

126. *Chicago Daily Tribune*, August 7, 1921, pG3, "He Makes Eyes 'Cause He Can't Make 'em Behave" by Mae Tinee.

127. *Fort Worth Star-Telegram* (TX), August 10, 1921, "Fire Fighter Ball Players Bar Ben Turpin As Umpire…"

128. *Fort Wayne News-Sentinel* (IN), August 18, 1921.

129. *Cleveland Plain Dealer* (Ohio), August 21, 1921, "Turpin Travels."

130. *Detroit Free Press* (MI), August 21, 1921, pD6, "Funny Ben Turpin Coming to Adams In Person."

131. *San Diego Union*, August 28, 1921, "Signs of the Times."

132. *Toledo News-Bee* (Ohio), September 2, 1921, "Ben Turpin to Give Show for Newsies."

133. *Indianapolis Star* (IN), September 8, 1921, "Bees Like Ben Turpin."

134. *Lima News & Times Democrat*, September 11, 1921, "Movie Secrets Are Revealed."

135. *Motion Picture Classic,* February 1921, pgs 26-28, "Eye-Eye!" by Gladys Hall.

136. *Boston Daily Globe* (Mass.), September 18, 1921, "Ben Turpin's Mission In Life Is To Create Laughter."

137. *Philadelphia Inquirer* (PA), September 13, 1921, "Ben Turpin at the Globe."

138. *Philadelphia Inquirer* (PA), September 20, 1921, "Ben Turpin at Cross Keys."

139. *The New Sentinel* (Fort Wayne, IN), September 25, 1921, "Ben Turpin Claims He's Permanently Beautiful…"

140. *Boston Daily Globe* (Mass.), September 25, 1921, p59, "Ben Turpin of the Funny Eyes Here Next Week."

141. *Cleveland Plain Dealer* (Ohio), August 4, 1923, by W. Ward Marsh.

142. *Variety*, September 30, 1921, p39, "Turpin at Capitol; New for Times Square…"

143. *New York Telegraph*, October 2, 1921, article by Louella Parsons.

144. *Denver Post* (CO), September 26, 1921, "Ben Turpin Plans to Leave Movies."

145. *Boston Daily Globe* (Mass.), October 3, 1921, p13, "Ben Turpin Greets Friends In Person…"

146. *Boston Daily Globe* (Mass.), October 4, 1921, p6, "Ben Turpin on Job for Jobless. Will Serve Good Supper…"

147. *Cleveland Plain Dealer* (Ohio), October 14, 1921, article by W. Ward Marsh.

148. *New Orleans Item*, October 16, 1921, "Notes from the Palmolive."

149. *Movie Weekly*, October 22, 1921, p19, "A Cross-Eyed View of New York" by Beverly Crane.

150. *Cleveland Plain Dealer* (Ohio), October 18, 1921, "Ben Turpin Is A Riot…"

151. *Capital Times* (WI), November 8, 1921, "Newsy Notes from Hollywood" by Daisy Dean.

152. "Motion Picture Directing, The Facts and Theories of the Newest Art" by Peter Milne, *Some of the Arts of Slapstick Comedy*, pgs 97-98, Falk Publishing Co., Inc.

153. *Kansas City Star*, November 17, 1921, "Ben Turpin Fears the Worst…"

154. *Camera*, November 19, 1921, "Turpin Dons His Little Brown Derby."

155. *New York Tribune*, November 27, 1921, "The Heartbreaking Game of Being Funny…" by Malcolm Oettinger.

156. *The Atlanta Constitution*, February 5, 1922, p6, "Ben Lands the Kale."

157. *Pantomime*, March 25, 1922, pgs 26 & 30, "Breakfast With Ben Turpin" by Bob Dorman.

158. *The Oregonian*, March 5, 1922, "Ben Turpin in Action."

159. *New Orleans States*, March 26, 1922, "Ben Steps Lively."

160. *Atlanta Constitution*, April 16, 1922, pF5 "Turpin Off."

161. *Los Angeles Times*, April 16, 1922, "Ben Turpin Is Pantages Headliner."

162. *Baltimore American*, April 23, 1922, "Honor Ben Turpin."

163. *San Jose Mercury*, May 17, 1922, "Ben Turpin Umpires; Beauties Root."

164. *New Orleans State*, June 6, 1922, "Success On Stage."

165. *Odgen Standard-Express* (UT), August 20, 1922.

166. *Moving Picture World*, August 22, 1922, p80.

167. *New York Tribune*, September 3, 1922, "Around the World On the Sennett Lot."

168. *Salt Lake Telegram*, September 20, 1922, "Ben Turpin In Person at Pantages Today."

169. *Exhibitors Herald*, December 2, 1922, p37, "Turpin Convalescing Following Operation."

170. *New Orleans Item*, December 3, 1922, "Ben in Hospital."

171. *Los Angeles Times*, February 27, 1923, "To Start Producing Campaign."

172. *Los Angeles Times*, March 15, 1923, pii22, "Pathe Will Distribute Comic Film."

173. *Los Angeles Times*, March 24, 1923, pi8, "Pathe Signs for Comedies."

174. *Cleveland Plain Dealer* (OH), September 17, 1923.

175. *Picture Show* (England), August 4, 1923, p21, "The Expressions of Ben Turpin."

176. *Cleveland Plain Dealer* (OH), August 4, 1923, "More Punishment for Ben Turpin" by W. Ward Marsh.

177. *San Diego Union*, August 19, 1923, "Asleep at the Switch."

178. *Los Angeles Times*, August 1923, "Even Turpin's Wife Will Not Know Him."

179. *Los Angeles Times*, August 26, 1923, pIII37, "Naming the Brainchild."

180. *Los Angeles Times*, September 4, 1923, pII9, "Dominoes Double-Crossed."

181. *Los Angeles Times*, September 13, 1923, pIII1, "Turpin's Shoes Puzzle Repairer."

182. *Chicago Daily Tribune*, September 30, 1923, pD1, "News of Screenables."

183. *Chicago Daily Tribune*, October 9, 1923, p21, "Closeups."

184. *Chicago Daily Tribune*, November 7, 1923, p21, "Mrs. Ben Turpin…"

185. *Clown Princes and Court Jesters* by Kalton C. Lahue and Sam Gill, A.S. Barnes & Co., Inc., 1970.

186. *The Republic*, December 4, 1923, "Real and Unreel Ben Turpin…" by Don H. Eddy.

187. *Hartford Courant* (CT), December 30, 1923, p8X, "Stars Life No Bed of Roses, Says Ben Turpin."

188. *Los Angeles Times*, 1923, "No Discord in Ranks of the Turpin Family" (advertorial).

189. *Los Angeles Times*, April 21, 1924, pA9, "Flashes by Grace Kingsley."

190. *Atlantic Constitution*, Jan. 6, 1924, pC6, "Ben Turpin."

191. *San Francisco Chronicle*, Jan. 20, 1924, "Stars Thrill Hero Fans…"

192. *International News Service*, Jan. 18, 1924, "Spars With Seven At Once…"

193. *Amarillo Globe* (TX), March 31, 1924, "The WAMPAS Ball…"

194. *Davenport Democrat* (IA), Jan. 20, 1924, "Ben Turpin at Work On Comedy."

195. *American Weekly*, December 5, 1941, "Mack Sennett's Glamour Girls" by Adela Rogers St. John.

196. *Los Angeles Examiner*, February 10, 1924, "Stars Are Insulted When Identity Is Confused."

197. *Sioux City Sunday Journal*, June 8, 1924, "Ben Turpin Suffers From Snowblindness."

198. *Los Angeles Times*, April 2, 1924, pA11, "Flashes by Grace Kingsley: Ben Turpin to Flit."

199. *Mansfield News* (OH), April 22, 1924, "Rain Dampens Snow."

200. *Los Angeles Times*, March 3, 1924, Billy Armstrong death

201. *Quebec Daily Telegraph*, March 31, 1924, "No Comedy in Turpin's Visit…"

202. *Montreal Gazette*, April 10, 1924, "Wife of Comedian Regained Hearing."

203. *Montreal Gazette*, April 12, 1924, "Longs for Tragic Roles, Looks Lacking, Ben Turpin Admits."

204. *New York Daily News*, April 19, 1924, p1, "RESTORED."

205. *Los Angeles Times*, April 27, 1924, p34, "Turpin Tea Taster."

206. *Moving Picture World*, May 3, 1924, p53, "Maine; Joseph Gagnon…"

207. *Riverside Daily Press* (CA), May 2, 1924, "Ben Turpin To Be At Bazaar."

208. *Riverside Daily Press* (CA), May 5, 1924, "Ben was present the final night…"

209. *San Antonio* (TX), May 25, 1924, "Four companies are at work…"

210. *Davenport Democrat and Leader* (IA), June 1, 1924, "Burlesque Is Popular In The Movies…"

211. *Sioux City Sunday Journal*, June 8, 1924, "Alice Day Becomes Rapid Change Artist."

212. *Davenport Democrat and Leader* (IA), June 15, 1924, "Sennett Busy On Four Big Films."

213. *Davenport Democrat and Leader* (IA), July 6, 1924, "Cashing Checks Easy For Turpin."

214. *Los Angeles Times*, July 6, 1924, pB19, "Fun. From The Seamy Side."

215. *Los Angeles Times*, (date?) 1924, "Are Cross-Eyes Bad Luck? Ask Ben Turpin."

216. *Lowell Sun* (Mass), August 2, 1924, "Turpin, In Latest, Apes Von Stroheim" by A.H. Frederick.

217. *Lowell Sun* (Mass), August 6, 1924, "Under the supervision of F. Richard Jones…"

218. *Los Angeles Times*, August 4, 1924, "Turpin Breaks Ankle. X-Ray Discloses…"

219. *San Antonio* (TX), August 31, 1924, "Turpin has just completed his new burlesque…"

220. *Los Angeles Times*, August 21, 1924, pA6, "Ben Turpin Reported Recovering Rapidly."

221. *Moving Picture World*, September 13, 1924, Three Foolish Weeks review by T.W.

222. *Picture Play*, March 1925, "Slap 'em Down Good!" by Don Ryan.

223. *Los Angeles Times*, December 9, 1924, pB3, "Ben Turpin Picked to Referee Fights."

224. *Modesto Evening News* (CA), December 13, 1924, "Ben Turpin May Leave Screen Soon" by Jack Jungmeyer.

225. *Los Angeles Times*, December 23, 1924, pA11, "Flashes by Grace Kingsley, Stars in Their Orbits."

226. *The Republic*, December 24, 1924, "Catholic Movie Actors' Guild Builds Church."

227. *Davenport Democrat & Leader* (IA), December 28, 1924, "At Last! Ben Turpin Grants An Interview" by Ben Turpin.

228. *Oakland Tribune*, Jan. 4, 1925, "Sennett Cameraman Will Proffer New Trick Photography."

229. *Moving Picture World*, September 13, 1924, p322, The Wild Goose Chaser review

230. *Sunday State Journal* (Lincoln, NE), March 1, 1925, "Turpin About To Retire."

231. *Chicago Daily Tribune*, April 9, 1925, p9, "Ben the Clown Is Scullion to Sick Mrs. Turpin."

232. *Alton Evening Telegraph* (IL), April 10, 1925, "Our Favorite Movie Star Quits."

233. *Variety,* April 14, 1925, "Ben Turpin Must Lay Off…"

234. *Massillon Evening Independent* (OH), April 15, 1925, "Ben Turpin's Retirement."

235. *Picture Play,* June 1925, p90, "Each Fault A Virtue" by Helen Klumph.

236. *Variety,* September 2, 1925, "It was understood that when Ben Turpin quit Mack Sennett…"

237. *The Evening Independent,* October 2, 1925, "Ben Turpin's Wife Dies After A Long Vigil Kept By Husband."

238. *The Evening Independent,* October 3, 1925, "Cross-Eyed Ben Turpin A Tragic Figure…" by John P. Miles

239. *Paris and Hollywood Magazine,* April 1926, "Tragedy Halts Ben Turpin's Comic Roles."

240. *Olean Evening Times* (NY), October 5, 1925, "A Clown. And A Man."

241. *Trenton Sunday Times Advertiser* (NJ), October 18, 1925, "Despite Fabulous Wealth, Cross-Eyed Comedy Star…" by Betty Morris.

242. *Los Angeles Times,* October 5, 1925, pA2, "Funeral Service Conducted for Mrs. Turpin."

243. *Appleton Post Cresent* (WI), October 5, 1925, "A Hollywood Family."

244. *Variety,* October 7, 1925, pA2, "Mrs. Ben Turpin Dies; Ben Devoted To Her."

245. *Galveston Daily News,* October 7, 1925, p4, "The End of One Hollywood Romance."

246. *Hartford Courant,* October 7, 1925, p16, "Ben Turpin's Affliction."

247. *Roanoke Times* (VA), October 21, 1925, p16, "A Comedian's Sorrow."

248. *Cleveland Plain Dealer* (OH), October 25, 1925, "Ben Turpin cried two or three times…"

249. *The Film Daily,* November 3, 1925, "Turpin Rejoining Sennett Soon."

250. *San Diego Union,* November 13, 1925, "Movies Make Yukon Jake Tough As Steak."

251. *Seattle Daily Times,* November 15, 1925, "Film Comedian's Genius Is Amusing Off Screen."

252. *Los Angeles Times,* November 13, 1925, "Ben Turpin Goes Under Knife at Santa Barbara."

253. *The Film Daily,* November 17, 1925, "Ben Turpin Better."

254. *Los Angeles Times,* December 5, 1925, "Turpin Taking Sun Baths at Santa Barbara."

255. *The Film Daily,* December 13, 1925, "Turpin Improving Rapidly. Back to Work Soon."

256. *Los Angeles Times,* May 16, 1926, "Ben Turpin Says Cupid Cross-Eyed…"

257. *Los Angeles Times,* June 30, 1926, "Ben Turpin Will Be There."

258. *Atlanta Constitution,* July 9, 1926, p1, "Turpin Joins Benedict Cast For Second Time…"

259. *Los Angeles Times,* July 11, 1926, "After a three week honeymoon…"

260. *Oakland Tribune,* July 11, 1926, "Suit Contemplated Over Use of Name."

261. *Variety,* February 23, 1927, "In February 1927 Tommy Turpin…"

262. *Photoplay,* July 1926, p115, "Ben Got Huffy" by Babette Turpin.

263. *Moving Picture World,* 1926, p364, "Alf Goulding and Harry Connett…"

264. *Moving Picture World,* August 14, 1926, p423, "Pie Throwing Is Passing Out."

265. *Milwaukee Sentinel,* August 25, 1926, column by Louella Parsons.

266. *St. Petersboro* (FL), August 28, 1926, "Ben Turpin Back In Movies Again."

267. *Variety,* September 29, 1926, "They're speculating as to the future of Ben Turpin…"

268. *The Oregonian*, December 22, 1926, "Ben Turpin To Appear."

269. *The Oregonian*, Jan. 1, 1927, "Band Meets Ben Turpin…"

270. *The Oregonian*, Jan. 2, 1927, "Hood Draws Motorists…"

271. *The Oregonian*, Jan. 2, 1927, "Ben Turpin Likes Snow…"

272. *Seattle Daily Times*, Jan. 11, 1927, "Ben Turpin Hats Popular."

273. *Moving Picture World*, February 5, 1927, p434, "A Hollywood Hero."

274. *Evening Independent*, Jan. 8, 1927, "May Be Able To See Joke…"

275. *Moving Picture World*, April 16, 1927, p654, "The Jolly Jilter."

276. *Los Angeles Times*, March 20, 1927, "Ben Turpin and Traffic Officer."

277. *Los Angeles Times*, April 10, 1927, "Good Short Stories…"

278. *Moving Picture World*, May 2, 1927, p838, "Broke in China."

279. *Niagara Falls Gazette*, June 24, 1927, "Ben Turpin Here, Jests…"

280. *Daily Movie Service*, July 6, 1927, by Dan Thomas.

281. *Hartford Courant* (CT), August 7, 1927, pD1, "Ben Turpin Rose from Janitor's Job."

282. *Oakland Tribune* (CA), September 18, 1927, "Turpin Signs Contract."

283. *Davenport Democrat Leader* (IA), May 2, 1928, "Ben Turpin Now in Vaudeville."

284. *Cleveland Plain Dealer* (OH), June 24, 1928, "Ben Turpin Plans Film Return" by Louella O. Parsons.

285. *Dallas Morning News* (TX), September 5, 1928, "Ben Turpin Will Sell Keys at State Fair."

286. *San Antonio* (TX), September 9, 1928, "Ben Turpin at Majestic…"

287. *Kansas City Star* (KS), August 1928, "On Looking Ben Turpin In the Eye" *(in part)*.

288. *San Antonio* (TX), September 9, 1928, "Turpin's Eyes Rest…"

289. *Winnipeg Free Press*, October 6, 1928, "Eye & Ear Enjoyment."

290. *New Orleans Times-Picayune*, October 8, 1928, "Ben Turpin at Orpheum, New Orleans" by K.T. Knoblock.

291. *New Orleans Times-Picayune*, October 11, 1928, "Ben Turpin is Given Memento…"

292. *New Orleans Times-Picayune*, October 14, 1928, "Ben Turpin Lands on Top of World…" by K.T. Knoblock (in part).

293. *Atlanta Constitution*, October 30, 1928, p12, "Ben Turpin Heads Good Card…" by Ben Cooper.

294. *Van Nuys News*, Jan. 18, 1929, "Ben Turpin Company Use Van Nuys…"

295. *Syracuse*, July 15, 1929, "Film Comics Booked for Keith Dates…"

296. *Variety*, August 10, 1929, "State Lake Theater…"

297. *Decatur Review*, August 16, 1929, "The Big Thrill Due…"

298. *Variety*, August 29, 1929, "Turpin has refused Keith time…"

299. *Trenton Evening Times*, September 1, 1929, "Ben Turpin Plays Bit In New Talkie…"

300. *Reno Evening Gazette*, September 23, 1929, "Tom Sims Says."

301. *Variety*, October 9, 1929, 6th Street Theater review.

302. *Los Angeles Times*, February 27, 1930, pA3 "Haywire Optics to Take Tour…"

303. *Big Spring* (TX), March 27, 1930, "Hollywood Sights and Sounds" by Robbin Coons.

304. *Oakland Tribune*, April 13, 1930, "Turpin Returns to Pictures in Speaking Role."

305. *Charleston Gazette*, April 20, 1930, "Turpin Is About Through" by Hubbard Keavy.

306. *Motion Picture News*, April 26, 1930, p46, "Voice of Hollywood."

307. *Rochester Evening Journal*, December 29, 1930, "The Christmas Holidays…"

308. *Los Angeles Times*, April 26, 1931, p15, "Knife Employed On Ben Turpin…"

309. *Oakland Tribune*, September 19, 1931, "Film Actors Now Woo Fame…" by Jessie Henderson.

310. *Los Angeles Times*, Jan. 20, 1932, "Ben Turpin to Play On Stage."

311. *Syracuse* (NY), March 5, 1932, "Ben Turpin will stage a comeback…"

312. *Dallas Morning News*, May 11, 1932, "Ben Turpin Himself."

313. *Zanesville Signal* (OH), November 6, 1932, "Cross-Eyed Children Not For the Screen."

314. *Toronto Daily Star*, November 11, 1932, p15, "Ben Turpin Just Itching To Show World A Hamlet…" by Gordon A. Sinclair.

315. *Cleveland Plain Dealer*, February 27, 1930, "Turpin Fears Europe."

316. *Cleveland Plain Dealer*, April 23, 1931, "Cock-Eyed Ben's Return Suggests A Brighter Day" by W. Ward Marsh.

317. *Cleveland Plain Dealer*, February 25, 1934, "One Moment, Please!" by W. Ward Marsh (Women's Magazine/ Amusement Sect., p9).

318. *Trenton Sunday Times*, October 18, 1925, "Despite Fabulous Wealth, Cross-Eyed Comedy Star…" by Betty Morris.

319. *The Pittsburgh Press*, November 18, 1932, "Turpin, Cock-Eyed Comedian, Asserts World Is Cock-Eyed."

320. *The Hollywood Reporter*, May 24, 1933, "Small Town Idol Just An Antique."

321. *Variety*, May 30, 1933, "Ben Turpin's Cafe."

322. *Variety*, June 20, 1933, "Ben Turpin's Error. Opens New Night Joint…"

323. *United Press*, June 23, 1933, "Ben Turpin Sued Over Club Opening."

324. *Variety*, July 18, 1933, "Turpin Nitery Folds In Quick Order with Wage Troubles Next."

325. *Oakland Tribune*, November 27, 1933, "Ben Turpin's Cafe In San Francisco Is Burned."

326. *Cleveland Plain Dealer*, March 18, 1934, "Ben Turpin Invests Film Earnings in Property…" by Inez Wallace.

327. *The Oregonian*, April 21, 1934, p10, "Ben Turpin's Strabismus Cost of Fame" by David W. Hazen.

328. "In A Door, Into A Fight, Out A Door, Into A Chase" by William Whitney.

329. *Springfield Republican*, July 15, 1934, "Old Comedians No Longer In Demand."

330. *Chicago Daily Tribune*, May 24, 1935, p24, "Turpin Returns to Films…" by George Shaffer.

331. *Sunday Morning Star*, July 28, 1935, "Back Come the Keystone Cops…" by Jeanette Meehan.

332. *New Orleans Times-Picayune*, August 2, 1935, "Hollywood in Review" by George Shaffer.

333. *The Great Movie Shorts*, Bonanza Books, 1972, by Leonard Maltin.

334. *Pittsburgh Post-Gazette*, October 10, 1935, "A screen version of the old time melodrama…"

335. *San Jose News*, November 29, 1935, "Ben Turpin Back. Of the Butcher Counter."

336. *Variety*, February 12, 1936, "Ben Turpin Sues on Rent."

337. *Niles Township Register*, March 19, 1936, "Ben Turpin Accepts Invitation to Niles."

338. *The Modesto Bee*, December 22, 1936, "Turpin Thinks He Would Be Colossal As Gateman."

339. *San Diego Union*, April 16, 1937, "Turpin Announced As Ringmaster of Antlers' Circus."

340. *Evening Independent*, February 2, 1938, "Turpin Forgotten By Studio Guard."

341. *The Oregonian*, May 6, 1938, "Cock-Eyed Comic, Ben Turpin, Here" by David W. Hazen.

342. *Spokane Daily Chronicle*, May 6, 1938, "Ben Turpin Tops Orpheum Billing."

343. *Los Angeles Times*, April 30, 1939, "Six stores fronting on San Fernando Blvd…"

344. *Seattle Post-Intelligencer*, May 31, 1938, p22, "Ben Turpin Star of Palomar Bill."

345. *Seattle Daily Times*, May 31, 1938, p14, "Turpin Applauded on Palomar's Bill" by J. R. R.

346. *New Orleans Times-Picayune*, September 14, 1939, "Talk about odd hobbies!…"

347. *Oakland Tribune*, December 5, 1939, "Wood Soanes" column.

348. *Screen & Radio Weekly*, October 22, 1939, "The World Needs Laughs" by Ben Turpin.

349. *Syracuse Herald-Journal*, March 4, 1940, "Turpin in Sea Farce."

350. *Old Mack Sennett Police Force Team Will Tour Country*, March 29, 1940, by Franklin Arthur.

351. *St. Petersburg Times*, July 2, 1940, "Death Ends Long Career of Ben Turpin, Star Comedian."

352. *The Charlotte News*, July 2, 1940, "CLOWN, Memories of Days When Turpin Was in Flower."

353. *Reno Evening Gazette*, July 2, 1940, "BEN TURPIN."

354. *Brooklyn Daily Eagle*, July 3, 1940, "Ben Turpin."

355. *Syracuse Herald Journal*, July 3, 1940, "Ben Turpin, whose crossed eyes were insured…"

356. *Amarillo Daily News*, July 4, 1940, "Turpin's Death Ends An Era" by John DeMeyer.

357. *Spokane Daily Chronicle*, July 6, 1940, "Ben Turpin Laughed Back At Life."

358. *Brooklyn Daily Eagle*, July 7, 1940, p8, "The Sound Track: Ben Turpin, Cross-Eyed Comic, Lived A Real-Life Romance That Was Cherished by Hollywood" by Herbert Cohn.

359. *The Chicago News*, July 13, 1940, "Timely Editorial. Ben Laughs Last."

360. *New Orleans Times-Picayune*, December 15, 1940, "Warners Will Show Sennett Comedies."

361. *Variety*, August 21, 1940, p3, "Turpin's Estate of $100-200G To Widow."

362. *Los Angeles Times*, May 30, 1944, pA2, "Beverly Hills Jewel Theft Suspect Held."

363. *Syracuse Journal*, August 22, 1929, "Insures Eyes to Stay Funny & Turpin Brings Crowds Into Keith's."

Additional articles, newspapers and magazines, and books consulted:

"Ben Turpin Reminisces," 1937 (source?).

"Ben Turpin's Tale of Woe," (unid) circa 1919.

Billboard magazine, various issues.

Chicago Daily Tribune, February 22, 1893; August 20, 1916.

The Chicago Sun, Jan. 26, 1947 (unid).

The Courier (New Orleans), December 8, 1859 & July 11, 1860.

The Denver Post, 1909.

Des Moines Register, August 31, 1916.

Deseret Evening News (UT), October 20, 1906.

Detroit Free Press, The (MI), August 26, 1921, p 6, "The Theater" by Len G. Shaw.

Essanay News, 1914-1916.

The Evening Independent, Jan. 6, 1910; October 3, 1925.

Film Daily, The, 1919-1932, various issues.

Films in Review, October 1977, "Ben Turpin" by Barry Brown.

The Hartford Courant, August 7, 1927, "Ben Turpin Rose From Janitor's Job" (anon).

Los Angeles Record, December 3-13, 1924, "Thos. H. Ince's Own Life Story" via: *www.public.asu.edu/~bruce/Taylor92.txt*

Los Angeles Times, various dates.

Mack Sennett Weekly, 1917-1920.

The Mansfield News, February 16, 1909.

The Mayville Evening Bulletin, February 16, 1909.

Motion Picture, March 1917, "Falling — On and Off the Screen by Robert Francis Moore."

Motion Picture Classic, February, June, and November 1917; February 1921.

Motion Picture Studio Directories, 1916, 1917.

Motography, November 20, 1915, p 1093; December 5, 1914, p 797; December 26, 1914, p 918; May 6, 1916, p 1024; May 27, 1916, p 1200; July 1, 1916; July 4, 1916, p 47; July 8, 1916, p 82; September 2, 1916, p 544; October 28, 1916, p 983.

"Movies Demand" by Louella Parsons, 1916 (ref p 26-27).

Moving Picture World, Jan. 14, 1911, p 93; September 23, 1916; August 10, 1918, p 830.

New Orleans Commercial Bulletin, December 10, 1860.

New Orleans Item (LA)

New Orleans States (LA)

New Orleans Times-Picayune (LA)

New York Clipper, Jan. 9, 1904; September 24, 1910.

New York Dramatic Mirror, 1910.

Oshkosh Daily Northwestern, May 16, 1896.

Oxnard Daily Courier, July 12, 1922.

Pantomime, various issues.

Picture Play, April 1919, "The Hard-Luck Twins" by Harry C. Carr.

Picture Play, June 1925, "Each Fault a Virtue" by Helen Klumph, p 90.

Piqua Daily Call, November 10, 1909.

The Police Gazette (NYC), May 26, 1906.

Reel Life, various issues, 1916 and 1917.

The Roanoke Times, October 21, 1925, "A Comedian's Sorrow" (anon).

St. Petersburg Times (FL)

Salt Lake City Inter-Mountain Republican, October 21, 1906.

Variety, various issues including March 10, 1906; November 3, 1906; August 28, 1909; April 16, 1910 .

The Waterloo Times Tribune, March 28, 1915.

The Woodland Daily Democrat, December 29, 1908.

Xenia Daily Gazette, November 16, 1909.

Broncho Billy and the Essanay Film Company by David Kiehn, Farwell Books, 2003.

A Chicago Firehouse; Stories of Wriggleyville's Engine #78 by Karen Kruse, Arcadia Publishing, 2001 (page 20).

Clown Princes and Court Jesters by Kalton C. Lahue & Samuel Gill, A.S. Barnes & Co., Inc, 1970.

Essanay Film Manufacturing Company, Snakeville Comedies, 1911 to 1917 by David Kiehn & Sam Gill, 2000.

Father Goose by Gene Fowler, Covici Friede Publishers, 1934.

The Films of Mack Sennett compiled & edited by Warren M. Sherk, Scarecrow Press, 1998.

The Gay Illiterate by Louella Parsons, Doubleday, Doran and Co., Inc., 1944.

The Great Movie Comedians by Leonard Maltin, Crown Publishers, 1978.

Keystone — The Life and Clowns of Mack Sennett by Simon Louvish, Faber and Faber, Inc., 2003 (pgs 147, 148, 198-200 from the Academy of Motion Picture Arts & Sciences, Ben Turpin files).

King of Comedy by Mack Sennett as told to Cameron Shipp, Doubleday and Co., Inc., 1954.

Kops and Custards, The Legend of Keystone Films by Kalton C. Lahue & Terry Brewer, Univ. of Oklahoma Press, 1968.

Mack Sennett's Fun Factory by Brent E. Walker, McFarland & Company, Inc., 2010.

Mack Sennett's Keystone, The Man, the Myth and the Comedies by Kalton C. Lahue, A.S. Barnes & Co., Inc., 1971.

Movieland by Robert Florey, 1927.

Twinkle, Twinkle, Movie Star! by Harry T. Brundidge, E.P. Dutton & Co., Inc., 1930.

World of Laughter — The Motion Picture Comedy Short, 1910-1930 by Kalton C. Lahue, Univ. of Oklahoma Press, 1966.

US Federal Census: New York, NY; New Orleans, LA; Houston, TX; Buffalo, NY; Chicago, IL.

City Directories: New York, NY; Buffalo, NY; New Orleans, LA; Chicago, IL.

1958 TV game show, Dotto, *with Jack Narz and a familiar canvas.*

Index

Numbers in bold indicate photographs

Handwritten margin notes: "GISH" 296   GOLF 276

436   FOR ART'S SAKE: THE BIOGRAPHY & FILMOGRAPHY OF BEN TURPIN

Lord for a Day, A 371
Lost — A Cook 83-84, 393
Lost and Found 388
Louder Please 371
Louis, Willard 405
Love and Doughnuts 112, 128-129, 199, 401
Love and Trouble 381
Love, Bessie 396, 407
Love Loops the Loop 87, 174, 394
Love Parade, The 334, 335, 409
Love's False Faces 397
Lovesick Bandit, A see Roping Her Romeo
Love's Languid Lure **233**, 324, 407
Love's Outcast 107, 110, 111-112, 400
Love Versus Sledge Hammers 104, 383
Lowe, Edmund 341, 407
Lowe, Marcus 401
Lowery, William 289, 404
Loy, Myrna 409
Lubitsch, Ernst 334, 335, 409
Lucas, Jackie 277, 403
Lucas, Wilfred 410
Lynn, Charlie 87, 88, 89, 91, 92, 97, **174, 175, 176, 177, 178, 179, 180, 181**, 395, 397, 398
Lynn, Hillary 413

"MAH JONGG" 270

MacAvoy, May 407
MacDonald, Jeanette 335, 409
Mack, Hughie 67, 396, 397
Mack, Marion 327, 407
Mack Sennett-Paramount 393-398, 399, 411
MacLean, Douglas 350, 410
MacLean, Kenneth 394, 405, 406
Madame Double X 379
Magic Pool see Poultry a la Mode
Maines, Donald 323, 406
Maison, Alice 393, 394, 398
Make Me A Star **243**, 341, 411
Maljan, Abdul 394, 396
Malone, Molly 408
Maltin, Leonard 290, 354
Mankiewicz, Joseph 411
Mann, Hank 83, **252**, 352, 353, 355, 358, 359, 361, 395, 407, 412, 413
March, Fredric 342, 411
Marriage Circus, The **220**, 291, 297-298, 404
Married Life 100-101, 102, 103, 104, 129-130, 184, 185, 399
Marshall, Maurice 407
Martell, Harry 408
Martin, Al 284, 403, 405, 412
Mascot Pictures 250, 349, 412
Masked Mirth 80, 392
Mason, Shirley 407
Maxwell, Edwin 410
Mayberry, Mary 406

McCall, William 301, 404, 405, 406, 407, 408, 410
McCarey, Ray 240, 356, 406
McCoy, Harry 321, 405, 406, 407, 410
McCoy, Ruby 408
McGowan, Dorothy 396
McGowan, J.P. 396
McGowan, Roxanna 393, 394, 395
McGrath, Larry 394
McGuire, Kathryn 137, 138, **184, 199, 205**, 294, 397, 398, 399, 400, 402
McGuire, Mickey see Rooney, Mickey
McKenzie, Bob 156, 382, 383, 384, 385, 386, 413
McKenzie, Eva 156, 383, 385, 386
McKinnon, Al 86, 393, 394, 395, 396, 397
McNeil, Allen 400, 402
McPhail, Addie 239, 408
McQuire, Paddy 63, 69, 70, 71, 72, 74, 75, 76, 77, 81, 97, **159, 160, 164**, 386, 387, 388, 390, 391, 394, 395, 396
Meek, Donald 413
Meins, Gus 300, 402
Merry Models, The 65, 104, 384
Merton of the Movies 272, 411
Metropolitan Pictures 313, 405
Mexican's Gratitude, A 375
MGM 410, 412, 413,
Midnight Disturbance, A 47, 374
Milland, Ray 410
Miller, Ernest 412
Miller, Patsy Ruth 346, 405
Miller, Rube 69, 70, 72, 74, 75, 77, 83, 161, 388, 389, 390, 391
Million Dollar Legs **244**, 342, 411
Milner, Victor 409
Mineau, Charlotte 265, 286, 377, 378, 379, 380, 381, 382, 397, 398, 399, 400
Mintz, Sam 411
Mitchell, Belle 384, 385, 386
Mix, Tom 278, 315
Moffit, Jefferson 284, 301, 404, 405, 406, 407
Molly O' 292, 401
Mong, William V. 405
Monsieur Don't Care see Marriage Circus, The
Montague the Magnetic see Hollywood Hero, A
Montgomery, Peggy 233, 324, 407
Montgomery, Robert 339, 412
Moon, Arthur 70, 71, 72, 74, 75, **158, 162**, 386, 387, 388, 390, 391
Moore, Dickie 411
Moore, Owen 53, 54, 376
Moran, Lee 239, 336, 409
Moran, Patsy 413
Moran, Polly 85, 86, 88-90, **169, 171, 173**, 349, 392, 393, 394, 395, 411
Moran, Sam 404
Moreno, Antonio 83, **250**, 346, 347, 348

"MUSIC" 125, 127-8

"OPERATION" 339-40

"OLDER" 349-50

"PALESTINE" 334, 336

"PALMOLIVE" 125
"PICTURES" 356, 359, 360

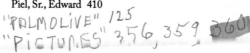

Pierce, Barbara 285, 286
Pitfalls of a Big City **209**, 267, 270, 403
Pitts, ZaSu 411
Plumbers, The see His Blowout
Pollard, Daphne 240, 409
Pollard, Snub 11, 63, 138, **245**, 328, 352, 358, 359, 361, 381, 382, 411, 413
Porter, The see Wicked City, The
Potel, Victor 55, 63, 64, **149**, **154**, **155**, 352, 361, 381, 382, 383, 384, 385, 386, 411
Poultry see Poultry a la Mode
Poultry a la Mode 99, 389
Powell, Paul 396
Powell, Russell 69, 391
Powers, Francis 45, 57
Pratt, Gil 301, 350, 406, 413
Preview Murder Mystery 355
Prevost, Marie 90, 91, 105, 106, 121, 130, **175**, **176**, **177**, **180**, **182**, **187**, **252**, 277, 345, 352, 355, 394, 395, 396, 397, 398, 399, 400, 401, 412
Price, Kate 249, 350, 399
Pride of Pikeville, The **231**, 316, 323, 406
Prieste, Hal 393, 394
Prince Consort, The 409
Prodigal Bridegroom, The **227**, 313, 318
Professor's Love Tonic, The 373
Prouty, Jed 413
Pure and Simple 338
Purviance, Edna 63, 380, 381, 385

Quack Doctor, The 399
Quiet Little Game, A 104, 383
Quillan, Eddie 12-13, 15, 81, 266, 319, 346, 347, 361
Quirk, James R. 396

Raguse, Elmer 410
Ralston, Jobyna 407
Rand, John 199, 385, 396, 398, 400
Rankin, Arthur 407
Rankin, Caroline 85, 393
Raspberry Romance, A **220**, 296-297, 404
Rathmell, John 412
Ray, Albert 75, 81
Ray, Charles 75, 100, 354, 396, 398, 401
Raymaker, Herman 83, 265, 266-267, 392, 403
Rea, Marvel 393, 394, 395, 396
Redway, Eddie 55, 57
Reel Virginian, The **217**, 289, 290, 404
Regan, Tom 400
Reid, Wallace 83, 90
Reiger, Margie 381, 382
Revenge Is Sweet see He Died and He Didn't
Rex, the King of Wild Horses 412
Reynolds, Vera 313, 405
Richards, Charles 240

Richardson, Jack 199, 213, 270, 285, 301, 400, 401, 402, 403, 412
Rich, Irene 294, 334, 336
Ridgely, Cleo 396
Rin Tin Tin, Jr., 412
Ripley, Arthur 284, 290, 300, 406, 410
Ritchie, Billy 67, 83
Roach, Bert 100, 105, **183**, **239**, 336, 395, 396, 397, 398, 399, 400, 409, 412
Roach, Hal 279, 280, 290, 317, 340, 359, 410, 413
Roach, Joseph Anthony 378
Robbins, Jess 103, **146**, 408
Roberti, Lyda 411
Roberts, Arthur 407
Roberts, Florence 411
Robin's Nest, The see Step Forward
Robinson, Dewey 412
Robinson, Kitty 377
Rodgers, Dora 392
Rodney, Earle 406, 410
Rogers, Buddy 410
Rogers, Charles 410, 413
Rogers, Gene 38, 86, 393, 394, 395, 396
Rogers, Ginger 342, 411
Rogers, Rena 70, 71, **158**, **160**, 386, 387
Rogers, Walter 389
Rogers, Will 243, 340, 343, 410
Roland, Ruth 294, 348, 407
Romeo and Juliet **214**, 284, 285, 286-287, 302, 404
Room 23 see Bedroom Blunder, A
Rooney, Mickey 11, 338, 356, 409, 413
Roping Her Romeo **169**, 393
Rosee, Rosie 390
Ross, Bud 199, 210, 211, 227, 231, 269, 400, 401, 403, 404, 405, 406, 408
Ross, Churchill 407
Roth, Lillian 409
Rowland, Roy 413
Rowlands, Arthur 403, 405, 406, 408
Royal Romance, A 409
Rube and the Bunco Men, The 49, 375
Rubin, Benny 338, 410, 411
Ruggles, Wesley 385
Running Hollywood 410-411
Ryan, Maurice 407

Safe Arrangement, A see Pawnbroker's Heart, The
Safe Proposition, A 104, 385
Sale, Chic 285, 349, 411
Sale, Virginia 411
Salome Vs. Shenandoah 97, 183, 398
Santley, Joseph 240, 337, 409
Santley, Seymore 409
Saps at Sea **257**, 358-359, 413, **414**
Sauber, Harry 410
Saucy Madeline 87-88, 171, 394

Saville, Ruth 383, 384, 385, 386
Saving the Innocents 376
Saxon, Hugh 75, 81
Sayers, Marion 410
Schaefer, Armand 412
Schertzinger, Victor 409
Scheurich, Victor 398, 399, 400
Schofield, Violet 400
Scott, Fred 240, 337, 409
Scott, Homer 402
Screen Snapshots #7 399
Screen Snapshots #10 399, 401
Screen Snapshots #11 401
Screen Snapshots #17 401
Screen Snapshots #25 402
Screen Snapshots, Series 9, #4 407
Searby, Bill 407
Sedgwick, Ed 386
Seeing Stars 401
Seeing Things 408
Sellon, Charles 411
Semon, Larry 81, 352, 353
Sennett, Mack 12-13, 31, 35, 40, 59, 62, 69, 79, 80, 81-140, **166**, 167, 172, 174, 176, 184, 186, 203, 219, 226, 228, 232, 233, 263, 264-265, 266-267, 268, 269, 270, 271, 272, 274, 276, 277, 278, 279, 280, 281, 284, 285, 286, 287, 288, 289, 290, 291, 292, 293, 294, 295, 296, 297, 298, 300, 301, 302, 303, 304, 306, 308, 311, 312, 313, 314, 316, 317, 318, 319, 320, 321, 323, 324, 325, 327, 328, 329, 336, 337, 338, 340, 341, 347, 348, 349, 350, 351, 352, 353, 355, 356, 357, 358, 359, 360, 361, 392-400, 402-407, 410, 411
Seymour, James 240
Shaw, Eugene 392
Sheean, Vincent 410
Sheehan, John 240, 409
She Landed a Big One 278
She Loved Him Plenty 89-90, 175, 395
Sheriff Nell's Tussle 87, 171, 394
Sherman, Evelyn 404
She Said No 408
She Sighed by the Seaside 109, 112, 115, 187, 400
Shot in the Fracas 80, 390-391
Show of Shows, The **239**, 336, 409
Shriek of Araby, The **205**, 263, 272, 402
Shriek, The see *Shriek of Araby, The*
Sidetracked see Asleep at the Switch
Sidney, George 54-55, 410
Skyrocket, The see *Masked Mirth*
Sleeping Tonic, The 49, 375
"SLEEP" 274-5, 331
Sleuths! 90, 176, 395
Slow But Sure 370
Small Town Idol, A 104-106, 107, 110, 111, 127, 187, 345, 355, 358, 400
Smith, Sid 266, 285, 286, 392
Smith, Vernon 284, 290, 404, 405, 406, 407
Snakeville Comedies 55, 63, 64, 65, 66, 104, 154, 156, 382, 383, 384
Snakeville's Champion 65, 104, 156, 384
Snakeville's Debutantes 104
Snakeville's Hen Medic 104, 154, 383
Snakeville's Twins 64, 104, 154, 382
Snow, Ross 30, 103
Sole Mates 83, 167, 392
Some Bravery 104, 385
Some Jazz Baby see *Musical Marvel, The*
Some Liars 73, 80, 161, 388
Somnambulist, The 373
Sophie and the Fakir 104, 382
Soul Kiss 372
Sovern, Whitey 392, 393
Speak-Easy, The 398
"SPEEDING" 313-14
Spear, George 403, 404
Special Delivery 104
Spencer, Fred 403
Spoor, George K. 35, 41, 43, 50-51, 56, 57, 61, 114
Sprotte, Bert 409
Squawk Man, The 405
"STAGE/SHOWBIZ" 343
Stafford, Earl 405, 406
Standing, Joan 407
Stanton, Eli 403, 404
Star Boarder, The 99, 183, 398
Starke, Pauline 409
Starlit Days at the Lido **253**, 412
STEELE, BOB 368
Starr, Jimmy 406
Starr, Sally 240
Staub, Ralph 351-352, 353, 354, 412
St. Clair, Mal 81, 111, **174**, 357, 393, 395, 397, 401, 413
Steadman, Vera 350, 393, 394, 395
Steel Preferred 301, 311, 313, 405
Stengel, Leni 410
Stengler, Mack 410
Step Forward 133, 135, 136, 137, 201, 402
Sterling, Ford 67, 90, 101, 129, **174**, **207**, **252**, 350, 352, 353, 354, 395, 396, 397, 398, 399, 402, 412
Stevenson, Charles 402
Stewart, Anita 249
Stine, Charles 380
St. John, Al 352, 359, 361
Stolen Booking, The 74, 80, 389
Stone, Arthur 341, 411
Stone, George E. 411
Stout, George W. 82
Street Fakir, The 44-45, 370
Street Urchin, The 370
Stuart, Nick 240,
Studio Stampede, A **163**, 391
Stung! Or Who Can It Bee? 372
Stunt Man, The see *The Dare-Devil*
Sulky, Leo 231, 403, 404, 405
Sullivan, Helen 405
Summerville, Slim 83, 85, 86, **169**, 393, 394
"SUNSHINE SAMMY" (MORRISON) 316

Sutherland, Dick 402
Suzanna 137, 293
Swain, Mack 83, 85, 267, 341, 352, 393, 403, 411
Swanson, Gloria 81, 308, 330, 377, 380, 401, 407
Sweedie and Her Dog 380
Sweedie and the Double Exposure 377
Sweedie and the Hypnotist 379
Sweedie and the Lord 377
Sweedie and the Sultan's Present 379
Sweedie at the Fair 59, 378
Sweedie Collects for Charity 379
Sweedie Goes to College 380
Sweedie in Vaudeville 382
Sweedie Learns to Ride 381
Sweedie Learns to Swim 378
Sweedie's Clean-Up 59, 377
Sweedie's Finish 382
Sweedie's Hero 382
Sweedie's Hopeless Love 380
Sweedie Springs a Surprise 377
Sweedie's Skate 377
Sweedie's Suicide 379
Sweedie, the Laundress 378
Sweedie the Swatter 58, 377
Sweedie the Troublemaker 378
Sweet, Harry 285, 404
Swing High 240, 241, 337, 409
Symonds, Harry R. 407

Tag Day 46, 374
Taking the Count 104, 239, 385, 408
Talmadge, Constance 399
Talmadge, Norma 399
Taming Target Center 87, 168, 394
Tarron, Elsie 403
Tashman, Lilyan 407
Tavares, Arthur 164
Taylor, Ruth 230, 301, 316, 319, 406
Taylor, Sam 410
Teare, Ethel 83, 393
Tearle, Conway 299, 355
Tec-Art Studios 338, 409
Teddy the dog 86, 90, 91, 99, 121, 166, 174, 204, 277, 394, 395, 397, 398, 399, 400, 402
Templeton, George 411
Templeton, Margaret 75, **162**, **164**, 386, 390, 391, 392
Ten Dollars or Ten Days **211**, 276, 403
Tennant, Barbara 229, 406
Tennyson, Gladys 403
Terry, Frank *see* Forde, Pat
Tetzlaff, Ted 409
Thatcher, Eva 73, 388, 392, 393, 394, 395, 396, 397, 398, 399
That Night 393
Their Cheap Vacation 379
Thompson, Edmund 382
Thorton, Frank 410
Thousand Dollar Bill, A 379
Three and a Half Weeks see *Three Foolish Weeks*
Three Foolish Weeks **214**, **215**, 287, 288, 289, 404
Three Stooges, The 11, 270, 349, 411
Three Weeks 286, 287, 288, 289
Thurman, Mary 86, **167**, **174**, 353, 393, 394, 395
Tic-Toc Girls 253, 412
Tiver, Irene 400
Todd, Harry 55, 63, 64, **149**, **154**, **155**, **156**, 381, 382, 383, 384, 385, 386
Too Much Dog Biscuit 373
Too Much Turkey 383
Total Loss, A see *Doctoring a Leak*
Towser the dog 131, 134, 200
Tracy, Lee 255, 413
Tragedian, The 371
Tramp Story, A 376
Trask, Wayland 174, 392, 393, 394, 395, 397
Traub, Joe 412
Treating 'em Rough 97, 397
Treed 391
Trevilla, Sibye 398
Triangle 69, 83, 85, 392-393
Tripped at the Altar see *Bright Eyes*
Trying to Get Along 97, 397
Tucker, George Loane 53, 54
Turner, Earl 412
Turner, Florence 249
Turpin, Babette 223, 224, 225, 257, 260, 312, 314, 315, 316, 361, 365-367, 368
Turpin, Bernard (grandfather) 19, 20, 21, 273
Turpin, Carrie see LeMieux, Carrie
Turpin, Dr. Charles Cyprien (uncle) 20, 26
Turpin, Ernest (father) 19, 20-21, 22, 24, 27, 29, 107, 273, 358
Turpin, Ernestine (sister) 20-21, 27, 120, **223**, 301, 307, 365, 366-367, 368
Turpin, Eugene (uncle) 19, 29
Turpin, Norma see Koch, Norma
Turpin, Octavia (sister) 21, 29
Turpin, Tommy see Knies, Julian Jerome
Twelvetrees, Helen 240, 337, 409
20th Century-Fox 351, 358, 410, 412, 413
Two Bold, Bad Men 381
Two Hearts That Beat as Ten 380
Two Laughs 84, 85, 104, 386
Two Lonely Knights 408
Two's Company see *Saps at Sea*
Two Tough Tenderfeet 88, 175, 395

Uncle Tom Without the Cabin 112, 182, 398
Undertaker's Uncle, The 63, 104, 382
Unger, Adolph 407
Unholz, George 404, 410
United Artists 263, 399, 413

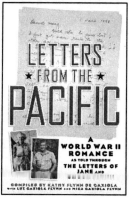

CPSIA information can be obtained at www.ICGtesting.com
Printed in the USA
BVOW01s2103041213

338146BV00004B/121/P